Live in Belgium, the Netherlands & Luxembourg

André de Vries

SERIES EDITORS VICTORIA PYBUS & DAVID WOODWORTH

Published by Vacation Work, 9 Park End Street, Oxford
www.vacationwork.co.uk

LIVE AND WORK IN BELGIUM,
THE NETHERLANDS AND LUXEMBOURG

First Edition 1992 André de Vries and Greg Adams
Second Edition 1998 André de Vries
Third Edition 2002 André de Vries

Copyright © Vacation Work 2002

ISBN 1-85458-286-0

No part of this publication may be stored, reproduced or transmitted
in any form without the prior written permission of the publisher

Publicity: Roger Musker

Cover Design by Miller Craig & Cocking Design Partnership

Text design and typesetting by Brendan Cole

Printed and bound in Italy by Legoprint SpA, Trento

CONTENTS

BELGIUM

– SECTION 1 –
LIVING IN BELGIUM

GENERAL INTRODUCTION
  CHAPTER SUMMARY 17
  DESTINATION BELGIUM 18
  PROS AND CONS OF MOVING TO BELGIUM 18
  POLITICAL AND ECONOMIC STRUCTURE – *Early years – Recent history – Economy – The modern economy* 21
  GOVERNMENT – *Federalisation – Political parties* 24
  GEOGRAPHICAL INFORMATION – *Area – Population – Climate* 26
  REGIONAL GUIDE – *General description of the regions of Belgium with details of major towns & information offices* 28

RESIDENCE & ENTRY REGULATIONS
  THE CURRENT POSITION – *EU nationality – Entry & residence for EU nationals – Entry on a self-employed basis – Entry & work permits for non-EU nationals – Nationality and citizenship – Summary* 40

SETTING UP HOME
  HOW DO THE BELGIANS LIVE? – *Estate agents* 47
  FINANCE – *Mortgages with Belgian banks – Registration & mortgage costs – Repayment conditions – UK & offshore mortgages* 49
  PURCHASING & CONVEYANCING PROCEDURES – *Finding a property – Professional assistance – the Compromis de vente – Registration tax – Buying an apartment.* 53
  RENTING PROPERTY – *Useful terms in French & Dutch – Tenancy agreements – Renting out your property – Short-term rented accommodation – Rental costs – Relocators* 55

INTERCULTURAL TRAINING 59
INSURANCE & WILLS 60
UTILITIES – *Electricity – Gas – Oil – Water – Telephones* 61
REMOVALS – *Customs regulations – Import procedures* 64
IMPORTING A CAR – *Buying a car – Car insurance* 66
IMPORTING PETS 68

DAILY LIFE
CHAPTER SUMMARY 69
THE BELGIAN LANGUAGES – *Language manners – Language study* 70
SCHOOLS AND EDUCATION – *The structure of the education system – Universities – International universities – International schools* 73
MEDIA AND COMMUNICATIONS – *Newspapers – Magazines – Books and bookshops – Television – Radio – Post – Telephones* 78
CARS & MOTORING – *Driving regulations – Breakdowns and accidents – Driving licences – Car registration* 82
TRANSPORT – *Trains – City transport – Air and sea travel* 85
BANKS & FINANCE – *Bank accounts – Transferring funds to & from Belgium – Money* 87
TAX AND THE EXPATRIATE – *The Question of Residence – Income tax – Local tax – Other taxes* 88
HEALTH CARE, INSURANCE & HOSPITALS – *The E111 – Emergencies – Private medical insurance* 92
SOCIAL SECURITY & UNEMPLOYMENT BENEFITS 95
CRIME & THE POLICE 96
SOCIAL LIFE – *Manners and customs – Making friends – Food and drink* 97
PUBLIC HOLIDAYS 100

RETIREMENT
RESIDENCE & ENTRY – *Possible retirement areas – Pensions – Taxation – Belgian pensions & health insurance – Wills and legal considerations – Death – Cohabitation – Churches – Hobbies & interests* 101

– SECTION II –
WORKING IN BELGIUM

EMPLOYMENT
CHAPTER SUMMARY 111
THE EMPLOYMENT SCENE – *Residence & entry – Skills and qualifications – Regulated professions* 112
SOURCES OF JOBS – *Newspapers – Professional associations – Specialist job publications & the internet – The UK employment service – UK recruitment agencies – Belgian state employment offices – Private employment agencies – Outplacement bureaux – Temporary employment agencies – Chambers of commerce – Letters of application – Transfers – The curriculum vitae – Interview procedure*..115
ASPECTS OF EMPLOYMENT – *Salaries – Benefits & perks – Working hours, Overtime & holidays – Trade unions – Employment contracts – Work practices Women in work* 125
PERMANENT WORK – *Employment prospects – Working for the European Commission – Translating & interpreting – Working or NATO – Teaching – Eurostar* 129
SHORT-TERM EMPLOYMENT – *Teaching English – Au pair work – Secretarial work – Tourism – Agricultural & industrial – Internships – Voluntary work*..134
BUSINESS & INDUSTRY REPORT – *Automotive – Banking & finance – Chemicals – Food & ariculture – Petrochemical – Retailing – Steel & non-ferrous metals – Textiles*..138
REGIONAL EMPLOYMENT GUIDE 144
DIRECTORY OF MAJOR EMPLOYERS 148

STARTING A BUSINESS
BASIC REQUIREMENTS..153
PROCEDURES INVOLVED IN STARTING A NEW BUSINESS –
Preparation from scratch – Accountants – Choosing an area – Raising finance – Investment incentives – Small & medium enterprises – Regional investment offices – Relocation agencies and business services – Business structures – Ideas for new businesses..154
RUNNING A BUSINESS – *Employing staff – Trade Unions – Employers' organizations – Taxation* 162

THE NETHERLANDS

– SECTION I –
LIVING IN THE NETHERLANDS

GENERAL INTRODUCTION
    CHAPTER SUMMARY 169
    DESTINATION THE NETHERLANDS – *Pros & cons of moving to the Netherlands*..170
    POLITICAL & ECONOMIC STRUCTURE – *History – Economy – Government – Political Parties*...173
    GEOGRAPHICAL INFORMATION – *Area – Population – Climate*............178
    REGIONAL GUIDE – *General description of the regions of the Netherlands with details of the provinces and major towns*...180
    GETTING TO THE NETHERLANDS – *Useful guides*........................189

RESIDENCE AND ENTRY REGULATIONS
    THE CURRENT POSITION – *Entry and residence for EU nationals – Entry on a self-employed basis – Non-EU nationals – Summary*...................191

SETTING UP HOME
    HOW DO THE DUTCH LIVE? – *Estate agents – Where to look for accommodation – Relocation agencies*..196
    MORTGAGES *Dutch mortgages – UK mortgages – Offshore mortgages – The purchasing and ownership of property – property-related taxes – The koop – Notaris and thetransport*...199
    RENTING PROPERTY – *The rental contract – Renting out property – Useful terms in Dutch*...203
    UTILITIES 206
    INSURANCE AND WILLS 207
    REMOVALS – *General import conditions* 208
    IMPORTING A CAR – *Buying a car* 209
    IMPORTING PETS 210

DAILY LIFE
    CHAPTER SUMMARY 212
    THE LANGUAGE – *Language courses – Courses in the Netherlands* 213
    SCHOOLS AND EDUCATION – *The structure of the education system – International Education*...215

MEDIA AND COMMUNICATIONS – *Newspapers & magazines –
Television & radio – The postal system – Telephones* 220
CARS AND MOTORING – *Roads – Breakdowns and accidents – Driving
regulations – Driving licences – Car registration – Insurance* 224
TRANSPORT *Waterways – Rail – Air – Public transport – Bicycles* 228
BANKS AND FINANCE – *Opening an account – Choosing a bank – Using
a Dutch bank account – Currency – Transferring funds to the Netherlands – Offshore
banking* 231
TAXATION – *Income tax – The Dutch tax system – Self employment –
Indirect taxes* 233
HEALTH INSURANCE AND HOSPITALS – *The E111 – Medical
insurance – Using the Dutch Health Service – Emergencies* 237
SOCIAL SECURITY AND UNEMPLOYMENT *Benefit*............................240
LOCAL GOVERNMENT 242
CRIME AND POLICE – *The judiciary* 243
RELIGION 244
SOCIAL LIFE – *The Dutch – Manners and customs – Making friends –
Entertainment and culture – Sport* 245
SHOPPING – *Dutch food and drink* 249
PUBLIC HOLIDAYS 251

RETIREMENT
BACKGROUND INFORMATION – *Residence requirements – Choosing
and buying a retirement home – Hobbies and interests – Entertainment –
English-language clubs – Pensions – Health – Wills – Death* 252

– SECTION II –
WORKING IN THE NETHERLANDS

EMPLOYMENT
CHAPTER SUMMARY 261
THE EMPLOYMENT SCENE – *Residence & work regulations – Skills and
qualifications*..262
SOURCES OF JOBS – *The Media – Employment organisations – EURES – Job
centres – The application procedure* 265
ASPECTS OF EMPLOYMENT – *Salaries – Working conditions – Etiquette in
the workplace – Trade unions – Women in work* 269
PERMANENT WORK – *Petrochemicals and Engineering – Information Technology
– Medicine and Nursing – Architects* 271
TEMPORARY WORK – *Teaching English – Au pair work – Secretarial work –*

Seasonal Work – Secretarial work – Voluntary Work..274
BUSINESS AND INDUSTRY REPORT – *Aerospace – Agriculture – Chemicals – Electronics – Food and beverages – Horticulture – Hydraulic engineering – Information technology – Motor Indistry – Oil & gas – Tourism – Transport*...279
REGIONAL EMPLOYMENT GUIDE 285
DIRECTORY OF MAJOR EMPLOYERS 291

STARTING A BUSINESS
PROCEDURES INVOLVED IN BUYING OR STARTING A NEW BUSINESS – *preparation from scratch – Chambers of commerce – Choosing an area – Raising finance – Small and Medium Enterprises – Investment incentives – Business structures* 295
IDEAS FOR NEW BUSINESSES – Exporters 303
RUNNING A BUSINESS – *Employing staff – Taxation – Accountancy and auditing advice* 304

LUXEMBOURG

– SECTION I –
LIVING IN LUXEMBOURG

GENERAL INTRODUCTION
Destination Luxembourg 311
Political and Economic Structure 312
Geographical Information 313
Regional Guide 313

RESIDENCE AND ENTRY REGULATIONS
Requirements for British citizens – Non-EU nationals 317

SETTING UP HOME
How do Luxemburgers live? – Purchasing property – Renting property – Utilities – Removals 319

DAILY LIFE
The languages – Schools and education – Media & communications – Transport – Banks & finance – Taxation – Health Insurance & Hospitals – Social Security & Unemployment Benefit – Local government – Crime & police – Religion – Social life – Public holidays 322

RETIREMENT *English-language clubs* 331

– SECTION II –
WORKING IN LUXEMBOURG

EMPLOYMENT
The employment scene – Residence & work regulations – Sources of jobs – Teaching English – Au pair work – Tourism – Aspects of work 332

BUSINESS AND INDUSTRY REPORT 336

STARTING A BUSINESS
Creating a new business – Buying an existing business – Business structures – Finance – Ideas for new businesses – Running a business – 337

MAPS
Belgium (including Luxembourg) Linguistic Regions & provinces......................................19
The Netherlands – Provinces, Main Towns & Water Barriers 171

APPENDICES
1 – Personal Case Histories – Belgium..243
2 – Personal Case Histories – The Netherlands 246

BIBLIOGRAPHY..249

THE EURO

On January 1st 2002 the Euro became the legal currency in Belgium, the Netherlands and Luxembourg: at the time of the change over in Belgium and Luxembourg one Euro was worth 40.3399 francs, and in the Netherlands one Euro was worth 2.2031 guilders. The value of the Euro against the UK £ and the US $ varies from day to day: at the time of going to press one Euro is worth UK £0.62 or US $0.87.

FOREWORD

Live and Work in Belgium, the Netherlands and Luxembourg was the fourth in a series of books identifying opportunities for work, starting a business, or retiring within the EU. Since the publication of the first edition in 1992, the introduction of the Single European Market in 1993 has made the freedom of movement of people, goods and services within the EU a great deal easier. Nevertheless, there are still complications inherent in buying or renting a new home and starting a new job in another EU Member State where laws and procedures are different from those at home. We hope that by using *Live and Work in Belgium, the Netherlands and Luxembourg* as a starting point, you will be able to take this major move in your stride. Each of the three countries in the book has two sections, one entitled *Living* and the other *Working*. These two sections cover all aspects of life, including how to find a job, work practices in the three countries, business opportunities, how to set up a business, renting and buying property, and retirement.

There are an estimated 72,000 UK and 16,000 US nationals in the Benelux countries, many of whom work for multinational companies in the large cities such as Brussels, Antwerp, Rotterdam, The Hague, Amsterdam and Luxembourg-Ville. In Belgium, a considerable number of Britons and Americans work for the EU Commission and NATO. In the Netherlands, many work on short-term contracts in the fields of construction and engineering or to gain experience of the latest developments in horticulture. As the climate in the Benelux countries is much the same as in the UK, it can be assumed that Britons go there to work rather than to sit in the sun. The main motivating factors are professional and business opportunities, good working conditions, excellent social welfare systems and a high standard of living. While there is a certain touch of the exotic about any foreign country, Belgium, the Netherlands and Luxembourg have more in common with the UK on the cultural level than any other European countries. Those from English-speaking cultures will find it easy to form long-lasting relationships.

Out of the three countries, Luxembourg has very few economic problems and the highest proportion of foreigners. Belgium has not been able to create large numbers of new jobs in the same way as the Netherlands, but prospects for qualified foreigners are still very good. The Netherlands has achieved an unexpected degree of economic success, much of it a consequence of opening up the economy along British and American lines, but without creating the same degree of social inequality. Since 1993 Belgium has gone down the road of federalisation, without knowing quite how far to go; the unitary Belgian state is still far from breaking up completely. The Netherlands is rated as the best place in the world to do business, and also scores highest along with Denmark in the 'happiness index' published by the World Values Survey.

The Benelux countries have always been pioneers in breaking down European trade and cultural barriers; the success of the Belgium-Luxembourg Economic Union (1922) and the Benelux Union (1948) contributed to a large degree in the creation of the Common Market. Their commitment to the European Union is second to none. Those who are prepared to take the opportunities offered by these countries will be amply rewarded. This book tells you how, where and why to make it in Belgium, the Netherlands and Luxembourg.

André de Vries
March 2002

ACKNOWLEDGMENTS

I would like to thank the following for their invaluable help in compiling the Belgian section of this book: René and Jacqueline Batslé, and Mary Jackson for their hospitality in Belgium; Christel Mertens, Gordon McKay, Mel Andrews, Myriam Friedman and Robert Adams for advice on setting up home and starting a business; and Michael Kingshott for information on buying and selling property in Belgium. Also to Caroline Bee of Commercial Union for shedding light on the mysteries of insurance in Belgium. Special thanks go to Gordon McKay (Hastings-McKay Associates) and Peter Burnett (EU Commission) for contributing their experiences of living and working in Belgium to the case studies section. The Belgian Embassy in London, the National Institute of Statistics and the Ministry of Economics in Brussels were also very generous in providing prompt information.

For their generous assistance with the sections on the Netherlands and Luxembourg, we would like to thank: H.E. the Ambassador of the Grand Duchy of Luxembourg; Nicholas Braun for information on Luxembourg; the *Luxembourg News*; the *Central Bureau of Statistics in the Netherlands*; the NVM (National Association of Estate Agents in the Netherlands); Estata Makelaars; the Netherlands Foreign Investment Agency (NFIA); the British Embassy in The Hague; the Royal Netherlands Embassy in London; and Greg Adams, who wrote much of this section for the first edition. Special thanks for help and advice to ACCESS; Helen Rietveld (Relocation Services); and Charles van Beuningen. Many thanks also to Ann Campbell-Lord and Simon Edwards for agreeing to provide case histories of their own experiences of living and working in the Netherlands.

Finally, I would like to dedicate this book to the memory of my late father, Dr Isidoor de Vries, who always encouraged my literary aspirations.

The author and publishers have every reason to believe in the accuracy of the information given in this book and the authenticity and correct practices of all organisations, companies, agencies etc. mentioned: however, situations may change and telephone numbers, regulations, exchange rates etc. can alter, and readers are strongly advised to check facts and credentials for themselves. Readers are invited to write to Vacation Work, 9 Park End Street, Oxford OX1 1HJ, with any comments, corrections and first hand experiences. Those whose contributions are used will be sent a free copy of the next edition or the Vacation Work title of their choice.

TELEPHONE NUMBERS

Please note that the telephone numbers in this book are written as needed to call that number from inside the same country. To call these numbers from outside the country you will need to know the relevant international access code; these are currently 00 from the UK, Belgium, the Netherlands and Luxembourg and 011 from the USA.

To call Belgium: dial the international access code + 32 + the complete number as given in this book.

To call The Netherlands: dial the international access code + 31 + the complete number as given in this book.

To call Luxembourg: dial the international access code + 352 + the complete number as given in this book.

To call the UK: international access code +44 + the complete number as given in this book – *but omitting the first 0 in the British number.*

To call the USA: international access code +1 + the complete number as given in this book.

Belgium

Section I

LIVING IN BELGIUM

GENERAL INTRODUCTION

RESIDENCE AND ENTRY REGULATIONS

SETTING UP HOME

DAILY LIFE

RETIREMENT

General Introduction

CHAPTER SUMMARY

- Belgium packs great linguistic and cultural diversity into its small area, which is shared between the Dutch-speaking Flemish and French-speaking Walloons.

- **What to expect.** Perhaps because of their internal divisions the Belgians are welcoming to foreigners.

  - Most of the English-speaking foreigners in Belgium are found in and around Brussels and Mons where the multi-national organisations are concentrated.

  - These cosmopolitan areas offer new immigrants life in ready-made expatriate communities.

- Job opportunities for English speakers remain good despite the weak economy; prospects are even better for linguists.

  - The country offers the immigrant its mild climate, rich cultural life, and leading cuisine plus cheaper housing costs than Britain.

- **Background.** Belgium has only existed in its present form since 1830, when it gained independence from the Netherlands.

  - As with most other European countries in Europe Belgium's manufacturing industry has declined in recent years, but its high tech industries are prospering.

- **Geography.** Belgium is the third smallest country in the EU after Luxembourg and Denmark.

- **Politics.** The use of proportional representation prevents any one group dominating the political stage; most governments since 1919 have been coalitions.

  - Federalistic Belgium has five levels of government, each with its own direct elections.

DESTINATION BELGIUM

BELGIUM IS ONE of the UK's closest neighbours, both in terms of location (65 miles away), and its historical and economic links with this country, yet to most Britons it remains largely unknown. It is not one of our main tourist destinations, and most of us would be hard-pressed to name any important Belgian cultural figures beyond the fictional Tintin and Hercule Poirot.

Those who do take the trouble to look more closely at Belgium will find extraordinary linguistic and cultural diversity packed into an area about half as large again as Wales, or about the same size as the state of Maryland. Belgium has now become a decentralised, federal state, where many institutions are divided into Dutch-speaking, French-speaking, Catholic, socialist and liberal. The two main communities – the Dutch-speaking Flemish and the French-speaking Walloons – are moving further apart while the European Union moves ever closer towards becoming a federal superstate. Belgium only came into existence in approximately its present form in 1830, and there have always been those who felt that it should have remained unified with France or the Netherlands, or been divided up in some other way. Even so, Belgium is definitely here to stay.

The Belgian people themselves, disregarding their linguistic quarrels, are exceptionally welcoming to those from other countries. The feelings of nationalism and cultural superiority prevalent in other European countries are generally absent. Having been variously occupied by the French, Spanish, Dutch, Austrians and Germans, the Belgians have learned to get along with other people, while maintaining a good-humoured cynicism towards all and sundry. Rather than blowing their own trumpets they would rather get on with enjoying life in their own down-to-earth way. Outsiders should always remember that Belgium has its own unique traditions and cultural identity, even if the locals do not make a great deal of fuss about these things.

Belgium is certainly a country which should not be overlooked, because it really is the Crossroads or Heart of Europe. If you are looking for a somewhat exotic and highly internationalised environment without going very far from home, then this could be the country for you.

PROS AND CONS OF MOVING TO BELGIUM

THOSE MOVING TO BELGIUM will be able to enjoy a lifestyle as good as anywhere in Europe. Not surprisingly, Belgium is seen as an attractive country by immigrants, who now make up 9.1% (920,000) of the population. 26,000 British and 12,000 US citizens actually reside in Belgium (2001), and the number is increasing, so the potential migrant will find a well-established expatriate community. British television stations are now easily available, as are newspapers.

Belgians are still very favourably disposed to the British, with the exception of football hooligans. Even though Brussels, in particular, is virtually saturated with foreigners, the locals are generally friendly and helpful. The Belgians are certainly not as outgoing as the French and other Latin peoples, and place more emphasis

Belgium: Linguistic Regions and Provinces

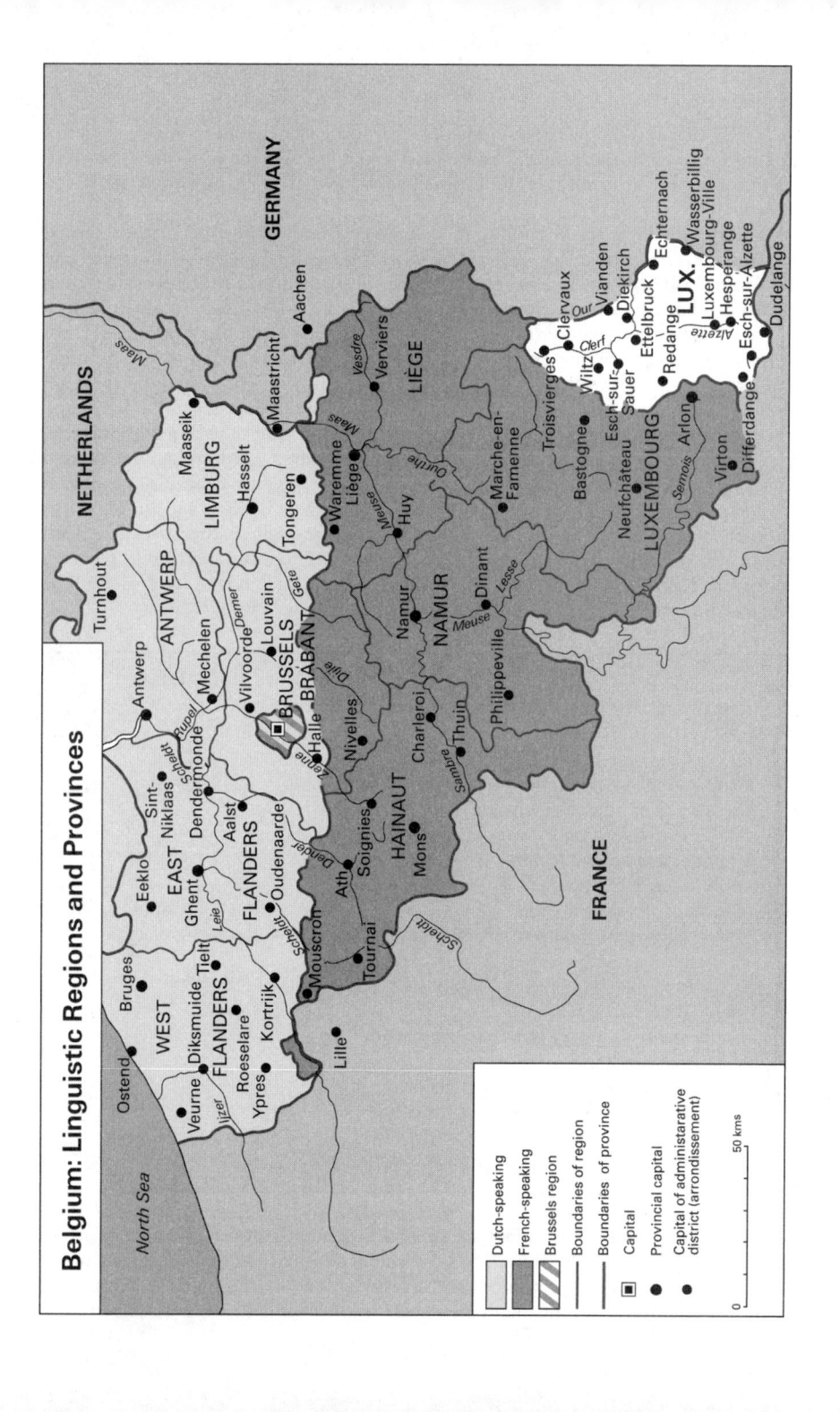

on family ties and long-term friendships than on casual acquaintances; societies and clubs play an important role in Belgian social life. On the other hand, with so many foreigners around, it is quite possible to have an exciting social life if you want one.

Working practices are becoming more relaxed than before, and Britons should not find too many problems here. The working week is generally 38 hours and minimum holidays are four weeks per year. Starting times may be earlier than in Britain, but this varies. Employees are afforded a large measure of protection by the law, but this has its disadvantages as well. One should not expect a lot of overtime work – your employer has to give you time off in lieu. The most important consideration for those wanting to work in Belgium must be the high level of both direct and indirect taxation there. Many items carry 21% VAT, and someone on a moderate salary may be paying 48% tax. Those with a high income, or multiple sources of income, who can use tax advisers, will do much better than someone whose taxes are deducted at source. There is, for example, no capital gains tax in Belgium. Those working for the EC pay very little tax at all. Earnings often include a company car, and other benefits, as well as the so-called '13th month', all of which have to be taxed, of course (see *Taxation* section in Chapter Four *Daily Life*). On the plus side, once you are established in Belgium, you will be able to enjoy the benefits of its generous social security system.

THE PROS AND CONS OF LIVING IN BELGIUM

PROS
- Good employment prospects for the well-qualified.
- Multinational organisations requiring English speakers.
- Possibility of supplying services to other foreigners.
- Multicultural environment.
- Friendly and helpful locals.
- Very favourable treatment of EU nationals.
- Excellent job security and benefits.
- Fascinating history with much to offer in all areas of culture. Highly regarded cuisine.

CONS
- Some sectors unlikely to employ foreigners.
- Excessive red tape.
- Rental agreements tend to be inflexible.
- Direct taxes on the high side and hard to avoid.
- Non-EU citizens require a work permit.
- Not the best place to save a lot of money in a hurry.

Job opportunities for English-speakers are generally good and at a constant level, in spite of the overall weakness of the economy (unemployment stands at about 8.5%). There are possibilities in most sections of the market. Temporary work is quite plentiful, although the trade unions tend to keep foreigners out of some jobs. On the other hand, all EU nationals have the right to use the services of the state employment offices to look for work, whether temporary or permanent. Trying to work without paying taxes/social security is not advisable, as the authorities are fairly zealous in seeking out illegal workers, of whom there are many.

There are always openings for language teachers, au pairs, secretaries, and so on, and these jobs are frequently advertised in the British press. Those with good language skills (any EU language is useful) are always in demand, and should consider going to job agencies and job fairs (see Chapter Six, *Employment*) in Belgium itself. Those with good qualifications will be able to make arrangements from Britain.

Rented accommodation is not hard to find, although expensive in Brussels. Rental agreements tend to require a minimum three-year commitment, with possible expensive penalties if you move out. Accommodation is usually unfurnished. There is no housing shortage at all in Belgium – at any one time 3%-4% of houses are empty – and prices are about half of those in Britain. Further information on property is given in Chapter Three, *Setting Up Home*.

The physical environment is much more varied than one might think. The 40 mile North Sea coast has some of the best and safest beaches in Europe. In the south there are the unspoiled hills and forests of the Ardennes Plateau which offer skiing in the winter. Belgium is particularly rich in medieval architecture and art, and there are numerous châteaux and parks to visit. It has preserved a considerable amount of its folklore; Belgians love to hold carnivals and festivals where everyone can join in. The climate is similar to Southern England's, but rather more consistent, with predictably warm summers and snow in winter.

POLITICAL AND ECONOMIC STRUCTURE

The key to understanding Belgium's political development lies in its long and complex history, which is characterised by frequent invasions and occupations. For more detailed studies, see the *Bibliography*.

The Early Years

Belgium takes its name from the Belgae, a Celtic tribe who moved here in prehistoric times. Julius Caesar conquered the area in 56 BC and made it into the Roman province of Gallia Belgica. The racial and linguistic division of what was to become Belgium started in the third century AD, as Germanic tribes moved into the north of the country, while the romanised Celts continued to occupy the south. As a result, there is an almost straight line across Belgium dividing the Dutch- and French-speakers, with Brussels a largely French island in the Dutch area. There are also 62,000 German-speakers in the east from the incorporation of the German areas of Eupen and Malmédy after World War I.

Dutch-speakers are often called 'Flemings' and their region Flanders, which includes the provinces of Limburg and Antwerpen, which were not part of medieval Flanders. The Flemings these days usually say that they speak Dutch

(*Nederlands*), the standardised form which is identical in most respects in Belgium and the Netherlands. The term 'Flemish' can be applied to the many dialects of Dutch spoken in Belgium, but not to the official language. The French-speaking area – Wallonia – has its own Walloon dialects, but the inhabitants would always claim to be speakers of French. The first thing to remember about Belgium is that the Dutch-speakers outnumber the French-speakers by 3 to 2. Contrary to widespread belief, French is not the only language spoken in Belgium.

Medieval Flanders had close relations with England, while the rest of the country was ruled by an assortment of dukes, counts and prince-bishops. The major event of this period was the defeat of the French nobility at the Battle of the Golden Spurs in 1302 by the Flemish towns, which is still celebrated on 11 July in Flanders. Without this victory Belgium would probably not exist today. Nevertheless, Belgium gradually came under the domination of the Burgundians, the Habsburgs, and finally Spain. Spanish efforts to suppress the Reformation in the Low Countries were entirely successful in Belgium, while the Netherlands managed to break free. As a result, Belgium's Christians are 95% Catholic. Although fewer than 10% of the population go to church, the Catholic church still wields considerable influence through political parties, trade unions and sickness funds.

Recent History

Following the Battle of Waterloo (near Brussels) in 1815, Belgium and Holland were unified for 15 years under the King of the Netherlands. Many objected to unequal treatment by the Dutch, and Belgium finally gained its independence in 1830, with Queen Victoria's uncle installed as King Leopold I. While Leopold I's grandson, Albert, fought heroically in World War I, his son, Leopold III, was compelled to surrender to the Germans in World War II, and decided not to escape abroad. The king's credibility was severely diminished and he eventually abdicated in 1950, to be succeeded by his son Baudouin I, who did much to restore the prestige of the monarchy. The latter's brother, Albert II, succeeded him on his death in 1993. The heir to the throne is Crown Prince Philippe.

Economy

Following independence the industrial revolution took off in Belgium in the 1840s, centred around coal, steel, textiles and other manufacturing industries. As it happened, most of the country's natural resources were to be found in the French-speaking south. Since education and government were conducted entirely in French, the Dutch-speakers became second-class citizens, tied to the land and denied any opportunities for advancement. Some Dutch-speakers looked to Germany for support, given that the Walloons (French-speakers) always looked to France, but after two occupations their pro-German feelings tended to diminish. Other factors eventually tipped the balance towards the Dutch-speaking community, without eliminating their lasting feeling of bitterness towards the French-speaking élite.

Manufacturing industries suffered severely during the Depression, while at the same time agriculture in the north prospered, and the Flemish majority increased more and more. Dutch finally gained equal status with French in 1932, so that Dutch-speakers could deal with the authorities in their own language.

Belgium and Luxembourg entered into a pioneering economic union in 1921 – the BLEU (Belgo-Luxembourg Economic Union) – after Luxembourg decided it no longer wanted to be tied to Germany. In 1948, a further free-trade area was created – the organisation of the Benelux countries (Belgium, the Netherlands and Luxembourg), which anticipated the creation of the Common Market in 1957.

Belgium also benefited greatly from its acquisition of the Congo (also known as Zaïre), which was initially run by King Leopold II as his private property from 1885 until 1908, when it became a Belgian colony. The immense natural resources of the Congo were crucial in Belgium's rapid recovery from World War II, and are still helping to support Belgium's prosperity, even though the Congo became independent in 1961.

Following the war, Flanders became more and more prosperous, while the heavy industry of the south continued to decline. Relative political stability after the crisis over the monarchy helped to attract immense foreign investment, a lot going into developing the port of Antwerp and the surrounding area. In spite of its position 54 miles/85 km inland from the sea on the Scheldt estuary, Antwerp is now the second biggest port in Europe after Rotterdam and reputedly has the fastest ship turnaround time in the world. It is also the world's leading centre for the trading and polishing of diamonds. Belgium also has a number of other ports, some of them inland, thanks to its highly developed network of canals.

The Modern Economy

Investment in Belgium is largely concentrated in manufacturing industries, where regulations are liberal and a well-trained workforce already exists. The United States is the largest foreign investor – Ford and General Motors both have factories here – and you will find that some of the leading department stores are American-owned. Volvo has a car-factory outside Ghent, and has found the workers more reliable than those in Sweden.

Traditional industries such as textiles and steel have declined as elsewhere in Europe. On the other hand, biotechnology, chemicals, pharmaceuticals, electronics and other high-tech industries are growing impressively, which has served to increase the prosperity of the Dutch-speaking north rather than of the south. Belgium now exports 70% of its GDP, one of the highest ratios in the world. In spite of its concentration of manufacturing, 47% of the land is still used for agriculture, but employs only 2.5% of the workforce.

International banks and financial institutions are also very active in Belgium although regulations are not very liberal. Because of the level of taxes and complex rules, tax evasion is rampant, and many Belgians put money into banks in the Netherlands and Luxembourg, or go there to claim their dividends and interests tax-free.

The boom years of the 1960s and 1970s were followed by a severe recession in 1979-1980, when the country appeared to be on the verge of bankruptcy. Extraordinary economic austerity policies led to a remarkable turnaround by 1985. A new recession in 1993 saw unemployment shoot up to 15.9%, leading to a wage freeze which is still in place. The economy started to grow strongly again from 1997, helped by the weakness of the euro. Unemployment is down to 8.5% although growth is now only at 1%. The balance of trade has, however, remained in surplus since 1992. Progress has been made towards meeting the Maastricht criteria for European monetary union; there was a small government budget surplus in 2001, the first time in 50 years. The national debt has gone down considerably, although it still remains alarmingly high, at 106% of GDP.

GOVERNMENT

BELGIUM HAS ALWAYS been a fragmented country, and as a result its politics have largely revolved around working out a satisfactory balance between the interests of the different communities. The system of proportional representation used in Belgium is designed to ensure that no one group becomes completely dominant. In earlier times Belgian governments fell with astonishing regularity, often for quite trivial reasons, but these days governments generally last their full four years.

Thanks to progressive federalisation, Belgium now has five levels of government: national, regional, community, provincial, and communal, with direct elections to all of them. Following the 1993 Sint Michiels agreement, which supposedly finalised the distribution of powers among the different levels of government, the Chamber of Representatives now has 150 members divided between Dutch- and French-speakers. At the same time, the Senate has had its numbers reduced to 40, plus 31 co-opted members, and has had its legislative powers substantially curtailed. Members of the royal family have the right to sit in the Senate unelected if they so wish. The government rules by decrees which must be countersigned by the King. The 10 provinces also have their own councils, and then there are 589 communes with mayors and councillors elected every six years. The nine provinces are also divided up into 45 administrative units known as *arrondissements/arrondissementen* (see map) for which there is no electoral representation.

Almost all Belgian governments since 1919 have been coalitions, with the Christian Social Party (Catholic party or Christian Democrats) in alliance with the Socialists or Liberals; the current government, elected in 1999, does not include the Christian parties. The major trends of the 1960s were the decline of the Liberals (actually a secularist right-wing party) and the rise of regionalist parties. By the 1970s the three major parties had split along linguistic lines, and a further polarisation had taken place, whereby the Christian party had become dominant in Flanders, and the traditionally anti-clericalist Socialists' power base tended to shift to Wallonia. Henceforth the leader of the Flemish Christian party inevitably became the Prime Minister as well. The French-speakers were now threatened with permanent Flemish domination as well as a rapidly declining economy.

The 1980s saw frequent changes of government, while Wilfried Martens headed every government from 1981 to 1992. In 1992, a new coalition was formed comprising Christian Democrats and Socialists, which was returned to power in

May 1995. Public confidence in the state was deeply shaken by the paedophile scandal of 1996, and the revelations of police incompetence that came in its wake. The different branches of the police have now been brought together into one organisation, although the problem of underfunding still remains. Another scandal broke in 1999, when carcinogenic dioxins were found in animal feed. The result was that, after the election of 1999, the Christian Democrats no longer formed part of the ruling coalition, the government now being composed of Socialists, Liberals and Green parties, under the Flemish Liberal leader Guy Verhofstadt.

The other major threat to political stability is the increasing popularity of the extreme right, the Vlaams Blok and the Front National, whose demands for tough action against immigrants and asylum seekers gave them almost 10% of the vote in 1999. The Vlaams Blok has also gained popularity by demanding that more of the functions of central government, in particular social security, should be placed in the hands of the regions, so that Flemish taxes do not end up in the hands of the more impoverished French-speakers.

Federalisation

Demands for devolution go back to the early days of Belgium's existence. Starting from the 1870s the Flemish gradually received the right to be tried before Dutch-speaking courts, to be educated in Dutch and to have Dutch-speaking officials in the central government. The German policy during two occupations of favouring the Dutch-speakers, as well as the pro-German tendencies of some Dutch-speakers had the unintended effect of discrediting Flemish separatism until the 1950s; serious discussions on meeting the aspirations of the language communities only began in the 1960s. The task of federalisation has been addressed in several reforms of the constitution, mainly in 1970, 1980, 1988 and 1993. The first reform fixed the boundaries of the language communities (Dutch, French and German), and created community cultural councils. It also stated that the Cabinet must have equal numbers of Dutch- and French-speaking ministers. Three regions were also created: Flanders, Wallonia and Brussels. Later revisions transferred more and more of the power of the central government to the Communities and Regions. Direct elections to Regional Assemblies finally took place in 1995. Members of the Community Assemblies are essentially the same as those of the Regions; the members of the Brussels Regional Assembly are co-opted to the French and Dutch Community Assemblies depending on their linguistic status. The German-speaking community also has its own assembly whose members sit in the French Regional Assembly. The German-speaking area comes under the control of the French Region: it would be impracticable to give such a small population group the same degree of autonomy as other regions.

The biggest problem has been to decide who is responsible for what amongst the five tiers of government: National, Regional, Community, Provincial and Communal; and complex institutions have been set up to arbitrate on disputes. At the moment, certain taxes are allocated to the Communities and Regions, and between them they now spend 60% of the national budget.

The distribution of government functions is roughly speaking as follows: the national level retains general control over policy-making and regulatory functions as well as defence, much of foreign relations, justice, social security, agriculture, the railways and other nationalised industries. The three Regions have a large degree of power in deciding their own economic policies, and are responsible for public works, state-owned industries, employment, housing, traffic, harbours and water. The Communities deal with education, the media, scientific research, social services, the arts and the defence and promotion of their respective languages. They also have control over the health service, on the basis that everyone should have the right to be treated in a hospital speaking their language. The Provinces also have certain powers, in particular in relation to public health and law and order, and are allocated some taxes.

The decisions of the Sint Michiels Accord of 1993 were meant to mark a pause in the process of federalisation. Many French-speakers fear that the next phase could be 'confederalism', namely virtual independence for the regions. French-speakers who want a strong central government greatly outnumber the few *rattachistes* in Parliament (those who wish to join Wallonia to France). There is little support for joining Flanders to the Netherlands (the so-called *orangiste* tendency). Rather Belgium is in effect going back in time, from the centralised Napoleonic constitution of 1830, to the situation under the Dukes of Burgundy in the 14th and 15th centuries, where towns and counties had to be persuaded to work together as a common unit.

Political Parties

After the last election there were 11 political parties in the Chamber of Representatives, all but one also present in the Senate. Traditionally there have been three main political parties: the Christian Social Party, the Liberals, and the Socialists. Dividing them into Dutch- and French-speaking wings, leaves the current coalition members, the PVV (Partij voor Vrijheid en Vooruitgang – Party for Freedom and Progress) and the PRL (Parti réformateur libéral – Liberal Reformist Party) together with the SP (Socialistische Partij) and PS (Parti socialiste), and the junior partners, the Dutch- and French-speaking Green parties, Agalev and Ecolo. Unusually, the Christian parties, the CVP (Christelijke Volkspartij) and the PSC (Parti social-chrétien) are, for once, not part of the government.

Parties promoting the interests of the French-speakers, notably the Brussels-based FDF (Front démocratique des francophones) are now allied to the PRL. The ultra-right Vlaams Blok has 15 representatives in Parliament; its Walloon counterpart, the Front National, has one. Some past governments have also included the Flemish nationalist VU (Volksunie).

GEOGRAPHICAL INFORMATION
Area

BELGIUM OCCUPIES 11,781 sq miles/30,541 sq km, a little larger than the American state of Maryland, making it the second smallest country in the EU after Luxembourg. It is bounded to the north by the Netherlands, to the east by

Germany and Luxembourg, and to the south by France; on the west it has a 40-mile/66 km coast on the English Channel/North Sea. At its closest Belgium is only 65 miles/104 km from the English coast. The longest distance from east to west is 175 miles/280 km and from north to south 140 miles/222 km. The land is cut into three by the two main rivers – the Scheldt (Dutch Schelde, French Escaut) and the Sambre/Meuse (Dutch Maas), which rise in France and enter the North Sea through the Netherlands. The Scheldt and Meuse are joined by a canal which runs roughly along the southern border of the Netherlands, so that Belgian shipping has access to the Rhine and other major river systems of Europe. West of the Sambre/Meuse line the country is mostly flat, fertile agricultural land; to the east it is hilly and forested, with its highest point reaching 2313 ft/694 m at the Signal de Botrange in the Hautes Fagnes region near Germany. Belgium does not have any foreign territories or offshore islands.

Regional divisions and main towns

There are three official regions and 10 provinces:

- FLANDERS – West Vlaanderen, Oost Vlaanderen, Vlaams Brabant, Antwerpen, Limburg
- WALLONIA – Hainaut, Namur, Brabant Wallon, Liège, Luxembourg
- BRUSSELS

Population

The current population of Belgium is just over 10 million, with a negligible rate of increase of 0.1%. This makes the population the third smallest in the EU after Luxembourg and Denmark. Belgium is the second most densely populated country after the Netherlands, with 858 inhabitants per sq mile/330 per sq km. The Flemish region accounts for 58% of the population, Wallonia for 33%, and Brussels for 9%. There are also 69,000 German speakers in the eastern area of Eupen and Malmédy. Belgium is more urbanised than most European countries, with 30% of the inhabitants concentrated in the urban areas of Brussels (952,000), Antwerp (480,000), Ghent (230,000), Liège (200,000), and Charleroi (210,000). Even so, 47% of the land area is given over to agriculture, and 20% is wooded. Apart from the original division into Celtic French-speakers and Germanic Dutch-speakers, and the various invaders who remained behind, Belgium has recently become a racially more and more diverse country. Of 922,000 foreigners living in Belgium, 554,000 come from the EU, most of them from Italy (38%), France, Spain and Germany. Of the rest, many are Moroccans and Turks, most of whom are likely to remain in Belgium.

Climate

Belgium's climate is generally similar to that of England, with slightly hotter summers and slightly colder winters. The highest recorded temperature in the last twenty years was 33.5° and the lowest minus 26. Average annual rainfall in Brussels is 838 mm (33 inches), which is similar to the east of England. Rain falls on about 220 days per year. Temperatures in the east of the country tend to be slightly more extreme; snow on the Ardennes plateau makes it possible to ski in some years. Table 1 (courtesy of the Belgian National Tourist Office) gives average temperatures for each month of the year:

TABLE 1	AVERAGE TEMPERATURES	
Month	Brussels °F/°C	Ostend °F/°C
January	42/6	42/6
February	42/6	42/6
March	48/9	48/9
April	55/13	52/11
May	65/18	61/16
June	69/21	65/18
July	74/23	68/20
August	72/22	69/21
September	66/19	65/18
October	56/14	56/14
November	46/8	48/9
December	42/6	45/7

REGIONAL GUIDE

MOST ENGLISH-SPEAKING foreigners in Belgium will be found in and around Brussels and Mons (where SHAPE – Supreme Headquarters Allied Powers Europe is situated). Other immigrant concentrations are to be found in the industrial areas of Antwerp, Brussels, Ghent, Charleroi and Liège.

Belgium is now divided up into the three regions of Flanders, Wallonia and Brussels, as well as the three language communities of Dutch, French and German-speakers, and the bilingual community of Brussels. Since 1993 it has become a federal state, with regional assemblies. The regions pursue their own development policies and have separate representative offices abroad. These moves all reflect the fact that most Belgians have little to do with members of the other linguistic community and would rather their taxes were spent on their own community. Everyone agrees that there is little sense of national identity. The most important entity is one's town or village rather than any larger unit, just as it was in medieval times. The visitor should at least try to be aware of the language spoken wherever they happen to be, which should not be difficult outside Brussels, given that the provinces reflect linguistic boundaries.

Information Facilities

A good starting point for information is the Belgian Tourist Office (BTO) in your home country for a supply of national maps, railway maps, and brochures on the main Belgian towns. In Belgium itself you will find tourist offices in most towns and they will usually have free maps of the town, information on places to visit and how to get there, etc. They will also be very willing to find and book a hotel room for you. You should not expect them to carry information on places outside their own region. Some railway stations have information offices which will book hotel rooms for you.

Useful Addresses

Tourism Flanders-Brussels, 31 Pepper Street, London E14 9RW; ☎ 020-7867-0311; fax 020-7458 0045; www .toerismevlaanderen.be.
Belgian Tourist Office Brussels Wallonia, 217 Marsh Wall, London E14 9FJ; ☎ 020-7531 0390; fax: 020-7531 0393; e-mail: consumer@belgiumt

heplaceto.be; www.belgiumtheplaceto.be, www.opt.be.
Belgian Tourist Office: 780 Third Avenue, Suite 1501, New York, NY 10017; ☎ 212-758 8130; fax 212-355 7675; e-mail info@visitbelgium.com; www.visitbelgium.com.

Belgium on the Internet

Belgium has been somewhat slower than some countries to switch on to the information superhighway. Most of the information available is rather factual and serious, much like the rest of the Belgian media. There are cybercafés in most Belgian towns now, including one in Deinze which serves (potato) chips to its customers. A useful starting point for Internet surfers is the website www.belgacom.be. For online telephone directories try www.infobel.be (White Pages) and www.goudengids.be (Yellow Pages). The Belgian Federal Government maintains some interesting pages at: www.belgium.fgov.be. For a guide to going out try www.uit.be, and for tourist sites www.plug-in.be.

The national telecoms company, Belgacom, offers subscription-free internet access (see www.belgacom.be). Skynet and Telenet are the most popular subscription services.

FLANDERS – THE DUTCH-SPEAKING REGION

West Vlaanderen (West Flanders)

Main tourist office: Burg 11, 8000 Brugge; ☎ 050 44 86 86; www.flanderscoast.be; www.brugge.be.
Main towns: Brugge (Bruges), Oostende (Ostend), Ieper (Ypres), Kortrijk, Knokke, Zeebrugge.

West Flanders is the fifth largest province with over 10% of the land area and population. It has all of Belgium's seacoast and therefore many of its tourist/ holiday resorts. These became fashionable in the last century with the French-speaking élite following royal patronage, and many French-speakers still spend their summer holidays there. For this reason, the coastal area is the only part of Dutch-speaking Belgium where French is widely used. During the winter the coastal resorts are quiet and some hotels close down. The Belgian seaside offers excellent sandy beaches, restaurants and sporting facilities. Inland, West Flanders is largely agricultural, one of the typical features being the pollarded willow trees. Towards the French border the landscape becomes more hilly in the area known as the West Vlaams Heuvelland.

There are high-speed ferry services from Ostend and Zeebrugge to Dover and Hull respectively; there is a small airport near Ostend – Middelkerke – but no flights to the UK. Zeebrugge is also a large container port. There are direct trains linking Ostend to Cologne via Ghent, Brussels and Liège. The E40 motorway links Ostend and Brugge to Brussels and Calais, thus providing quick access to the Channel Tunnel.

West Flanders was the site of some of the fiercest battles of World War I; the area of Ypres is dotted with memorials to the dead. Ypres was largely destroyed in World War I and it took almost 50 years to rebuild the cathedral. East of Ypres is the town of Kortrijk, the centre of the flax and linen industry, just a few miles from the French industrial city of Lille-Roubaix. The capital of this province is Brugge (often known by its French name of Bruges), more or less on the way from Ghent to Ostend, which has an unusually well-preserved medieval city centre and some world-famous art museums.

West Flanders has the lowest unemployment in Belgium and offers a very good living environment. Industrial textiles and the food industry are major employers. The textile industry has difficulty in finding enough workers. There are very good chances of finding work in the tourist sector, especially in Bruges during the summer, where there is always a shortage of staff. The youth hostels in Bruges employ English-speaking foreigners.

East Flanders (Oost Vlaanderen)

Main tourist office: Woodrow Wilson Plein, 9000 Gent; ☎09 267 70 20; www.oostvlaanderen.be; www.gent.be.

Main cities: Ghent (Gent/Gand), Sint Niklaas, Dendermonde, Oudenaarde.

East Flanders comprises 10% of the land area of Belgium and 13% of the population. It has much the same topography as West Flanders – a fertile alluvial plain intersected by rivers – the Scheldt, Leie and Dender. During the Middle Ages it reached the height of its prosperity and power through importing wool from England and then exporting it back as finished cloth. Religious wars and declining political fortunes eventually reduced the area to a backwater, many of its citizens emigrating to the Netherlands and England.

Ghent has many superb medieval buildings and is as attractive as Brugge, with more varied architecture. There are regular festivals, in particular the Floraliën, a five-yearly horticultural festival (last held in 1995) and the Festival van Vlaanderen or European Music Festival, held over three weeks in August-September every year. In July there are the Gentse Feesten with traditional processions and carnivals.

Although Ghent is the capital of the Flemish area there are a significant number of middle-class French-speakers and the local dialect shows distinct French influences. Some of the 'high-class' shops still have French-speaking staff, but in general speaking French in shops here is likely to meet with a stony response.

East Flanders was at the forefront of developments in agronomy in the 19th century, and now has a world-leading biotechnology sector, some of it foreign-owned. Horticulture is also an important employer. The traditional textile industry which once reigned supreme has now given way to textile technology and industrial fabrics. There is a wide range of industries, including car manufacturing, with a strong emphasis on high-tech. There is scope for temporary work for foreigners; a lot of extra staff are taken on for the big festivals, especially in July.

Antwerp

Main tourist office: Grote Markt 15, 2000 Antwerp; ☎03 232 01 03; www.visitantwerp.be.

Main towns: Antwerp (Antwerpen/Anvers), Turnhout, Mechelen (Malines), Lier, Geel, Herentals.

The province of Antwerp includes Belgium's largest port of the same name, and covers 9% of the land area. Most of the population of 1,600,000 live in and around Antwerp, employed in the docks or in the numerous factories which have sprung up nearby. From the early 16th century until 1648, Antwerp was Belgium's main port and commercial centre. The Protestant leanings of the inhabitants, however, brought down the wrath of the Spanish King Philip II, who eventually forced all Protestants to leave and incorporated it into the Spanish Netherlands. It took almost 200 years before the city began to recover its former status.

There is a saying that 'Antwerp is not Belgium', meaning that the city looks out towards the Netherlands and the outside world rather than towards the rest of the country. It has both very prosperous and rather seedy areas; the bohemian atmosphere attracts many artists and designers. There are some fine museums, the most popular being the home of Rubens. Antwerp also has an international airport at Deurne 4 miles/6 km to the east of the city centre with daily flights to England.

Going east of Antwerp there is the area known as the Kempen/Campine, originally a desolate area of sandy heaths, marshes and forests considered almost worthless for agriculture until it was developed by religious communities in the Middle Ages. Towards the Dutch border, 6 miles/10 km east of Geel, is Mol, the home of Belgium's nuclear research programme. On the southern edge of the province of Antwerp, halfway to Brussels, is the historic city of Mechelen (or Malines). During the First World War its Cardinal-Archbishop, Cardinal Mercier, won worldwide respect for his resistance to the German occupiers. Along with Leuven, it is still the powerhouse of the Belgian Catholic faith.

There are frequent trains from Antwerp to destinations in the Netherlands and Lille in France. The high speed train from Paris to Amsterdam, the Thalys, passes through here (see website www.thalys.com). There are daily flights from Antwerp to London.

Employment opportunities are mainly concentrated in Antwerp itself, which is by far Belgium's most prosperous city. A variety of industries have established themselves around the docks, including oil refineries, chemical and car factories. The transportation industry employs a number of English-speakers. Most of all, Antwerp is the centre of the world diamond trade – 95% of uncut diamonds pass through here, and 50% of cut diamonds. It has also recently become world-famous for its school of textile design.

In recent years the better-off inner-city inhabitants have been leaving at the rate of 4,000 a year for the suburbs, which, coupled with the threat of new ports being built closer to the mouth of the Schelde estuary, and the political difficulties caused by the extreme right Vlaams Blok, leads one to question whether the city can maintain its prosperity.

Limburg

Main tourist office: Lombardstraat 3, 3500 Hasselt; ☎ 011 23 95 40; www.hasselt.be.
Main towns: Hasselt, Sint Truiden (St. Trond), Tongeren, Genk, Heusden.

Limburg has 8% of Belgium's total surface area and 7% of the population. Although it has some notable tourist attractions it is by far the least well known area of the country, a situation which the provincial government is trying hard to remedy. In earlier times the Duchy of Limburg was a major power in the Lowlands – there is a Dutch province of Limburg across the border – but it was permanently partitioned after the 1830 revolt against the Dutch. The northern part of Limburg is a continuation of the Kempen, with sandy plains, moorlands and forests. The southern part, the Haspengouw (Hesbaye), is more fertile and undulating, with a large concentration of fruit-growing.

The provincial capital, Hasselt, is a modern town, notable as the centre of the Belgian *jenever* (gin) industry. To the northwest the racetrack at Zolder is sometimes the site of the Belgian Grand Prix and nearby is the holiday resort of Heusden. Southeast of Hasselt is the Roman town of Tongeren (Atuatuca Tongrorum). West of Tongeren the town of St. Truiden has substantial medieval remains. These days the area is something of an unemployment blackspot.

Limburg is mostly Dutch-speaking but there are some French-speakers in the commune of Les Fourons/De Voeren, an enclave separated from the rest of Limburg by part of Liège. De Voeren has been the subject of bitter disputes since it elected a French-speaking mayor who refused to take an examination in Dutch. In 1986 this resulted in violent scenes in the national parliament and the fall of the government.

There are motorways linking Hasselt and Genk to Germany and Liège, and a frequent train service from Hasselt and Genk to Maastricht in the Netherlands and to Brussels and Ostend. The regional government is keen to build a north-south motorway to Eindhoven, in order to stimulate more economic activity. The main attraction of Limburg is that it still has a large amount of land available for building. The most prosperous areas are around Hasselt and Genk, with their car factories, and the north around Overpelt, one of the centres of the steel industry. The rest of Limburg suffers from high unemployment because of the ending of coal mining.

Vlaams-Brabant (North Brabant)

Main tourist office: Diestsesteenweg 52, 3010 Kessel Lo; ☎016 26 76 20; www.vl-brabant.be.

Main towns: Leuven (Louvain), Tienen (Tirlemont), Halle (Hal), Vilvoorde.

Including the conurbation of Brussels, Brabant has 2.2 million inhabitants and covers 11% of the land area. It has now been split into three provinces, with Brussels a separate region and the rest divided between the Flemish and Walloon executives. The provincial capital is still Brussels. North Brabant's capital is Leuven (or Louvain) whose origins may well go back to Julius Caesar's time. It was a prosperous cloth city in the 13th and 14th centuries; it has Belgium's most prestigious university, dating from 1425. During the 1960s the Flemish community agitated for the university to become purely Dutch-speaking. In the end it split into two sections and a French-speaking university was established at Louvain-la-Neuve south of Brussels in 1970. The Katholieke Universiteit Leuven is now a major centre for Flemish Catholic academics. Leuven's other great claim to fame is the Stella Artois brewery.

To the northeast of Leuven is the town of Aarschot, the centre of asparagus-growing in Belgium, and to the southeast Tienen (Tirlemont) the sugar-producing capital of Belgium. West of Leuven, in the northern suburbs of Brussels, is the industrial town of Vilvoorde, where William Tyndale was burnt at the stake as a heretic in 1535. In 1997 it was at the centre of industrial unrest when Renault suddenly closed its factory. There are also many chemical factories in the area. West of Brussels is the agricultural region of the Pajottenland.

Vlaams-Brabant benefits from having Belgium's international airport at Zaventem. There is a dense network of motorways and railways in the area. The mixed economy offers various employment possibilities, with a dense concentration of foreign companies, such as IT, accountancy and transportation.

WALLONIA – THE FRENCH-SPEAKING REGION

Brabant-Wallon (South Brabant)

Main tourist office: Place Albert Ier 1, 1400 Nivelles; ☎067 21 54 13; www.brabantwallon.be.

Main towns: Nivelles, Wavre, Braine l'Alleud, Louvain-la-Neuve.

The south of Brabant shares much of the same history as the north and was partly Dutch-speaking at one time. These days it is a fashionable area for wealthier locals and foreigners, with plenty of international schools. The landscape of rolling meadows dotted with small woods and châteaux makes it an attractive environment to live in.

Nivelles (Dutch Nijvel), on the way from Brussels to Charleroi is famous for its convent, founded in 650 AD, but for most foreigners the most important thing to see in this area is the site of the battle of Waterloo. There are few actual physical remnants, and one would have to visit the museums and souvenir shops to understand much of what happened. The British made sure to build the biggest memorial, an artificial hill with a lion on the top. In general, the Walloons took the side of Napoleon and the Flemings the British-Dutch-German side.

South Brabant shares the same advantages as North Brabant as regards communications and proximity to Brussels. Expatriates who favour French culture will appreciate being a short drive away from the French border. Job opportunities are varied; the area has the highest concentration of foreign schoolteachers, au pairs and nannies in the country. Banking and related activities are another major employer.

Hainaut (Henegouwen)

Main tourist office: Grand Place 22, 7000 Mons; ☎065 33 55 80; www.hainaut.be.
Main towns: Mons (Bergen), Charleroi, Tournai (Doornik), Mouscron (Moeskroen), Ath (Aat).

The province of Hainaut, bordering France, makes up 12% of the land area and 13% of the population of Belgium. Much of the province is agricultural, while having a heavy concentration of engineering industry. The recorded history of the capital, Mons or Bergen in Dutch (population 90,000) goes back to the seventh century. It shared in the prosperity of other cloth-making towns as well as in their frequent wars. It was the site of one of the great opening battles of World War I. Nowadays it is the command centre for NATO troops in Europe, which is located five miles away at Casteau. Several thousand Americans and other foreigners live in the area, and English is widely spoken.

Much the largest city in Hainaut is Charleroi (population 212,000). It was made into a fortress by the Spanish in 1666 named after Charles II of Spain. It is significant as one of the centres of Belgium's traditional heavy industries, but is now at the centre of the Walloon rustbelt along with La Louvière. In earlier days, along with mining and engineering, pottery and glass-making were major activities. On the more positive side, Charleroi has the cheapest housing in the country. Since 2001 there are direct flights from Brussels South Charleroi airport to London Stansted, Glasgow, Dublin, Shannon, Pisa, Venice and Carcassonne with Ryanair.

Mons has good rail connections and is on the high-speed railway line from Paris to Cologne, but unfortunately there is only one train a day to these destinations.

Hainaut's efforts at regenerating its economy have had only limited success. There is some overspill from the more successful Flanders, but further development will inevitably have a negative impact on the environment.

Namur (Namen)

Main tourist office: Place Léopold, 5000 Namur; ☎081 24 64 49; www.ciger.be/Namur.
Main towns: Namur, Dinant, Philippeville, Gembloux.

Namur province is relatively lightly populated, with 12% of the land area and 4% of the Belgian population. The Ardennes plateau begins here and extends through the provinces of Liège and Luxembourg, as well as through parts of France, Luxembourg and Germany. Namur is cut through by numerous rivers such as the Meuse, Sambre and Lesse and their tributaries, which have formed deep ravines amongst the forests, giving the region a wild, scenic beauty. Caves and grottoes are another natural feature. Communications here are less developed than in neighbouring provinces and it is useful to have your own transport if you want to explore. Visitors are mostly attracted by the small towns perched on the sides of ravines and the numerous châteaux and churches. Restaurants and hotels are to be found here in abundance.

Chimay, near the French border, is famed for its dark beer brewed by Trappist monks. Otherwise the Meuse valley has always been famous for its metalwork, called Mosan. Namur (Dutch Namen), the provincial capital, lies at the confluence of the Sambre and Meuse near the Brussels to Luxembourg motorway. There is an impressive fortified citadel.

17 miles/28 km south of Namur, built into a gorge on the river Meuse, is the tourist town of Dinant, which, like ', has a citadel and cable-car railway to the top. It is noted as the birthplace of the inventor of the saxophone, Adolphe Sax. The restaurants are highly rated.

Namur has never been a heavily industrialised province; the attractive and peaceful environment has brought a number of foreign companies to the area, who require IT and finance specialists. Namur lies on the main line from Brussels and Luxembourg. Access to France by road or rail is not all that good.

Liège (Luik)

Main tourist office: Féronstrée 92, 4000 Liège; ☎ 04 221 92 21; www.liege.be.
Main towns: Liège, Verviers, Waremme, Huy, Spa.

The province of Liège, bordering on Holland and Germany, comprises 12.6% of the land-area and 10% of the population of Belgium. Surrounded by rich deposits of lead, zinc, iron and coal, the capital city, Liège, developed into a centre for steel and weapon making from the 12th century. While the steel industry is only a shadow of its former self, non-ferrous metals and mechanical engineering are still doing well.

Liége province was unique in Belgium, in that it remained independent under the Prince-Bishops of Liège from the 10th century until 1794, when French revolutionaries expelled the Prince-Bishop and razed the Gothic cathedral to the ground, leaving a huge hole in the centre of the city. Liège still retains a great deal of original charm, with its wide boulevards and open-air cafés. It is also a major cultural centre. The composer César Franck and the writer Georges Simenon originated from here.

The highest area of Belgium, the Hautes Fagnes (German Hohes Venn), the High Fens, is in the east of Liège, on the German border. The German-speaking towns of Eupen and Malmédy are also worth visiting. Nearby is the town of Spa, which gave its name to all the other towns named Spa, and the racing circuit of Spa-Francorchamps.

Liège city benefits from being on the high-speed rail line from Paris to Cologne. There are also frequent conventional trains to Maastricht in the Netherlands, and to Cologne. All the motorways in the province converge on the city; there is nowhere very remote in the province.

The metallurgy industry in this province is a world-leader, but it is the only industry that is doing well in the area. Liège has a dynamic cultural life, with its own special identity, but it is far from an obvious place to look for work, unless you have specialised skills.

Luxembourg (Luxemburg)

Main tourist office: Rue des Faubourgs 2, 6700 Arlon; ☎ 063 21 63 60; www.ftlb.be.
Main towns: Arlon, Bastogne, Libramont, Neufchâteau.

Luxembourg (not to be confused with the Grand Duchy) is by far the largest and also the most sparsely populated province of Belgium, with 14% of the land area and 2% of the population. The ancient Ardennes forest extends over the whole province, and has some of Belgium's most scenic rivers, popular with campers and hikers. Luxembourg also offers several ski-ing locations, provided enough snow falls. The far south of the province, known as La Gaume, or the Belgian Lorraine, is a tobacco-growing region. It is also well-known for its beer.

During the medieval period the Duchy of Luxembourg extended much further to the west and south than it does today, and was linked to the Holy Roman Empire. After 1815 Luxembourg lost all its eastern territories and was compensated with parts of Bouillon and Liège. It then came under the Dutch, but was split into two in 1839, with the French-speaking west becoming the Belgian province of Luxembourg, and the more Germanic east eventually becoming independent.

The provincial capital, Arlon is relatively small (22,000 inhabitants), but particularly significant as one of the major Roman settlements in Belgium. 40 km/25 miles to the north, still right by the border of the Grand Duchy, is the town of Bastogne, the site of the Battle of the Bulge in December 1944.

While being the most scenic of Belgium's provinces, Luxembourg also has a certain amount of industry. There are motorways to Liège and Luxembourg City. The rest of the province has few main roads and access to France is not particularly easy.

Brussels Region (Bruxelles/Brussel)

Main tourist office: Hôtel de Ville, Grand Place, 1000 Brussels; ☎ 02 513 89 40; www.eurobru.com.

Brussels, with almost 1,000,000 inhabitants, is not only the capital of Belgium and the administrative centre of both language communities, but also houses the European Commission and the headquarters of NATO. As a result, many more international organisations have set up offices in Brussels, bringing thousands of expatriate workers along with them.

Brussels began as a small settlement on an island in the middle of the marshy river Senne, hence its early name, Bruocsella, the dwelling in a marsh. Thanks to the large numbers of irises that grew around the Senne, this flower is now the symbol of Brussels. In 979 a fortress was built on the island, for which reason Brussels celebrated its millennium in 1979.

At first a small staging post on the road from Ghent to Cologne, Brussels developed into a town under the Dukes of Brabant, and eventually was made the capital of the Spanish Netherlands in the 16th century. Louis XIV devastated the city in 1695, but many magnificent buildings took the place of what was lost. As the capital of Belgium, Brussels was beautified with parks and wide boulevards, and the river Senne covered over. In recent times a metro system has been built. From an architectural point of view, Brussels has a rather odd mix of styles. The Grand-Place is justly famous for its harmonious style, but many other buildings have been put up without much regard for their surroundings. The city still retains a number of fine art nouveau buildings.

Apart from its national and international organisations, Brussels is also the business capital of Belgium, with the Bourse (stock market) and the National Bank located here. For the visitor there are many museums (such as the superb Musée des Beaux-Arts and the Cartoon Museum) and some of the best and most expensive restaurants in Europe. The real heart and soul of Brussels, however, is hard to find; the city has a rather confused identity, since so many of the inhabitants switched from speaking Dutch to speaking French relatively recently. At the present time, some 30% of the population are foreigners, with the proportion rising to 35% in the central commune and 75% in St Gillis. EU nationals make up 50% of the foreigners in the Brussels agglomeration. Of the Belgian inhabitants, about 15% are Dutch-speakers, and 85% French-speakers. The status of Brussels is the major obstacle to splitting Belgium completely. It is now an autonomous region, with an assembly and government like Flanders and Wallonia.

As one would expect of a capital city, one can pursue almost any interest in Brussels. As capital cities go, Brussels is quite small, and it is certainly more cosmopolitan than most. The locals are friendly and hospitable.

For job-seekers, Brussels is an obvious place to consider, but it must be borne in mind that Brussels is by far the most expensive place to live in Belgium. It is easy enough to commute from the surrounding area, but public transport ends at midnight. On the other hand, Brussels is already joined by high-speed trains to London, Paris, Amsterdam and Cologne, so one can travel far and wide at the weekends.

GETTING TO BELGIUM

THERE ARE MANY ways to get to Belgium, none of them very expensive. The Eurostar high-speed passenger train service from London Waterloo to the centre of Brussels, via Ashford and Lille, has encouraged many more Britons to take short breaks in Belgium. By the year 2003 there should be a high-speed service between London and the Channel Tunnel, and possibly a direct service to Antwerp. Those wishing to continue on to other destinations in Belgium need to change at Brussels for the moment. See their website for regularly updated information. Belgian Railways also has a website: www.nmbs.be. Car drivers should contact Le Shuttle.

The Irish low-fares airline, Ryanair, changed the face of travel to Belgium when it started flights to Charleroi from London and Glasgow in 2001. Depending on when you book, it is possible to pay less than a quarter of the price charged by other airlines, but it is necessary to check their website daily for the best fares.

The introduction of high-speed ferries, or HSS, has made sailing more attractive. The crossing from Dover to Ostend takes 120 minutes, Dover to Calais 45 minutes. Calais is the favoured point of entry for motorists. The cheapest way to get to Belgium (if one leaves aside special offers by Ryanair) is by coach with Eurolines/National Express or Hoverspeed with a choice of Ghent, Antwerp, Brussels or Liège as destinations.

Direct flights from North America to Brussels are limited to three airlines. American Airlines flies from Chicago to Brussels daily; Delta from New York and Atlanta to Brussels; and United from Washington DC to Brussels. At the time of writing, the Belgian airline DAT, which took over some routes from the defunct national carrier Sabena, had no scheduled services to North America.

Train Services
Eurostar: ☎ 08705-186186; www.eurostar.com.
Le Shuttle: ☎ 08705-353535 (bookings); 08000-969 992 (inquiries); www.eurotunnel.com.

Ferry Services
Hoverspeed: International Hoverport, Dover CT17 9TG; ☎ 08705-240241 (UK); 059 55 99 11/13 (Belgium); www.hoverspeed.com. Dover to Ostend/Calais.
P&O North Sea Ferries: King George Dock, Hedon Road, Hull HU9 5QA; ☎ 0870-129 6002; fax 01482-706438; www.ponsf.com. Hull/Zeebrugge.
P&O Stena Line: Channel House, Channel View Road, Dover CT17 9TJ; ☎ 01304-203388; www.posl.com. Dover/Calais.

Air Services
British Airways: Waterside, POB 365, Harmondsworth, UB7 0GB; ☎ 0845-77 333 77 *or* 0845-606 0747; www.britishairways.com; Heathrow/Gatwick/Manchester/Birmingham/Glasgow to Brussels.
British European: Exeter Airport, Devon EX5 2BD; 0870-567 6676; www.flybe.com; Newcastle/Edinburgh/Birmingham to Brussels.
bmi British Midland: Donington Hall, Castle Donington, Derby, E. Midlands DE74 2SB; ☎ 0870-60 70 555 (reservations); 01332-854000 (switchboard); www.flybmi.com. Birmingham/Brussels; East Midlands/Brussels; Heathrow/Brussels.
DAT: 0870-735 23 45; www.dat.be. Heathrow/Birmingham/Bristol/Manchester/Newcastle to Brussels.
Ryanair: ☎ 08701-569 569; www.ryanair.com. London Stansted/Glasgow/Dublin/Shannon to Brussels.
VLM: London City Airport, Royal Docks, London E16 2PX; ☎ 020-7476 6677. London City to Antwerp.
Virgin Express: ☎ 0800-891199; www.virgin/express.com. Heathrow to Brussels.

Coach Services
Eurolines (UK): 4 Cardiff Rd, Luton, Beds LU1 1PP; ☎ 08705-143219; e-mail welcome@eurolines.co.uk; www.eurolines.co.uk. London to Ghent/Antwerp/Brussels/Liège.

USEFUL GUIDES

Brussels, Ghent, Bruges and Antwerp: Cadogan Guides.
Cities of the Imagination: Brussels: Signal Books. In-depth cultural and literary guide.
Flemish Cities Explored: Pallas Athene. For serious enthusiasts.
Frommer's Belgium, Holland and Luxembourg: Macmillan Travel. Detailed information on places to visit, hotels, history and so on.
Insight Guides Belgium: APA Publications. Colourful guide with emphasis on history and folklore.
The Rough Guide to Belgium and Luxembourg: Rough Guides/Penguin.
Time Out Brussels.

RESIDENCE & ENTRY REGULATIONS

THE CURRENT POSITION

WITH THE COMING of the Single Market from 1993 and continuing moves towards a federal European state, it might seem that this chapter could soon be irrelevant. The Single Market allows all EU nationals freedom of movement and residence in the EU, but of course this does not mean that there are no regulations governing EU nationals who wish to live and work in another EU country. As regards EFTA countries, citizens of Iceland and Norway have the same rights as those from the EU, but the Swiss do not. Together the EU and EFTA countries constitute the European Economic Area (EEA).

In the case of Belgium, EU citizens receive the kind of favourable treatment that one would expect, even if there is still a degree of red tape to go through. The law states that no work permit is required. As regards residence, there is a graduated series of stages going from just being a temporary visitor, through permanent resident, right up to becoming a Belgian citizen. While the authorities retain the right to deport undesirables, the EU guarantees your basic right to live in Belgium. For most other non-EU citizens without very good reasons for being in Belgium the situation is more difficult.

EU NATIONALITY

THE RIGHT TO LIVE and work in Belgium is extended to all EU citizens, including Austria, Finland and Sweden, who are now full members, as well as Norway and Iceland.

It is not sufficient to be the holder of a passport of an EU country: you must also possess right of abode in that country. This will be indicated in the passport, in the case of a UK national, by the wording 'British Citizen'. Those who fulfil these criteria should follow the procedure for EU nationals shown below; those who fulfil the first but not the second requirement must follow the procedure for non-EU nationals described below. Anyone in any doubt about their status should check with the passport authorities in their own country or with the local Belgian consulate.

Entry and Residence for EU Nationals

In order to enter Belgium a UK national must have a full valid passport. The need to have the right papers should not be underestimated: in 1996 a 76-year-old British woman was held in jail for not having her passport. It is not necessary for EU nationals to apply for a visa or other permission before going to Belgium with a view to living or working there. Such persons can enter Belgium as tourists and then take the necessary steps to change their status to resident. If you wish to do voluntary work with a recognised institution for less than three months there is no need to register with the authorities.

EU nationals who know that they are going to stay in Belgium for more than three months for any purpose must register within eight days at the local town hall (*maison communale/stadhuis*). There are 589 communes in Belgium with their own maison communale: the names are listed at the beginning of the Yellow Pages for the relevant area. In the past there were over 2,000 communes, which were reduced to the present number in 1977. Large cities have generally absorbed many former communes, now renamed 'districts' or 'localities', with their former town halls still providing some services to local residents. Foreigners need to go to the main town hall, and ask for the 'Aliens' bureau' (*Bureau Administratif des Etrangers/Administratief Vreemdelingenbureau* or *Dienst Vreemdelingenzaken*).

When registering at the town hall, you should take your passport and three passport-sized photographs. At this point you will be placed on the Aliens' Register (*Registre des Etrangers/Vreemdelingenregister*) and issued with 'Mauve card Model B' (*Attestation of Immatriculation*), which is valid for three months and can be renewed for a further period of three months. This card is to be used until one receives permanent resident status and applies to those staying between three months and a year who wish to work. You may be asked to produce an attestation of work signed by your employer to prove you can support yourself. There is a small charge to pay, and you may be asked to give fingerprints. If for some reason you wish to remain in Belgium, but you do not have sufficient funds, it is possible for a Belgian or EEA citizen resident in Belgium to undertake to support you for a period of two years.

Although you are not likely to be asked for them at the outset, there are a number of documents which you may sooner or later have to produce, the main one being your birth certificate. A British birth certificate has to be legalised with the 'apostille' by the Legalisation Office, Foreign and Commonwealth Office, Old Admiralty Building, The Mall, London SW1A 2LG; ☎020-7008 1111; www.fco.gov.uk. Other documents include your marriage/divorce certificate and health insurance documents.

Once you have a fixed abode and a regular income, and if you decide that you would like to stay in Belgium for more than a year, you should then move on to apply for a 'Blue card' or 'EU Residence card' (*Carte de séjour de ressortissant d'un Etat-membre de la CEE/Verblijfskaart van onderdaan van een Lid-staat der EEG*) which is valid for five years. This confirms your right to stay in Belgium (which you always had in any case). If your employment is permanent, then one could apply for this card after three months. In any case, the law states that the card must be issued to you within six months of your application. It is then renewable indefinitely.

If you know in advance that you are going to spend a year or more working in Belgium you have to apply for a 'Blue card' at the outset, taking along your employment contract or an attestation of work signed by your employer, or, if self-employed, documents and diplomas required for your profession. While you are waiting for your blue card, you will be issued with the mauve one mentioned above.

Acquiring the blue card means that you have been placed on the Population Register of the local commune and that you have permanent resident status (*Etablissement/Vestiging*). In general, you must continue to be gainfully employed and able to support yourself. The commune must always be informed if you move your place of residence and you will have to re-register with your new commune. If you decide to leave Belgium for more than a year, you must inform the commune how long you intend to be away for. Any doubts can be clarified by the immigration service offices shown below.

EU nationals who go to Belgium to study will be issued with a mauve card, which is then renewed for as long as they are in Belgium. EU citizens not intending to work or study in Belgium can remain in Belgium as long as they have some means of support. They can go on to the Population Register of the commune, and are given another type of identity card – the 'Yellow card' – which is also issued to non-EU dependants of EU nationals working in Belgium.

The Citizens First campaign operated by the EU provides information on residence and employment for EU citizens in other member countries. You can obtain a guide to rights of residence in Belgium by calling Freephone 0800-581591. Information on legal and human rights questions is available from the AIRE Centre (Advice on Individual Rights in Europe) on 020-7831 3850. You can also look at the website http://citizens.eu.int. General information about residence and work permits can be found on the Brussels-Europe Liaison Office website: www.blbe.irisnet.be.

Entry On A Self-Employed Basis

EU citizens have the right to self-employed status in Belgium. If the area you wish to work in is one where trade unions are very active, for example, building, then obstacles may be put in your way. Those in the professions will have to deal with the relevant professional body in order to become established in Belgium. In order to obtain a residence permit, a self-employed person must show that they are making social security payments. Where necessary they must also go onto the Commercial Register and with the VAT authorities.

Those from outside the EU planning to be self-employed in Belgium need to obtain a Professional Card (*Carte professionnelle pour étrangers/Beroepskaart voor vreemdelingen*) from the Ministry of the Self-Employed (see below) via the Belgian Consulate in their country. This procedure can last up to a year. Applicants are only likely to be successful if they are planning to do work which could not be done by a Belgian or EU national. There is a fast-track procedure for journalists and investors.

ENTRY & WORK PERMITS FOR NON-EEA NATIONALS

NON-EEA NATIONALS may require a visa to enter Belgium as tourists. US citizens will receive a stamp on arrival which allows them to spend a total of 90 days out of six months in Belgium. It is not necessary to obtain a visa prior to travelling. A US citizen who plans to stay in Belgium for more than three months must apply for an 'Authorisation of Provisional Sojourn' or APS (*Autorisation de Séjour Provisoire/Vergunning tot Voorlopig Verblijf*) before entering Belgium. The applicant has to supply evidence that they do not have a criminal record, undergo a medical examination, and show that that they can support themselves in Belgium. Once in Belgium, they can go on to the Register of Aliens and will obtain the provisional 'Orange card model A' (Attestation of Immatriculation) or the 'White card' known as the CIRÉ in French (*Certificat d'Inscription dans le Registre des Etrangers* or Certificate of Inscription in the Register of Aliens) or BIVR in Dutch, which is a 'Title of residence' valid for one year and renewable thereafter. Both these cards show that you have gone on to the Register of Aliens. Non-EU nationals working in Belgium, or residing in Belgium for a certain period of time can apply to go on to the Population Register and, if successful, will obtain the 'Yellow card' mentioned before.

According to a law of 1985, which is still in force, the six central communes of Brussels (see below) and the City of Liège will only register Belgians and EU nationals. There may be exceptions.

You should be aware that it is difficult to sign a lease or to get public services without an identity card (blue, white or yellow card). The Belgian authorities attach a great deal of importance to one's birth certificate (with apostille), so it is essential to have this to hand. It is advisable to know the date and place of birth of one's parents and grandparents as well, something you are likely to be asked sooner or later. Whichever card you are issued with, it should be kept on your person at all times. If you fail to provide identification when asked by a police officer you may be detained at a police station until your identity has been established. Police officers are not allowed to take away your identity card.

THERE ARE THREE CLASSES OF WORK PERMIT (*PERMIS DE TRAVAIL/ARBEIDSKAART*) IN BELGIUM: A, B AND C.

- **Work Permit A** is the most favourable in that it permits the worker to work in any sector of the economy, change jobs, and is for an unlimited period, unless the worker leaves the country for more than one year. Permit A is granted to long-term residents from non-EU countries and to non-EU dependants of EU workers.
- **Work Permit B** applies to non-EU nationals, such as US citizens. Permit B is valid for only one employer and that employer must obtain an 'Authorisation of Employment' (*Autorisation d'occupation/Arbeidsvergunning*) in advance. Workers from countries with bilateral labour agreements with Belgium – Algeria, Malta, Morocco, Tunisia, Turkey, Switzerland, Slovenia, Croatia, Macedonia and Bosnia are given Work Permit B if they are offered a job.

> ○ **Work Permit C** applies to non-EU nationals the nature of whose work involves multiple employers, such as musicians and film crews, and is very rarely used these days. The basic principle for foreigners is that you must have a work permit before you can get a residence permit. Journalists, seamen, flight crews and some other categories are exempted from the above restrictions.

If you believe that you need a work permit, the relevant application forms can be obtained from any Sub-regional Employment Office (see Chapter Six, *Employment*).

NATIONALITY AND CITIZENSHIP

FOREIGN NATIONALS can, after at least five years, apply for Belgian citizenship, although this would serve little purpose for anyone from the EU. Children born of foreign parents in Belgium take the father's nationality. Foreign nationals with children born in Belgium should register the birth with their local embassy/consulate. A child with one Belgian parent can have dual nationality (as long as they apply for the nationality of the other country) but is treated as a Belgian citizen by the authorities. Fortunately, military service was abolished in 1995.

For the first time in 1999, foreign residents were allowed to vote in local elections, after a great deal of opposition, but only 15% of foreigners bothered to register. Some Belgian cities have in the past set up foreigners' councils, an idea first pioneered in Liége in 1968. These are known as *Conseils Communals Consultatifs des Immigrés* (Foreign Residents' Consultative Councils). These days their main function is to help non-EU immigrants who are in dispute with the immigration authorities.

SUMMARY

WHILE THE RULES governing EU residents in Belgium have been simplified by the introduction of the Single Market in 1993, their actual application can vary considerably between different Belgian communes and it is best to be prepared for this. Town halls in big cities are used to dealing with aliens and will certainly have some English-speaking staff. The Belgian Embassy can also provide you with a booklet on living and working in Belgium.

Once resident in Belgium, it is essential to register with your local Consulate. This enables UK authorities to keep you up to date with new information for overseas residents and to trace you in the event of an emergency. You also need to make sure that your passport remains valid while you are abroad. Consulates do not act as employment bureaux and are not a source of general help and advice. If you are thinking of living in Belgium then your first port of call is always the Belgian Consulate in your own country. There are consulates to represent the interests of the individual once in Belgium, while embassies represent their country.

Useful Addresses

Belgian Embassies:
103 Eaton Square, London SW1W 9AB; ☎020-7470 3700; fax 020-7470 3710; e-mail London@diplobel.org; www.diplobel.org/uk.
Shrewsbury House, 2 Shrewsbury Rd., Ballsbridge, Dublin 4, Eire; ☎01-269 20 82; fax 01-283 84 88.
3330 Garfield St. N.W., Washington D.C. 20008; ☎202-333 6900; fax 202-333 3079; e-mail Washington@diplobel.org; www.diplobel.org/usa.

In Belgium:
British Embassy: Rue d'Arlon 85, 1000 Brussels; ☎02 287 62 11; fax 02 287 62 70. Consular Section: ☎02 287 62 11; fax 02 287 63 20; www.britishembassy.be.
British Consulate: c/o Immobiliën Hugo Ceusters, Frankrijklei 31-33, 2000 Antwerpen; ☎03 213 21 25; fax 03 213 29 91.
British Consulate: Rue Beeckman 45, 4000 Liège; ☎04 223 58 32.
Irish Embassy: Rue de Luxembourg 19, 1000 Brussels; ☎02 513 66 33.
US Embassy: Bvd du Régent 27, 1000 Brussels; ☎02 508 21 11; www.usembassy.be.
City of Brussels Commune Administration Centre: Aliens' Bureau, Bvd Anspach 6; ☎02 279 35 20.

Brussels communes only registering EEA nationals, and the telephone numbers of their Aliens' Bureaux:
Anderlecht: Place du Conseil 1, 1070 Brussels; ☎02 558 08 00.
Forest/Vorst: Rue du Curé 2, 1190 Brussels; ☎02 370 22 59.
Molenbeek Saint Jean/Sint-Jans-Molenbeek: Rue du Comte de Flandre 20, 1080 Brussels; ☎02 412 36 73.
Saint Gilles/Saint Gillis: Place M. van Meenen, 1060 Brussels; ☎02 536 02 11.
Saint-Josse-Ten-Noode/Sint Joost-Ten-Noode: Av. de l'Astronomie 13, 1210 Brussels; ☎02 220 26 28.
Schaerbeek/Schaarbeek: Place Colignon 2, 1030 Brussels; ☎02 244 70 54.

For Professional Cards and information on self-employment:
Ministère de l'Agriculture et des Classes Moyennes/Ministerie van Agricultuur en Middenstand, World Trade Centre III, Bvd S. Bolivar 30, 1010 Brussels; ☎02 208 51 33; fax 02 208 51 47; www.cmlag.fgov.be.

Foreign Residents' Consultative Council:
Conseil Consultatif des Bruxellois d'Origine Etrangère, Bvd Maurice Lemonnier 162, 1000 Brussels; ☎02 511 34 37.

SETTING UP HOME

WHILE THE BRITISH press and certain politicians enjoy whipping up anti-European sentiment, many British citizens have voted with their feet and successfully set up home in another EU country. Britons have been migrating to Belgium ever since the battle of Waterloo, in far larger numbers than one might imagine. The original population of British expatriates who settled in Belgium at the end of World War II has now been replaced by large numbers of young professionals sent to work there who decide to stay on. At present an estimated 26,000 Britons and 12,000 US citizens reside in Belgium, a substantial number in relation to the total population.

The areas where foreigners are mostly likely to buy property are those within easy commuting distance of major cities, which, given Belgium's small size, covers about half the country. Property in Belgium is plentiful and relatively cheap; even so property has always outperformed the Brussels stock market over the years. Between 1987 and 1991, property prices in Brussels soared to undreamt-of levels by Belgian standards. From 1992 and 1996 prices rose more gradually; with the economic recovery and lower interest rates prices have gone up more quickly (although still only at a rate of 5% a year in Brussels) since 1996. The average house in Brussels now costs about €129,000 (£82,500 or $116,000). Apartments in Brussels are relatively cheap compared to the Flemish region, at an average of €75,000 (£48,000 or $68,000). In less fashionable locations within 20 miles of Brussels it is still possible to buy a flat or terrace house in good condition for less than €50,000. There is also an active market in properties on the Belgian coast for holidaymakers. For property prices in Belgium, see Tables 1 and 2 below.

While property prices may look cheap, potential buyers should be aware of the particular conditions of the market in Belgium. In the first place, estate agents in Britain do not deal with Belgian property, since the Belgian property market is generally buoyant and does not need to look for foreign buyers. The buyer is therefore obliged to go to Belgium and to deal with local estate agents and/or a notary (*notaire/notaris*). A notary is essential for the registration of the house purchase and for a mortgage agreement as well. Estate agents are now regulated by the Ministère des Classes Moyennes (Ministry of the Middle Classes) and have to be qualified before they can conduct a business. All estate agents must be registered with the *Institut Professionel des Agents Immobiliers* or *Beroepsinstituut van Vastgoedmakelaars* (☎ 02 505 38 50; www.biv.be). They may also be members of another professional association such as the *Confédération Immobilière Belge (CIB)*, the association of Belgian real estate agents (☎ 02 347 29 87; www.cib.be).

In many cases you will find that the house sale is being handled by a notary on behalf of the seller. You should by all means engage your own notary to look after your interests. If the buyer and seller each have their own notary the fee has to be split, so this will not add to your costs. Notaries will try to pressure both sides into using only one notary, even though there is a clear conflict of interest. In any case, you will need professional advice; otherwise you could end up paying over the odds.

There are now a large number of British property companies in Brussels dealing with offices and investment property. Limiting your search to English-speaking estate agents or to the English press is a doubtful strategy, since you will not have a wide choice of properties to look at. The best source of properties, especially at the bottom end of the market, is the local press (see below).

If you intend to buy or invest in property in Belgium, it would be a good idea to obtain a copy of *A Practical Guide to Property Purchase and Arranging Mortgage Finance in Belgium*, published by Michael Kingshott & Associates, 22 rue de Hocaille, 1390 Archennes, Belgium (☎ 010 84 42 50; fax 84 25 25; michael.kingshott@yucom.be), which can be paid for with a UK cheque for £15.00. The above company will provide assistance not only with house purchase and mortgages, but also with other investments in Belgium. Another possibility is to ask a reputable relocation company to handle matters.

When looking at property prices it is essential to take into account the costs of registration (12.5%) and a notary (a fixed fee of about 1-4%). If you sell within two years you can get 60% of the costs of registration back, but otherwise these are lost. Mortgages also attract legal fees and duties. If you buy at auction the notary's fees will be twice as high as with a normal sale, and you will be obliged to complete the purchase and arrange a mortgage within one month. Buying a new property entails paying 21% VAT for the property and 12.5% for the land. If you build a property yourself, labour and materials are also subject to 21% VAT, and there is the added complication of planning permission. You will also have to prove that you did all the work yourself; any work done by someone else attracts VAT.

On the face of it, property in Belgium appears to be cheap, but one should always bear in mind that because of the high costs associated with buying, prices are never likely to go up as quickly as they may do in Britain. Most expatriates rent properties first; as many of them are on fixed-term contracts in Belgium, the question of buying a property does not arise. If you are thinking of settling in Belgium permanently then paying rent would be money down the drain, and the difference between the price of your UK/US home and the one in Belgium could generate a substantial amount of capital as well.

HOW DO THE BELGIANS LIVE?

THE FAMILY UNIT is still very much in evidence in Belgium; stastically at least, the average Belgian lives in his or her own house – 66% of dwellings are owner-occupied and the number is still increasing. Houses are either detached or terraced – semi-detached houses are not all that common. The Belgians like a considerable amount of personal space; statistically, the average Belgian has more floor space than anyone else in Europe. Almost 75% of houses are occupied by just one family, and the rest are mostly apartments.

The number of occupants per property at the moment stands at 2.3 and is tending downwards, largely because the divorce rate has shot up. There is generally no shortage of housing, and accommodation for single people is quite readily available. Unfurnished accommodation here means unfurnished – you will probably have to buy your own cooker and fridge as well as everything else. Mobility is even further restricted by the strict nature of rental agreements. The average Belgian tends therefore to stay in one place, and to invest a considerable amount in equipping their flat or house.

Belgians are rather houseproud by our standards, as you will notice when you are invited to a Belgian home. A visit to a Belgian home has a certain formality which may surprise foreigners. Dropping in on people unexpectedly is considered a bit eccentric. In apartment blocks people tend to keep themselves to themselves, with the result that single elderly people can be very isolated. On the plus side apartment blocks often have a live-in *concierge*, whose task is to keep an eye on things, as well as to deal with the dustbins and clean communal areas.

**ARE YOU LOOKING FOR A HIGH CLASS PROPERTY IN BRUSSELS...?
...CALL NOW OUR RELIABLE AND PROFESSIONAL TEAM**

LARGE SELECTION OF HOUSES, VILLAS AND APARTMENTS FOR RENT AND FOR SALE. IN BRUSSELS AND SURROUNDING AREAS

DELTA CONSULTANTS
ESTATE AGENCY

TELEPHONE 32 2 - 880.41.51
TELEFAX 32 2 - 770.31 57

Second homes or holiday homes are a popular institution with the better-off; many French speakers own apartments on the coast. For others their second home may be a short drive away.

Estate Agents

Centrale Informatique Immobilière: Boulevard A. Max 5, Brussels; ☎02 219 61 21; www.cii-br.be.

Delta Consultants: 62 Av.du Bois de Sapins, 1200 Bruxelles; tel 32 (0) 2 770 41 51; fax 32 (0) 2 770 31 57; e-mail Delta-Consultants@wol.be; www.Delta-Consultants.be

Immo V: Drève Richelle 274, 1400 Waterloo; ☎02 354 09 48; fax 02 354 77 36; www.immov.be.

Propriétés Immobilières SA: Av. Molière 202, 1050 Brussels; ☎02 343 59 59; www.pim.be.

Rainbow Properties: Av. de Tervuren 37, 1040 Brussels; ☎02 732 37 24; www.rainbow-careers.be/properties.html.

Union Professionelle des Immobiliers; Av. Albert 29, 1190 Brussels; ☎02 344 57 52.

Useful Websites

http://woneninbrussel.vgc.be; 0800 20 4000. Adverts in Dutch for rented property, and helpline, run by the Flemish Regional Commission.

www.xpats.com. Lists property agents, and adverts for properties; website of *The Bulletin*.

www.notaire.be. Lists of properties being auctioned in the French-speaking area; run by the Belgian notaries organisation.

www.test-achats.be. Run by Belgian Consumers Association, with model contracts and useful links.

www.belgimmo.be. Lists estate agents, enables searches by price for properties, and advertisements by prospective buyers.

Useful Publications

- *AZ:* Free weekly in Charleroi and Mons.
- *De Gazet van Antwerpen:* Antwerp daily; www.gva.be.
- *De Nieuwe Gazet:* Antwerp daily with property advertisements on Saturdays.
- *De Streekkrant:* Free weekly in Flemish towns; www.streekkrant.be.
- *La Libre Belgique:* French-language daily with property section on Thursdays; www.lalibre.be.
- *Le Soir:* French daily; www.lesoir.com.
- *The Bulletin:* English weekly available in Brussels newsagents; www.xpats.com, www.ackroyd.be.
- *Vlan:* Free weekly published in Brussels and Wallonia; www.vlan.be.

FINANCE

Mortgages with Belgian Banks

TAKING OUT A MORTGAGE (*hypothèque/hypotheek*) is just as common in Belgium as it is in Britain as a way to purchase property. At the time of writing Belgian mortgage interest rates are between 5% and 7%, but one should always bear in mind that currency fluctuations can affect the relative value of your house abroad and what you have to repay.

Mortgages in Belgium come in many shapes and sizes. Building societies, as such, do not exist in Belgium. Savings banks (*banque d'épargne/spaarbank*) are similar institutions and generally offer the best mortgage loan terms. If the savings bank you deal with is linked to an insurance company, however, they may try to impose expensive mortgage protection insurance on you. The best-known savings banks are Axa Bank, Centea, Argenta and Spaarkrediet. You can also deal with ordinary high-street banks such as the Fortis, BBL, Dexia and KBC Bank, but generally their interest rates are less competitive than those of savings banks. Another option worth looking at is to arrange a mortgage with a Dutch bank.

These banks are not allowed to advertise their mortgages in Belgium, so one needs to approach them through a broker.

TABLE 2 HOUSE PRICES IN URBAN AREAS (IN EUROS)

	65 sq m (1 bedroom)	140 sq m (2 bedrooms)	250 sq m (3 bedrooms)
Antwerp	56,000	81,000	98,000
Brugge	64,000	79,000	98,000
Brussels-Anderlecht	79,000	104,000	126,000
Brussels-Evere	103,000	128,000	156,000
Brussels-Schaarbeek	83,000	113,000	137,000
Brussels-Watermaal/Woluwe	120,000	112,000	146,000
Charleroi	25,000	39,000	48,000
Gent	47,000	80,000	95,000
Hasselt	49,000	82,000	88,000
Kortrijk	30,000	53,000	76,000
Liège	36,000	58,000	70,000
Mons	34,000	46,000	52,000
Namur	77,000	85,000	92,000
Oostende	55,000	80,000	96,000

Figures based on Gids der onroerende waarden *– June 2001 publ. Fortis Bank.*

TABLE 3 APARTMENT PRICES IN URBAN AREAS (IN EUROS)

	Studios 1 bedroom	2 bedrooms
Antwerp	36,000	63,000
Brugge	68,000	104,000
Brussels-Anderlecht	51,000	80,000
Brussels-Evere	103,000	128,000
Brussels-Schaarbeek	57,000	83,000
Brussels-Watermaal/Woluwe	90,000	120,000
Gent	59,000	80,000
Hasselt	54,000	84,000
Knokke	104,000	144,000
Mons	47,000	78,000
Oostende	63,000	86,000

Figures based on Gids der onroerende waarden *– June 2001 publ. Fortis Bank.*

It is also possible to take out a mortgage which is linked to an endowment or life insurance policy (known as a *vie mixte* policy in Belgium). This type of mortgage entails paying interest on what you borrow and life insurance premiums until you retire, whereupon the sum borrowed is repaid. The length of time you have to pay interest (even though the interest might seem low) and the high life insurance premiums in Belgium make this a very poor option. Borrowing money from an insurance company for house purchase is not advisable in any event, as you will be obliged to buy house insurance and mortgage protection insurance at a high premium from the same firm. Anyone looking for the best mortgage deal should get hold of the monthly magazine *Je Vais Construire* which shows the latest offers in tabular form.

Useful Addresses

Michael Kingshott & Associates: Rue de Hocaille 22, 1390 Archennes, Brabant; ☏ 010 84 42 50; e-mail michael.kingshott@yucom.be. Advice on mortgages, real estate and international investments.

Sohr & Son: 172 rue de la Station, 1640 Rhode St. Genèse, Brussels; ☏ 02 380 93 60/380 93 85; fax 02 380 94 20; www.sohretfils.com. Specialise in arranging mortgages and house insurance for foreigners.

Registration and Mortgage Costs

Under current Belgian law mortgages are registered for a 30-year term. Previously, mortgages ran for 15 years so that those with a mortgage of 20 or 25 years had to be pay the registration fees a second time. It is perfectly possible to negotiate a mortgage for a much shorter term, even as short as three years (with Banque Bruxelles Lambert), but if you sell your house or want to pay in full before the mortgage term is up you will incur considerable 'withdrawal fees' *(frais de mainlevée)* and a penalty of three months' interest on the remaining capital. You will therefore be saving money if you decide on the period of the mortgage and then stick to it. If you expect to pay off your mortgage early, then it is best to negotiate a no-penalty clause if you can; in practice, few banks will do this.

A mortgage agreement between a house buyer and a bank must be registered by a notary and this registration is subject to legal fees and taxes. Tax is levied at 1.3% of the amount borrowed while the notary's fees are on a sliding scale. On a loan of €50,000 the registration tax and notary's fee will come to about 3% of the whole, but this amount decreases considerably for higher sums, down to about 1.8% on a loan of €250,000. In addition a surveyor is often called in to value the property, thus adding at least €125 to the cost of the mortgage. A few Belgian banks add on a negotiation fee of 0.5% payable when the sales agreement is signed. In some cases this fee may be deducted from the loan at the last minute, so that the customer ends up paying interest on money he or she has not received. Although this appears to be highly dishonest it is not illegal.

A major pitfall is mortgage protection insurance. The main mortgage lenders are now tied to insurance companies, so it is difficult to avoid paying high Belgian mortgage insurance premiums. Only the small Flemish HBK bank does not impose such premiums. The only possibilities are to try to take out mortgage protection insurance with a British insurer based in Belgium, such as Commercial Union, or find a mortgage lender in the UK.

Repayment Conditions

Most banks will now lend up to 100% of the value of the property, and some will go up to 125%. Properties are sometimes valued at the price they would fetch if sold privately (*valeur vénale*) within six months, and sometimes at what they would fetch at auction (*valeur vente publique*) which effectively reduces the value by about 10%. The advantage of borrowing more than 100% of the value of the house is that all sales costs will then be covered. The disadvantage is that you will be obliged to pay very heavy insurance premiums.

The rate of repayment depends on the net monthly income of the individual or husband and wife, including investment income and family allowance payments. Repayments cannot exceed one-third of this figure. It is a standard practice to fix the interest rate on the mortgage for five years at the outset, and then to raise or lower the interest rate if there has been a change of more than 1% in the prevailing rate. Very often the interest rate for the entire term of the mortgage is fixed at the outset, which involves paying a somewhat higher rate, but is certainly worth considering if you think that interest rates are going to rise.

UK and Offshore Mortgages

Some British building societies and banks will lend money for the purchase of property abroad, including the Abbey National, Barclays, Norwich & Peterborough BS and the Woolwich. A number of people have managed to buy homes abroad by remortgaging or taking out a second mortgage on their UK property in order to pay for a property in cash in another country. The property owner should be aware that he or she is liable to lose some UK tax relief if a UK property is remortgaged and if part of the original loan was used for home improvements or capital raising.

The principle of offshore mortgages involves turning a property into a company, the shares of which are held by an offshore bank based in a tax haven such as Gibraltar or the Channel Islands as collateral against a mortgage. It is then possible to sell your property by confidentially transferring the shares in the company to a new owner, thus avoiding Belgian transfer taxes. In practice there seems to be little to be gained from such a scheme in view of the high administrative costs and the efficiency of the Belgian tax authorities. A more workable scheme would be to form a company in Belgium itself to buy a property if you can show that you are working from home in some way. Further details can be found in Michael Kingshott's *Practical Guide to Property Purchase and Arranging Mortgage Finance in Belgium* mentioned above.

PURCHASING AND CONVEYANCING PROCEDURES

Finding a Property

A MAJOR CONSIDERATION for many expatriates is finding a house close to their children's school. Apart from this you also need to decide how close you want to be to the centre of town, given the parking difficulties in many Belgian towns. The further you are prepared to commute, which does not have to be that far, the more likely you are to find a cheap property. The best way of finding a place is to look in the local free newspapers which carry thousands of advertisements from real estate agents (*agence immobilière/makelaar*) and notaries. Although there are some British estate agents operating in Belgium, they generally only deal with commercial property or high-priced investment property, so they will not be able to help. Many Belgian estate agents speak English and are used to dealing with expatriates.

Professional Assistance

Whichever way you go about buying a property in Belgium, the services of a notary are obligatory. Notaries are listed under 'Liberal professions' (*Professions libérales/Vrije beroepen*) in the Yellow Pages; someone who speaks and writes English is evidently going to be the most useful. There is also the regulatory body for notaries, the Fédération Royale des Notaires de Belgique (Rue de la Montagne 30-34, Brussels; ☎ 02 505 08 11; www.notaire.be). The notary's fees are fixed by law and are on a sliding scale depending on the value of the purchase. It is important to remember that the notary is also a kind of tax collector. During the property sale he or she will make a fiscal search, and if it becomes clear that either the buyer or the seller is liable for back taxes these sums will be seized by the notary at the moment of sale. If you are aware that you owe any taxes you should not buy or sell any property.

In addition to dealing with a notary you will also need to have the property surveyed. There are two organisations of quantity surveyors:
UGEB-ULEB – *Société Royale de Géomètres Experts Immobiliers:* ☎ 02 217 39 72.
Fédération Royale des Géomètres Experts: fax 02 644 94 69; www.geometre.be.

Charges start at €125, depending on the thoroughness of the survey.

The Compromis de Vente

The most common way to buy is through personal sale – *gré à gré/uit de hand*. It is also possible to buy a house at public auction (*vente publique/openbaar verkoop*; see the website www.notaire.be for examples), although this entails high costs at the outset.

House prices are negotiable. It is usual to make an offer (in writing) below the asking price and perhaps save a considerable amount of money. Once agreement is reached, the buyer and seller will sign the *compromis de vente* (sales agreement), which is then legally binding on both parties. You may use a model agreement favoured by the professional organisations, but this is not obligatory. The plus side of the *compromis* is that the seller cannot then withdraw if they receive a higher offer: gazumping is impossible. On the downside, the buyer must be absolutely sure that they want the property before signing anything binding. If you change your mind you could be liable for 10 to 15% of the purchase price. After the *compromis de vente* has been signed, the notarial act will be drawn up. If a dispute arises then an arbitrator may be appointed by agreement of both parties, or you may go to court.

If you intend to apply for a mortgage it may be wise to append a clause to the sales agreement stating that the sale is conditional on obtaining mortgage finance. If you then fail to obtain a loan you may be able to withdraw from the sale without penalty. The agreement usually allows you up to four months to arrange finance. Normally, you will have to pay a 10% deposit to the seller, but this is not an inflexible rule.

If you have doubts about the purchase or the mortgage, it is possible, for a small fee, to buy an option on the property at an agreed price. If you then pull out, you will only lose the fee for the option.

Registration Tax

The high level of registration tax (*droit d'enregistrement / registratierecht*) on house purchases is a major factor in discouraging speculation in property in Belgium. Most property purchases are subject to a tax rate of 12.5%. New property is subject to VAT at 21%. If you build a property yourself, you pay 21% VAT on the labour and materials, as well as 12.5% on the land. Because of these taxes, the seller sometimes takes some of the purchase price under the counter, but this is a potentially dangerous procedure for foreigners. The Belgian authorities will levy tax on what they consider to be the real worth of the property if they suspect any irregularity, and any cash payment made to the seller could be lost for good.

If a foreign purchaser has reason to believe that they may sell the property again within five years, then it is possible to recover part of the registration tax. Doing this with a new property is far more difficult, however. Another possibility is to buy an older house and renovate it, in which case the registration tax is only 6% and VAT on the renovation, labour and materials 6% as well. For this to work, the property must be over 20 years old, and the *revenu cadastral* (a hypothetical annual rental value used to calculate property tax) below €750 (£500).

Buying an Apartment

Apartments may be an attractive proposition, but it is important to be aware of the annual charges levied by the managers of the building. These can cover communal hot water, heating, cleaning of corridors and staircases, lift operating expenses, and maintenance of the building and gardens. Difficulties can arise with other owners of apartments in the same building. It is also necessary to have a third-party insurance policy which all the owners contribute to, in case of accidents occurring in the communal space. Another possibility is to buy an apartment from plans. If you buy before the building is finished then the notary's fee is based on only half the price of the apartment.

Registration tax is calculated at 12.5% of the purchase price; in addition one has to add on legal fees which start at around €750 for a €25,000 house. There is always a fixed charge of €600 for 'miscellaneous costs' added on to the notary's fees. The estate agents' website – www.belgimmo.be – has a convenient ready reckoner to help work out your costs.

RENTING PROPERTY

THOSE WHO ARE EMPLOYED by British or other foreign companies in Belgium will most probably have their accommodation arranged for them as part of their job package. In order to minimise the amount of time taken up with settling in, executives are often given the services of a relocation company. In the case of large companies there may be an in-house relocation department. If you are not in a position to use a relocator, you can easily find rented accommodation by looking in the newspapers mentioned for property purchases. English advertisements can be found in the weekly *The Bulletin*. Otherwise you can look for signs in windows saying *A Louer* (French) or *Te Huur* (Dutch), meaning 'To Rent', or notices in newsagents. The third possibility is to go to an estate agent (*agence immobilière/makelaar in onroerende goederen* or simply *makelaar*). In addition, there is now a computerised database of properties in Brussels which an estate agent may have access to. For a small fee your requirements can be fed in and a list of suitable properties will come out.

When looking at advertisements it is often difficult to understand the peculiar abbreviations in Belgium, which come in two languages of course. Firstly it is necessary to know if a property is furnished (*meublé/gemeubeld*) or not. Furnished property in Brussels is now becoming quite common. A further consideration is whether monthly 'charges' are included or not.

TABLE 4	USEFUL TERMS
French	
appt/appartement:	a flat with at least one bedroom.
bail loyer:	rental agreement.
buanderie:	washhouse.
cave:	cellar.
chf.maz./chauffage mazout:	oil central heating.
ctre.chf./chff.centrale/chauffage centrale:	central heating.
cuis.éq./cuisine équipé:	kitchen with a sink and built-in cupboard.
cuis.sup.éq./cuisine super équipé:	kitchen with cooker, fridge, dishwasher and more.
ent rén./entièrement rénové:	completely renovated.
étg/étage:	floor.
fermette:	a house done up in rustic style.
flat:	flat with bed in living room and limited cooking facilities.
grenier:	attic/loft.
pas de chgs/pas de charges:	no monthly maintenance charges.

sdb/salle de bain:	bathroom.
studio:	very small studio flat; or a room to be hired by the hour, if there is a number after the word studio.
terr./terrace:	terrace or balcony.
villa:	a detached house in the countryside surrounded by a garden.

Dutch

bdk/badk/badkamer:	bathroom.
cv/centraal verwarming:	central heating.
cv mazout/centraal verwarming met mazout:	oil central heating.
kamer:	room.
kelder:	cellar.
keuken:	basic kitchen.
inger.keuken/ingeriefd keuken:	kitchen equipped with cooker and fridge.
rijw./rijwoning:	terraced house.
slk/slpk/slaapkamer:	bedroom.
verdiep./verdieping:	floor.
voll.vern./volledig vernieuwd:	completely renovated.
zolder:	attic.

Tenancy agreements

Finding a place to live is only the beginning of the intricate process of renting a property. If you deal with estate agents you will probably find yourself visiting the same place several times. This is because the landlord does not use one estate agent's services exclusively, but decides when an estate agent has found a tenant. You should on no account give any money to an estate agent – this is entirely the landlord's responsibility.

A landlord is legally obliged to provide you with habitable accommodation. Before a lease can be signed the parties must agree on the condition of the property, which requires an expert to perform an *état des lieux/staat van de huis* (state of the premises). This protects the tenant from having to pay for existing damage, but it also means that you may be forced to pay to bring the property back to its original condition. A lease with a clause requiring you to return the property to 'perfect' condition should be avoided.

The basic form of lease is now one of 9 years, or a so-called 3-6-9 year lease. According to a law of 1991, a lease of indefinite duration is not permitted. The tenant pays a deposit of three months' rent. For expatriates it is important to have a so-called 'diplomatic clause' in the lease, which allows you to break the rental agreement with three months' notice and the payment of an indemnity. If you give notice within a year, you lose three months' rent, in the second year, two months' rent, and in the third year, one month's rent. At the end of three years, it is possible to leave without paying any indemnity, if you give three months' notice. When you leave, damage will be paid for out of your deposit, and you will have to wait until all utilities and other outstanding bills are settled before your money is returned.

The owner can eject you with six months' notice if he can show that he needs the property for himself or his immediate family, or pays a large indemnity. Every three years the owner can undertake building work and ask you to leave with six months' notice. If the property passes to a new owner, that person is obliged to continue the lease in the same manner, as long as it is in a written form. The tenant or owner can have recourse to a court of law if there are repeated breaches of the rental agreement. In the first place, the tenant should send a registered letter (*recommandée*) to the owner detailing any complaints.

Any rental agreement of any complexity or duration should be in writing. The Belgian consumers' association supplies model leases as well as the book *La Location de A à Z* telling you about clauses to watch out for (Test Achats/Test Aankoop, Rue de Hollande 13, 1060 Brussels; ☎ 02 542 32 11; www.test-achats.be). This organisation publishes invaluable monthlies such as *Test Achats/Test Aankoop* and *Budget et Droit/Budget en Recht* and will help non-members and members alike. Agreements in English are also valid if legally certified. Many rental agreements are far more informal, of course, and not of nine years' duration. If matters remain amicable, then owner and tenant can make whatever agreement they choose. The law states, however, that illegal clauses are null and void. It should be noted that a 'diplomatic clause' in a three-year lease may not stand up in a court of law, and that from this point of view the 3-6-9 lease has advantages. In any case, it is in the tenant's own interest to be aware of what they are signing at all times. If you are looking for advice or help then you can contact the National Tenants' Association (Office National des Locataires) on 02 218 75 30; other tenants' association numbers include: 02 201 03 60 (Brussels); 03 272 27 42 (Antwerp); 016 25 05 14 (Leuven).

Renting out your property

In the past, investors found Belgium an attractive place to buy property to rent out because the income was virtually tax-free, apart from the moderate property tax (*revenu cadastral*) which is about €800 annually for an average Brussels property. Renting out property at the seaside is an attractive possibility. Rental income is now taxable, however, and rent increases are limited to the rate of inflation. The inflexible nature of Belgian rental agreements means that it can take a long time to get rid of undesirable tenants even though the law is in many ways on the side of the owner. The owner of a property is responsible for redecorating every nine years, the replacement of carpets, wiring and boilers, amongst other things, but the tenant is generally responsible for making good wear and tear.

Precise information about the conditions attached to renting out can be found in *La Location de A à Z*, obtainable from Test Achats, Rue de Hollande 13, 1060 Brussels; ☎ 02 536 64 11. There is also information in the *Newcomer* magazine and in Michael Kingshott's *Practical Guide to Buying Property*.

Short-term rented accommodation

In order to avoid the problems associated with long rental agreements, it may be easier to rent an apartment from a company specialising in short-term lets. Many of these are located near the up-market shopping area of Avenue Louise in Brussels, close to the Eurostar terminal at the Gare du Midi. They come in all sizes, with rents starting at around €600 per month. The following companies offer this type of accommodation:

Immobe SA: Av. Louise 137, 1050 Brussels; ☎02 538 71 51; fax 02 538 77 99; e-mail info@immobe.be; www.immobe.be.
New Continental Flat Hotel: Rue Defacqz 33, 1050 Brussels; ☎02 536 10 00; fax 02 536 10 15; www.newcontinental.be.
Rue Souveraine Furnished Apartments: Rue Souveraine 40, 1050 Brussels; ☎02 512 34 00; fax 02 511 20 29; e-mail rue.souveraine@btinternet.com; www.ruesouveraine.com.

Rental costs

In this respect Brussels is in a class of its own, for the obvious reason that there is intense competition for accommodation near the EU Commission and other major offices. Bargains are becoming hard to find, especially near English-language schools, but at least the rise in rents has flattened out since the boom of the early 1990s. Rents are index-linked and may be raised annually but the landlord must give written notice to the tenant. A one-room flat in a suburb will cost at least €100 (£60 or $90) per week. Three-bedroom flats in better areas (east and south of Brussels) exceed €300 per week. Well-appointed houses (known as 'villas') in the surrounding countryside cost €500 per week or more. In the case of apartments maintenance charges or share of facilities can add 10-20% to the rent and can be a source of dispute if they are not clearly stated at the outset. Apart from these charges, the tenant is responsible for the electricity, gas, telephone and cable TV.

Relocators

The purpose in using professional relocation firms is to minimise the cost, time and hassle for an executive or other employee to settle into Belgium. In order to make the best use of their services, it is important to contact the relocator as far in advance as possible. A good relocator will advise on education and spouse employment and know how to cope with the multitude of regulations and formalities. In the past they were able to negotiate a lower rental, but this has not been possible during the recent flat property market. They can negotiate for improvements and better equipment for your property. Once the relocator has the customer's requirements they can canvass owners and agents to produce an exhaustive list of likely properties and then invite the customer over to Belgium. They then accompany you on a highly concentrated tour over several days and advise on fair rental prices. While relocation fees range from €1,000 to €4,000 for the complete process (some invoice their services by the hour) they generally save their customers many times more than that and make the expatriate's transfer far easier. There is also now a developing market in 'delocating', where the relocation firm handles all the formalities when an employee moves out of Belgium, often at short notice and with consequent problems in applying the vital 'diplomatic clause' which allows you to break the rental lease agreement.

Not all relocation firms are totally independent of other interests. Some are little more than escort services who provide a cultural tour but are not experienced enough to negotiate better deals on their customers' behalf. In some cases relocators function as estate agents on the side and collect commissions from the landlord (or agent) as well as the fee from the person whose interests they are supposedly defending.

Many relocators belong to the European Association of Relocators; see the website www.eura-relocation.com. It may be worth finding out if a relocator is a member and whether they are linked to any real estate brokers. There is a clear line between residential and office relocators. The profile of a person moving to Belgium can be either 'cold', someone with no acquaintances there, or 'warm' if they are joining an established company. They are likely to use a relocator when looking to rent a property upwards of €1,500 per month.

The London-based relocator, T.W.G. Estates, can arrange for the purchase, management or letting of a property in London and the Home Counties, for investment purposes, or if you need a property for when you move back to the UK. They can also manage your property for you while you are abroad.

Relocation Firms

Belgian Relocation Centre: Professional Relocation & Orientation Services, Leopoldlei 6/b2, 2930 Brasschaat; ☎03 650 05 10; fax 03 650 05 11; e-mail vivhermans@pro-relocation.com.

Brussels Relocation SC: Bvd Henri Rolin 3, 1410 Waterloo; ☎02 353 21 01; fax 02 353 06 42; e-mail brussels.relocation@skynet.be; www.publisite.be/brussels.relocation.

Living Abroad: Kraaienheuvel 19, 2950 Kapellen; ☎03 665 42 39/40; fax 03 665 42 41; e-mail info@livingabroad.be.

Management Relocations: Chemin de Dadelane 4, 1380 Lasne; ☎02 633 36 21; fax 02 633 30 27; e-mail mgtreloc@skynet.be.

Relocation Assistance. M. Friedmann: Promenade du Val d'Argent 5, 1310 La Hulpe; ☎02 353 04 56; fax 02 351 07 98.

T.W.G. Estates Ltd: 36/37 Maiden Lane, Covent Garden, London WC2E 7LJ; ☎020-7420 0300; fax 020-7836 1500; twg.estates@virgin.net.

INTERCULTURAL TRAINING

STAFF GOING ABROAD can benefit from training in intercultural awareness. The leading organisation in this field, the Centre for International Briefing, at Farnham Castle, offers a wide range of services including language country briefings and language tuition for those going abroad on short- or long-term assignments. Business overview briefings are also available for home-based managers with international responsibilities. Further details from: The Centre for International Briefing, ☎01252-720416; fax 01252-719277; e-mail marketing@farnhamcastle.com; www.cibfarnham.com.

INSURANCE AND WILLS

BELGIUM IS NOTORIOUSLY EXPENSIVE for insurance, which can cost 200% to 300% of UK rates. House and contents insurance is essential. Under Belgian law the tenant is liable for damage to leased property caused by fire, explosions, lightning, water and so on. House insurance is often called 'fire insurance', but there is in fact no separate category for fire. Insurance is calculated after an inspection by a surveyor, usually at the rate of 0.1% of the total value of house and contents per annum, plus 15.75% tax. Both rises in property prices and depreciation must be taken into account. Your insurance company will guide you as to the amount you should insure for. A personal third-party liability policy is also necessary because of a person's high degree of responsibility under Belgian law for damage to other people and their property. The advantage of this type of policy is that you receive free legal assistance in the event of a claim against you. Those in communally owned apartment buildings will also have to contribute to a policy covering accidents in the communal space. Insurance is renewed annually, but you must give three months' notice by recorded delivery letter if you wish to cancel the arrangement at the time of renewal.

Since 1993 it has been theoretically possible to take out an insurance policy in the UK which is valid in other EU countries, but in practice there is very little cross-border underwriting. A law regulating the qualifications of insurance brokers in Belgium has only been in existence since 1997 and many expatriates are dissatisfied with the level of service offered by Belgian insurers. One way around this is to deal with one of the UK-based companies which have set up in Belgium. On the scale of best buys in Belgium the British-based Commercial Union has been recommended by the consumers' magazine *Budget et Droit*. Out of Belgian insurance companies, the following have received favourable mentions: ABB, ASLK, Royale Belge and DVV. *Budget et Droit* is available from the Belgian Consumers Association at Rue de Hollande 13, 1060 Brussels (02 536 64 11; www.test-achats.be).

Useful addresses

Commercial Union Belgium SA: Av. Hermann-Debroux 54, 1160 Brussels; ☎ 02 676 61 11.
General Accident Plc: Brusselstr. 59, 2018 Antwerp; ☎ 03 221 57 11.
Royal & Sun Alliance Insurance, Bvd de Woluwe 64, 1200 Brussels; ☎ 02 773 03 11; e-mail info@royalsun.be.

WILLS

BELGIAN LAW SUBJECTS the value of an inheritance from a 'habitant' of Belgium to inheritance tax, and there is also a tax on change of ownership when real estate located in Belgium is inherited from a non-habitant of Belgium. If at the time of your death you administered your wealth or managed your business from somewhere in Belgium then you are a habitant, regardless of your nationality, legal domicile or place of death. This means in effect that any property or other assets in Belgium are subject to Belgian inheritance laws. In principle your property and half of your assets go to your spouse, and the rest is divided equally amongst your children. Legacies to other relatives or strangers are taxed very heavily indeed. If you die without leaving a will, then complications will ensue. It is therefore advisable to register a will with a notary and to appoint an executor to carry out your wishes. A will made under Anglo-Saxon or Scottish law can be taken into account by the Belgian authorities, but any unusual requests or conditions could be invalid if they affect assets in Belgium. See *Retirement* chapter below for further details.

UTILITIES

IF YOU ARE PLANNING to move to Belgium, you should be aware of the potential delays and costs involved if gas, electricity and telephones are not already connected to your property. It is also legally necessary to be connected to the sewage system, even if you have your own well, unless you are in a remote location where cess-pits are still in use.

Utility companies in Belgium issue estimated bills every two months; the meter is read once a year and a refund or extra bill is then issued. Bills must be paid promptly – generally within 10 days – otherwise the service will be cut off without warning. In the case of telephones you have to pay within five days. It is easiest to do this with a standing order (*domiciliation des paiements/domicilie*).

If you are taking over from a previous occupant you should obtain forms from the company concerned and fill in the meter reading together with the previous occupant. The form is then sent to the company by the previous occupier with a copy of your identity card. A copy of your passport may be acceptable instead. If it is necessary to have a company representative to read your meter, they must be given adequate advance notice. When a property has been left uninhabited for some time, the power will have been disconnected, but reconnection can easily be arranged with two or three days' warning.

Electricity

Almost all electricity in Belgium is produced by Tractebel, which is controlled by the French utilities giant Suez-Lyonnaise des Eaux. Local distribution is dealt with by the communes, who have formed various local electricity companies. If the name of your supplier is not on your meter, and your landlord does not know, then you can enquire at the town hall, or look in the ordinary telephone book under *Electricité/Electriciteit*. If all else fails you can find out by calling 02 549 41 11.

Electricity in Belgium is 220 volts AC 50 cycles. British 240 volt appliances run quite satisfactorily, except for those with motors such as record turntables and washing machines, which run more slowly. American equipment needs a transformer to convert from 110 to 220 volts, but equipment meant to be run on 60 cycles AC will not work properly. In general two-pin round plugs are used in Belgium; you should make sure that your appliances are properly earthed. Most houses have a fuse-box (*coupe-circuit/zekering*) which you should become familiar with.

One problem which often arises is that the electrical capacity, or amperage, for your property is too small. You can have a larger meter installed by the utility company for a fee. A lot of Belgian houses do not have a hot water tank, but rather water is heated by a gas burner when you turn on the tap. In more dilapidated houses the hot water supply can be virtually non-existent. A dishwasher or washing machine has the advantage of heating its own water, but you should first determine the power capacity of the socket if you want to use any high-amperage equipment; you may need heavy wiring. Connecting appliances to the mains must be done by a qualified electrician; the electricity company's responsibilities end at the meter. In the event of moving into a brand-new house, the wiring will have to be checked by an inspector from the electricity company before you can have the power connected.

Gas

Natural gas is widely used in Belgium for cooking, central heating and heating water. Bottled propane and butane gas are also widely used – you can find a local distributor by looking under 'Gas – household' in the Yellow Pages. A gas bottle is a *bouteille de gaz* or *gasfles*. The name of the local gas company (of which there are many) can be found at the town hall, under *gaz/gas* in the ordinary phone book, or by calling 02 549 41 11 as a last resort. Also see the Electrabel-Sibelgaz website www.electrabel.be. The name may be on your central heating or other equipment. As with electricity, the utility company's responsibilities end with the meter, and you will need the services of a plumber (*plombier/loodgieter*) for the installation of appliances.

Some bathrooms in Belgium are equipped with gas water heaters which were designed for use in kitchens and which will generate carbon monoxide if used for too long in an unventilated room. Make sure that your local gas distributor checks for potential hazards when they turn on your supply.

When renting accommodation, you must inform your landlord if you are planning to change the power supply or install new appliances. You should also confirm that the landlord will pay for the repair of the central heating or the water heater when signing the lease.

Oil

Oil (*mazout/stookolie*) is widely used for central heating, and can be obtained from companies such as BP and Esso Belgium. You will find the fuel tank in the courtyard or garden, often under the grass, with a metal lid, and there will also be a long metal ruler for measuring the fuel level to be found in your cellar or garage. The procedure for lighting oil heaters needs to be handled with some care. Mazout is cheaper than gas or electricity, but still attracts 21% VAT. The cost also varies depending on the world price of oil.

Water

Water is in plentiful supply in Belgium and safe to drink, if not always very palatable. The name of your local water company can be found under *Eaux/Water* in the white phone directory. In Brussels contact the Compagnie Intercommunale Bruxelloise des Eaux, Rue aux Laines 70, 1000 Bruxelles; ☎(02) 518 81 11; e-mail cibe@pophost.eunet.be. The emergency number in Brussels is (02) 739 52 11. Cold water is charged for and the meters read once a year. The bill, which could amount to about €185 for an average dwelling, is also issued annually, or in some areas quarterly. You may be asked to pay some of your bill in advance when moving in. Installations are the domain of the plumber; for leaking mains contact the water company.

If you are lucky enough to have your own well (*puits/put*) you will enjoy much better-tasting water than that from the public supply, and a high level of nitrates. The water in Brussels has such a high calcium content that many apartment blocks have communal water softeners, which adds to your monthly charges. Not surprisingly, bottled water is popular.

Telephones

Until 1998, the partly privatised Belgacom enjoyed a monopoly in Belgium, with the consequence that Belgians were paying the highest telephone charges in Europe. With the liberalisation of the telecommunications market from 1998 matters have improved a little, although prices have only come down about 10%. Your first telephone line still has to be installed by Belgacom; the other phone companies rent their lines from Belgacom. You can rent or buy a handset from Belgacom or from another source. Having a telephone installed is now supposed to take place within a week, whereas in the past it took up to six months. Installation costs €65.99 plus 21%; additional lines cost €32.99. If work has to be done within your house you may have to pay another €100. For enquiries in English about services, phone the free number 0800 55 800 or look at the website www.belgacom.be/expats. For faults call 0800 55 700; for bills 0800 55 900.

When moving into accommodation with an existing phone, the quickest solution is to go with the previous tenant to the local Téléboutique/Teleboetiek and sign a transfer agreement. If you are in less of a hurry, call 0800-55 800 and ask for the transfer forms, which you can then return by post. Directories and Yellow Pages (*Guide d'or/Gouden Gids*) are provided free annually. Belgian phone subscribers can be found via the website www.infobel.be; the Yellow Pages are under www.goudengids.be. The main mobile phone companies are Proximus, Mobistar and Orange.

The cost of the monthly subscription for a landline is €16.20 in Brussels. Telephone bills are sent out every two months and it is necessary to pay within five days. This should not pose a problem since electronic transfer of money is instantaneous. You should make arrangements to pay if going abroad, or inform Belgacom well in advance.

REMOVALS

WHILE IT COULD save money to take some of your possessions from home with you it is worth bearing in mind that electrical equipment may not function well in Belgium, and it is expensive to ship goods back and forth. With the implementation of the Single Market in 1993 the movement of goods became much easier; in principle moving from the UK to Belgium should (with a few exceptions) be no different from moving from the North of England to the South. There are numerous international removals firms; it is important to check that they have the necessary experience.

Membership of the BAR (the British Association of Removers) provides a guarantee that you are dealing with a reputable company which is not likely suddenly to go bankrupt. Companies with offices in Belgium as well as in the UK are generally the safest bet. The BAR can provide a list of international removers in your area and other information in return for an SAE (BAR, 3 Churchill Court, 58 Station Road, North Harrow, Middlesex HA2 7SA; ☎020-8861 3331; fax 020-8861 3332; e-mail info@bar.co.uk; www.barmovers.com). Removals can be done door-to-door or your possessions can be put into a warehouse in Belgium. Charges start around £500 for three cubic metres, but the exact price depends very much on the total distance involved at both ends, and whether you are flexible about the delivery time. Some removers dealing with Belgium include:

Allied Pickfords: Heritage House, 345 Southbury Road, Enfield, Middlesex EN1 1UP; ☎0800-289 229; www.allied-pickfords.co.uk (UK) www.alliedintl.com (USA).

Capital Worldwide: Kent House, Lower Stone Street, Maidstone ME15 6LH; ☎01622-766380 (UK) *or* 02 535 74 30 (Belgium); e-mail moving@capital-worldwide.com; www.capital-worldwide.com.

Crown Worldwide Movers: Security House, Abbey Wharf Industrial Estate, Kingsbridge Road, Barking Essex IG11 0BT; ☎020-8591 3388; fax 020-8594 4571; www.crownww.com.

Gosselin World Wide Moving: Keesinglaan 28, 2100 Antwerp; ☎+32 3 360 55 00; fax +32 3 360 55 79; e-mail comm@gosselin.be; www.gosselin.be.

Customs Regulations

If you are an EU citizen entering the country with your household effects you should have some proof that you have registered with your local commune. There are restrictions on the importation of firearms, alcohol, tobacco and medicines. HM Customs and Excise has a Helpline on 0845 010 9000, or look at the website: www.hmce.gov.uk.

Import Procedures (non-EU citizens)

Assuming that you have registered with your commune and are planning to move your residence to Belgium, you are entitled to import household goods, your car and tools needed for your work without paying import duty, as long as you can

Moving to the UK?

THEN CALL PETER McEWAN ON BRUSSELS 02/535.74.30

Capital WORLDWIDE

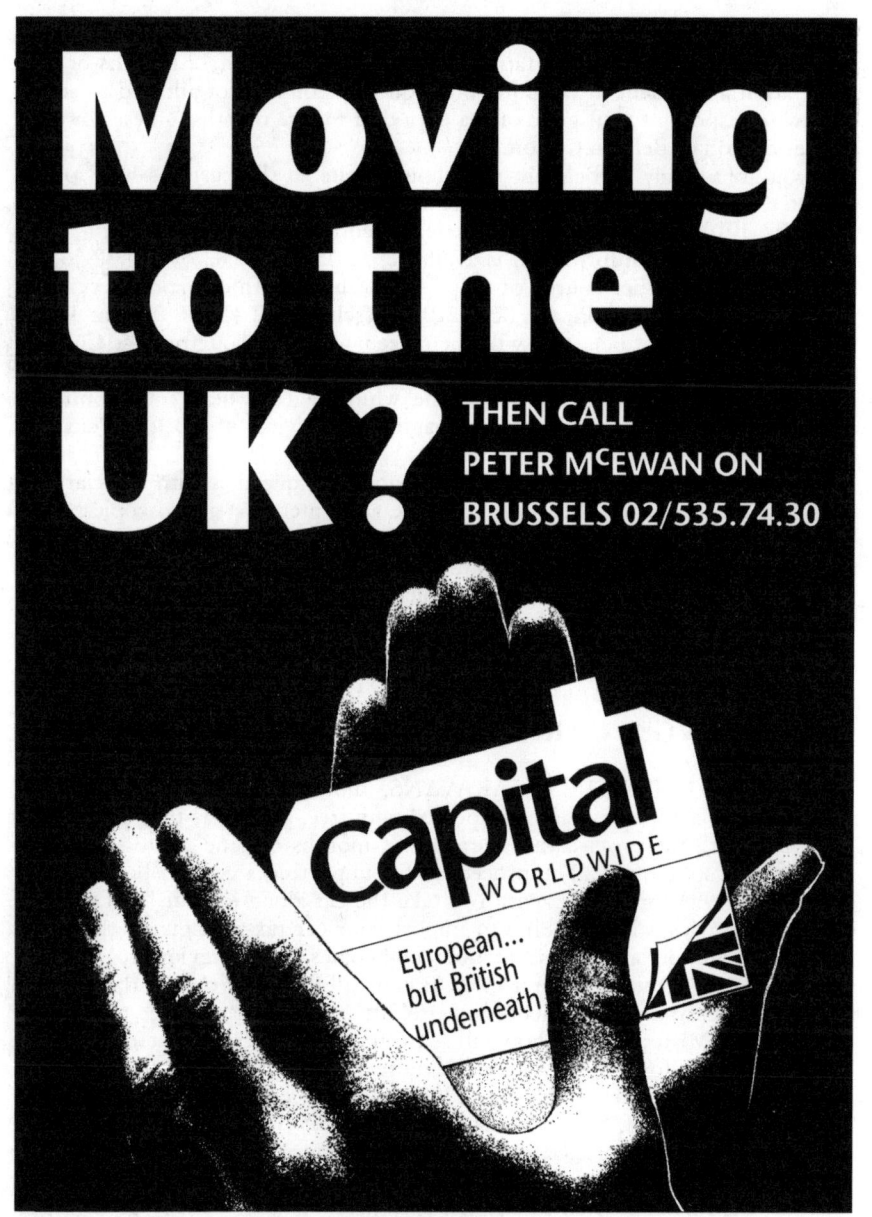

European... but British underneath

For moves from the UK
call Maidstone (01622) 766380

email: peter.mcewan@skynet.be   web: www.capital-worldwide.com

show that you have owned these items for over six months or if there is some wear and tear on them. Importation must take place within 12 months of your registration as resident in Belgium. Subsequently you are not allowed to sell or otherwise dispose of your goods for a period of twelve months, unless you have the permission of Belgian Customs.

If you are already in Belgium you should write to the customs head office: Ministère des Finances, Direction Générale des Douanes, Bvd du Jardin Botanique 50 bte 37, 1010 Brussels and obtain the leaflet entitled *Notice déménagements/Notitie verhuizingen*. General information is available on 02 210 31 82 or 210 32 16, fax 02 210 32 76. Another source of help is the Customs Information Service, at Bureau de Douane, Rue Picard 1-3, 1210 Brussels (☎ 02 421 38 30; fax 421 37 94; www.minfin.fgov.be). You will then need to locate your nearest Customs and Excise Office (look for *Douane et accises/Douanen en accijnzen* under *Ministère des Finances/Ministerie van Financiën* in the white pages) where you submit the paperwork. You can save trouble by engaging the services of a Belgian 'customs broker' (*agence en douane/douane agentschap*).

You then draw up a complete list of the goods in question with a declaration in French or Dutch that the list is accurate and enter five signed copies at the customs office, along with a copy of your residence registration card. Sometimes an English list is acceptable, or your removal firm will supply a standardised multilingual list. Insurance policies, invoices and proof of where you have been living are all useful documents.

IMPORTING A CAR

CARS, MOTORCYCLES, CARAVANS, mobile homes and even private boats and aeroplanes can be imported duty free, as long as they are on your inventory, with the proviso that they are six months old and you do not resell them within six months. The procedure for importing a car has become a lot easier since 1993 for EU citizens. You take the car along to your local customs office, along with a letter asking to import your car tax-free, giving the make, registration number and chassis number, and copies of the previous registration, your residence permit, and the invoice (if you still have it). You will then receive the customs clearance document 'vignette 705' and the rear licence plate (a car shop, DIY or Mister Minute shop will sell you the front licence plate).

The procedure for non-EU citizens is more complicated. In the first place you have to obtain the forms D5 and 139B from the customs office at Tour et Taxis, Rue Picard 1-3, 1020 Brussels (☎ 02 421 37 11). Having returned these with copies of the invoice, registration and insurance as well as proof of your previous residency and your residence permit, you can drive for six months. Your car must then be converted to Belgian specifications after which you will need a Certificate of Conformity from the local importer. After going through the *Contrôle Technique/Technische Kontrole*, and taking out Belgian insurance you will receive Belgian number plates. Final permission to import a car tax-free can take anything from nine months to two years.

Buying a Car

Belgium was at one time well-known in the U.K. for its low car prices, but with changes in EU regulations there is now little advantage in buying a new car in Belgium. Second-hand luxury cars are, however, a very good deal, because of the more rapid depreciation in Belgium. To find out current prices for new and second-hand cars look in the monthly *Moniteur de l'Automobile/Autogids* or look for the biweekly *Auto-occasion*. If you are not resident in Benelux it is possible to buy a vehicle 'in transit'. Dealers have their own 'transit departments' or customs broker who knows all the formalities. If everything is in order you will be granted exemption from paying VAT for long enough to take your car home with Belgian transit documents and number plates. You can also escape VAT if you have been resident in Belgium and can show that you are about to leave. Further information about cars is given in Chapter Four *Daily Life*.

Insurance

Car insurance in Belgium is expensive and comprehensive, partly thanks to the high level of traffic accidents. You cannot even get a licence plate without third-party insurance (*responsabilité civile/wettelijke aansprakelijkheidsverzekering*), which must be taken out with a Belgian company. You also need to be insured against fire and theft, and for legal costs in the event of court cases, which are frequent after accidents. Your policy will not necessarily cover you for injury to the driver. Belgian insurers may demand the installation of a car alarm. On the plus side you can transfer your no-claims bonus from the UK. Since 1993 car insurance policies taken out with a UK company have been valid in other EU countries, but in practice UK companies will not insure you outside the UK in the long term and you will still have to get Belgian insurance. Possession of the traditional Green Card for overseas insurance is no longer a legal requirement but it is still recommended that you have one. You will have to inform your UK insurance company about your intention to go abroad in any case.

Useful Addresses

Automobile Association (AA): Overseas Department, PO Box 2AA, Newcastle-upon-Tyne, NE99 2AA; ☏0870 606 1615; www.theaa.com.

RAC Motoring Services: Travel Services, PO Box 1500, Bristol BS99 1LH; ☏0800-550055; www.rac.co.uk.

Royal Automobile Club de Belgique (RACB): Rue d'Arlon 53, 1040 Brussels; ☏02 287 09 11; www.racb.com.

Sohr & Son: Rue de la Station 172, 1640 Rhode St. Genèse; ☏02 380 9360; fax 02 380 9420; www.sohretfils.com. Insurance brokers.

IMPORTING PETS

Many expatriates would like to have their four-legged friends with them abroad, and this should not be a difficult procedure. Dogs and cats being exported to Belgium must be vaccinated against rabies at least 30 days and not more than 12 months before export. In the case of dogs and cats vaccinated before the age of three months the validity of the rabies vaccination certificate is three months. After that the validity of the vaccination certificate is one year. Rabies is present in Belgium to the south of the Sambre and Meuse rivers, and annual inoculation will be needed if you are in this area. You can bring your pet back into the UK without entering quarantine as long as you follow the rules laid down by the UK Department of Food, Environment and Rural Affairs (DEFRA) in the Pets Travel Scheme (PETS). It does, however, take at least seven months from the initial insertion of a microchip and rabies injection before you can get a re-entry certificate from your vet. Call the PETS Helpline on 0870-241 1710 or look at the Website www.defra.gov.uk for further information.

The Independent Pet and Animal Transportation Association International Inc members around the world can arrange for transportation of animals and advise on local rules; the website is www.ipata.com. IATA rules on animal transport can be found at: www.iata.org/cargo/live.htm. If you are bringing a pet from the United States, then vaccination against rabies is necessary, unless it is under three months old. See the above websites for further details. There is a club for US residents who want to take their pets abroad: www.takeyourpet.com.

With birds and other animals certificates of good health are needed. The UK Department of Food, Environment and Rural Affairs (DEFRA) can provide forms for specific countries. If you are thinking of exporting animals other than cats and dogs the PETS Helpline will give you the number of the section you need to call.

When in Belgium, dogs have to be registered annually at your local town hall. Your dog will be given a disk to wear. As in Britain, there are charitable societies for the protection of animals, and organisations which provide a 24-hour animal ambulance service. There is a 24-hour animal helpline on 0903 40 040. For regular services look under *médecin vétérinaire/dierenarts* for vets, and *clinique vétérinaire/dierenkliniek* for animal hospitals in the yellow pages.

Useful Addresses

Animaux sans frontières ASBL – Ambulance animalière: ☎02 427 42 75; www.psynet.net/asf.

Animal Ambulance S.A.V.U.: ☎0475 39 91 10 (emergencies) 0903 40 040 (helpline).

Clinique Vétérinaire: Av. d'Auderghem 240, 1040 Brussels; ☎02 640 1161.

Société Royale Protectrice des Animaux-Veeweyde: Av. Itterbeek 600, 1070 Brussels; ☎02 527 59 58 *or* 527 10 50; www.veeweyde.be.

Vlaamse Vereniging voor Dierenbescherming (Flemish Society for the Protection of Animals): Langdorpsesteenweg 95, Aarschot; ☎016 56 77 07; www.vvdb.be.

DAILY LIFE

CHAPTER SUMMARY

- **Languages.** The key to succeeding in daily life in Belgium is speaking French or Dutch reasonably well.
  - Dutch speakers are in the majority at around 58% of the population, against 40% speaking French; only 20% of the population is bilingual.
  - Both languages are spoken in Brussels: elsewhere broadly speaking French is spoken in the south and Dutch in the north.
- **Education.** Belgium has an excellent education system and claims to be the only western country offering free schooling from the age of 2.
  - School attendance is compulsory between the ages of 6 and 18.
  - Those not planning to settle in Belgium should consider sending their children to one of the many international schools in Belgium which offer English and American curricula.
- Most British newspapers are available in Belgium on the morning of publication.
- Belgian drivers have a reputation for being dangerous – perhaps because there was no driving test until 1967.
- The Belgian railway system is one of the most comprehensive in the world, and urban public transport systems are highly integrated.
- Belgium has double taxation agreements with the UK and the USA so you should not have to pay taxes twice on the same income.
- The Belgian medical services are amongst the world's best, but private medical insurance is advisable to cover its cost.

WHEN GOING TO LIVE in a foreign country, one will find straight away that there is a multitude of daily rituals, which now pose a seemingly insurmountable challenge. The intention of this chapter is to provide all of the practical information required to cope successfully with various aspects of life in Belgium. The key to dealing with daily life in Belgium lies to some extent in being able to speak French or Dutch reasonably well. The first section of this chapter covers this area, with subsequent sections dealing with all those aspects of daily life, which, if handled successfully, can make living in another country an exciting rather than a daunting experience.

THE BELGIAN LANGUAGES

KNOWING WHICH LANGUAGE to speak to whom is of considerable importa nce if you want to get on with the Belgians. There are three languages with official status: Dutch, French and German, and speakers usually occupy a well-defined region of the country. In Brussels, Dutch and French have equal status. Brussels is surrounded by (officially) Dutch-speaking communes, in six of these there are French-speaking 'minorities' with special status. Foreigners should bear in mind that Dutch-speakers are in the majority in Belgium as a whole. Discounting immigrants, close to 58% of the population speak Dutch and 40% French. The number of German-speakers comes to 69,000.

Dutch spoken in Belgium (sometimes known as Flemish, or Vlaams) is basically the same as in Holland and this common language is called *Algemeen Beschaafd Nederlands (ABN)* or Common Civilised Dutch. Dutch in Belgium preserves certain archaic features in its spoken form not used in the Netherlands and also uses French and English loanwords in a different way. The most notable of these archaisms is the use of *gij* ('thou' or 'you', pronounced like 'hay') by many speakers, which is in between *jij* and *U* in terms of formality; *gij* is not used at all in the Netherlands, except in the Bible. The Belgians are also more aware of the difference between masculine and feminine gender than the Dutch. The differences are clearly explained in Bruce Donaldson's *A Comprehensive Grammar of Dutch* (see below).

If you speak Dutch you will be aware that almost every town in Belgium has its own dialect and some of these can sound like a different language to the untrained ear. Some older people may only speak their own dialect; Dutch spoken by younger people tends to be closer to the standard language, and it appears that many dialects are on the way to extinction.

In spite of its very different pronunciation and appearance, Dutch is closely related to English. It is not a dialect of German although it shares the same basic vocabulary. The relationship between the spelling and pronunciation is very logical but the sounds of the language take some getting used to.

In the case of French, Belgians naturally aspire to speak and write standard French, and many of them do so very well indeed. Wallonia has its own dialects, and you will soon become aware of a Walloon accent and peculiarities in grammar and vocabulary in dealing with French-speakers. The words for 'seventy' and 'ninety' are invariably *septante* and *nonante* in Belgium, unlike in France. A telephone directory is a *bottin* and not an *annuaire*; a zip is a *tirette* rather than a *fermeture éclair*, and so on. Very noticeable is the tendency of Belgian French speakers to make mistakes with verbs, especially the subjunctive.

Language Manners

Foreigners tend to fall into the trap of assuming that Dutch- and French-speakers are perpetually at war with each other. In reality, most Belgians have little contact with members of the other language community or much knowledge of their culture. Most of the bilingual Belgians are in and around Brussels or in the Flemish area. Since the Dutch-speakers have now gained the upper hand, their feelings of inferiority have dissipated somewhat. The language issue has been heavily exploited by the media and by unscrupulous politicians seeking to further their own careers, much to the detriment of their country. It is generally best to avoid making simplistic judgements about a complex and changing situation.

You cannot be expected to know automatically which language the person you are speaking to uses. In the case of Dutch-speakers, they will usually be keen to speak English to you. In Brussels many Dutch-speakers do not mind using French. In Dutch-speaking areas French is becoming more acceptable, but it is still best avoided in shops (the coast is an exception). Do not try German.

French-speakers are not as good at English as Dutch-speakers. It is important to remember that only 20% of Belgians are actually bilingual in Dutch and French. The Flemish are, statistically, some of the best linguists in Europe – speaking four or five languages is considered quite normal amongst educated people. Belgium is an ideal place to study any of the EU languages since there are plenty of teachers and people to practise on.

Language Study

Before paying a lot of money for a language course or lessons, it is a good idea to look at what your local library has to offer. You will probably be able to borrow a book and cassettes in the language you want to learn. In the case of Dutch it may be the only way to proceed until you arrive in Belgium. Dutch courses available in Britain are invariably from the Netherlands; you will soon notice that the spoken language in Belgium is rather different from what you might expect from the textbooks. The following beginner's books are recommended: *Praatpaal*, by Anne Schoenmakers (publ. Stanley Thornes); and *Colloquial Dutch* (publ. Routledge). Linguaphone have one course for Dutch at £279.90. Living Language produce a CD-Rom for Dutch, entitled *In-Flight Dutch*. The works of W.Z. Shetter are essential for more serious study (see Bibliography). The standard work on Dutch grammar is *A Comprehensive Grammar of Dutch*, by Bruce Donaldson (Routledge).

For French there is a wide choice of courses available. At the basic level there is the BBC Multimedia language course, *The French Experience* which includes cassettes or CDs (see www.bbc.co.uk/education/languages. Another highly rated course is *A Vous la France*. W.H. Smith and AA Travel Shops stock a variety of French language courses. *Linguaphone* (111 Upper Richmond Rd, London SW15 2TJ; ☎ 020-8333 4898; http://www.linguaphone.co.uk, www.linguaphone.com/usa) distribute self-study courses with cassettes, CDs, Videos, CD-Roms and On-line courses with prices ranging from £19.99 to £345.00 (order directly). There are free on-line dictionaries for Dutch and French at: www.yourdictionary.com.

Part-time Courses

Local colleges of further education often run day and evening classes in EU languages, which range in length from three months to a year. A-level courses, costing from £100.00, usually start in October, so you need to register in September. The *Alliance Française* in your area will also run courses in French. There is no Belgian equivalent of the *Alliance Française*.

Courses in Belgium. In Belgium you can follow residential courses of varying length in rural surroundings. Céran hold courses in various languages for all ages in Belgium, France, Ireland, Spain, the USA, England and Japan (Céran Lingua, Av. du Château 16, 4900 Spa, Belgium; ☎087 79 11 22; fax 087 79 11 88; e-mail customer@ceran.be; www.ceran.com). For French, Dutch and German, Pro-Linguis, Rue de l'Eglise 19, 6717 Thiaumont (☎063 22 04 62; www.prolinguis.be) offer courses which include sport. There are more official summer courses, such as four-week courses in French Language and Literature at the Free University of Brussels, Av. F.D. Roosevelt 50, 1050 Brussels; and two-week courses in Dutch Language and Flemish Culture held at the Limburg University Centre in Hasselt (contact L.U.C. Universitaire Campus Gebouw D, 3590 Diepenbeek; ☎011 26 80 10; fax 011 26 80 19). For general information on Dutch courses see the Dutch Language Union site www.taalunie.be.

Apart from residential courses there are numerous language schools operating in Belgium of varying quality. You could just as well try to find a sympathetic conversation partner and arrange a 'language exchange' which costs nothing. In the case of formal lessons most experts agree that a group lesson is just as good as learning one-to-one; it is also a great deal cheaper. Language courses are also organised by some local communes starting every September.

Useful Addresses

For French:
Alliance Française: Av. de l'Eméraude 59, 1030 Brussels; ☎02 732 15 92; Rue d'Arlon 24, 1050 Brussels; ☎02 502 46 49.
Amira: Av. Louise 251, 1050 Brussels; ☎02 640 68 50; www.amira.be.
CLL, Université Catholique de Louvain: Passage de la Vecquée 17, 1200 Brussels; ☎02 771 13 20; www.cll.be.

For Dutch:
College of Europe: Dijver 11, 8000 Brugge; ☎050 44 99 11; fax 050 34 75 33; e-mail info@coleurop.be; www.coleurop.be.
Nederlands Taalinstituut: Rue de l'Association/Verenigingsstraat 56, 1000 Brussels; ☎02 219 03 27; e-mail nti@village.uunet.be.

SCHOOLS AND EDUCATION

THE DECISION ON HOW and where to educate one's children is always a difficult one wherever or however you live. Moving abroad with children of a young age is in some ways easier than moving with teenagers, as younger children are far more adept at picking up languages and fitting into new situations. As their education has not yet begun in earnest, the problem of juggling two different curricula does not arise. Switching over to a new and unfamiliar language can set a teenager back a year in their schooling. Belgium has an excellent education system and claims to be the only country in the western world that offers free schooling from the age of 2½. This does not of course mean that a child being educated in the British system would immediately function well in a Belgian school. For this reason many parents choose to send their children to international schools. Luckily, Belgium has a great concentration of such schools where children can mix with different nationalities, and receive part of their schooling in another language as well.

The Belgian regions have made education one of their top priorities, and spend 20% of their budget on this sector. School attendance is compulsory between the ages of 6 and 18. With the latest moves towards federalisation, most of the responsibility for education has now moved from the central government to the Communities (the tier of government concerned with language and culture). General policy is still decided by the central state, but in other respects there are divergences between the regions.

There are two types of publicly-funded schools in Belgium: 'official' and 'free' (*libre/vrij*). In the French-speaking area a little over half of all secondary schools are 'free schools'; in the Flemish area almost three-quarters. In the official sector most schools come under the Community but some are run by the Provinces or Communes.

Most 'free' schools are linked to the Catholic church, but a few belong to other religious groupings or to none at all. A major difference between official and free schools is that parents have to pay for some equipment and activities at the latter.

The Structure of the Education System

Pre-school: This is divided into playschool (2½-4 years of age) and kindergartens (2½-5) which are often attached to a primary school. Playschools (*prégardienne/ peuterschool*) are not usually free, whereas kindergartens (*jardin d'enfants/kleuterschool*) often are. The advantage of enrolling a child in a kindergarten, amongst other things, is that he/she will be better prepared in terms of reading and sociability than if he/she stayed at home. Kindergartens are not compulsory, but more than half of the children in primary school have been to one. Some international schools also have pre-school classes.

Primary: Children are usually six when they enter primary school (*école primaire/ lagere school*), although they may be allowed to enter at five if the school thinks they are ready. Primary education lasts six years and concentrates on the mother tongue and mathematics. There are regular tests and students can be made to repeat an entire year if their performance is below standard. In the last year children are assessed by the 'psycho-medical-social centre' who will advise them on which type of secondary school is most suitable for them.

Secondary: Having obtained a primary school pass certificate, children then go on to the six-year secondary system (*école secondaire/middelbare school*) where specialisation begins in earnest. While there are some schools offering technical or vocational education at this level, called *institut/instituut*, most offer a wide range of options as well as vocational training. Secondary schools are generally known as *athénée/atheneum*, *lycée* or *collège* in the case of Catholic schools.

Since 1978 the revised system of education known as Type I has become the norm in state schools. The traditional humanities-based system (Type II) is still followed in some non-state schools. In the revised system students are continuously evaluated and specialisation is introduced gradually. During the third year students go into a transitional period and can decide to take up technical and vocational studies which more or less excludes the possibility of going to university, or to select a curriculum chosen from up to 24 different options.

In the traditional system, choice is considerably more limited and pupils must commit themselves to their specialisation at the age of 12. There is again a choice between general and technical/vocational streams. In the general section there are options such as Latin and Greek, Latin maths, Latin sciences, scientific A (pure sciences), scientific B (science and modern languages), economics with modern languages and social sciences. After six years of secondary school students in the Flemish area receive a Diploma in Secondary Education (*Diploma van Secundair Onderwijs*). In the French area this is known as the Certificate in Secondary Education (*Certificat d'Etudes Secondaires*).

Universities

Belgian universities have a worldwide reputation for excellence in a number of scientific fields, in particular in biotechnology. The Katholieke Universiteit Leuven (KUL) is the oldest and best-known, with 25,000 students of whom 10% are foreigners (website: www.kuleuven.ac.be). The system is open to anyone who has gained a high school diploma and universities are to a large extent regulated by the State. As one might expect, institutions of higher learning are divided between French and Dutch, and the official and 'free' (Catholic) systems. About 26% of Belgians go on to higher education (compared with 20% in the UK) and of these about half pursue full-length university courses. These are divided into 'cycles' of two or three years each, with some institutions offering only one cycle. In a full (*complet/kompleet*) university course there is a preparatory cycle – the *candidature/kandidaatschap* followed by a second cycle leading to the equivalent of a bachelor's degree – the *licence/licentiaat*. In some fields a graduate will be awarded the title of medical doctor, civil engineer, and so on, after completing the second cycle. Beyond the level of 'licence' there is a third possible cycle conferring a master's degree or doctorate.

All instruction at Belgian universities is given free of charge, but there is an annual registration fee of about €500 (£300). As far as living expenses are concerned, students receive grants according to the financial circumstances of their parents or they can take out loans from the state. EU citizens are legally entitled to attend EU universities and are also eligible for grants in another country if they qualify in their home country. Grants in Belgium are so low (£150 a month), however, that poorer students usually live at home and commute to the university.

EU citizens can enter university courses if they have a secondary school leaving certificate and can pass a language test. All the six major universities offer courses in the medium of English, in particular at postgraduate level. For information on courses at secondary and university level contact the following institutions:

CSBO: Centrum voor Studies en Beroepsorientering: Chaussée de Ninove 339, 1070 Brussels; ☎ 02 414 14 10.

CEDIEP: Centre de Documentation et de l'Informatique sur les Etudes et les Professions: Rue Philippe Baucq 18, 1040 Brussels; ☎ 02 649 14 18.

SIEP: Service d'Information pour les Etudes et les Professions: Av. de la Couronne 224, 1050 Brussels; ☎ 02 640 18 51.

International Universities

Belgium has an unusually high concentration of universities and colleges offering courses in management, law and politics with a European or international slant, in order to prepare students for possible careers in the European Commission and other international organisations. The College of Europe offers a Diploma in Advanced European Studies or a Masters in European Studies. The entry requirement is a good first degree and good French; grants are available. For American-style university education there is Vesalius College, Brussels which works in cooperation with the Flemish Vrije Universiteit Brussels. United Business Institutes offers a four-year Bachelor of Business Administration course, and five one- or two-year MBA courses. The European University, founded in 1973 in Antwerp, has programmes in most EU countries. The British Open University also runs business courses. For a study of university education in Belgium consult *Selected Links: Business and Academia in Belgium,* available from Focus Career Services, Rue Lesbroussart 23, 1050 Brussels; ☎ 02 646 65 30; www.focusbelgium.org.

Useful Addresses

International Universities

Boston University Brussels: Bvd du Triomphe 36, 1160 Brussels; ☎ 02 629 27 07; www.bostonu.be.

College of Europe: Dijver 7, 8000 Brugge; ☎ 050 44 99 11; e-mail info@coleurop.be; www.coleurop.be.

European University: Amerikalei 131, 2000 Antwerp; ☎ 03 238 10 82.

Open University: Av. Emile Duray 38, 1050 Brussels; ☎ 02 644 33 72; www.open.ac.uk.

Vesalius College – VUB: (mailing address) Pleinlaan 2, 1050 Brussels (visiting address) Triomflaan 32, 1160 Brussels; ☎ 02 629 26 26; e-mail vesalius@vub.ac.be; www.vub.ac.be/VECO.

Business Schools
International Management Institute: Rue de Livourne 116-120, 1050 Brussels; 02 644 33 72.
Solvay Business School: Dept NEW 3/99, Av. F. Roosevelt 50, 1050 Brussels; 02 560 41 83.
United Business Institutes: Av. Marnix 20, 1000 Brussels; ☎02 548 04 80; fax 02 548 04 89; e-mail info@ubi.edu; www.ubi.edu.

UBI — **THE NUMBER ONE BUSINESS SCHOOL IN BRUSSELS**

United Business Institutes

BBA & MBA

BBA: four-year undergraduate degree (full-time) starting September or March.

MBA: one or two-year graduate degree (evening classes) starting October, January or April.
Concentrations and/or certificates:
- International Business Management,
- Corporate Intelligence & Knowledge Management,
- Global IT & Telecommunication Management,
- Lobbying & Business Representation,
- Leadership & Change Management.

UBI - United Business Institutes
Avenue Marnix, 20 B-1000 Brussels - Belgium
Tel.: +32-(0)2-548 04 80 - Fax: +32-(0)2-548 04 89
E-mail: info@ubi.edu - WebSite: http://www.ubi.edu

International Schools

Parents abroad have three main options for their children: to send them to local Belgian schools, to send them to boarding schools in Britain or elsewhere, or to use one of the many international schools in Belgium. These can offer British and American curricula, as well as the European and International Baccalaureate programmes. One major advantage of such a school is that your child can be prepared to enter university in their own country if they do not intend to go into higher education in Belgium. The following is a list of schools with English-speaking pupils and their annual fees. Unless otherwise stated there is some provision for British GCSE:

American School Elementary: Kiestraat 1, 3670 Meeuwen Gruitrode; ☎011 79 25 27.

Antwerp British School: Korte Altaarstraat 19, 2018 Antwerp (03 271 09 43; e-mail antwerpbritschool@pandora.be; www.antwerpbritschool.org) 2½-14.

Antwerp International School: Veltwijcklaan 180, 2180 Ekeren, Antwerp (03 543 93 00; www.ais-antwerp.be) 3-18.

British Junior Academy of Brussels: Bvd St. Michel 83, 1040 Brussels (02 732 53 76; e-mail bjabrussels@yahoo.com; www.bjab.org) 2½-11.

British Primary School: Stationstraat 3, 3080 Tervuren (02 767 30 98; e-mail sky74988@skynet.be; www.users.skynet.be/british.primary) 3-8.

British School of Brussels: Leuvensesteenweg 19, 3080 Tervuren (02 766 04 30; e-mail principal@britishschool.be; www.britishschool.be) 3-18. Some assisted places.

Brussels American School: John F. Kennedylaan 12, 1933 Sterrebeek (02 717 95 52) 5-18. School for NATO and US personnel. US curriculum.

Brussels English Primary School: Av. Franklin Roosevelt 23, 1050 Brussels (02 648 43 11/fax 02 687 29 68; www.beps.com) 2½-11.

Brussels English Primary School (BEPS-2 Limal): Rue L. Deladrière 13, 1300 Limal (010 41 72 27; www.beps.com) 2½-11.

Brussels English Primary School (BEPS-Waterloo): Chaussée de Waterloo 280, 1640 Rhode St-Genèse (02 358 06 06; www.beps.com) 2½-10.

The City International School: Bvd Louis Schmidt 101-103, 1040 Brussels (02 734 44 13) 3-18.

Ecole Internationale Le Verseau: Rue de Wavre 60, 1301 Bierges (010 23 17 15) 3-18.

EEC International School: Jacob Jordaen Straat 77, 2018 Antwerp (03 218 54 31) 3½-20.

International School of Brussels: Kattenberg 19, 1170 Brussels (02 661 42 11; www.isb.be) 3-18. US curriculum.

Children's House Montessori School: Av. Dolez 458B, 1180 Brussels (02 375 61 84; 375 12 65) 2½-5½.

The European Montessori School: Av. Beau Séjour, 1410 Waterloo (02 354 00 33) 1½-12.

Montessori House Belgium: Rue Pergère 117, 1420 Braine-L'Alleud (02 385 15 03; www.montessorihouse.net) 2-9.

International Montessori School Tervuren: Rotselaerlaan 1, 3080 Tervuren (02 767 63 60; e-mail montessoritervuren@online.be) 3-12.

Montessori Children's Centre (International): Mechelsesteenweg 79, 1933 Sterrebeek (02 784 27 84; montessoritervuren@online.be) 1½-6.

St John's International School: Drève Richelle 146, 1410 Waterloo (02 352 06 10; www.stjohns.be) 3-19. US curriculum, GCE 'O'-Level and International Baccalaureate.

Further information from:

Council of British Independent Schools in the European Community (COBISEC): Lucy's, Lucy's Hill, Hythe, Kent CT21 5ES; tel/fax 01303 260857; e-mail cobisec@cs.com; www.cobisec.org.

European Council of International Schools: 21 Lavant Street, Petersfield, Hants GU32 3EL; ☎01730-268244; fax 01730-267914; e-mail ecis@ecis.org; www.ecis.org.

ECIS North America: 105 Tuxford Terrace, Basking Ridge, New Jersey 07920, USA; ☎908-903 0552; fax 908-580 9381; e-mail malyecisna@aol.com; www.ecis.org.

MEDIA & COMMUNICATIONS

Newspapers

Belgian newspapers, as with everything else in Belgium, are divided by regions and languages, and by their attitude towards the hegemony of the church and state. In general French-speakers do not read Dutch language newspapers, while some Flemings read the French press. The Belgians are not great newspaper readers in the British tradition – even the most widely read newspaper, the Dutch *Het Laatste Nieuws*, has a circulation of less than 300,000. Newspapers are serious and accurate in their reporting; nothing like the British tabloid press. The popular press concentrates more on human interest stories and sport, but is still rather sober by any standards.

Newspapers rely to a large extent on subscribers (*abonnés*) for their income with a subscription (*abonnement*) generally costing about €200 per year. Single issues are around €0.80 for most papers. The most important edition of the day is in the evening, with updates in the morning. Subscribers receive their copies through the letterbox in the afternoon. The weekend edition is delivered on Saturday morning.

National newspapers based in Brussels are *Le Soir*, *La Libre Belgique* (French), *Het Laatste Nieuws* and *De Standaard* (Dutch). Newspapers published in Antwerp, for example *De Gazet van Antwerpen*, are widely read in the Flemish area for their financial reporting.

The state pays subsidies to the press which are mainly taken up by Catholic newspapers. Most papers are pro-Christian or pro-Liberal (free-market secularist). Those claiming to be 'neutral' or 'independent' combine respect for Christian values with economic liberalism. Leftist papers such as *De Morgen* and *Le Peuple* have a more limited appeal.

Most British newspapers are available in Belgian cities during the morning of publication at prices ranging from €1.60 to €4.00. A subscription to *The Times* will guarantee you same-day delivery in certain areas of Belgium; call 01733-588 494 (UK). The *International Herald Tribune* costs €1.60; subscriptions can be ordered on-line: www.iht.com. The *Financial Times* International Edition costs €2.25 and is obtainable by subscription from Financial Times Benelux, Rue Ducale 39, 1000 Brussels; ☎02 548 95 55.

Major Newspapers

Dutch
Het Laatste Nieuws. Liberal. Colourful and middlebrow. Circulation 300,000.
Het Nieuwsblad. Christian/Liberal. Circulation 300,000.
De Gazet van Antwerpen. Business-oriented. Circulation 191,000.
Het Volk. Owned by Catholic trade union. Circulation 190,000.
De Standaard. Christian/Liberal. Circulation 80,000.
De Financieel Economische Tijd. Independent. Economic and news reporting. Circulation 38,000 (www.tijd.be/tijd). Published from Antwerp.
Trends en Beleggen. Deals with financial trends and investments. Also French version *Trends et Tendances*. Circulation 60,000 (www.roularta.be).

De Streekkrant. Dutch. Free weekly newspaper with various editions in different Flemish towns. Ghent edition has a circulation of 400,000 (www.streekkrant.be).

French

Le Soir. Christian/Liberal. Serious news and comment. Owned by same company (La Régie Rossel) as *La Meuse-La Lanterne* in Liège and *La Nouvelle Gazette* in Charleroi. Circulation 147,000 (www.lesoir.com).
La Dernière Heure. Liberal. Colourful and middlebrow, with emphasis on sport. Same owners as *La Libre Belgique* (SIPM). Circulation 97,000.
La Libre Belgique. Christian. Stodgy and serious. Heavy emphasis on culture. Useful economic pullout section on Saturdays *La Libre Entreprise.* Circulation 90,000 (www.lalibre.be).
L'Echo de la Bourse. French. Founded 1881. Independent stock market paper. Circulation 31,000 (www.echonet.be).
Vlan/Vlan+. French. Main group of free weeklies in Wallonia. Brussels edition has a circulation of 400,000 (www.vlan.be).

Magazines

Since 1970 there has been a huge increase in the number of weeklies and monthlies published in Belgium; the total is now over 8,000. The major evolution in the magazine market has been the decline of women's magazines. The most popular magazines are now those that appeal to the whole family, such as the Dutch *Blik* (circulation 180,000) and the French *Le Soir Illustré* (120,000), and TV-listings magazines with interviews and articles, such as the Dutch *Humo* (www.humo.be) and the French *Télémoustique.* Sales of weeklies with political comment and international news, in particular *Knack* (Dutch) and *Le Vif-L'Express* (French) (see www.roularta.be for both) have increased considerably as young Belgians look for more and more sophisticated reading matter. For the expatriate, the English-language weekly *The Bulletin* is essential reading, particularly if you live in Brussels; available from large newsagents in main Belgian towns. A year's subscription costs €99.00 and single issues €2.35.

Books and Bookshops

The Belgian reading public benefits considerably from the large influx of books published in neighbouring Holland and France. Highbrow French literature is widely read, including by Dutch-speakers, and there is also a ready market for all kinds of translations from English into Dutch or French. Academic and scientific books in English are indispensable for university students and widely available, and you will also find a section of English novels and coffee-table books in any large bookshop. Naturally, English books in Belgium are expensive. The cheapest bookshops in Belgium are those run by De Slegte in Brussels, Ghent and Antwerp (main branch: Rue des Grands Carmes 17, 1000 Brussels). The French-owned FNAC chain has an excellent range of books sometimes with discounts. There are some specialist English bookshops in Brussels, including: Waterstones (Bvd Adolphe Max 71-75, 1000 Brussels; ☎ 02 219 27 08) which has English magazines and newspapers; Sterling Books, Fossé aux Loups 35, 1000 Brussels (☎ 02 223 62 23) equally large; and The Reading Room (Ave Georges Henri 503, Woluwé-St. Lambert, 1200 Brussels; ☎ 02 734 79 170). Stone Manor (Steenhofstraat 28, 3078 Everberg, ☎ 02 759 49 79; fax 759 24 88) stocks English books and magazines, as well as videos, games and a wide range of groceries. For a complete listing of bookshops look in the yellow pages under *Librairies/Boekhandels*.

Television

Belgium is ideally located to receive foreign TV broadcasts; with cable television it is now possible to receive up to 30 different channels. With a satellite dish it is possible to pick up anything up to 400; FilmNet and Canal Plus are the two main suppliers. Because of the limited resources of Belgian TV companies, viewers have always preferred Dutch and French stations for more interesting programmes. Commercial television only started in 1989. In the Flemish area, the commercial stations VTM (*Vlaamse Televisie Maatschappij*), Kanaal 2 and VT4 have about one-third of viewers, and the Flemish state channels BRTN-TV1 and TV2 under 30% (website: www.brtn.be). The programme which attracts most viewers is the 7.30 evening news on TV1 with a maximum of 1,200,000. TV1 mostly consists of general interest information programmes and homegrown drama along with the inevitable American films and series. TV2 covers sport and cultural programmes. VTM consists mostly of game shows and American imports. In Wallonia, RTBF 1 has similar programmes to the Flemish TV1, while RTBF 2 is a more serious cultural channel. The French-language Luxembourg station, RTL TV1, has a mix of game shows and American and French-language imports.

Foreigners do not need to watch Belgian television – programmes from France, the Netherlands, Germany, Italy and Britain are readily available, as well as the American news channel CNN, the music channel MTV and Eurosport. To obtain this wealth of viewing, look under *Cable/Kabel* in the Yellow Pages for your local cable TV company. The main company in the Brussels area is Coditel. Apart from any cable fees, owners of TVs have to pay a licence fee. The office which collects licence fees can be found under *Radio et Télévision Redevances (RTR)* or *Kijk en Luistergeld (KLG)* in the Yellow Pages; in Brussels call 02 207 74 11. A colour TV licence costs about €190. A licence is also required for a car-radio (about €28).

Radio

Belgian radio has three channels for both languages. Radio 1 is mostly a news and cultural channel, and gives traffic information as well. Radio 2 is the most popular channel, and is much like British Radio 2 – light music and other bland entertainment. Radio 3 is a highbrow channel with a great deal of classical music and heavy academic discussions. The Brussels station *Studio Brussel/Bruxelles* offers continuous music. Because of Belgium's geographical position it is easy to pick up British radio broadcasts, and those of many other countries.

Post

Postal services, together with telephones and telegraphs, are run by the national ministry known as the PTT. The Belgian postal service is more efficient than many of its EU counterparts: it aims to deliver letters in Belgium the following day. Most post offices are open from Monday to Friday from 9am to 12 noon and from 2pm to 5pm. Only main post offices open on Saturday mornings and stay open through the lunch break. The post office at the Gare du Midi/Zuidstation in Brussels is open from 7am to 11pm Monday to Saturday, and from 12pm to 8pm on Sundays and public holidays. Post offices are also often closed the day before or after a public holiday (the notorious so-called *pont* or 'bridge'). Service at post offices can be infuriatingly slow because of the large number of financial and fiscal transactions which one can carry out. You should first check that you are standing in the right queue. There is a board with window numbers – the correct window is the one with *Timbres postales/Postzegels* (stamps) next to it.

Internal letters cost €0.42. Postcards and letters up to 50 grams to EU countries are €0.52; to the US €0.84. The Belgian post office makes a big deal about postcards and envelopes being of a standard size; non-standard sizes are charged at higher rates. Letters to the UK take anything from two days to a week; letters to the USA take about a week. Rates for express letters can be found on the website www.emstaxipost.be. A registered letter *(lettre recommandée/aangetekend schrijven)* costs €3.72 and is absolutely necessary if legal proof of postage is required. When addressing mail in Belgium the PTT requires addresses to be written in the form in which they are given in this book, namely street first, and house number second, even if the French-speakers tend to do the opposite.

Small parcels in Belgium will be delivered the next day. An even faster service is offered by EMS-Taxipost, a service also run by the Belgian post office (see www.ems-taxipost.be). For a complete list of courier services, look under *Courrier (service de)/Koerierdiensten* in the yellow pages.

If you want to send a telegram you can simply phone 1325 (for French) and 1225 (Dutch) and dictate your message, even from a public call box. Otherwise you can send your telegram from a post office or railway station. A ten-word telegram from Belgium to the UK costs about €20, to the US €26. Faxes can be sent from any one of the 'Bureaufax' offices around the country.

Telephones

For installation and billing of telephones look under *Telephones* in Chapter Three, *Setting Up Home*. Call boxes are not that plentiful; in central Brussels many are broken. The minimum cost of a call is €0.25. Telephone cards can be bought at post offices, railway station ticket offices, and some kiosks and banks. There are also other cards on offer which may save money on foreign calls if one uses them from a private phone rather than a call box. Beware of rip-off cards which give no number to call if you have a complaint. Calls from private telephones cost 5 cents per minute for a national call at peak rate, 2 cents at cheap rate, plus a connection charge of 5 cents. A 5-minute call to the UK, US or Canada costs 95 cents at peak rate.

There are two rates of charge at the present time: peak rate is from 8am to 7pm, cheap rate from 7pm to 8am and at weekends. Further information can be found in the telephone directory or on from the website www.belgacom.be.

Mobile telephones are known as GSM in both languages. The three main brands are Mobistar, Proximus and Orange.

Dialling in Belgium is different from dialling in the UK, in that the area code is required within the same zone. Area codes within Belgium and some codes for abroad can be found at the front of the white pages, under *Indicatifs interurbains/ Netnummers*. Directory enquiries in English are on 1405 for all countries. Note that all telephone information services in English begin with 14, in French with 13 and in Dutch with 12. Reverse charge calls are on 1324/1224. For operator-assisted international calls, dial the same numbers. To make an international call from Belgium you dial the access code 00 followed by the country code followed by the subscriber's number minus the initial zero.

Note that Belgians are in the habit of quoting telephone numbers in pairs or even threes, thus a Brussels number such as that of the American Chamber of Commerce (02 513 67 70) comes over as *zéro-deux cinq-cent-treize soixante-sept septante* in French and *nul-twee vijfhonderd-en-dertien zeven-en-zestig zeventig* in Dutch. Unless you are very good at numbers in Dutch and French you should therefore insist on numbers being quoted in single figures, or in English.

CARS AND MOTORING

BELGIANS HAVE A REPUTATION for being dangerous and aggressive drivers which is well deserved. Part of the problem stems from the fact that there was no driving test at all until 1967, and a hands-on test was not introduced until 1979. The Belgian driving test is now one of the stiffest in the world, and there are numerous rules and regulations drivers have to be aware of. One feature of the Belgian test is that it is possible to take the theoretical test before taking the practical. The Belgian Road Safety Code has been translated into English as *The Illustrated Highway Code*. Other essentials are *Driving in Belgium from A to Z*, published by New Traffic Books Edition and *Driving Training Theory and Practice*, by Garant, available from Waterstone's in Brussels.

Belgium has an excellent system of motorways (French *autoroute*; Dutch *autosnelweg/autostrade*) which costs nothing to use. Within older towns there are still some cobbled streets (*kassei/pavé*) which provide a somewhat hazardous driving surface. Road signs use the local language (except in Brussels where there are two) with the result that a place name may suddenly take on an unfamiliar form (e.g. Antwerpen becomes Anvers in French, Liège becomes Luik and Mons becomes Bergen in Dutch).

The most important traffic law is *priority to the right* (*priorité à droite/voorrang aan rechts*) which is an obsession with Belgian drivers. When coming to any intersection, which includes any side road however small (in theory), you must give way to vehicles coming from the right. Equally, you must take your priority where it applies. When coming to a main road you are likely to see one of two signs telling you to give way – a white triangle edged in red with a black arrow with a line through it, or a yellow diamond edged in white. You may also see a row of white shark's teeth painted on the road pointing towards you telling you to give

way. At roundabouts entering traffic has right of way, unless indicated otherwise.
Another cause of accidents involving foreigners is misunderstanding what is meant by flashing headlights at someone. This signifies 'Get out of my way' or 'I have priority' – not 'Please go ahead'. Trams are another unfamiliar hazard. Overtaking a tram on the inside when it is at a stop, or pulling up next to it, is illegal – you could hit passengers trying to get off – so watch out for tram stops (particularly in Brussels). Trams have priority at all times in any case. While you cannot avoid parking near tramlines you must make sure that trams can get past.

Driving Regulations

There are two police forces which deal with traffic violations: the local *police communale* or *gemeentepolitie* and the *police fédérale/federale politie*. The two police bodies are expected to fulfil similar roles as of January 2002. No decision had yet been taken on differentiating their uniforms at the time of writing.

Seat belts are compulsory, front and back. Children under 12 must travel in the back. Tyres should have a minimum tread of 1.6 millimetres. You are also legally obliged to carry the following: a fire extinguisher with the logo *Bénor V*; a red triangular danger signal; a rear fog lamp; and an approved first-aid kit. You must also carry your identity card, car registration papers (*carte grise/grijze kaart*) which is a pink A4 form with a grey card in the middle; driving licence and insurance papers.

Most drivers break the speed limits on the motorways in the knowledge that the police do not have the resources to catch offenders. You are four times more likely to be caught speeding in the Netherlands than in Belgium. On four-lane highways there is a minimum speed limit of 70 kph (44 mph) and a maximum of 120 kph (75 mph). Other out-of-town roads usually have a 90 kph (56 mph) limit. In built-up areas the limit can vary between 40 and 80 kph (25-50 mph) but 60 kph (37.5 mph) is the norm.

Parking is regulated by meters, or by the display of a special disc if in a 'blue' zone in towns. Sometimes parking is on one side of the street 15 days of the month and on the other side the rest of the month. This will be shown by a sign with Roman numerals on it.

Drinking and Driving. The permissible blood/alcohol level has now been fixed at 50 milligrams per 100 millilitres of blood, lower than the British level of 80 milligrams. Serious cases of drink driving can result in your licence being withdrawn and a jail sentence. Breath tests are becoming more and more frequent, and about 10% turn out positive. The only crumb of comfort is that you can request a 30 minute wait before being breathalysed to allow the alcohol in your mouth to dissipate.

Breakdowns and Accidents

Thanks to the introduction of driving tests and stricter police regulation the number of deaths and injuries on the roads has fallen somewhat since the 1970s, nonetheless you are twice as likely to be killed on the road in Belgium as you are in the UK. If you do have an accident it is only necessary to call the police (on 101) if someone is injured or there is a disagreement with the other driver about the circumstances. If there is no disagreement you can fill in a standard form supplied by your insurance company called a *Constat à l'amiable* – an 'amicable account of the accident' – with details of car registration, type, and so on. Otherwise the police will have to draw up a written account of the accident. If a car cannot be moved or someone is injured, call 100, the number for both the fire brigade (*pompiers/brandweer*) and ambulances (*ambulance/ziekenwagen*).

Should you break down on a motorway you will find telephones every three kilometres by the side of the road from where you can call the local or federal police who will put you in touch with a breakdown service. There are three motoring organisations in Belgium which offer 24-hour-a-day breakdown services all over Benelux. RAC and AA members get help from their sister organisations in Belgium – the RACB and TCB – provided that they have taken out extra insurance cover for Europe. If you are not covered at all you can join one of the Belgian organisations on the spot at a surcharge. These are (together with the name of the service they offer and emergency numbers):

Royal Automobile Club de Belgique/Koninklijke Automobiel Club van België (RACB/KACB): Rue de Trèves 828, 1000 Brussels; ☎ 02 287 09 11; www.racb.com. SOS Dépannage/Pechdienst – (National number) 078 15 20 00.

Touring Club de Belgique/Touring Club van België (TCB): Rue de la Loi 44, 1040 Brussels; ☎ 02 233 22 11.

Touring Secours/Touring-Wegenhulp – Antwerp 03 353 88 88; Brussels 02 233 22 11; Liège 041 368 79 91; Namur 081 22 78 45; Ghent 09 225 89 59.

Vlaamse Automobilistenbond (VAB): Pastor Coplaan 100, 2070 Zwijndrecht; ☎ 03 253 61 30; www.vab.com.

Wacht op de Weg (Road Watch) – 03 253 64 64.

Driving Licences

Anyone visiting Belgium can continue to use the driving licence of their home country. For Britons this means the pink EU licence. Since 1996 EU licences have been fully transferable and so there is no need to exchange yours for a Belgian licence.

Only a few non-EU licences are recognised by the Belgian authorities. If you do not hold a recognised licence you may continue to drive on an international one for a limited period of time, but you will then have to take the Belgian driving test. US licence holders only need to hand in their licence, residence permit and two passport photos, and they will receive a Belgian licence within seven days.

Car registration

If you plan to take your car out of the UK for more than 12 months, you must notify its export to the Driver and Vehicle Licence Agency in Swansea; they will send you a certificate V561 for registering abroad. If you are going abroad for less than a year, you need to take the registration document with you, or apply for a temporary certificate of registration from the DVLA. See website www.dvla.co.uk for further information.

When importing your own vehicle, you need to see that your car conforms to Belgian norms. You can check first with a dealer for your particular model if a change needs to be made. Your car must then be inspected at a Technical Inspection (TI) centre (look in the Yellow Pages under *Auto-inspection technique et centres d'examens/Automobielinspectie en rijbewijscentra*). If they are satisfied that your car is roadworthy, the TI centre will issue a Certificate of Inspection and ask you to fill in a pink registration (*immatriculation/immatriculatie*) application form. You then take out an insurance policy with a Belgian company, with at least third-party protection. An insurance contract runs for a year and is automatically renewed. Notice of cancellation must be given three months before the renewal date. In the case of foreign residents it is possible to insert a clause into the contract making it possible to cancel before the usual date. Belgian car insurance is expensive and a comprehensive policy costs at least €1,000.

Once you have an insurance policy the insurance company will pass on your application for registration to the relevant authority – the *Direction pour l'Immatriculation des Véhicules/Direktie voor Immatriculatie der Voertuigen* (DIV) (Résidence Palace, Rue de la Loi 155, 1040 Brussels; ☎02 287 43 43; www.vici.fgov.be) – who will send you the rear registration plate and your registration card (*carte grise/grijze kaart*). You then have a copy made of the number plate at a car shop or Mister Minute shop and attach it to the front of your car. The DIV will also send a demand for payment of the road tax (*verkeersbelasting/taxe de circulation*), which is calculated on the basis of the car's nominal horsepower. For an average-sized car this comes to about €180 per year.

The procedure outlined above is much the same for buying a new or second-hand car in Belgium. If you require guidance the DIV has an information service on 02 287 43 23 (French) or 02 287 43 22 (Dutch).

TRANSPORT

Trains

BELGIUM HAS ONE of the densest railway networks in the world, noted for its punctuality and safety (and strikes), run by the nationalised SNCB/NMBS. Trains are coded according to the number of stations they stop at. Local trains (L) stop at every station, and peak-hour trains (P) at most stations. Inter-city and Inter-regional trains (IC and IR) miss out most small stops. Supplements (*supplément/toeslag*) have to be paid on international trains marked EC. International trains marked INT do not require a supplement.

Tickets must be bought before getting on the train. Prices are calculated on the basis of total distance. A 100 km journey, for example, costs €10. The price of a return ticket (*aller retour/heen en terug*) is double that of a single ticket (*aller simple/enkel*). Reduced rates on return tickets are generally only available at weekends. One very good deal, however, is the B-Tourrail Card which offers unlimited travel in Belgium on five days within a month for €56.52. Under-26s can benefit from the Go-Pass which offers 10 one-way journeys for €38.42; the equivalent for over-26s is the Rail Pass, at €56.52. Train times and prices (including international trains) are available on 02 555 25 55 or on the website www.b-rail.be.

City Transport

Urban transport systems are highly integrated, with metros in Brussels and Antwerp. A ticket is usually valid for one hour on the whole system in a particular city. A single ticket costs €1.40 in Brussels, and a ten-ticket card (*carte réseau urbain/stadskaart*) €9.00. In other towns tickets cost less. It is preferable to buy your ticket in advance – they are sold in stations and bookshops – or to have the right change on you, as tram/bus drivers do not like wasting time. In general, you get on at the front of the tram or bus and get off at the back. If you already have a ticket then it is acceptable to get on at the back or middle (on the newer trams it is now compulsory). Once you get on, your ticket has to be 'invalidated' (*obliteré/ontwaardt*) so that the time is printed on it. If you change tram or bus, then you invalidate your ticket again; no money will be deducted from the ticket within the one-hour time period. This is so that the driver can see that you are not trying to travel for nothing.

Air and Sea Travel

Belgium's main international airport (Brussels National) is at Zaventem, on the northwest side of Brussels. There are also international airports at Middelkerke (Ostend) and Antwerp. The national airline, Sabena, went out of business in 2001. Airlines serving Belgium from the UK have seen a considerable fall in their traffic since the opening of the Channel Tunnel; their fares should become cheaper with greater deregulation. The main advantage of flying is the wide variety of destinations in the UK. For details of airlines serving Belgium see the section 'Getting There' in the *Introduction*.

About half of UK travellers now use the Channel Tunnel in order to get to Belgium. When the high-speed rail links have been completed in the UK and Belgium the journey time will be reduced to 2½ hours. The French ports of Calais and Dunkirk are very close to the Belgian border; ferry services to Ostend and Zeebrugge (closer to Holland) take rather longer.

Useful Addresses

Belgian Rail (SNCB-NMBS), Rue de France 85, 1060 Brussels; ☎ 02 555 25 25; www.sncb.be, www.b-rail.be.

Tourism Flanders-Brussels, 31 Pepper Street, London E14 9RW; ☎ 020-7867-0311; fax 020-7458 0045; www.toerismevl aanderen.be.

Belgian Tourist Office Brussels Wallonia, 217 Marsh Wall, London E14 9FJ; ☎ 020-7531 0390; fax: 020-7531 0393; e-mail consumer@belgiumtheplaceto.be; www.belgiumtheplaceto.be, www.opt.be.

Belgian Tourist Office: 780 Third Avenue, Suite 1501, New York, NY 10017; ☎ 212-758 8130; fax 212-355 7675; e-mail info@visitbelgium.com; www.visitbelgium.com.

BANKS AND FINANCE

IF YOU HAVE BECOME used to the dismal service offered by UK high street banks, you will be in for a pleasant surprise if you settle in Belgium. Not only does it lead the world in the use of electronic banking, but it also has the largest number of bank branches per head in the world. The use of paper cheques has largely died out – 95% of transactions are carried out electronically. If you work in Belgium your employer will expect you to have a bank account so that your salary can be paid into it.

Bank Accounts

Most people have accounts with one of the three major banks – Fortis Banque/ Fortis Bank, Bank Brussel Lambert/Banque Bruxelles Lambert, and Kredietbank – or a Post Office cheque account. Bank opening hours are 9.00am to 3.30pm, Monday to Friday, but there are variations, and some banks are open on Saturdays. If you bank with the post office, you will benefit from the longer opening hours (9 to 5). Anyone can open a current or checking account (*compte à vue/ zichtrekening*) by presenting their identity card or passport. You will receive a 12-figure bank account number which is unique in Belgium and identifies your bank and branch.

Your cheque guarantee card is also a debit and cash card. Not only can you make automatic electronic payments at over 20,000 terminals in retail outlets, but you also have access to the Bancontact and Mister Cash networks of cash dispensers, where you can withdraw cash 24 hours a day to a maximum of €250 in one day. If you have a card you can run up an overdraft of between €250 and €1,250, depending on the bank. If you exceed the limit all transactions will be stopped until you resolve matters. Bank statements (*extraits de compte/rekeninguittreksels*) can be sent daily, weekly or monthly and cost very little.

Instead of using cheques, bills are usually paid by bank transfer (*virement/overschrijving*) using the red form attached to the bill or invoice. You can also use a direct debit (*domiciliation/domicilie*) or standing order (*ordre permanent/bestendige opdracht*).

In spite of the sophistication of electronic banking in Belgium, credit cards are also popular, in particular Visa, American Express, MasterCard and EuroCard.

Debit Cards: A recent development in banking is the Proton card, the most advanced debit card in the world. The card can be 'charged up' with €125 at a time and then used in thousands of retail outlets. It can also be charged up and used for making calls at 10,000 public telephones.

Transferring Funds to and from Belgium

There are no foreign exchange controls in Belgium. When transferring a amounts over €2,500 (£1,620) to another country customers are asked to inform the financial institution what the nature of the transaction is. This is for statistical purposes to help calculate Belgium's balance of payments; the information is supposedly not made known to the tax inspectors.

Sending money from the UK should only take three days. It is worth checking if the bank uses the SWIFT system of electronic transfer of money.

Money

The Belgian Franc ceased to be legal tender at the end of February 2002. Old banknotes and coins can still be exchanged at banks, but there may be a charge. One euro (€) is made up of 100 cents. 1, 2, 5, 10, 20 and 50 cent, and 1 and 2 euro coins are in use. Banknotes come in 5, 10, 20, 50, 100, 200 and 500 euro denominations.

Useful Addresses

Banque Bruxelles Lambert: Av. Marnix 24, 1050 Brussels; ☎ 02 547 21 11, 0800 99 399; www.bbl.be.

Banque Bruxelles Lambert (UK): 6 Broadgate, London EC2; ☎ 020-7247 5566.

Fortis Banque: Montagne du Parc 3, 1000 Brussels; ☎ 0800 16 789; www.fortis.be.

Fortis Bank: 23 Camomile Street, London EC2; ☎ 020-7444 8000.

KBC Bank: Havenlaan 2, 1000 Brussels; ☎ 02 429 11 11; www.kbc.be.

KBC Bank: Exchange House, Primrose St, London EC2; ☎ 020-7638 5812.

Brewin Dolphin Ltd: 5 Giltspur Street, London EC1A 9BD; ☎ 020-7246 1062; fax 020-7246 1093. Offer a variety of services, including investment management and financial planning; contact Victoria Le Sueur.

TAX AND THE EXPATRIATE

AS A RESULT OF the different tax regimes which exist in different countries there are major complications involved in a move overseas. This does not just apply to tax affairs in the host country; a move will conjure up many tax implications in one's home country also. Many globetrotters simply leave home without informing the tax authorities in their own country. While the UK tax authorities have always been quite indulgent, as long as you can show that you were away for a whole tax year, the Internal Revenue Service in the US is much stricter. If you have already arranged a job in advance in Belgium, then it would be advisable to obtain some information from the tax authorities in your home country before leaving, thus ensuring that no unnecessary tax is paid. If your tax affairs are complex, e.g. you own property or you have income in more than one country, then you will probably need to consult a tax adviser. These can be found in specialised magazines such as *FT-Expat* or *The Expatriate*.

The Question of Residence

Anyone who is domiciled or who has their principal wealth in Belgium is liable for Belgian taxes on his or her worldwide income, from the point of view of the Belgian tax authorities. Taxable income includes income from work, letting and leasing, trade enterprises, returns on investment, annuities and speculative capital gains. Before moving abroad it is important to consider where one's main residence will be for tax purposes. The important point to note is that one does not necessarily escape one country's income tax and become subject to another's just by moving there. It all depends on where the tax authorities consider one is resident for tax purposes, and also where one is ordinarily resident or domiciled – not necessarily the same thing. The terms resident, ordinarily resident and domiciled are not defined in the UK Tax Acts but are based on legal precedent.

Procedure for UK Residents. The situation is reasonably straightforward if you are moving permanently abroad. You should inform the UK Inspector of Taxes at the office you usually deal with of your departure and they will send you a P85 form to complete. The UK tax office will usually require certain proof that you are leaving the UK, and hence their jurisdiction, for good. Evidence of having sold a house in the UK and having rented or bought one in Belgium is usually sufficient. If you are leaving a UK company to take up employment with a Belgian one then the P45 form given by your UK employer and evidence of employment in Belgium should be sufficient. You may be eligible for a tax refund in respect of the period up to your departure in which case it will be necessary to complete an income tax return for income and gains from the previous 5 April to your departure date. It may be advisable to seek professional advice when completing the P85; this form is used to determine your residence status and hence your UK tax liability. You should not fill it in if you are only going abroad for a short period of time. Once the Inland Revenue are satisfied that you are no longer resident or domiciled in the UK, they will close your file and not expect any more UK income tax to be paid.

If you are moving abroad temporarily then other conditions apply. You are not liable for UK taxes if you work for a foreign employer on a full-time contract and remain abroad for a whole tax year (6 April to 5 April), as long as you spend less than 183 days in a year, or 91 days a year averaged out over a four-year period, in the UK. Several part-time jobs abroad may be considered as full-time employment. If you are considered a UK resident and have earned money working abroad then taxes paid abroad are not deductible. If you spend one part of a year working abroad and the rest in the UK you may still be considered non-resident for the part spent abroad, the so-called split tax year concession; this only applies to someone going abroad for a lengthy period of time.

Belgium has a double taxation agreement with the UK, which makes it possible to offset tax paid in one country against tax paid in another. While the rules are complex, essentially, as long as you work for a Belgian employer and are paid in Belgium then you should not have to pay UK taxes, as long as you meet the residency conditions outlined above. For further information see the Inland Revenue publications IR20 *Residents and non-residents. Liability to tax in the United Kingdom* which can be found on the website www.inlandrevenue.gov.uk. Booklets IR138, IR139 and IR140 are also worth reading; these can be obtained from your local tax office or from:

Non-Resident Claims: Fitz Roy House, PO Box 46, Nottingham NG2 1BD; ☎ 0115-974 1919; fax 0115-974 1919; www.inlandrevenue.gov.uk.
Centre for Non-Residents (CNR), Residence Advice & Liabilities Unit 355: St. John's House, Bootle, Merseyside L69 9BB; ☎ 0151-472 6202; fax 0151-472 6003.

Procedure for US Citizens The US Internal Revenue Service (IRS) expects US citizens and resident aliens living abroad to file tax returns every year. Such persons will continue to be liable for US taxes on worldwide income until they have become permanent residents of another country and severed their ties with the USA. If you earn less than a certain amount abroad in one tax year then you do not need to file a tax return. The amount in 2001 was $7,200 for a single person; other rates apply for pensioners, married persons, heads of household, etc.

Fortunately the USA has a double taxation agreement with Belgium so you should not have to pay taxes twice on the same income. In order to benefit from the double taxation agreement you need to fulfil one of two residence tests: either you have been a bona fide resident of another country for an entire tax year, which is the same as the calendar year in the case of the US, or you have been physically present in another country for 330 days during a period of 12 months which can begin at any time of the year. Once you qualify under the bona fide residence or physical presence tests then any further time you spend working abroad can also be used to diminish your tax liability.

As regards foreign income, the main deduction for US citizens is the 'Foreign Earned Income Exclusion' by which you do not pay US taxes on the first $80,000 of money earned abroad (as of 2002; the amount of the exclusion has in recent times gone up by $2,000 every year). Investment income, capital gains, etc. are unearned income. If you earn in excess of the limit, taxes paid on income in Belgium can still be used to reduce your liability for US taxes, either in the form of an exclusion or a credit, depending on which is more advantageous. The same will apply to Belgian taxes paid on US income.

The rules for US taxpayers abroad are explained very clearly in the IRS booklet: *Tax Guide for US Citizens and Resident Aliens Abroad*, known as Publication 54, which can be downloaded from the internet on www.irs.gov.

Income Tax

The Dutch term for a tax demand is an *aanslag*, which also means an assassination attempt, which more or less sums up the Belgian view of taxation. Belgians have long suffered from excessively high levels of taxation, and therefore often try to hide some of their assets abroad; this may soon be a thing of the past with the expected abolition of banking secrecy in the EU from 2003. The Belgian state has come to realise that high taxes contribute to high unemployment, and has therefore started a process of reducing some taxes in order to motivate more people to work. This includes eventually abolishing the top two tax rates (52.5% and 55%) and introducing a tax credit for the very low-paid. By the year 2006 the annual tax burden should have been reduced by €3.3 billion per year. Belgians are notorious tax evaders, but for most foreigners the scope for tax evasion is limited, since most taxes are withheld at source.

The tax year is the same as the calendar year. By the beginning of April you should receive a tax return (*déclaration/aangifte*) for the previous year's income, which is to be returned by the end of June. There are two sections to the tax return. The first is sent out automatically, while the second applies to more unusual categories such as occasional income, profits from the sale of property, sub-letting etc., and also for people who run a shop or a small business on the side, which you have to request from the authorities by the end of May. Income tax (*impôt personnes physiques/belasting natuurlijke personen*) is deducted by your employer from your monthly salary, so this is an opportunity to adjust the total amount. The date by which the form has to be returned will be printed on the form. You have two months to pay any tax demand or face interest penalties. If you have not received a form by the end of May you are obliged to request one from the Finance Ministry (*Ministère des Finances/Ministerie van Financiën*). You are entitled to make a complaint if you believe the authorities have made an error. On the other hand, if you fill in the return incorrectly so that your liability appears to be higher than it really is, you have to pay up.

Foreigners working in Belgium can be treated as residents or non-residents. A resident is taxed on their worldwide income, whereas a non-resident is only taxed on income earned in Belgium. Foreign executives and researchers who are temporarily assigned to Belgium, benefit from a special tax regime whereby they are treated as non-residents so that double taxation can be avoided. If you are in this category you will inevitably need the services of an accountant. There is also a special office for non-residents: Ministère des Finances, Contrôle des Contributions de Bruxelles Etranger, Jan Jacobsplein 10, 1000 Brussels; ☎ 02 548 57 96, 548 58 06, 548 59 56.

Professional expenses and social security payments are deducted from the gross salary in order to calculate taxable income. It should be noted that fringe benefits, bonuses and so on all count as taxable income. The basic single person's allowance (which is index-linked) in 2002 stood at €5,350 (£3,320) and for a married couple at €4,240 for each partner. A number of allowances are applicable, including insurance payments, private pension schemes, mortgage repayments, and so on. There are also generous allowances for children – €1,140 for one child, €2,920 for two children, and so on. It is important to understand that allowances take you into a higher tax bracket and rate of tax and so save you less than you might think. Tax brackets for income earned in 2002 are listed in table 5.

TABLE 5		TAX BRACKETS	
Bracket	Taxable Income	% Tax	Total tax (in euro)
1	0 - 6,570	25%	1,642.5
2	6,571 - 8,710	30%	2,284
3	8,711 - 12,420	40%	3,768
4	12,421 - 28,540	45%	11,022
5	28,541 - 42,810	50%	18,156
6	42,811 - 62,790	52.5%	28,656
7	62,791 -	55%	

There is a surcharge, the 3% 'crisis contribution' added on to the amount of tax to be paid, which will be abolished as from tax year 2003. A single person with taxable income of €35,000 (after deduction of social security at 13.07%), claiming €2,000 for working expenses pays about €13,036 (including 6% local tax and 3% crisis contribution). A married person earning a gross salary of €70,000 with two children and claiming professional expenses pays about €26,664 in tax, assuming the spouse does not work. A single person with the same salary would pay €32,900. Those with salaries over €75,000 will save a great deal of money if they can constitute themselves as a limited company, and thus pay the corporate tax rate of 39%.

Self-employed workers usually arrange to pay income tax in advance at quarterly intervals on the basis of their predicted income, as there are substantial savings on interest to be made.

Local Tax

Quaintly called *centimes additionnels* or *opcentiemen* (additional centimes), this is paid to the commune and is calculated as a percentage of your income tax. The usual rate is between 7% and 10%, depending on how up-market the commune is.

Other Taxes

VAT: TVA (*Taxe Valeur Ajoutée*) or BTW (*Belasting Toegevoegde Waarde*) is levied at four different rates. These are: 1% on gold, 6% on basic foods, publications, travel costs and soap; 12% on pay television and public housing; and 21% on new buildings, vehicles, petrol, clothes, services, beer, wines, spirits, cigarettes, televisions, audio equipment and cosmetics.

Précompte immobilière/Onroerende voorheffing: Withholding tax on non-movable assets. If you own any property or land you will be sent a demand for this in the first half of the year. This is a percentage of the nominal annual rental value of your property, the *revenu cadastral/kadastraal inkomen*, which is reviewed every 15 years. This tax is distributed between the region, province and commune.

Droit de succession/Erfenisrecht: Inheritance tax. This is dealt with in the next chapter *Retirement*.

Plus values/Meerwaarde: Capital Gains. There is no Capital Gains Tax as such. If you happen to make a profit on the sale of private property, shares, goods, etc. and can argue you were not speculating in them you will not be taxed. Profit on the sale of land, however, is taxed at 33% plus 3% if you owned the land for less than five years. Any regular buying and selling is considered a business activity and comes under income tax.

HEALTH CARE, INSURANCE AND HOSPITALS

BELGIAN MEDICAL SERVICES are some of the best in the western world. All doctors are trained for at least seven years, and specialists for 12. While you will not be refused medical treatment on the grounds of inability to pay, the financial implications of falling ill without proper cover are serious.

The E111

Until such time as you join a health insurance scheme in Belgium you will need to make provision for medical costs. It is possible to obtain refunds of some of the cost of urgently needed medical treatment received in Belgium, if you have a form E111 with you. This form is available in leaflet T6 *Health Advice for Travellers* from your post office. The leaflet SA29 *Your social security insurance, benefits and health care rights in the European Community, and in Iceland, Liechtenstein and Norway* is also available from the Inland Revenue.

If you are already in Belgium you can have your E111 sent to you by International Services, Inland Revenue, National Insurance Contributions Office, Longbenton, Newcastle upon Tyne NE98 1ZZ (☎ 0845-915 4811 *or* 44 191 225 4811 from abroad; fax 0845 915 7800 *or* 44 191 225 7800 from abroad). Allow one month for International Services to process your application. Details are also available on the Inland Revenue website: www.inlandrevenue.gov.uk/nic/intserv/osc.htm.

If you go to a doctor or dentist, check that they are *conventionné/gekonventioneerd*, i.e. linked to a sickness fund. Only 17% are not *conventionné*. The sickness funds (*mutualité/ziekenfonds*) keep lists. Show them your E111 and make sure you obtain a receipt for treatment (*Attestation de soins donnés/Getuigschrift voor verstrekte hulp*); if you buy medicines from a pharmacy, get a receipt and ask your pharmacist to stamp your copy of the prescription. You will then be able to obtain a refund of 75% of your treatment costs from the local sickness fund office (less for medicines).

If you need hospital treatment, ask a sickness fund to recommend a hospital. They will then issue a certificate stating that they will pay part of your hospital costs. If you cannot contact a *mutualité* before entering hospital, show your E111 to the hospital and ask them to contact the *mutualité* for you. Ambulance costs are not refunded. As a rule of thumb, it is best to choose a university hospital (*hôpital/ziekenhuis*) which has a wide range of services, rather than a clinic (*clinique/kliniek*) which has more limited services and is likely to be private.

An E111 is only valid for three months. It loses its validity once you are registered as resident in Belgium. Since the E111 is meant primarily to cover emergency medical care you would be well advised to take out private medical insurance for all eventualities (see below).

Emergencies

In the event of an emergency, dial 100 and ask for an ambulance (*ambulance/ziekenwagen*). If you are unable to speak, your call will be traced in five seconds if you leave the phone off the hook. If you think it is necessary, you can request a doctor to come with the ambulance. The ambulance will take you to the nearest hospital with an emergency service, which can lead to problems if you want to be transferred to a cheaper hospital. Most Belgian doctors understand English. If you have a chronic illness, you could carry an account in English of the nature of your ailment. If you need to consult a doctor at the weekend or at night, you can go to the emergency section of any hospital. There are also pharmacists on duty

24 hours a day. The name is posted on every pharmacist's door. Needless to say, you should keep your E111 or *carnet de mutuelle* (sickness fund card) with you at all times.

Private Medical Insurance

If you hold a private health insurance policy in the UK, you will find that most companies will switch this for European cover when you are in Belgium. Private health insurance can be arranged through organisations such as the following.

British United Provident Association (BUPA): Russell House, Russell Mews, Brighton BN1 2NR; tel 01273-208181; www.bupa-intl.com. BUPA International offers a range of worldwide schemes for individuals and companies of three or more employees based outside the UK for six or more months.

Expacare: email info@expacare.net or visit www.expacare.net. Specialists in expatriate healthcare offering high quality health insurance cover for individuals and their families, including group cover for five or more employees. Cover is available for expatriates of all nationalities worldwide.

As a resident of Belgium, you will pay contributions into a Belgian sickness fund, but you need to pay six months' contributions before you can claim. Even then you still have to pay a part of your medical costs – 25% of treatment, and anything up to 100% of medicines. You could therefore consider paying your sickness fund for extra cover. If you work in Belgium as a non-resident, it is legal to continue using a private medical insurance scheme from your home country.

Useful Addresses

Recommended hospitals:

Academisch Ziekenhuis Jette: Av. de Laerbeek 101, 1090 Brussels; ☎02 477 41 11 emergencies 02 477 51 00; www.vub.ac.be.

Clinique Universitaire Saint Luc: Av. Hippocrate 10, 1200 Brussels; ☎02 764 11 11 emergencies 02 764 16 02.

Hôpital Erasme: Route de Lennik 808, 1070 Brussels; ☎02 555 31 11 emergencies 02 555 34 05.

Institut Jules Bordet: Rue Heger-Bordet 1, 1000 Brussels; ☎02 535 31 11.

Sint-Vincentius Ziekenhuis: St Vincentiusstraat 20, 2018 Antwerpen; ☎03 285 2000.

THE WORLD HEALTH SERVICE

Choose from our flexible range of individual & company schemes. For more information or a quote, visit www.bupa-intl.com or complete the coupon below.

TO: BUPA International, Russell Mews, Brighton BN1 2NR. Tel: +44 (0)1273 208181

Name _____ Address _____

Telephone _____

Email _____

BUPA International

ExpaCare – high-quality health insurance cover, for individuals or families living abroad. To find out more...

For a copy of the **International Health Plan** brochure for individuals or groups (minimum of 5 employees) please email **info@expacare.net** or visit **www.expacareworld.net**

ExpaCare is a trading name of JLT Healthcare Limited. Regulated by the General Insurance Standards Council.

24-hour helplines in Brussels (French/Dutch):
Accidents/Fire/Ambulance/Medical Emergency: 100 (112 from a mobile)
Police: 101 (112 from a mobile)
Community Help Line: 02 648 40 14;.
Dentists: 02 426 10 26; 02 428 58 88.
General practitioners, 02 479 18 18; 02 242 43 44.
Pharmacists: 0900 105 00.
Veterinary surgeons: 02 538 16 99 (outside working hours).

SOCIAL SECURITY AND UNEMPLOYMENT BENEFIT

BELGIUM AIMS TO PROVIDE a high level of social security. For every 100 working people there are 106 recipients of benefits, compared with 80 in Great Britain. The level of social security contributions is staggeringly high. As an employee you pay 13.07% of your salary for social security. Your employer, on the other hand, pays about 35%. Note that the latter figure is not included in the salary quoted in job advertisements.

You do not have to pay social security if you are a temporary worker in Belgium. This refers to high-level executives and researchers who pay social security in their home country. The time period covered by the word 'temporary' could extend to several years. US citizens, for example, can be exempted from social security payments for up to five years.

Social Security Benefits.

The minimum monthly wage for Belgian workers is about €1090 (£680). You are legally entitled to 20 days' paid holiday a year, plus an added holiday payment of one month's earnings. If you are unable to work because of illness, the sickness fund pays 60% of your salary for a year; thereafter you receive a disability allowance of 45% of your salary. If you have dependants you will receive 65%. Pregnant women get 75% of their last wages for a period of up to 15 weeks plus a single payment per child. There are minimum and maximum payments in all these cases.

The notice for terminating employment is generally a matter of mutual agreement between the employer and employee. For the low paid (under €24,200 p.a.) it is legally fixed at three months, plus three months for every five years' service. You are usually entitled to severance pay related to length of service.

Unemployment.

If you become unemployed against your free will, register at the local *Caisse Auxiliaire de Paiement des Allocations de Chômage/Hulpkas voor Werkloosheidsuitkeringen* (Unemployment Benefit Office), and you will be paid 60% of your former salary, or up to €35.45 per day. There are a number of conditions attached to this. Before making a claim you have to be registered at an employment office (see *Service de l'Emploi/Tewerkstellingsdienst* in the Yellow Pages) as seeking work. You will not receive any benefit for up to three months if you left of your own accord, or caused your own dismissal. Benefit is reduced after one year. If you are a member of a trade union payments will initially be made via your union.

If you are thinking of going to Belgium to look for work, it is worth knowing that you can continue to receive UK unemployment benefit at UK rates for three months in Belgium. This is only applicable if you have already been unemployed for a month in the UK. It is essential to apply as soon as you can, as entitlement to transfer benefit expires within three months of becoming unemployed. You will need to have paid full Class 1 contributions during the two tax years previous to the one you are claiming in. You should contact your usual benefit office who will in turn contact the International Services branch of the Inland Revenue (see above for address). They will issue a form E303, the document which is needed to claim benefit in another EU country. In order to receive the medical care you are entitled to under Belgian regulations for unemployed people you should also ask for the form E119 at the same time. For general information about benefits and social security in EU countries, ask for forms SA29 and JSAL22, either from your Jobcentre or from the Pensions and Overseas Benefits Directorate, Department for Work and Pensions, Tyneview Park, Whitley Rd, Benton, Newcastle-upon-Tyne NE98 1BA.

If you have paid Class 1 contributions for the previous two years, you may also try to sign on directly in Belgium itself; conditions may be less stringent than in the UK.

CRIME AND THE POLICE

BELGIUM HAS A LOW level of crime compared with neighbouring countries, but there has been an alarming rise in muggings and car thefts in Brussels recently. Following the bungled investigations into the paedophile Marc Dutroux, and other scandals, it was decided that the different police services would be integrated into one body, a process that was supposed to be complete by January 2002. The decision to reorganise the police was reached in 1998 by eight main political parties, hence it is known as the Octopus Accord. As of 2002 Belgium is divided up into 196 zones where the *police communale* or *gemeentepolitie* and the *police fédérale/federale politie* (formerly known as the gendarmerie) should fulfil similar roles. Which of the two police services responds to a call-out is a matter that the two bodies decide between them on a day-to-day basis. Both of the services are armed and have the same powers. At the time of writing no decision had been taken on the style of uniforms for the two police services.

You must keep your identity card with you at all times; otherwise you could be arrested and held for up to 12 hours until you can prove who you are. The police cannot hold anyone without an arrest warrant from an examining magistrate for more than 24 hours. If you are arrested, you should inform the Consul of your country immediately. You also have the right to free legal representation – the so-called *Pro Deo* lawyer. The police can only search your home between 5am and 9pm, and then only with a search warrant. You can refuse entry to the police between 9pm and 5am even if they have a search warrant.

SOCIAL LIFE

THE KEY TO UNDERSTANDING the Belgians undoubtedly lies in their strong respect for the Catholic church. Even when dealing with avowed atheists, as an outsider you should not criticise the church or the Pope. It is also just as well not to comment on politics, which are inextricably linked with religion, unless you are quite sure of your host's sympathies. Belgium's colonial past is another area to avoid. On the other hand, it is always safe to talk about one's family or about sport.

The Belgian view of life may well seem serious and austere to Anglo-Saxons – frivolity and eccentricity are not greatly appreciated or understood. Work in particular is taken very seriously and is kept quite separate from social life. A more positive side of the Belgians' Catholic piety is a strong sense of social justice, which has led them to create an all-embracing welfare state, and a less materialistic attitude towards life than in neighbouring countries. The attempt to create social justice has, however, also led to excessive bureaucracy and regimentation. It is also true to say that the Belgians have a strong tendency to try to rebel against authority, which may explain why it is so difficult to do anything without official permission.

Manners and Customs

On a personal level, Belgians are friendly and accommodating, but some petty officials can be very rude. Servile behaviour is not expected from anyone: it is a general rule that the lower someone's status is the ruder they are likely to be. You should adopt a respectful attitude when dealing with the authorities. When addressing people you do not know well, it is usual to use their titles – Mr and Mrs are *Monsieur/Madame* in French and *Meneer/Mevrouw* in Dutch – on the end of greetings and questions. With superiors at work, you are not likely to get onto first name terms. In spite of this formality, Belgium is not a class-ridden society in the British sense. Modesty and realism are the archetypal Belgian virtues. Social status is largely related to one's profession, and one's reputation as a respectable member of society.

If you go to work in Belgium the first thing you will notice is a great deal of hand-shaking in the office and anywhere else when people meet and part. Between men and women, or women and women who know each other well, the *trois bises* or three pecks on the cheeks, are still customary when meeting socially. Two pecks are sufficient for more casual acquaintances.

In their own homes, the Belgians tend towards formality. They prefer to be told in advance if you are planning a visit, so that they can be sure to have sufficient food and drink available. Since they are hearty eaters, you should be prepared for a big meal if you are invited to dinner. Even on informal occasions it is a good idea to offer flowers (but not chrysanthemums or carnations which are unlucky) or chocolates to the hostess. Gifts should in any case be in proportion to the occasion. It is not usual to take wine or spirits, unless you know your hosts very well; otherwise they may take this as a criticism of their taste in drinks. If you cannot invite someone round to your home, then taking them to a restaurant is always greatly appreciated.

Making Friends

Outsiders, especially Americans, will have the impression that friendships take a long time to develop in Belgium. Because of their close involvement with their families and long-established family friends, Belgians feel less need for a large circle of more casual acquaintances. They are also reluctant to invade other people's privacy, which might mean that you do not get to know your neighbours very well. On the other hand, when you have made friends with someone, you will find them to be very loyal and supportive when needed.

In a place like Brussels there are great numbers of foreigners who form their own groups and clubs. It is very easy to locate groups of compatriots if you feel the need to meet people from back home. *The Bulletin* (from main newsagents in Brussels) publicises their meetings. Belgians love joining societies and clubs, so foreigners should do the same.

Food and Drink

Eating and drinking assume an importance in Belgian life which is difficult for Anglo-Saxons to comprehend. Fresh produce is cheap and of a very high quality. The multiplicity of local delicacies and beers is well covered in tourist handouts. For beers, check out website www.beerparadise.be. A lot of Belgian food is fried in butter or lard, so it might be a good idea to avoid high-cholesterol food in between going out for meals. Belgium is famous as the country which invented potato chips; they are known as French fries because American soldiers stationed in Belgium at the end of World War II thought they were in France. Other well-known dishes are *carbonades flamandes/stoverij* (beef cooked in beer) and *waterzooi* (chicken in a creamy sauce). Also famous are waffles (*wafels/gaufres*) and cinnamon biscuits (*speculoos*).

METRICATION

CONVERSION CHART

LENGTH (NB 12 inches 1 foot, 10 mm 1 cm, 100 cm 1 metre)

inches	1	2	3	4	5	6	9	12	
cm	2.5	5	7.5	10	12.5	15.2	23	30	

cm	1	2	3	5	10	20	25	50	75	100
inches	0.4	0.8	1.2	2	4	8	10	20	30	39

WEIGHT (NB 14lb = 1 stone, 2240 lb = 1 ton, 1,000 kg = 1 metric tonne)

lb	1	2	3	5	10	14	44	100	2246
kg	0.45	0.9	1.4	2.3	4.5	6.4	20	45	1016

kg	1	2	3	5	10	25	50	100	1000
lb	2.2	4.4	6.6	11	22	55	110	220	2204

DISTANCE

mile	1	5	10	20	30	40	50	75	100	150
km	1.6	8	16	32	48	64	80	120	161	241

km	1	5	10	20	30	40	50	100	150	200
mile	0.6	3.1	6.2	12	19	25	31	62	93	124

VOLUME
1 litre = 0.2 UK gallons   1 UK gallon = 4.5 litres
1 litre = 0.26 US gallons   1 US gallon = 3.8 litres

CLOTHES

UK	8	10	12	14	16	18	20
Europe	36	38	40	42	44	46	48
USA	6	8	10	12	14	18	

SHOES

UK	3	4	5	6	7	8	9	10	11
Europe	36	37	38	39	40	41/42	43	44	45
USA	2.5	3.3	4.5	5.5	6.5	7.5	8.5	9.5	10.5

BELGIUM USES THE METRIC SYSTEM in all respects: the standards of measurement are recognisable to English speakers. Temperature is always measured in celsius.

In the long run it is much easier to learn and think in metric rather than to always try to convert from metric to imperial. To facilitate this process a metric conversion table (including clothes and shoe size conversions is) given: see table 12.

In all cases measurements are quoted as a decimal and not a fraction; for example, on road signs, 'Ostend 12.7 km'.

TIME

THE 24-HOUR CLOCK SYSTEM is used for all times in Belgium. For example, shop opening hours are given as 09.00 à 17.30 (9am to 5.30pm) or train times as 20.20 (8.20pm) or 00.15 (12.15am).

Belgium follows Continental European Time (CET) as do most EU countries with the exception of Greece, the UK and Eire. Summer time lasts from the last Sunday in March at 2am to the last Sunday in September at 3am, when clocks are advanced one hour. Consequently Belgium is one hour ahead of the UK for most of the year, whether the UK is operating to Greenwich Mean Time (GMT) or British Summer Time (BST). However, clocks in the UK are changed later in the autumn than in Belg so for a time, in September and October, the two countries are actually sychronised: there are currently proposals to synchronise the times throughout the EU.

PUBLIC HOLIDAYS

ON THE FOLLOWING days banks, offices, schools, etc. are closed.

1 January – New Year's Day (*Nouvel An/Nieuwjaar*)
Easter Monday (*Pâques/Pasen*)
1 May – (*Jour du Travail/Dag van de Arbeid*)
Ascension Day (*Ascension du Seigneur/Hemelvaart*)
Whit Monday (*Pentecôte/Pinksteren*)
21 July – National Day (*Jour National/Nationale Dag*)
15 August – Assumption (*Ascension de la Vierge/Maria Hemelvaart*)
1 November – All Saints' Day (*Toussaints/Allerheiligen*)
11 November – Armistice Day (*Armistice/Wapenstilstand*)
15 November – King's Name Day (*Jour de la Dynastie/Dag van de Dynastie*)
25 December – Christmas (*Noël/Kerstmis*)
26 December – Boxing Day (*Deuxième Jour de Noël/Tweede Kerstdag*).

11 July is a holiday in Flanders commemorating the defeat of the French at the Battle of the Golden Spurs in 1302. The anniversary of the defeat of the Dutch in the 1830 revolution – 27 September – is celebrated by the Walloons.

Retirement

BELGIUM IS NOT AN obvious place to retire to unless you have some prior connections there. You would not be short of company, however, as there is a well-established community of retired Britons who have spent some part of their working life in Belgium and put down roots there. One obvious attraction of being retired in Belgium is the high level of amenities provided for senior citizens and the convenience of never being far away from essential services. Retirement properties are still cheap and plentiful. If you are looking for good food and culture this is the place to be. The climate, on the other hand, is much like that of England – the number of days you can sit on the beach in a deckchair is limited.

Financially you will not be at a disadvantage living in Belgium as both company and state pensions are honoured in Belgium at the UK rate (further details below). As a Belgian resident, you will be taxed on any pension you receive from abroad.

RESIDENCE AND ENTRY

FROM 1 JANUARY 1992 EU countries have been obliged to allow pensioners who can support themselves to settle anywhere in the EU without asking them to make prior arrangements before leaving their own country. This directive has applied in Belgium for some time in any case. If you know that you are going to stay in Belgium for over three months, then you should register at the commune within eight days of your arrival. You are then issued with the mauve card mentioned in Chapter Two, *Residence and Entry*, and placed on the Register of Aliens. The first three months of your stay are a sort of trial period, during which you have to show that you are receiving a pension or have some other kind of income. While the state does not prescribe a standard figure, it is usually reckoned that you need €24,000 (£15,000 or $22,000) per year to live comfortably in Belgium. Arranging health insurance is an absolute necessity. Since Belgian sickness funds (*mutualités*) are very reluctant to take on clients who are over 65 when they first apply for sickness cover, this means continuing your own private health care plan from the UK.

Assuming that you are able to show sufficient funds, you will be able to exchange your mauve card for the yellow card of a non-working EU citizen which is valid for five years. If you intend to engage in any kind of work other than voluntary, then you are entitled to a blue card for EU workers, also valid for five years. Should you not be able to show sufficient funds after three months, you can expect to be asked to leave the country even as an EU citizen.

If an EU national resides in Belgium for three years and reaches the age of retirement they can then stay on permanently, provided they worked during the year just before retirement. The same right to remain is extended to the spouse and family of an EU worker if the worker dies after two years of residence.

Non-EU Nationals

Entry for non-EU nationals is heavily restricted, as stated in Chapter Two, *Residence and Entry*. The first step in this case is to contact the Belgian Embassy or nearest Consulate in your home country. To obtain permission to enter Belgium as a non-worker, you have to show, at the very least, that you are financially completely independent and covered by health insurance, as well as being able to prove that you have no criminal record. A medical examination by a doctor appointed by the Embassy is obligatory. It is also necessary to give convincing reasons for wanting to live in Belgium with documentary evidence. If your application is approved you will receive the APS (Authorisation of Provisional Sojourn) and can go to live in Belgium.

POSSIBLE RETIREMENT AREAS

THOSE WHO ALREADY KNOW Belgium may have some idea of where they would like to retire to, and those who do not should try to find out something about the way of life as well as looking at different regions. There is no particular area with a large number of British retired people. A major consideration concerns the proximity of services. The only area of Belgium which could be described as remote from public services is the southeastern province of Luxembourg, but even here the distances involved are not that great.

The Coast

This is a popular area in the summer for tourists. The advantages are excellent sports facilities, such as golf courses and tennis courts, a concentration of convalescent homes and medical facilities, and superb restaurants. In winter the area is quiet, but most facilities remain open. Property prices vary depending on how fashionable a resort is. At the top end, a three-bedroom apartment in Knokke, near the Dutch border, costs about €270,000 (£165,000) while a similar apartment in De Panne, near France, is only €125,000 (£75,000). In less fashionable areas, three-bedroom apartments can be found for under €75,000 (£45,000). The cheapest prices of all are in unfashionable Ostend, which is the most conveniently located and most interesting of all the seaside towns, and the most British visitors.

The Ardennes

Undoubtedly the most scenic part of Belgium, the area around Bastogne and St Vith is strongly associated in American minds with the Battle of the Bulge of World War II. The most popular retirement home in this area is the so-called *fermette*, a converted farmhouse or farm cottage. One could also consider a chalet or villa (often a large bungalow). The drawback to the Ardennes is the relative isolation and lack of public transport. Unless you have a car, living out in the sticks here would be out of the question. If you are energetic and enjoy horse-riding or similar pursuits, this would be a good area to look at.

Flanders

In this case referring to Flanders proper, i.e. the provinces of East and West Flanders, rather than the whole Dutch-speaking region. This area has traditional close links with the UK. Bruges and Ghent have great artistic heritages; if you enjoy painting or drawing you might find one of the artists' communities close to these cities a congenial place to live. Although this is not a region with wide open spaces, there are plenty of retirement villas and bungalows with large gardens where you can be at a reasonable distance from your neighbours.

Brussels

The area to the south of Brussels is very much favoured by wealthy expatriates. The landscape is more hilly than in Flanders; the best houses have woods and artificial lakes attached. If you are in this league you can enjoy a very good social life indeed with other émigrés living all around you. A further advantage of this area is that you will be able to use French all the time if you are not inclined to try speaking Dutch.

PENSIONS

THERE IS NO REASON why a move to Belgium should affect the provision or rate of state pension for most people. The main point to remember is that if a pension is sourced from the UK it will always be pegged at UK levels. The value of the pound against the franc is more or less up to the same level where it was in 1991 at the time of writing; in the somewhat unlikely event that Britain is part of the first phase of European Monetary Union, this rate of exchange will in effect become permanent.

Some time before you retire abroad, you need to find out how many different pensions you are going to receive. For many people this can be a complex combination of state pensions, occupational pensions and private pension plans. If you find that the total sum is short of expectations, it is possible to pay additional voluntary contributions (AVCs) into your company pension during your last few years of work. If you are going to live in an EU country such as Belgium, there should be no problem about having your pension paid abroad.

TAXATION

THE DEPARTMENT OF WORK and Pensions will, in principle, pay your gross pension direct into a Belgian bank account without any deductions, as long as you have a declaration from the Belgian tax authorities that you are paying taxes in Belgium. Contact the DWP Pensions and Overseas Benefits Directorate, Newcastle-upon-Tyne NE98 1BA (☎ 0191-218 7777) for further details. It would be advisable to inform the Inland Revenue office with which you last dealt about your plans; they will supply leaflet IR138 *Living or Retiring Abroad? A guide to UK tax on your UK income and pension* or you can contact the Inland Revenue's two specialist offices for non-residents (Non-Resident Claims, Fitz Roy House, PO Box 46, Nottingham NG2 1BD; ☎ 0115-974 1919; fax 0115-974 1919; www.in landrevenue.gov.uk; or Centre for Non-Residents (CNR), Residence Advice & Liabilities Unit 355, St. John's House, Bootle, Merseyside L69 9BB; ☎ 0151-472 6202; fax 0151-472 6003). US citizens thinking of retiring in Belgium can contact the Federal Benefits Unit, American Embassy, 27 Bvd du Régent, 1000 Brussels; ☎ 02 508 2388; fax 02 513 0409.

If you are quite certain that you are going to become a Belgian resident, then the situation should be straightforward in that you will only be liable for Belgian income tax. At the present time pensions up to €10,510 (£6,300) are tax free for single people with no dependants, and most pensioners are exempt from property taxes. A more complex situation arises if one intends to divide one's time between the UK and Belgium. In this case specialist advice is essential. In particular you cannot totally escape UK taxes if more than 183 days are spent in the UK in the first year of possessing a residence abroad. It should also be remembered that the Belgian tax year runs from January to December, whereas the UK tax year runs from April to April. The date of moving could affect your tax liability.

BELGIAN PENSIONS AND HEALTH INSURANCE

IF YOU HAVE WORKED in Belgium for any time, you will be entitled to Belgian pension payments in proportion to the years worked. The general procedure is that your social security records will be exchanged by the British and Belgian authorities, and the amount of pension payable by each country worked out. You are entitled to receive all your pension at the rate payable in Belgium, which is higher than the UK rate. The Belgian pension equals 60% (for single people) and 75% (for those with dependants) of the average annual gross salary multiplied by the number of years worked, and then divided by the maximum number of possible years worked. The maximum total of years worked is reckoned to be 45 years for men and 40 years for women. The minimum pension for someone who has worked a full 45 years now stands at €815 a month (approximately £500) for a single person. A single pensioner is guaranteed an income of €500 a month in any case, and this provision is extended to foreigners who have been in Belgium for more than five years before retirement. Pensions are index-linked.

A potential problem could arise in that Belgian *mutualités* (sickness funds) do not generally take on clients who are already retired. You are expected to remain with the same *mutualité* you dealt with when you were working, and they cannot refuse to insure you once you are established with them. There are special sickness insurance plans for the over-50s – the price depends on the level of benefits and can vary from €135 to €400 (£80-£250) per year. The *mutualité* is likely to place a limit on the maximum weekly amount it will pay out and this is rarely enough to cover your costs. For retired British people the only option could be to continue with a private health plan from the UK.

WILLS AND LEGAL CONSIDERATIONS

MOST PEOPLE OF RETIREMENT age have either already made, or are intending to make a will. This step assumes even greater importance if one intends to move abroad. If a will has not been made then take the advice of a UK solicitor with knowledge of Belgian law. If a will has been made it must be reviewed before any move takes place.

In Belgium itself, it is vital to draw up a will with the help of a *notaire* (notary). Writing down your wishes without consulting a notary is hazardous, as your intentions could well be overridden by Belgian inheritance laws. Once you have drawn up your will, the notary will register it with the Register of Testaments.

A major consideration affecting inheritance tax is the domicile of the deceased. The British Inland Revenue (or IRS) will have to make wide-ranging and detailed inquiries before they will accept that you are domiciled in Belgium. Inheritance taxes are much heavier in Belgium than in Britain (the USA does not have inheritance taxes as such), however, so that your heirs would be disadvantaged if you were domiciled in Belgium. The greatest difficulty lies in the fact that the Belgian fiscal authorities could try to tax you on property and assets held outside Belgium if you were domiciled in Belgium at the time of death. Domiciled here means that you were a Belgian resident and administered your affairs from Belgium. By the same token the British Inland Revenue can tax British citizens on their worldwide assets, unless it is agreed that they are not domiciled in the UK. Further explanations can be found in leaflet IHT16, *Inheritance Tax. Foreign Aspects*, available from the UK Inland Revenue (see www.inlandrevenue.gov.uk); or from the IRS (see www.irs.gov).

If you have interests in both the UK and Belgium, you will evidently need a will for both countries. In Belgium, a notary acts as a trustee after your decease and draws up lists of creditors, claimants and heirs. The heirs are required to file an inheritance tax return within five months of death and to pay the tax within two months thereafter. Taxes are on a sliding scale with a tax-free allowance of €12,500 (£7,600) for descendants, ascendants and spouses. They are quite modest for the spouse and children (no more than 30%) but very heavy for more distant relatives and unrelated persons (anything up to 80%). Rates have recently been simplified and slightly reduced in the Flemish region; they are heavier in Brussels and Wallonia. Taxes can be partly avoided by transferring assets to your children at least three years before you die. The way in which this is done is crucial, and you will have to go to a notary who specialises in such matters.

There are strict laws concerning the way inheritances are divided up between family members. The spouse is entitled to half your assets, including the family home. A single child also has a right to half your assets; if there are two children, each receives at least a third; three children receive a quarter each, and so on. If your will is unclear or there is a conflict between your heirs, the result is that your heirs will have to argue their case before a judge resulting in extra legal costs. The moral therefore is to know what the laws are when drawing up your will.

COHABITATION

SINCE 1998 IT HAS been possible for two people living together to draw up a declaration that they are legally cohabitating – a *contrat de vie commune* – according to article 1476 of the Belgian Civil Code, which can be registered at the town hall. The sex or relationship of two such persons is entirely irrelevant. While such a contract can have far-reaching consequences as regards taxes, social security and right of abode, it does not guarantee the surviving partner any special status as regards the inheritance laws. The children and other family members of the deceased still take precedence over the surviving partner. It is usual to engage a notary to draw up a suitable contract.

DEATH

THIS IS AN EVENTUALITY WHICH should be planned for. The fact that one's close relations may not be at hand complicates matters, and makes it all the more important that one's wishes are known in advance. It is as well to realise that having one's body shipped home for burial is very expensive, and there may be no alternative but to make arrangements in Belgium itself.

Deaths must be certified by a doctor and registered within 24 hours at the commune, with the death certificate and identity papers. In the case of foreigners the main consulate also issues a death certificate. A funeral director will help with formalities concerning the commune. Funerals (whether burials or cremations) cost from £1200 upwards. Because Belgium is virtually entirely Catholic, those of other Christian denominations are likely to be buried in a Catholic cemetery. Cremations are becoming more and more usual. There should be no difficulty in having a Protestant church service if you want one. Some names of churches are given below.

CHURCHES

APART FROM BEING INDISPENSABLE for births, marriages and deaths, going to church services is a very good way of meeting expatriates. Sunday services in English are held in the churches given below (Anglican unless otherwise stated).

St Boniface: Grétrystraat 39, 2018 Antwerp; ☎03 239 33 39.
St Peter's Chapel: Keersstraat 1 (off Philipstockstraat), 8000 Bruges.
Pro-Cathedral of the Holy Trinity: Rue C. Crespel 29, 1050 Brussels; ☎02 511 71 83.
St Andrews Church of Scotland: Chaussée de Vleurgat 181, 1050 Brussels; ☎02 672 40 56.
St Anne's Church: Place de la Sainte Alliance 10, 1180 Brussels; ☎02 354 53 43. Catholic.
St Anthony's Roman Catholic Parish: Oudstrijderslaan 23-25, 1950 Kraainem, Brussels; 02 720 19 70.
Synagoge de Bruxelles: Rue de la Régence 32, 1000 Brussels; ☎02 512 43 34.
Protestant Church: Bvd Audent 20, Charleroi; 08 584 44 82.

St John's: Edmond Boonenstraat 4, 9000 Ghent; ☎09 222 76 91.
St George's: Zoutelaan 77, 8300 Knokke.
Protestant Church: Quai Marcellis 22, 4000 Liège; ☎08 584 44 82.
International Chapel Centre: SHAPE, 7000 Mons; ☎065 44 56 93. Anglican and Episcopalian.
The English Church: Langestraat 101, 8400 Ostend.
Notre Dame d'Argenteuil: Chaussée de Louvain 563, Ohain, Waterloo; ☎02 384 35 36. Episcopalian.
St Paul's: Dorpsplein, 3080 Vossem, Tervuren; ☎02 767 34 35.
St George's Memorial Church: Elverdingsestraat 1, 8900 Ypres; ☎05 721 56 85. Sunday evening service only.

HOBBIES AND INTERESTS

RETIREMENT IS THE ideal time to pursue old and new interests. Finding some part-time work is also a possibility, although your income could be very heavily taxed. There is also considerable scope for doing charity work, another excellent way of meeting new friends. Homesickness should be less of a problem in Belgium than elsewhere in Europe. English-language TV channels are available by cable, and British newspapers are delivered on the morning of publication. The *Wall Street Journal* and the *International Herald Tribune* have European editions and can be ordered by subscription (see section on Newspapers, *Employment* Chapter. Unless you have a very good radio the only British radio channels you are likely to get are Radio 5 Live and the World Service.

There are numerous clubs for English-speaking expats:

Antwerp
American Women's Club of Antwerp: PO Box 20, 2930 Brasschaat; ☎03 658 13 00; www.fawco.org.
Antwerp British Community Association: ☎03 541 92 21.
Royal British Legion: 03 542 12 65.
Brussels
American Women's Club of Brussels: ☎02 358 47 53; www.fawco.org.

American Club of Brussels: ☎02 542 47 80; www.americanclubbrussels.com.
British and Commonwealth Women's Club of Brussels: ☎02 772 53 13.
Brussels British Community Association: 02 344 68 77.
Brussels Hash House Harriers: 02 734 45 60.
Irish Club of Belgium: ☎02 742 27 37; e-mail icb@skynet.be.

Royal British Legion: ☎ 02 345 61 56.
Other
Australian Society: ☎ 02 648 47 95.
National Trust Association of Members in Belgium: www.come.2/ntab.

Liège Rencontre: Palais des Congrès, Esplanade de l'Europe 2, Liège.
Vlaams-Caledonische Society: http://users.skynet.be/caledonia; www.caledonian.be.

SECTION II

WORKING IN BELGIUM

EMPLOYMENT

BUSINESS AND INDUSTRY REPORTS

TEMPORARY WORK

STARTING A BUSINESS

Employment

CHAPTER SUMMARY

- **The potential.** Belgium is an excellent place for to look for work for those with appropriate qualifications who can speak French or Dutch.

  - There are possibilities for finding work with 1,000+ international organisations based in Brussels

  - The European Commission employs 16,500 people in Brussels and the British are currently under-represented there.

- Most UK professional qualifications are acceptable in Belgium.

- **Finding work.** Sources of information about jobs include the pan-European job information network EURES, professional organizations, online job resources and chambers of commerce.

  - There are large numbers of temporary employment agencies for those prepared to look for a job on the spot.

- Salaries in Belgium are generally lower than in Britain, France and Germany.

- The workers most in demand in Belgium are sales engineers, systems analysts, software engineers, and project leaders.

- Possibilities for short-term work include teaching English, au pair work and work in the tourist industry: bilingual secretaries should have little difficulty in finding a good job.

THE EMPLOYMENT SCENE

AS WITH MUCH of Europe, Belgium suffered severely during the recession of 1993-1994. Business confidence recovered from 1997. While the outlook from 2002 is less positive, the implementation of the euro may also give a boost to the economy. Translating the improved economic climate into new jobs has proved difficult. This is down to a generally inflexible labour market which does not allow for changing economic conditions at home and abroad. Productivity levels in Belgian industry are some of the highest in the world; at the same time the minimum wage and strict levels of seniority pay make it difficult for wages to reflect productivity. Recently, salaries have been rising rapidly for executives and other highly qualified staff, driven by skill shortages and competition from foreign companies. The planned reduction in direct taxation may have an impact on unemployment, which stood at a seasonally adjusted average of 6.8% in 2001; fortunately much of this is in sectors where English-speaking foreigners are not likely to want to work.

Present economic conditions in Belgium have no effect on the number of workers employed by the European Commission (EC) in Brussels (about 16,500), and it is well-known that Britain is under-represented as regards numbers of EC employees. As more countries join the EU, and more governmental functions are transferred to the Commission, the number of staff is bound to rise. Along with posts for translators and administrators, numerous posts for clerical and technical support staff could be filled by British workers, even those who are not very good linguists. A similar situation exists with NATO and its affiliated organisations, such as the North Atlantic Assembly and the Supreme Headquarters of Allied Powers in Europe (SHAPE). NATO does not employ as many foreign workers as the EC, but there are opportunities which tend to be overlooked by the insular British.

Belgium is an excellent place to look for work, provided that what you have to offer is what Belgian employers are looking for. In the main this means relevant training and qualifications, and a commitment to acquiring French or Dutch. A desire to work hard is also indispensable. If you go to Belgium without arranging employment beforehand you can use the numerous temporary employment agencies. Because of the sky-high social security contributions employers have to pay, and the difficulties involved in dismissing workers from their jobs, many employers would prefer to employ you on a trial basis for six months to see if you are the kind of worker they want to commit themselves to. This creates the ideal opportunity for anyone who wants to prove that they can do a good job. This does not mean that Belgium is a land of temporary workers: 95% of employment contracts are permanent. If you are prepared to stay in Belgium for some time, you will profit from the exceptionally generous social security and pensions, as well as a high degree of job security.

RESIDENCE AND ENTRY

THE BELGIAN AUTHORITIES apply EC directives in full as far as foreign residents from the EU are concerned. What few formalities there are for EU citizens going to Belgium to look for work are detailed in the chapter Residence and Entry. If you hold an EU passport it should be unnecessary to go to the Belgian Embassy before you leave home. Non-EU citizens cannot obtain a residence permit before they have a work permit, a process which can take up to a year.

SKILLS AND QUALIFICATIONS

MANY DIRECTIVES HAVE appeared over the years concerning mutual recognition of professional qualifications, for instance those of doctors, veterinarians and nurses, in all EU countries. Such directives give every Community national certain rights to have their qualifications and experience recognised or taken into account in another member state where entry to particular jobs is regulated by law or other administrative provisions. This means that there should be no unnecessary barriers to practising your profession in another member state. Where there are significant differences in the training required to exercise a profession the directives provide for the need to take an aptitude test or for an assessed period of supervised practice.

There are two main directives concerning mutual recognition of education and training (89/48/EEC and 92/51/EEC). The first concerns higher education, the second qualifications gained through any post-secondary course of more than one year or work experience. This means that National and Scottish Vocational Qualifications (NVQs/SVQs) and their equivalents are now recognised by the EU. The UK organisation responsible for providing information on the comparability of all academic qualifications is the National Academic Recognition Information Centre (NARIC), which can be contacted at UK NARIC, ECCTIS Ltd, Oriel House, Oriel Road, Cheltenham, Glos GL50 1XP; ☎01242-260010; fax 01242-258611; e-mail naric@ecctis.co.uk; www.naric.org.uk. You should first ask the jobcentre in the UK, or in Belgium, if you have already there, to approach NARIC on your behalf. You can also approach NARIC directly, but there will be a charge for the service.

If you have experience but no formal qualifications, it is possible to obtain a European Community Certificate of Experience. For EU citizens in the UK this is issued by the DTI. Since the Certificate costs £80 to process, you should first make sure that your type of work experience is covered by an EC directive by asking the authorities in Belgium or the DTI, who will try to send you a copy of the relevant directive, together with an application form and any available literature. There is an enquiry line on 020-7215 4004 (fax 020-7215 4489) or you can write to: Certificates of Experience Unit, Department of Trade & Industry, Kingsgate House, 66-74 Victoria Street, London SW1E 6SW.

If your qualifications are vocational or in hotel and catering, the motor trade, travel and tourism or office work and you want to know how your qualifications stand up against the Belgian equivalent, you can consult the Comparability Co-ordinator through your local job centre or direct: Comparability Coordinator, Employment Dept., Qualifications and Standards Branch (QSI), Room E454, Moorfoot, Sheffield SP1 4PQ; ☎ 0114-2594144.

Study Abroad: If you are a student in higher education, you can obtain a grant to follow part of your course in another European country through the SOCRATES-ERASMUS programme. Your college or university should be able to advise you or you may look at the website www.erasmus-uk.net.

REGULATED PROFESSIONS

TABLE 6 — REGULATED PROFESSIONS

English	French	Dutch
Bicycle mechanic	Mécanicien de cycles	Fietsmecanicien
Bricklaying contractor	Entrepreneur en maçonnerie et béton	Metselwerkondernemer
Carpenter/joiner	Menuisier-charpentier	Schrijnwerker-timmerman
Electrician	Electricien-installateur	Elektricien
Glazing contractor	Entrepreneur de vitrage	Glazenmaker
Hairdresser	Coiffeur	Kapper
Insurance broker	Courtier d'assurances	Verzekeringmakelaar
Optician	Opticien-lunetier	Opticien
Painter and decorator	Peintre	Schilder
Photographer	Photographe	Fotograaf
Plasterer	Plafonneur-cimentier	Stukadoor
Plumber	Plombier	Loodgieter
Restaurant-owner	Restaurateur	Uitbater
Secondhand car dealer	Négociant en véhicules d'occasion	Okkazieautohandelaar
Stonemason	Tailleur de pierres	Steenhouwer
Upholsterer	Tapissier	Stoffeerder
Watch-repairer	Horloger-réparateur	Uurwerkmaker

A USEFUL STARTING POINT to research opportunities is to contact the International Trade Team at your local Business Link. You can find out their address by calling 0845-606 4466. Apart from the professions regulated by professional bodies, there are officially 44 non-salaried or independent trades which are subject to statutory conditions in Belgium. To become self-employed in one of these areas you will be expected to show managerial as well as work experience, and that you have the capital to start a business. You will also need a permit if your trade is considered likely to harm the environment. You will have to register your qualifications with one of the Chambers of Crafts and Trades (*Chambre des Métiers et Négoces/Kamer van Ambachten en Neringen*) whose address can be found in the Yellow Pages.

Some of the jobs concerned are listed in table 6.

SOURCES OF JOBS

DEPENDING ON YOUR PROFESSION, it may or may not be advantageous to go to Belgium to look for work on the spot. Someone who wants to work for the EU Commission, for example, can make their application from the UK; there is no advantage in going over to Brussels first. If you are going to go to Belgium without arranging work in advance, it is important to have enough money to support yourself for a few weeks. You should also make sure you have copies of all your diplomas and degrees with you. The British Embassy in Brussels is at pains to point out that British consulates have only limited resources to help British citizens. They cannot help you to find a job or give you legal advice. Belgian Embassies and consulates do not give help with finding work either.

NEWSPAPERS

National Newspapers

VACANCIES AT THE European Commission in Brussels, and in Belgium generally, are often advertised in the British press. *The Guardian*, for example, has a European Appointments page on Fridays. *The Independent* and *The Times* also advertise jobs in Belgium. Apart from EC jobs, dealt with under the section Working for the EC (see below), many of the advertisements are for secretaries and personal assistants to Brussels-based executives. Advertisements for executives, lawyers, accountants, financial analysts and so on also appear from time to time.

International Newspapers

These circulate editions across several national boundaries and carry a number of job advertisements for different countries. The following are numbers of subscription offices of three newspapers in this category:

Financial Times: ☎02 548 95 55 (Brussels); www.ft.com.

International Herald Tribune: ☎00 800 4448 7827; e-mail subs@iht.com; www.iht.com.

Wall Street Journal: 00 800 9753 2000; www.dowjones.com.

Magazines, Journals and Directories

Financial weeklies like *The Economist* often carry advertisements for jobs in Brussels. If you want to teach in Belgium you can sometimes find advertisements in the *Times Educational Supplement* published on Fridays. The specialist fortnightly publication, *Overseas Jobs Express* (available only by subscription from Overseas Jobs Express, 20 New Road, Brighton, East Sussex BN1 1UF; ☎01273-699611; www.overseasjobsexpress.com) boasts, in addition to many well-researched articles, a substantial *Jobs* section, covering a range of jobs: accountancy, banking, EFL teaching, computers, tourism, agriculture, equestrian work, secretarial work, nannies, au pairs, and so on *ad infinitum*. It is possible to put your CV on their database: e-mail to cv@overseasjobsexpress.co.uk

Many professional journals are available at public libraries where they can be consulted free of charge. Examples include *The Architects' Journal* and *The Bookseller*. Some journals are not actually tied to one specific organisation but are read by everybody in the trade, such as *Farmers' Weekly, Caterer and Hotel Keeper, Computer Weekly* and *Oil & Gas Journal*. You can find valuable leads in these publications, even if there are no jobs advertised for the country you want to work in.

Some journals and trade magazines are more obscure, so it is worth looking through a media directory, such as *Benn's Media* or the *European Media Directory*, to see what is available. One journal which is essential to English teachers is the monthly *EL Gazette*, which not only carries advertisements for jobs and training courses, but also has a lot to say about working conditions in foreign countries for English teachers. The *EL Gazette* can be found at specialist English teaching bookshops, or can be ordered direct from: EL Publications, Dilke House, 1 Malet Street, Bloomsbury, London WC1E 4JA; ☎020-7255 1969. In the USA contact: PO Box 61202, Oklahoma City, OK 73146; fax 405-557-2538.

A further source of jobs is directories. There are several worthwhile publications, including *Student Move Up*, an annual guide to potential employers, and *Executive Move Up*, a directory of recruitment agencies (see www.moveup.be); Move Up is ultimately owned by the Daily Mail group, via Hobsons Publishing. Academici Roularta Media publish the annual *GO* (see www.ar-media.be). Imediair produces the annual *JOB* (see www.azur.be).

A wide range of casual jobs, including secretarial, agricultural, tourism and domestic work, are advertised in the directory *Summer Jobs Abroad; Teaching English Abroad* lists schools all over the world which employ English language teachers. Both publications are available from Vacation Work Publications, 9 Park End Street, Oxford OX1 1HJ; ☎01865-241978; fax 01865-790885; www.vacationwork.co.uk.

Belgian Newspapers and Magazines

Numerous job advertisements appear in the newspapers and magazines mentioned in the Media section of Chapter 4, *Daily Life*. *Le Soir* is generally the only Belgian newspaper available in the UK outside Central London. This French-language newspaper carries most job advertisements on Tuesdays and Saturdays. The main weekly English-language publication for job advertisements is *The Bulletin*, which also has a Situations Wanted section. Advertisements can be placed in *Le Soir* and the Dutch-language *Het Laatste Nieuws* through their British representative: Powers Turner Group, 100 Rochester Row, London SW1P 1JP; ☎020-7630 9966; www.publicitas.com.

Useful Addresses

Le Soir: Rossel & Cie SA, Rue Royale 120, 1000 Brussels; ☎02 217 77 50; www.lesoir.com.
The Bulletin: Ackroyd Publications, Av. Molière 329, 1060 Brussels; ☎02 373 83 25; fax 02 373 99 09; www.ackroyd.be. English-language weekly for foreigners.

PROFESSIONAL ASSOCIATIONS

MANY PROFESSIONAL ASSOCIATIONS do not provide any official information on working overseas as such. However, most of them will have had contact with their counterpart association in other countries during negotiations over the question of EU recognition of qualifications, as required by the EU directives. Such associations should provide individual help if asked.

Details of all professional associations are to be found in the directory, *Trade Associations and Professional Bodies of the UK*, available at most reference libraries. It is also worth trying to contact the Belgian equivalent of UK professional associations. In addition, some trade unions have links with their counterparts in Belgium and may be able to supply addresses.

SPECIALIST JOB PUBLICATIONS AND THE INTERNET

SOME PUBLICATIONS IN BELGIUM contain only job vacancies and articles aimed at helping the unemployed. The most widely read recruitment supplement in Belgium is *Vacature* (Vacancy in Dutch), or *Vacature Références* (in French) published by the weekly *Financieel Economische Tijd* (www.vacature.be) which claims a readership of over 1.8 million. Another important publication is *Intermediair/Intermediaire* (www.intermediair.be) which appears every second Tuesday. The English-French-Dutch website www.nomad.be/Profiles, has a database of situations wanted and job offers; you can also put your CV on the database, and there are articles of interest to prospective employers and employees. There are numerous other jobs websites, e.g. www.jobstoday.be, www.jobs-career.be, www.monster.be, www.jobscape.be, www.work4u.be, www.jobworld.be, and so on. *La Libre Belgique* also has a site: www.lalibre.com/Emploi. The Belgian employment service publishes the biweekly *De Werkzoeker* in Dutch and *Offre d'Emploi* in French for jobseekers.

THE UK EMPLOYMENT SERVICE

THE EMPLOYMENT SERVICES of the 15 EU countries, including those of the UK and Belgium, are linked together by a computer network known as EURES (European Employment Services), by which information on specialist vacancies notified to the employment service in one country can be made available to the employment services in the others. At any one time there are over 5,000 vacancies on the system, including jobs for graduates and professionals. In addition the EU has trained 450 Euro-advisers, including six at British universities.

The British branch of EURES is based at the Overseas Placing Unit (OPU) of the Employment Service in Sheffield (Rockingham House, 123 West Street, Sheffield S1 4ER; ☎0114-259 6051/2). Most UK Employment Service offices have computer access to the vacancies held at Sheffield. The kinds of vacancies range from computer programmers, medical personnel, teachers and bilingual secretaries to florists, upholsterers, chefs and entertainers. Most employers are looking to fill posts as quickly as possible; at the same time, EURES has reported that the system has worked best for postgraduate vacancies. You can see the vacancies on-line at: http://europa.eu.int/jobs/eures.

The Employment Service produces the booklet, *Working in Belgium*, available from their offices nationwide or from the OPU (see above).

UK RECRUITMENT AGENCIES

THERE ARE SOME AGENCIES in the UK which specialise in finding overseas jobs for clients. In general, these agencies deal with a specific sector such as electronics, computers, secretarial, medical, English teaching, etc. and can only place people with suitable qualifications. As a rule, agencies are retained and paid by employers to fill specific vacancies and do not search on behalf of prospective workers, but there are also firms which maintain databases of jobs and will try to match you with the ones you are qualified for.

The Recruitment and Employment Confederation (36-38 Mortimer Street, London W1N 7RB; ☎ 020-7462 3260; www.rec.uk.com) issues a list of employment agencies who are members (see below). Human Resourcing Consultancies (Chancery House, 53-64 Chancery Lane, London WC2 A1QS; ☎ 020-7406 5154; www.careermanagement.co.uk) publishes a useful guide entitled *The Job Search: A Practical Guide* in two versions, for *Executive and Professional Staff*, and for *Supervisory and Support Staff*, which deals with job application procedures, from researching the job market, CV's and letters of application, to the all-important interview technique, as well as providing notes on self-employment and personal finance.

Useful Addresses

Beechwood Recruitment: 219 High St, London W3 9BY; ☎ 020-8992 8647; www.beechwoodrecruit.com. IT, technical, engineering, telecoms, etc.

Bilinguagroup Recruitment Consultants: 24 Maddox Street, London

W1S 2QF; ☎020-7493 6446; www.bilinguagroup.com. Office staff.
Comtex Solutions: Kingswood House, Woburn Road, Leighton Buzzard, Bedfordshire LU7 0AP; ☎01525-379111; www.comtexsolutions.com. IT professionals.
Coutts Career Consultants: 5-7 New Street, London EC2M 4TP; ☎020-7283 1229.
Dux International: 15 Princeton Mews, 167-9 London Rd, Kingston-on-Thames, Surrey KT2 6PT; ☎020-8547 0100; fax 020-8547 0400; www.duxrecruitment.com. Specialises in computer vacancies in Europe.
Euro London Appointments: 3 Kings Court, 150 Fleet St, London EC4A 2DQ; ☎020-7583 0180; www.eurolondon.com. Multilingual staff.
James Baker Associates: 46 Queens Road, Reading, Berkshire RG1 4BD; ☎01734-505022; www.jba.clara.net. IT, high-tech, personnel specialists.
Manpower: UK International House, 66 Chiltern Street, London W1M 9PB; ☎020-7224 6688; www.manpower.co.uk. Can supply information on Manpower branches in Belgium.
Merrow Language Recruitment: 3rd Floor, 23 Bentinck St, London W1U 2EZ; ☎020-7935 5050; fax 020-7935 5454; e-mail recruit@merrow.co.uk. Specialises in multilingual appointments.
Michael Page International: 50 Cannon St, London EC4N 6JJ; ☎020-7831 2000; www.michaelpage.co.uk. Banking.
Miller Brand Recruitment: 16 Wigmore St, London W1H 9DE; ☎020-7290 0985; fax 020-7290 0981; www.eurorecruit.com/miller. Middle and senior management.
OCC Computer Personnel: 108 Welsh Row, Nantwich, Cheshire CW5 5EY; ☎01270-627206; www.occ-computing.co.uk.
RenaissanceWorldwide Professionals, Abbey Court, St John's Road, Tunbridge Wells, Kent TN4 9PQ; ☎01892-513344; fax 01892-514477; e-mail ukjobs@rens.com; www.rens.com.
Track International: PO Box 1, Perranporth TR6 0YG; e-mail track@trackint.com. IT professionals in Europe.

BELGIAN STATE EMPLOYMENT OFFICES

EMPLOYMENT OFFICES are organised on a regional basis, the regions being Flanders, Brussels and Wallonia. The following offices will send you lists of local employment offices and can assist in your job-search:
ORBEM (Office Régional Bruxellois de l'Emploi) or BGDA (Brusselse Gewestelijke Dienst voor Arbeidsbemiddeling), Bvd Anspach 65, 1000 Brussels; ☎ 02 505 14 11; e-mail info@orbem.be *or* info@bgda.be; www.orbem.be or www.bgda.be.
Vlaamse Dienst voor Arbeidsbemiddeling en Beroepsopleiding (VDAB): Keizerslaan 11, 1000 Brussels; ☎ 02 506 15 11; e-mail info@vdab.be; www.vdab.be.
Office Wallon de la Formation Professionnelle et de l'Emploi: Bvd J. Tirou 104, 6000 Charleroi; ☎ 071 20 61 74; communic@forem.be; www.hotjob.be.

PRIVATE EMPLOYMENT AGENCIES

BRUSSELS HAS BECOME a mecca for recruitment agencies and executive search companies wanting to take advantage of the Single Market. There has also been an explosion in the number of firms offering human resource management, career evaluation, psychographology and other exotic-sounding services. Personnel recruitment companies can be found in the Yellow Pages under *Personnel (Recrutement et Selection de)* or *Personeelsrecrutering en -selectie*. A few recruitment companies are given below.

Useful Addresses

ACT Careers: Tweehuizenweg 63 bte 10, 1020 Brussels; 02 771 01 82.

Ashurst Morris Crisp: Rue Defacqz 72, 1060 Brussels; 02 539 34 37. Executive search.

Bosman EC Management Consultants: Av. de Tervueren 114a, 1040 Brussels; 02 732 25 10. Computer and DP professionals.

Computer Futures: Floor 8, The Blue Tower, Av. Louise 326, 1050 Brussels; 02 645 3355; fax 02 645 3366; e-mail contract@compfutures.be; www.compfutures.com.

DPSC Belgium: 126 Av. Milcamps, 1040 Brussels, 02 732 11 40.

Fontaine Archer Van De Voorde: Av. Général de Gaulle 47, 1050 Brussels; 02 649 43 08. Finance, accountancy, banking and legal.

Michael Page International: Av. Molière 262, 1060 Brussels; 02 347 02 10. Finance, accountancy and banking.

Mottet & Associates: Rue Vlasendael 25, 1070 Brussels; 02 527 03 09. Top and middle management.

PA Consulting Group: Av. M. Thiry 79, 1020 Brussels; 02 761 79 10.

Profile Group (The): Bvd L. Schmidt, 1040 Brussels; 02 732 01 75. Secretarial and administrative staff.

Rainbow Careers: Av. de Tervuren 37, 1040 Brussels; 02 735 41 54 (secretarial), 735 86 86 (executive); www.rainbow-careers.be.

Ray & Berndtson: Belgicastr. 7, Fountain Plaza, 1930 Zaventem; 02 725 0004. Executive recruitment.

Recruitment Partners (Computer Related Recruitment): Sq. Vergote 32, 1030 Brussels; 02 736 00 53.

Staff Selection and Services: Av. Brugmann 32, 1060 Brussels; 02 344 18 04.

OUTPLACEMENT BUREAUX

OUTPLACEMENT BUREAUX ASSIST those who are being made redundant to find new careers, by analysing the candidate's potential, advising on interview techniques, providing secretarial services, and so on. They are paid by the companies who are releasing their staff, not by the employee. Outplacement bureaux deal with groups as well as individuals. They sometimes advise blue-collar workers.

Useful Addresses

Coutts Alternative SA: Bvd Louis Schmidt 64, 1040 Brussels; ☎02 735 90 40.

Vlaamse Vennootschap voor Outplacement (V.V.O.): Antwerpsesteenweg 124, 2630 Aartselaar; ☎03 870 46 07.

Will also advise on spouse-employment and pre-retirement.

V.V.O. Outplacement International: Leuvensesteenweg 613, 1930 Zaventem; ☎02 757 90 24.

TEMPORARY EMPLOYMENT AGENCIES

ALTHOUGH TEMPORARY WORK is increasing rapidly in Belgium, only a little more than 1% of workers are engaged in this area, far fewer than in the UK, where the figure is over 3.3%. There are nevertheless a large number of temporary work agencies in Belgium. Often they are all to be found in one street in a city, which makes life convenient for the job-seeker. It is important to note that temping agencies usually have separate offices for manual and office workers. Some also have separate sections for computer personnel, nurses, and so on. Office workers should look under *Intérimaires – Travail Intellectuel* or *Uitzendkrachten – Hoofdarbeid* in the Yellow Pages. For manual workers the heading is *Intérimaires – travail manuel* or *Uitzendkrachten – Handenarbeid*. Agencies can offer not only daytime work, but also evening and weekend work. There is, however, a strict separation between agencies offering temporary and permanent work.

A temping agency receives the equivalent of up to a month's salary when it places a worker, so good workers are a very valuable commodity. If a worker should decide to accept a full-time job with a company, the temping agency is not allowed to charge the customer anything. A temporary worker has the same rights as a permanent worker, even as far as receiving holiday pay and compensation if he/she is dismissed without good reason. In many cases, temporary work can lead to a full-time job, so this is an excellent way to begin your career in Belgium.

The Belgian Ministry of Employment also runs a network of temporary work offices in 12 major towns, known as the 'T-Service'. T-Service offices are usually in a separate building from the permanent employment office and have a different telephone number. They can be found in the Yellow Pages under T-Service, or you can ask for a list from the Brussels office: Boulevard Anspach 69, 1000 Brussels; ☎02 511 23 85. T-Service has another Brussels office at Avenue des Arts 46, 1040 Brussels; ☎02 513 77 39.

Useful Addresses

Antwerp

Creyf's Interim: F. Rooseveltplaats 8, 2060 Antwerp; ☎03 234 28 08; www.creyfs.be.

Vedior Interim: Gemeentestraat 6, 2060 Antwerp; ☎03 229 08 79; www.vedior.be. Managerial, technical computer staff.

Manpower: Jezusstraat 17, 2000 Antwerp; ☎03 231 77 75; www.manpower.be.

Brussels

Adecco Interim: Bvd Adolphe Max 26, 1000 Brussels; ☎02 217 40 70;

www.adecco.be.
Creyf's Interim: Rue de l'Ecuyer 21-23, 1000 Brussels; ☎02 218 83 70; e-mail brussels@creyfs.be.
Creyf's Engineering: address as above; ☎02 218 82 85.
Vedior Interim Executive Secretaries: Place de Brouckère 21, 1000 Brussels; ☎02 344 98 19; www.vedior.be.
Manpower: Bvd Anspach 10, 1000 Brussels; ☎02 218 36 00; www.manpower.be.
Select Interim: Av. de la Joyeuse Entrée 1/5 bte 14, 1040 Brussels; ☎02 231 03 33; fax 02 230 12 10; e-mail select.interim@selectinterim.be; www.interimpartnership.be. Secretarial temps.

Liège
Creyf's Interim: Bvd de la Sauvenière 34, 4000 Liège; ☎041 22 39 22; e-mail liege@creyfs.be.
Vedior Interim: Bvd de la Sauvenière 90, 4000 Liège; ☎04 223 59 38.

CHAMBERS OF COMMERCE

CHAMBERS OF COMMERCE exist to promote the interests of companies trading in Belgium and the UK; they do not offer help in looking for work. However, they can be a useful source of information on companies operating in their geographical area and they will usually sell you a copy of their directory of members. Once you have a list of companies you can then make applications for current or prospective vacancies even if they are not being advertised in the press. The British Chamber of Commerce in Belgium Directory costs €90 (order online). The American Chamber of Commerce's Directory, which has information on 1,700 companies operating in Belgium, costs €123.95 from within Benelux.

Anyone setting up a business in Belgium must contact their local chamber of commerce (*Chambre de Commerce/Handelskamer*) on arrival. The chamber of commerce will tell you about the requirements that you have to fulfil before you can start up. A list of regional chambers of commerce is given in the section Regional Employment Guide, at the end of this chapter.

Useful Addresses

American Chamber of Commerce in Belgium: Av. des Arts 50 bte 5, 1000 Brussels; ☎02 513 67 70; fax 513 35 90; www.amcham.be.
British Chamber of Commerce in Belgium: Egmont House, Rue d'Egmont 15, 1050 Brussels; ☎02 540 90 30; fax 512 83 63; e-mail brit.cham@skynet.be; www.britcham.be.

LETTERS OF APPLICATION

WHETHER YOU ARE applying speculatively, or in answer to a job advertisement, in most cases it will be necessary to write a letter, and very often your curriculum vitae will be attached. Needless to say, the way your letter is presented can greatly influence your chances of success.

If you are making a speculative job application, your letter should be typed rather than handwritten. Belgian companies set a great deal of store by graphology, but at the initial stage it is more important to make your letter legible. Try to be brief, polite and to the point. Rather than a lengthy life history, a statement of your qualifications and professional interests is the most important thing. A photocopied letter is not likely to make a good impression; a word-processed letter is just as convenient and will receive a much more positive response.

If you are dealing with a Belgian company, it is vital to know which language to use. In central Brussels it is generally safe to use French or English, but if you are dealing with a Dutch-speaking company always use English. Letters to companies in Wallonia will probably be more successful if they are in French, as long as you remember not to give the impression that your French is much better than it really is. There are a number of books on how to write business letters in French, for example, *How to Address Overseas Business Letters* by Derek Allen (Foulsham). If necessary, have the letter professionally translated into French. The Institute of Translation and Interpreting (Exchange House, 494 Midsummer Boulevard, Central Milton Keynes MK9 2EA; ☎01908-255905; e-mail info@iti.org.uk) can put you in touch with a qualified translator, whose charges may range from £50-70 for 1,000 words. It is also worth contacting a college of further education for this purpose.

The letter of application can be written in much the same way as a letter in the UK, with the proviso that it is best to avoid using abbreviations, or, even worse, trying to be humorous. If your letter is speculative, the company in question may be surprised to hear from you. At the same time, the fact that you had the initiative to contact them gives a good impression. Belgian companies are usually good about replying to letters, however, they do not like to feel that their time is being wasted, so it is best to be very clear about your purpose in writing. On the whole, Belgians prefer to communicate by telephone or fax or e-mail. If you do establish a positive contact with a firm or agency in Belgium, you could well be asked to fax or e-mail a copy of your CV or diplomas.

TRANSFERS

THE ALTERNATIVE TO finding work directly in Belgium is to do this through the longer-term procedure of finding a position within a company in the UK which offers the prospect of being transferred to Belgium. If you go to work for one of the big accountancy or law firms you are more or less guaranteed to have the opportunity of working abroad if you want it. In other areas there is far less certainty that you will be posted to a specific country. The Single Market promotes mobility of labour in the EU but language barriers still remain. While English will remain the most widely spoken European language, the ability to speak French or another EU language will assume a crucial importance for those who seriously want to work abroad, so now is the time start learning.

The following types of company offer the option of transfer abroad:

Belgian Companies Operating in the UK. Belgian companies have quite a low profile in the UK, but there are far more of them than you might suspect. Two of the most significant are Solvay, the giant chemicals multinational, and Agfa-Gevaert, one of the world's leading photographic products suppliers. Belgian food producers are also expanding their UK presence, the biggest being Vandemoortele. The Belgian brewing giant, Interbrew, owns Bass and other brewers in the UK, and now rates as the world's second biggest brewer after Anheuser Busch. Subsidiaries of Belgian companies are also to be found in the engineering, glass and transport sectors. The Belgian Embassy can supply a list of Belgian companies with subsidiaries in the UK.

British Companies Operating in Belgium. Most major UK-based multinationals already have subsidiaries or branches in Belgium. ICI has its European headquarters in Everberg, near Brussels. British banks, estate agents, accountants and management consultants are all heavily represented. Numerous British law firms have opened offices in Brussels to offer advice on EU law to companies wanting to set up in Europe, and this will continue to be a growth area. A list of major British employers in Belgium is given at the end of this chapter.

International Companies. Belgium attracts multinationals in large numbers, not only because it is the centre of the EU, but also because of its liberal investment climate. American firms have been particularly drawn to Belgium, so that the USA is now the largest foreign investor with 40% of the total ($20 billion). Companies which set up 'co-ordination centres' in line with certain criteria benefit from generous tax-breaks, as well as exemptions from the rules governing work permits for their employees. A company setting up a co-ordination centre must have sales of more than €250 million (£170 million) a year.

It is not always easy to know the extent of a company's involvement in Belgium. Addresses can be found in the directories of Chambers of Commerce. If you can contact a subsidiary directly in Belgium you may well be able to obtain a brochure on their activities from them. While not many companies recruit with a transfer in mind, you can always discuss your long-term aims at interview.

International Organisations: More than 1,000 international, non-governmental organisations and associations are located in Brussels, including the Union of International Associations (UIA) which has been in Brussels since its foundation in 1910. Many of them are in Brussels to lobby or take part in the work of the EU Economic and Social Committee. A list of international organisations based in Brussels can be found at: www.uia.org.

THE CURRICULUM VITAE

A TYPICAL APPLICATION WOULD comprise a letter of application and a curriculum vitae (CV). There are agencies which will prepare your CV; some advertise in newspapers or you can look under 'Employment Agencies' in the Yellow Pages. A one-page graduate CV will cost from £25 upwards. You can save yourself time and money by producing your own CV and updating it every time you have something new to add to it. The layout of CVs is generally more old-fashioned in Belgium than it is in the UK and the US. For Belgian employers you need to go through your education and work experience in chronological order, with the most recent last. Trying to sell yourself with exaggerated claims about your abilities is likely to hinder your chances. It is not usual to put names of referees on the CV. You may either get advice from a careers service on writing your CV, or consult a specialist publication such as: *How to Prepare your Curriculum Vitae* by A.L. Jackson. Be careful to remove any abbreviations that could confuse a foreign employer. Keep the CV as succinct as possible. You can send more details later on.

INTERVIEW PROCEDURE

IF A COMPANY asks you to attend an interview in Belgium, then this should be taken as a sign that they are seriously interested in hiring you. Since Belgian companies operate on the philosophy that time is money, they are not keen to interview everyone whose application seems to be in order. Unfortunately you can expect to have to pay your own travel costs.

As stated earlier under Manners and Customs (*Daily Life* chapter) it is important to use the correct terms of address (*Monsieur/Madame* in French and *Meneer/Mevrouw* in Dutch). You can also expect to shake hands on arrival and departure. The degree of formality of an interview can vary between the language communities. Dutch-speakers tend to favour a more informal approach than French-speakers. If your interview is conducted in French, be prepared for a close scrutiny of your language abilities. Sounding polite will help your cause considerably.

One way to make a favourable impression is to find out something about Belgium and show some interest in the country. Belgians do not expect foreigners to know anything about their country, so they will be pleasantly surprised if you do. You should, however, avoid commenting on controversial matters such as the language question or Belgian politics. Remember also that modesty is the key virtue in Belgium and exaggeration a cardinal sin.

ASPECTS OF EMPLOYMENT

SALARIES

BELGIAN SALARIES HAVE risen less slowly than those in other EU countries in recent years. British managerial and executive salaries now exceed those in Belgium (at least at the current exchange rate); those at the top of the scale do considerably better in France and Germany, which is to a large extent a reflection of the fact that Belgian firms are smaller than those in neighbouring countries. Those at the lower end of the scale earn more than in Britain, but this must be balanced against the higher Belgian taxation, with the result that take-home pay may be less than in the UK. The cost of living is a little less than in the UK but about 25% more than in the US. Brussels is one of Europe's cheapest capitals; rents are about half those in London.

The statutory minimum wage for workers at age 21 is €1,060 (£650) per month. Employees are divided into blue-collar (*ouvriers/arbeiders*) and white-collar (*employés/bedienden*) workers, low and middle managers (*cadres/kaders*) and higher management (*gérants/zaakvoerders*). Wages are standardised in most industries by collective bargaining through Labour and Management Committees (*commissions paritaires/paritaire komitees*). They are usually index-linked, but at times of economic crisis, such as 1993-1997, indexation may be suspended. Minimum wages for clerical workers, for instance, depend on age and qualifications, and range from €13,600 (£8,200) p.a. to €27,200 (£16,400). The average wage outside Brussels for clerks and factory workers is about €21,800 (£13,100). Highly skilled workers in industry earn at least 50% more than this. In Brussels junior managers can expect to earn at least €41,000 (£24,600), middle-ranking executives €82,000 and the managing director of a medium-sized firm €165,000 (£100,000).

BENEFITS AND PERKS

SALARIES ARE PAID at the end of the month. Manual workers are usually paid every week, or every two weeks. It is a general practice to grant a 13th month (*treizième mois/dertiende maand*) and sometimes half of a 14th month, at the end of the year. This is also sometimes known as a yearly bonus (*prime de fin d'année/jaarpremie*). It is also common practice to pay a profit-related bonus (*participation aux bénéfices/aandeel in de winst*), which also sometimes goes under the name of a productivity bonus (*prime de productivité/produktiviteitspremie*).

Managers and executives also have the added attraction of company cars, enhanced sickness insurance and extra pension schemes. For low-paid workers the employer is obliged to subsidise their travel costs to and from work. Companies who reimburse their employees' commuting costs can claim tax rebates, on the grounds that the environment benefits from fewer cars on the road.

WORKING HOURS, OVERTIME AND HOLIDAYS

WORKING HOURS are limited by law to 40 hours a week in most cases, and 8 hours a day. In some industries the unions and employers have negotiated a longer working week or shift system. In a typical office the worker is contracted to do 38 hours a week, but in practice works 39 hours and receives one extra day's holiday a month. The working day lasts from 8.30am to 5.00pm, with a half-hour lunch-break. Work ends at 4.00pm on Fridays in most offices. As far as the statistics go, the average Belgian works 38½ hours a week, about two hours less

than in the UK.
Employees are not obliged to work overtime. If overtime is worked, this has to be paid at an additional 50%. Overtime on Sundays and public holidays is paid at double time. In addition to extra pay, workers are entitled to take time off.
All workers are entitled to 20 days' paid holiday, as well as public holidays. Those working a six-day week receive 24 days' holiday. Not only is salary paid during the holiday period, but a further 85% of a month's salary is paid at the time of the annual holiday.

TRADE UNIONS

BELGIUM IS ONE of the most heavily unionised countries in the Western world; 50% to 85% of workers are likely to be members of unions in any given industry. The percentage for the workforce as a whole is 70%. There is no such thing as a closed shop, however, and the unions generally co-operate with employers to ensure peaceful industrial relations. Strikes have been rare in recent years (except on the railways). Unions are organised by industry, and affiliated to one of three trade union federations, which are split up on linguistic and political/religious lines. The federations are:

CSC/ACV: *Confédération des Syndicats Chrétiens de Belgique/Algemeen Christelijk Vakverbond.* The most powerful confederation (especially in Flanders), with 1,350,000 members. Affiliated with the Christian Social parties.

FGTB/ABVV: *Fédération Générale des Travailleurs de Belgique/Algemene Belgische Vakverbond.* Has 1,150,000 members and is linked to the Belgian Socialist parties.

CGSLB/ACLVB: *Confédération Générale des Syndicats Libéraux de Belgique/Algemeen centrale van de Liberale Vakbonden van België.* Has only 200,000 members. Affiliated with the Belgian Liberal parties.

Every business with over 100 workers must have a Workers' Council (*Conseil d'entreprise/Ondernemingsraad*) made up of both management and workers, with elections held every four years. The workers' council mainly functions as a channel of communication between managers and personnel. Businesses with more than 50 personnel must also institute a health and safety committee.
Wages and salaries are determined by Labour Management Commissions (*commissions paritaires/paritaire komitees*) for entire industries. Pay levels are then made compulsory by royal decree.

EMPLOYMENT CONTRACTS

A WRITTEN EMPLOYMENT contract is not obligatory, but is usually desirable, given the complexity of the labour laws. A contract is only valid if it is in French or Dutch. There is usually a trial period of employment, not exceeding a year, during which an employee can be dismissed with one week's notice. After the trial period, a typical contract runs for an indefinite duration, and at least three months' notice has to be given. Length of notice increases with seniority; in some cases this goes up to three years. Employees are generally expected to give at least six weeks' notice if they intend to leave

WORK PRACTICES

BELGIANS LIKE TO work fixed hours and keep their work and home life strictly separate. It is considered bad form to telephone people about work matters during their free time, or to discuss work in front of outsiders. If you are in the habit of being unpunctual you could soon be out of a job. In general, taking tea-breaks or chatting on the office phone are frowned upon. There is a strong emphasis on being conscientious and being seen to be working hard. Amongst Flemish firms, management structures tend to be simple, and the boss will spend a lot of time on the shop floor. In French-speaking companies things tend to be more formal; to some extent there is the same liking for grand plans and hierarchies as in France, while the Flemings prefer a more flexible, consensual approach. The super-efficient Dutch do not have a high opinion of the Belgians' organisational capabilities, to the extent that chaotic situations are called *Belgische toestanden* (Belgian conditions) in Holland. It is also true to say that Belgian firms are far less concerned with keeping down costs than the Dutch.

The Flemish like to consider themselves more entrepreneurial and open to change than the Walloons, but in reality work practices are conservative throughout the country. Since the Flemings speak better English than the Walloons, they tend to be more aware of what is happening in the UK and the USA. Speaking French or Dutch is not always a necessity in order to work for a Belgian company, although making an effort is always appreciated.

WOMEN IN WORK

ONE OF THE MOST STRIKING facts about Belgium is how few women go out to work. Equality of opportunity for women is guaranteed by law in Belgium and barriers to professional advancement have largely been eliminated. In practice, there are very few women in higher management, except in family-owned companies. In more ordinary jobs women are at a disadvantage in some sectors since it is illegal for them to work at night (with the exception of nurses and barmaids). Most part-time work is done by women (85% in Flanders); taking the workforce as a whole, women earn 25% less than men, and are almost twice as likely to be on unemployment benefit.

PERMANENT WORK

EMPLOYMENT PROSPECTS

AS IN OTHER COUNTRIES, changing technology has resulted in changes in the demand for different types of workers. Workers most in demand are sales engineers, systems analysts, software engineers, project leaders – in fact, anyone with a university degree and experience in engineering or information technology. There is a notable shortage of IT graduates, and a vast surplus of graduates in agricultural engineering and environmental studies. There is also something of a surplus of technicians and electrical engineers, although the somewhat unfashionable textile industry finds it hard to recruit suitably qualified trainees. Supply and demand are more or less in balance for architects and chemistry graduates. International law and accountancy are growth areas.

Executive Recruitment Prospects

According to surveys carried out by the American Chamber of Commerce, the best job prospects are in marketing, finance, general management and IT. Law firms and consultancies on government affairs are also seen to be expanding rapidly. The worst areas to be in are personnel and administration.

As far as the country of origin goes, the European headquarters of US companies are looked on as the best sector for recruitment. Virtually any foreign company is looked on as a good job prospect. Belgian companies are not highly favoured, either because they do not have many openings for foreigners, or because prospects for advancement are not as good. Many Belgians prefer the security of working for a Belgian company to the perceived uncertainty of working for a foreign company. As a result, those employed by Belgian and foreign companies usually follow separate career paths.

If you do want to make your career in a Belgian-owned company, it is as well to be aware of the fact that in family-owned companies, promotion tends to go automatically to family members, rather than to the best-qualified people. This type of nepotism is often criticised but seems to be more or less part of Belgian culture.

WORKING FOR THE EUROPEAN COMMISSION

THE EUROPEAN COMMISSION, the central administrative body for the European Union, employs about 16,500 staff in Brussels. Because 11 languages are used in the Commission's work, there is an immense demand for translators and interpreters. Over 1,200 translators are employed by the

Commission in Brussels alone. However, all staff are required to have a good working knowledge of a second EU language. In practice, day-to-day work at the Commission is conducted in English and French; training in languages is offered where necessary. Perhaps because of the language requirements, British workers are under-represented in EU institutions.

EU officials enjoy good salaries, allowances and working conditions. They pay tax directly to the EU, not to member states. Those who work outside their own country receive a 16% expatriate allowance. Children of EU workers can have free schooling at one of the EU schools in Belgium.

Careers Structure

The Commission is divided into 24 policy Directorates-General administering different areas of policy. There are also various other services such as the Secretariat General, Translation Service, Joint Interpreting and Conference Service, and so on. EU Commissioners also have their own offices or 'cabinets'. The great majority of EU Commission personnel are located in Brussels, but some work in Luxembourg, and a small number in other EU member countries and elsewhere in the world.

There are four grades of workers in EU institutions, classified A, B, C and D. In order to apply for a post at the EU you must be an EU citizen, know one EU language at native speaker level and have a good knowledge of at least one other. When there is sufficient demand for staff, open competitive examinations are held in member countries. Successful entrants are then invited for interview in Brussels, and if they pass this hurdle, are placed on a reserve list of available staff. It can then take a further year before a post is actually offered. Posts are advertised in national newspapers such as *The Times*, *The Independent* and *The Guardian*. Details of competitions and application procedures appear regularly in the Official Journal of the European Commission, available from the Commission's Information Offices (see below). If you are a national civil servant, there is also the possibility of working for up to three years for the EC without giving up your UK job, as a 'detached national expert'.

Grade A: This grade is reserved for university graduates and includes administrators, scientists and advisory personnel. Candidates without work experience enter at Grade A8, while those with experience can enter at between A7 and A5. The starting salary for Grade A8 workers stood at about £29,000 in 2001.

Grade LA: This grade is reserved for graduates who work either as translators or interpreters. Candidates for the LA grade can have a degree in any discipline, not necessarily languages, but must have a very good knowledge of at least two other EU languages from which they translate or interpret into their mother tongue. Translators do not require a special qualification in translation but interpreters must have specialised interpretation training, usually at postgraduate level.

Grade B: Education up to A-level standard is required for this grade, which covers various levels of administrative assistants. Workers with a background in computers are particularly in demand for this grade. Basic pay at Grade B5 is £21,500.

Grade C: This is the grade for secretaries and clerical staff. Education to GCSE level and some work experience are required. Languages are important at this level as well. Basic pay at Grade C5 is £16,500.

Grade D: Workers in this category are manual and support service staff, for example, drivers, printers and messengers.

Entry via the Civil Service

Each year, 15-20 graduates with a second or first class honours degree are recruited into the British Civil Service and posted to government departments, where their work as a full-time civil servant, combined with special training, helps them to prepare for the recruitment competitions run by the EU institutions. Full information on the European Fast Stream is available on the website: www.faststream.gov.uk or from RAS, Innovation Court, New Street, Basingstoke RG21 7DP; ☎ 01256-383683.

Stagiaires

The European Commission in Brussels offers a five-month internship programme for young graduates known as the *stage*. This provides them with an opportunity to gain first-hand experience of working in an EU institution, but those wishing to work for the Commission on a permanent basis will still have to go through the open competition recruitment process. The European Commission is unable to offer any traineeships, industrial, summer or vacation placements to graduates or undergraduates, other than the five-month traineeship or *stage*. Recruitment for courses takes place at the beginning of February and September. Details and application forms can be found at: http://europa.eu.int/comm/stages/index.

One further possible entry route to an EU post is to take a one-year postgraduate course in European Studies at the College of Europe in Bruges (see Education section in *Daily Life*). Subject areas include Advanced European Economics, Administration and Law. Graduates whose qualifications are considered relevant to the Commission's requirements have a good chance of being recruited. The British government has 30 bursaries on offer each year for such courses.

Useful Publications and Addresses

The main website for general EU information is the Europe website: http://europa.eu.int. European Union recruitment information can be found at http://europa.eu.int/en/comm/dg09/dg9home.htm and on the website for the European Commission Representation in the UK which is: www.cec.org.uk.

Press and Information Offices of the European Commission:
8 Storey's Gate, London SW1P 3AT; ☎ 020-7973 1992.
Windsor House, 9/15 Bedford Street, Belfast BT2 7EG; ☎ 028-9024 0708.

4 Cathedral Road, Cardiff CF1 9SG; ☎ 029-2037 1631.
9 Alva Street, Edinburgh EH2 4PH; ☎ 0131-225 2058.
European Commission Representation in Ireland, Jean Monnet Centre, 18 Dawson Street, Dublin 2; ☎ 01-662 51 13; www.euireland.ie.

TRANSLATING AND INTERPRETING

TRANSLATORS CONVERT WRITTEN documents into their own mother tongue, and have usually mastered two foreign languages. They tend to specialise in certain subject areas, such as technical or legal translation. Some translators have worked in scientific or other fields before training as translators. A degree in languages is not enough to become a translator – further training at an institute for professional linguists or university is needed.

Interpreters have an even more difficult job than translators, in that they have to interpret while someone is actually speaking (simultaneous interpreting) or during pauses left by the speaker (consecutive interpreting). Sometimes the interpreter translates from and into two languages as people speak to each other. A full-time job as an interpreter is hard to find outside the EU Commission, so most interpreters are freelances who do translating and other work as well. Conference interpreters usually belong to either the *Association Internationale des Interprètes de Conférence (AIIC)* or the *Institute of Translation and Interpreting (ITI)*.

Further information on careers in interpreting and translating is available from:

Institute of Linguistics: Saxon House, 48 Southwark Street, London SE1 1UN; www.iol.org.uk.
Institute of Translation and Interpreting: Exchange House, 494 Midsummer Boulevard, Central Milton Keynes MK9 2EA; www.iti.org.uk.

WORKING FOR NATO

THE NORTH ATLANTIC TREATY ORGANIZATION (NATO) moved its headquarters to Brussels in 1967 after France withdrew from the military command structure. Its policy-making body is the North Atlantic Council of Ministers, and its parliamentary body the North Atlantic Assembly. NATO headquarters employs 3,000 workers from 16 different member countries; several thousand more are employed at Supreme Headquarters Allied Powers in Europe (SHAPE) at Le Casteau, near Mons. Workers at NATO are classified according to Grades A, B, C and L, in a similar way to EU workers (see above). Applications are made through the delegation of one's home country. In the case of British people, the address is: British Delegation NATO, Autosnelweg Brussel-Zaventem 1, 1110 Brussels; ☎ 02 707 72 11; fax 726 49 57; ukdelnato@skynet.be.

TEACHING

THERE ARE REGULAR opportunities for school and university teachers in Belgium. Names and addresses of potential employers can be found in the Schools and Education section in the *Daily Life* chapter. Some names of organisations in the UK and the USA which can place schoolteachers are given below.

Council of British Independent Schools in the European Communities (COBISEC): c/o Lucy's, Lucy's Hill, Hythe, Kent CT21 5ES; tel/fax 01303-260857; e-mail cobisec@cs.com; www.cobisec.org.
European Council of International Schools: 21 Lavant Street, Petersfield, Hants GU32 3EL; ☎01730-268244; fax 01730-267914; e-mail ecis@ecis.org; www.ecis.org.
ECIS North America: 105 Tuxford Terrace, Basking Ridge, New Jersey 07920, USA; ☎908-903 0552; fax 908-580 9381; e-mail malyecisna@aol.com; www.ecis.org.
Gabbitas Educational Consultants Ltd: Carrington House, 126-130 Regent St., London W1R 5EE; ☎020-7734 0161; fax 020-7437 1764; e-mail admin@gabbitas.co.uk; www.gabbitas.co.uk and www.teacher-recruitment.co.uk.
International Schools Services: PO Box 5910, Princeton NJ 08543; ☎609-452-0990; fax 609-452-2690; e-mail edustaffing@iss.edu; www.iss.edu.

EUROSTAR

EUROSTAR, WHICH RUNS THE CHANNEL TUNNEL train service, recruits on-board train managers and customer services team members on the ground for fast trains between London and Paris/Brussels on a permanent basis. You need to speak English and French (Dutch is also appreciated), and have experience of working with the public.

Momentum Services has the franchise for catering and service on the Eurostar to Brussels and Paris. The qualifications needed to be a steward or for catering staff are fluent French (and some Dutch if possible) and a background in catering, or another relevant industry. Positions are permanent. They have offices in the UK and in Belgium.

Eurostar (UK) Ltd: Personnel Dept., Eurostar House, Waterloo Station, London SE1 8SE.
Momentum Services: Waterloo International Terminal, London SE1 7LT; ☎020-7633 9416; fax 020-.
Cross-Channel Catering Company: Rue de France 52, 1060 Brussels, Belgium; ☎02 556 06 10.

SHORT-TERM EMPLOYMENT

TEACHING ENGLISH

THE DEMAND FOR ENGLISH language teachers is not as great as it was in the past, partly because of unfavourable economic conditions, but more so because many Belgians have already gained an adequate knowledge of English at school and would like to try other languages. In general, the French-speakers are less good at English than the Flemish; there is another potential market amongst the large numbers of citizens from other EU countries with time and money to pursue language studies.

Most prospective teachers look in the Yellow Pages and go round the language schools. Many language schools will offer you part-time work; what they will not do, however, is deal with your tax and social security affairs. Many English teachers therefore take their gross salary and never declare any of it. They should actually become self-employed *indépendants* and pay their taxes but, in practice, after about six months they move on elsewhere. Both the employer and the employee take the risk of being fined; nevertheless the practice seems to be tolerated by the authorities. Once you have worked *au noir/in het zwart* (in black) for a while it is difficult to become legal, as you would have to declare everything you had earned up until then, so it is important to decide whether you want to be legal or not, which largely depends on how long you want to stay in Belgium.

If you want to establish yourself as a language teacher it is a good idea to go along to your local *commune* to see if they run adult education classes in English. Another area where there is more demand for teachers is in primary education; if you have the necessary qualifications and experience then the following organisation may be of help: Worldwide Education Service (WES), Canada House, 272 Field End Road, Eastcote, Middx. HA4 9PE; ☎020-8582 0317; fax 020-8429 4838; e-mail wes@wesworldwide.com (include an SAE).

The best way to approach teaching is to obtain a recognised qualification in the UK or North America first. The minimum useful qualification is the CELTA (UK) or CTEFL (outside UK), a one-month course which costs up to £1,000. It is also possible to do this course in Belgium once you have managed to find work. Prospective employers tend to look not only for qualifications and experience, but also for an enthusiastic and outgoing personality. Teachers are hired locally; few schools reply to speculative letters. For further information on English-teaching, the publication, *Teaching English Abroad* (Vacation Work, £12.95) is an invaluable source of references. Also try the *Education* section of *The Guardian* on Tuesdays or the *Times Educational Supplement* on Fridays.

Useful Addresses
Language Schools in Belgium:
Berlitz Language Center: Av. Louise 306-310, 1050 Brussels; ☎02 649 61 75; e-mail info@berlitz.com.

Eurospeak: Rue de Stassart 49, 1050 Brussels; ☎ 02 511 89 12.
Fondation 9: Av. Louise 485, 1050 Brussels; ☎ 02 627 52 52; e-mail fondation9@ulb.ac.be.
May International: Rue de Bordeaux 55, 1060 Brussels; ☎ 02 536 06 70.

AU PAIR WORK

AU PAIRS are very much in demand among wealthier expatriate and Belgian families. In exchange for board, lodging and pocket money (at a minimum of £200 per month), au pairs are expected to devote a certain amount of time to their hosts' offspring, to attend a part-time language course at a local school and generally to promote cultural exchange. If you are lucky, the family you stay with will rent an apartment on the coast during the summer and take you along.

The status of au pairs is regulated by Belgian law and Council of Europe regulations. Although there are no legal obstacles to male au pairs, they are certainly very rare in Belgium. General rules are that the au pair should have her own bedroom and cannot be asked to do more than four hours of housework a day, in addition to one or two hours looking after the children. Au pairs are entitled to one free day a week. Employers are legally bound to pay pension contributions, sickness insurance and accident insurance for au pairs, whichever country they are from. British au pairs should take form E111 (see Section on E111 in *Daily Life* chapter) to cover for health insurance in the first three months.

Non-EU au pairs must obtain Work Permit B (see *Residence and Entry* chapter) from a Belgian Embassy before leaving. To qualify they must submit a document proving that they have a working knowledge of Dutch or French or that they are registered at an approved language school for at least 10 hours a week. EU au pairs only have to register at the local commune when they arrive in Belgium. They will then be given the mauve card model B which can be renewed every three months. Strictly speaking, no one can be an au pair for more than one year.

A good source of au pair jobs is *The Lady* magazine published weekly in the UK. It is possible to find an au pair position for the summer only, but you will have to start looking several months beforehand. Another way to find an au pair position is to go over to Belgium and look at notice boards or in the classified sections of newspapers and magazines, especially the English-language weekly *The Bulletin*. Meeting a family in advance helps to minimise the risks of exploitation or a personality clash. There are organisations in Belgium which can help you find a position as well (see below).

Many UK agencies arrange au pair posts abroad and the better-known ones are listed in the *Useful Addresses* section below. Remember that it is illegal for any agency to charge a registration fee to the prospective au pair, who is liable to pay only a reasonable charge to cover administration fees once a job has been organised and the contract actually signed. Because of changes in the law concerning fees, UK-based agencies may in the future no longer place au pairs abroad, so that you would have to approach an agency in Belgium. The Vacation Work publication, *The Au Pair and Nanny's Guide to Working Abroad* is an invaluable resource for those looking for au pair work abroad (see inside back cover).

Useful Addresses

Academy Au Pair and Nanny Agency: 42 Milsted Rd, Rainham ME8 6SU; ☎01634-310808; www.academyagency.co.uk.

Bond van Jonge en Grote Gezinnen (Association of Large and Young Families): Rue du Trône 125, 1050 Brussels; ☎02 507 88 11. Source of information.

Childcare International Ltd: Trafalgar House, Grenville Place, London NW7 3SA; ☎020-8959 3611; www.childint.co.uk.

House o Orange Au Pairs: Noordeinde 134, 2514 GN The Hague; ☎070-324 59 03.

Ligue des Familles: Rue du Trône 127, 1050 Brussels; ☎02 507 72 11. Source of information.

Nannies Incorporated: 317 The Linen Hall, 162-168 Regent Street, London W1R 5TB; ☎020-7437 8989; e-mail NanniesInc@aol.com; www.nanniesinc.com.

Services de la Jeunesse Féminine: Rue de Dave 174, 5100 Jambes; ☎081 30 99 80; fax 081 30 91 35.

Stufam VZW: Vierwindenlaan 7, 1780 Wemmel; ☎02 460 33 95; e-mail aupair.stufam@ping.be.

Windrose: Av. Brugmann 11, 1060 Brussels; ☎02 534 71 91; e-mail windrose@skynet.be.

SECRETARIAL WORK

THERE ARE GOOD OPPORTUNITIES for well-qualified bilingual secretaries in Brussels and other parts of Belgium. Bilingual here means that you are able to write letters and take shorthand or dictation in another EU language. The languages most in demand are French and Dutch, but there are good openings for other languages as well. The best way to obtain work is to go over to Belgium in person. Legal secretaries are particularly in demand. Salaries range from €1,500 to €2,500 per month (£1,000-£1,660). Secretarial temps can expect to earn from €15 to €25 per hour. A good source of jobs is the weekly *The Bulletin*, and its website: www.xpats.com. Names and addresses of agencies have been given under UK and Belgian Employment Agencies above.

TOURISM

ONE WAY OF WORKING in Belgium is to join a tour firm in the UK which sends coach drivers, couriers and tour guides over there. Knowledge of French and/or Dutch is often required. You can expect to work very long hours and have a lot of fun at the same time. For more information on training and employers, see *Working in Tourism*, published by Vacation Work (www.vacationwork.co.uk).

British Tour Companies Operating in Belgium:
3D Education and Adventure Ltd: Business Support, Osmington Bay, Weymouth, Dorset DT3 6EG; 01305-836226; fax 01305-834070; e-mail darren@3d-

education.co.uk. Activity instructors, watersports instructors, IT instructors.
Eurocamp: Overseas Recruitment Department (Ref SJ/02); ☎01606-787522. Campsite and children's couriers, with relevant experience and languages.
Holts Tours: Old Plough, High St, Eastry, Sandwich, Kent CT13 0HF; ☎01304-612248. Specialists in battlefield tours; applicants need to have a knowledge of military history.

Hotels and Restaurants: Hotel and catering work comes under the rather oddly named *Horeca* sector (*Ho*tels, *Re*staurants and *Ca*fés). Work in hotels is seasonal and not necessarily well-paid. The most likely areas for finding hotel work in Belgium are West Flanders, mainly on the coast, and in the provinces of Namur and Luxembourg, in the Ardennes. Lists of hotels can be obtained from Belgian Tourist Offices. Alternatively, local employment agencies will be able to put you in touch with prospective employers. Vacancies in catering can be found on the EURES website: http://europa.eu.int/jobs/eures.

AGRICULTURAL AND INDUSTRIAL

BELGIAN AGRICULTURE is highly mechanised and employs only 2% of the total workforce. Agricultural science is highly developed, especially in Flanders. A large number of young farmers from around the world come to study here, and there is the possibility of working on a farm for three to six months, as long as you already have at least two years' experience.

Belgian industry is always looking for highly qualified young graduates. The first point of departure is through the relevant federation; see the following section *Business and Industry*. Temporary jobs in industry are available through the regional employment offices and temporary work agencies.

INTERNSHIPS

INTEREXCHANGE INC. can arrange internships in Belgian companies for US residents. These last for one to three months. There is a $700 fee; interns may be paid a small wage; they pay for their own accommodation. For further information contact: InterExchange, 161 Sixth Ave, New York, NY 10013; ☎212-924-0446; fax 212-924 0575; www.interexchange.org.

VOLUNTARY WORK

BELGIUM HAS A LONG OF TRADITION of voluntary work, some of it under the auspices of the Catholic church. The International Building Companions (*Internationale Bouworde* in Dutch) have their headquarters in Brussels and sends volunteers to construction work camps for the underprivileged in different European countries including Belgium. Camps last from two to four weeks in the summer. Free board and lodging are provided, but you are responsible for your own travel costs. The *Service Protestant de la Jeunesse* (Protestant Youth Office) can place volunteers aged between 18 and 26 in Christian or other institutions in Belgium for nine to 12 months. Volunteers receive pocket money and free board and lodging. Placements begin in September.

Other kinds of voluntary work can be for much shorter periods and without any provision of accommodation. You may be asked to pay towards board and lodging where they are provided.

Possibilities for finding voluntary work are covered in depth in the book *The International Directory of Voluntary Work* (Vacation Work: www.vacationwork.co.uk).

Useful Addresses

Année Diaconale Belge: Service Protestant de la Jeunesse, Rue de Champ de Mars 5, 1050 Brussels; ☎02 510 61 61.
Archéolo-J: Av. Paul Terlinden 23, 1330 Rixensart; fax 02 654 19 17. Archaeological workcamps.
ATD Quart Monde: Av. Victor Jacobs 12, 1040 Brussels; ☎02 640 04 93.
Bouworde: Tiensesteenweg 157, 3010 Leuven; 016 25 91 44; www.bouworde-vzw.be. Flemish branch of *Internationale Bouworde*.
Compagnons Bâtisseurs: Rue des Carmes 24, 5400 Marche en Famenne; ☎084 31 44 13. Walloon branch of *Internationale Bouworde*.
Internationale Bouworde: Rue Amédée Lynen 8, 1030 Brussels.
NATUUR 2000: The Flemish Youth Federation for the Study of Nature and for Environmental Conservation: Bervoetstraat 33, 2000 Antwerpen; ☎03 231 2604.

BUSINESS AND INDUSTRY REPORT

BELGIUM HAS FEW NATURAL RESOURCES, apart from some small coal and iron deposits, and is highly dependent on the export of goods and services. The golden era of the Belgian economy was undoubtedly the 1960s, when strong economic growth brought a high level of prosperity to the whole country. The first oil crisis of 1973 brought this period of expansion to a sudden end and Belgian industry became less and less able to compete with its neighbours. The traditional heavy industries of Wallonia went into a steep decline. Industrial productivity and investment failed to keep up with levels in other EU countries; current account and budget deficits became a major problem, and unemployment soared. As a result of extraordinary fiscal measures, the situation rapidly improved and by 1986 the balance of trade was in the black for the first time since 1973, and has remained there ever since. Unit labour costs declined significantly in the 1980s and 1990s; Belgian workers are now among the most productive in the world. While exports continue to rise slowly, investment is rising only very slowly. The difficulties of the German economy tend to have a strong influence on Belgium's exports.

Thanks to the improved economic situation the state now has a small budget surplus and is planning to reduce taxes over the coming years to make Belgium more of an entrepreneurial society. The national debt has come down considerably but is still over 100% of GDP. Because the Socialists are part of the coalition government, painful measures needed to reduce the social security budget and other expenditures are not likely to be taken.

There are only a few state-owned industries in Belgium. These are mainly public services such as the post office, the semi-privatised Belgacom, and the railways. The Belgian National Bank is half owned by the state and half by private individuals. In recent years, the state, and with federalisation, the regional governments, have become increasingly involved in providing venture capital for private investment through its various credit institutions.

Belgium's major trading partners are its neighbours, Germany, the Netherlands and France. In 2001 these three countries alone accounted for 49% of imports and exports. The United Kingdom is Belgium's fourth largest trading partner with 9-10% of imports and exports. After the UK come Italy, the United States, Japan and Spain.

Out of the total population of 10 million, 4,180,000 are considered to be economically active. Men make up 59% of the workforce and women 41%. The employment rate of women is somewhat lower than the EU average. Industry now accounts for only 20% of the workforce, while the service sector employs 70%. Employment in industry is expected to contract further in the future with increasing automation.

European Monetary Union: During 1996 the Belgian government decided to begin the process of converting to the euro. Even if Belgium was not at the centre of the EU, the EMU would still be considered vitally important in a country largely dependent on exports for its economic survival. In 1999 the value of the Belgian franc was fixed at 40.3399 to the euro. The new notes and coins appeared on 1 January 2002, and the changeover was completed on 28 February 2002. Old notes and coins can be exchanged or deposited at banks until the end of 2002. The central bank (Banque Nationale de Belgique) will continue to exchange coins until the end of 2004, and notes for an indefinite period thereafter until further notice.

AUTOMOTIVE

CAR MANUFACTURING has always played a major role in Belgium's industrial success. From 1895 Belgian makers produced their own models, but the indigenous industry was all but obliterated by American competition during the 1930s. Except for coaches and buses there are no Belgian-owned car makers left. Car assembly is, however, still thriving. Belgium is a net exporter of cars

– 98% of production goes abroad. Numerous foreign-owned and local companies specialise in supplying the car industry with components, to the extent that cars could be manufactured entirely from Belgian-made parts. Three-quarters of car-related manufacturers are located in Flanders and the Brussels area, and only a quarter in Wallonia, which does not have a single car assembly plant as such.

Major firms operating in this area are:

- Ford, GM-Opel, Volvo, Volkswagen: passenger cars.
- Van Hool, Jonckheere, Eos: coaches and buses.
- Solvay, Du Pont De Nemours, Akzo-Nobel, Monsanto, Cockerill Sambre, Sekurit Saint Gobain, Uniroyal, Bell Telephone: components.

BANKING AND FINANCE

THE CENTRAL BANK is the National Bank of Belgium (*Banque Nationale de Belgique/Nationale Bank van België*), which is 50% owned by the state and 50% owned by the public. Its functions include issuing currency and controlling banks and financial institutions where necessary. There are about 85 commercial banks offering a full range of services, of which 63 are wholly or mainly foreign-owned. Of these 37 are European banks, most of them French.

As Belgium is the world leader in electronic banking, it is not surprising that two major bank clearing systems have established their headquarters in Brussels – SWIFT and Euroclear. As well as commercial banks, there are banks specialising in savings and loans to individuals, in particular mortgages.

The third sector of Belgian banks are the semi-public credit institutions which channel investment funds to industry and other businesses. Other banks under this heading are the General Savings and Pensions Fund (*Caisse Générale d'Epargne et de Retraite/Algemene Spaar en Lijfrentekas*) which deals with pensions and mortgages; and the *Credit Communal/Gemeentekrediet*, the bank used by the local and provincial governments.

There are four stock exchanges in Belgium – in Liège, Antwerp, Ghent and Brussels. The Brussels stock exchange (*La Bourse/De Beurs*) conducts 85% of business, but is still relatively small compared with some EU stock markets. There is still considerable scope for expansion for banking and financial services in Belgium – only 1.25% of workers are engaged in this sector.

Major commercial banks in Belgium: Fortis Bank, Banque Bruxelles Lambert, KBC Bank, Deutsche Bank, Banque Nationale de Paris, Banque Paribas, ABN-AMRO, Citibank.

CHEMICALS

BELGIUM HAS HAD a significant chemicals industry since the end of the 18th century. Mass production of photographic paper and plates was pioneered by Lieven Gevaert in 1890, and Agfa-Gevaert is still the largest chemicals company in Belgium. The forerunner of plastics – Bakelite – was invented by a native of Ghent, Léo Baekeland, in 1908. Belgian firms have also been innovators in pharmaceuticals, fertilisers and paints. During the 1980s the chemicals industry expanded rapidly and now accounts for some 15% of total industrial production. In 1999 Belgium had a foreign surplus in chemical products amounting to €6 billion (£3.6 billion).

In recent years the focus of the chemicals industry has shifted decisively towards Flanders, most of it based in or around Antwerp. Here it benefits from the proximity of refineries and seaports. Many chemical companies have sales or registered offices in Brussels, but 80% of production is located in the Flemish region. Of the large number of foreign chemical companies established in Belgium, many are American and British household names. French, German and Swiss pharmaceuticals companies also have a large presence.

Chemicals: Solvay, Solvic, UCB, BASF, ICI, Union Carbide, Dow Corning, Fisons, Rhône-Poulenc, Akzo-Nobel, 3M, Exxon.

Pharmaceuticals: Janssen, UCB, Boots, Bayer, GlaxoWellcome, Du Pont de Nemours, Monsanto, Sandoz, Schering, Smithkline Beecham.

FOOD AND AGRICULTURE

EMPLOYMENT IN AGRICULTURE has diminished far more rapidly in Belgium than in other EU countries over the last few decades, yet thanks to better training and scientific innovation, agricultural production has grown continuously. One agricultural worker is now reckoned to feed 80 consumers. Arable land takes up 25% of the total surface area of the country, the most important crops being potatoes, grains and sugar beet.

The food industry was one of Belgium's greatest success stories in the 1980s and 1990s, with production and exports rising at a 10% higher rate than in industry as a whole. It is now the second largest industrial employer in the country with 90,000 workers. There has been a determined drive towards finding new markets for well-known Belgian products such as chocolates, beers, soft drinks and waffles. The largest importer of Belgian food is France (over £1.5 billion annually). The Netherlands and Germany are next, followed by the UK and other EU countries.

Major food producers: United Belgian Mills, Kathy, Vandemoortele, Corman, Nutricia, Mabidic, Amylum, Delhaize-Le Lion, Jacobs-Suchard-Côte d'Or, Belcolade, Nestlé, Spadel, Soubry.

PETROCHEMICALS

BELGIUM HAS NO OIL reserves of its own, and is therefore entirely dependent on imports from abroad. Since the oil shocks of the seventies and the Gulf War, Belgium has reduced its dependence on the Arab states for its oil. The largest suppliers are now Iran, Great Britain, Norway, Russia and the Netherlands. Belgium has a refining capacity in excess of its own domestic needs and exports marginally more petroleum products than it actually uses. While it runs a large deficit with the Netherlands in this sector, it maintains a healthy surplus with the USA, Germany, France and Luxembourg. The largest surpluses are in car fuel (*essence/benzine*), fuel oils, lubricants and bitumens. Gas supplies come mainly from the Netherlands, Norway and Russia.

The *Fédération Petrolière Belge* (Belgian Petroleum Federation) has some 23 member companies, but only five of them are involved in refining, notably Fina Raffinaderij, Esso Belgium and the Belgian Refining Corporation. Major retailers in Belgium include: Aral, BP, Castrol, Elf Belgique, Exxon Mobil, Fina, Texaco, Belgian Shell and Total.

RETAILING

THE RETAIL SECTOR in Belgium is rather different from that in the UK. There are still traditional shopping streets in every Belgian town; it has been difficult to build shopping centres because land tends to be in the hands of many small owners and local governments have no wish to expropriate them. While there are hypermarkets and other specialised retailers on the edges of most towns, they are rarely very large as it is virtually impossible to obtain permission to build shops with a sales area of over 750 sq. metres outside town centres. Most retailing is still in the hands of small independent family-owned firms rather than chain-stores; department stores and other large sites are usually owned by foreign (often Dutch) multiples. The major Belgian group of supermarkets is GIB (*Grand Bazar-Innovation-Bon Marché*). An important development in the 1980s was the increase in the number of supermarkets selling food, led by the German chain Aldi, which has led to the closure of many (but not all) greengrocers. In many respects small- and medium-sized retailers have maintained their position. Belgian consumers are well-known for their insistence on quality products and have more faith in specialised outlets than chain-stores.

Chain stores: Delhaize, Innovation, GB, Hennes & Mauritz, Fnac, C&A, Mothercare, Witteveen, Hunkemöller, Hema, Blokker, Eram, 3 Suisses, Bally, Benetton.

STEEL AND NON-FERROUS METALS

BELGIUM HAS TRADITIONALLY been a world leader in metallurgy and still maintains this position today. Employment in the steel sector has fallen by more than half since 1979 to about 20,000, while production has tended to go up. Over half of steel products are destined for the Belgian railways. The situation in non-ferrous metals is healthier than in the steel sector, with production tending upwards, but there has been a marked shift in investment away from Wallonia to Flanders. Non-ferrous metal production directly employs 11,000 workers, most of them in Flanders. The giant new non-ferrous metals company formed in 1989 when ACEC-Union Minière took over Vielle-Montagne and Metallurgie Hoboken Overpelt is reckoned to be the world leader in the metallurgy of zinc, cadmium, germanium and cobalt, and the European leader in the metallurgy of copper and lead. Hoogovens Aluminium is now part of the Corus group (formerly British Steel).

Steel: Cockerill Sambre, Sidmar, Gustave Boël, Fabrique de Fer, ALZ, Thy Marcinelle, Ellwood Steel.
Metallurgy: Union Minière, Corus Aluminium, Bekaert, Remi Claeys Aluminium, Johnson Matthey, Boliden Cuivre et Zinc.

TEXTILES

THE TRADITIONAL TEXTILES sector went through a major crisis in the late 1970s and contracted substantially in the 1980s. The decline in clothing and knitwear manufacturing has proved to be irreversible and Belgium now imports a lot of finished goods from Asia. The clothing industry now employs about 22,000 workers. The main success story has been in women's *haute couture*, centred on Antwerp, which now has an international reputation. The design and manufacture of high-tech textile machinery is also of major importance.

More significantly, Belgium is now the world leader in synthetic floor coverings through such companies as Lano, Beaulieu and De Poortere and also exports large amounts of upholstery coverings, specialised industrial textiles and carpets, of which it is the world's largest exporter. 2000 showed a total surplus of €1.8 billion (£1.08 billion; excluding clothing) almost entirely made up of carpet exports. Employment prospects for technicians, chemists, etc. are excellent; there is an acute staff shortage and some companies are now thinking of moving production to northern France.

Textiles: De Witte-Lietaer, Louis De Poortere, Lano, Bekaert Textiles, Balta, Depraetere, Santens, UCO.
Clothing: Levi-Strauss, Lee Europe, Deltex, Van Overdijk, Staels Borco, Alcico.

REGIONAL EMPLOYMENT GUIDE

IN CHAPTER 1, the main cities and provinces of Belgium were discussed with a view to residence. In this section the same cities and provinces are covered, but this time with a view to the employment prospects available.

The information provided will give some idea of the dominant industries and which types of jobs are available in each area. In each case, further sources of information are given. The press listing is for the major newspaper in the area where job advertisements are most likely to be found. There is usually more than one Chamber of Commerce in each province. Many of these also have a Euro-Info Centre attached. All of these offices publish brochures and journals which they will supply on request.

ANTWERPEN

Major City: Antwerp.
Regional Newspaper: *De Gazet van Antwerpen.*
Chamber of Commerce: Markgravestraat 12, 2000 Antwerpen; ☎ 03 232 22 19; fax 03 233 64 42; e-mail info@kkna.be; www.dma.be/kkna/.
Industry/Other Comments: Antwerp is by far the wealthiest area of Belgium, producing 20% of its GNP. Industries favour the Antwerp area because of the port facilities and transport connections. Major activities: automotive, diamonds, chemicals, oil refineries, shipping, electronics, engineering, nuclear power, furniture-making, agricultural.

VLAAMS-BRABANT

Major City: Leuven.
Regional Newspaper: see Brussels.
Chamber of Commerce: Tiensevest 61, 3010 Leuven; ☎ 016 22 26 89; fax 016 23 78 28; www.ccileuven.be.
Industry/Other Comments: Dutch-speaking Brabant includes Vilvoorde and other industrial suburbs of Brussels, the national airport at Zaventem, and the university city of Leuven. The town of Tienen (Tirlemont) is the centre of the sugar industry. There is a high concentration of chemical factories around Brussels, in particular battery-makers. Major activities: chemicals, pharmaceuticals, telecommunications, distribution, agriculture, sugar-refining.

BRABANT WALLON

Major City: Nivelles.
Regional Newspaper: see Brussels.
Chamber of Commerce: Rue de la Science 16, BP 108, 1400 Nivelles Sud; ☎ 067 89 33 33; fax 067 21 08 00; www.knhb.be.
Industry/Other Comments: French-speaking Brabant, known locally as Brabant-Wallon, is a small but prosperous area with a large range of industries. Banking and finance are also important sectors. Major activities: steel, paper, pharmaceuticals, electronics, finance.

BRUSSELS

Major Newspaper: see Media section in *Daily Life* chapter.
Chamber of Commerce: Av. Louise 500, 1050 Brussels; ☎ 02 648 50 02; fax 02 640 93 28; www.ccibrussels.be.
Industry/Other Comments: Brussels has 10% of the Belgian population but employs 20% of the workforce, and generates 15% of GNP. Brussels is the third autonomous region of Belgium and has its own ministries, development board and so on. At the same time it functions as the capital of the Belgian state, of the Dutch- and French-speaking regions and of the province of Brabant. Most workers are employed in administration, finance and other services, but there are also 15 industrial and 4 science parks dedicated to keeping Brussels in the forefront of industrial development. While there are hundreds of representative offices of foreign companies, their production facilities are usually in other countries or other parts of Belgium. Major activities: finance, insurance, distribution, chemicals, car-assembly, aerospace, engineering, printing, publishing, furniture, food, tobacco.

EAST FLANDERS

Major City: Ghent.
Major Newspaper: *De Gentenaar.*
Chamber of Commerce: Martelaarslaan 49, 9000 Ghent; ☎ 09 266 14 40; fax 09 266 14 41; www.cci.be/gent.

East Flanders continues to be one of the most prosperous regions of Belgium, thanks to high levels of investment in automation and high technology. Some of its prosperity is a result of overspill from the Antwerp area. The province benefits from having Belgium's second largest port in Ghent, connected to the Scheldt estuary by the Ghent-Terneuzen canal, as well as the new port on the left bank of the Scheldt, the Waaslandhaven. The automotive industry is represented by the Volvo car factory on the outskirts of Ghent. The steel-producer Sidmar in Ghent is now one of the most efficient in the world. The textile industry has contracted but is still significant. Some household names in the chemicals and plastics industry are to be found here, such as Rhône-Poulenc, Bayer and Samsonite. A great deal of investment has recently gone into the area of electronics and computers. East Flanders also has one of the world's leading biotechnology centres in Plant Genetic Systems. Major activities: metal-working, automotive, textiles, chemicals, agriculture, horticulture, biotechnology.

HAINAUT

Major City: Charleroi.
Major Newspaper: *La Nouvelle Gazette*.
Chamber of Commerce: Av. Général Michel 1A, 6000 Charleroi; ☎071 32 11 60; fax 071 33 42 18; www.ccic.be.
Industry/Other Comments: The traditional industrial heartland of Wallonia, Hainaut is in the process of restructuring its entire economy. Mining has closed down completely in the province and the steel industry has shrunk considerably. Hainaut hopes to attract new high-tech industries but is finding it difficult to do so in the face of competition from the Flemish north. Major activities: steel, metallurgy, engineering, glass, plastics, rubber, cement, quarrying.

LIÈGE.

Major City: Liège.
Major Newspaper: *La Meuse*.
Chamber of Commerce: Palais des Congrès, Esplanade de l'Europe 2, 4020 Liège; ☎04 343 92 92; fax 04 343 92 67; www.ccilg.be.
Industry/Other Comments: The city of Liège was a world leader in heavy engineering and weapons manufacturing during the 19th century. The weapons industry is not as healthy as it was but other sections of the steel and metal-working industries have had to be rationalised in order to survive. The workforce in these sectors has fallen by more than two-thirds since 1974. Verviers has traditionally been a major textile-producing city, but has been adversely affected by competition from the Far East. The province of Liège includes the German-speaking area of Eupen, Malmédy and St. Vith, whose foremost employer is Kabelwerk Eupen, a leading manufacturer of electrical cables. Major activities: steel, weapons, machine tools, textiles, cables, telecommunications.

LIMBURG

Major City: Hasselt.
Major Newspaper: *Het Belang van Limburg*.
Chamber of Commerce: Gouverneur Roppesingel 51, 3500 Hasselt; ☎011 28 44 00; fax 011 28 44 06; www.khnl.be.

Industry/Other Comments: The province of Limburg, although historically an agricultural area, benefited along with Antwerp from the huge foreign investment of the 1950s and 1960s. The existing coal-mining industry expanded rapidly along with steel and car production. While other industries continue to thrive in Limburg, the local coal-mines became uneconomical and had to close down, thus spelling the end of the Belgian coal-mining industry for the time-being. Car-production is concentrated in Hasselt and Genk; Tessenderlo and its surrounding area has the largest concentration of chemicals factories. Major activities: automotive, chemicals, rubber, steel, engineering, electronics, fruit-growing, distilling.

LUXEMBOURG

Major City: Arlon.
Major Newspaper: *L'Avenir du Luxembourg.*
Chamber of Commerce: Grand rue 1, 6800 Libramont; ☎ 016 22 26 80; fax 061 22 40 20; www.ccilb.be.
Industry/Other Comments: Although thinly populated and better known for its scenic beauty than for its industries, Luxembourg has attracted its fair share of investment from abroad. As well as the traditional industries such as agriculture and forestry, chemicals and car components are represented here. The American firm Champion manufactures spark-plugs and windshield-wipers in Libramont. Major activities: paper, plastics, car-components, chemicals, packaging, agriculture, cosmetics, forestry, chocolates.

NAMUR

Major City: Namur.
Major Newspaper: see Brussels.
Chamber of Commerce: Av. Gouverneur Bovesse 117/b 7, 5100 Jambes; ☎ 081 32 05 50; fax 081 32 05 59; www.cciv.be.
Industry/Other Comments: The province of Namur was never heavily industrialised and was therefore shielded to some extent from the worst of the economic crises of the 1970s and 1980s. The work environment is more attractive than in neighbouring Hainaut and Liège. Tourism is a major industry here and half the surface area is devoted to agriculture; Namur is well-known for its food products. Since 1980 there has been a strong shift away from basic industries into the service sector which now employs 75% of the workforce. Another important feature of the local economy is the fact that 96% of firms employ less than 50 people; only six firms employ over 1,000 people. The largest growth has been in finance and insurance. A number of foreign firms have established themselves in Namur, including names such as Rank Xerox and Tandy (electronics), Siemens (software) and Gestetner (printing). Major activities: agriculture, food-processing, tourism, electronics, chemicals, computers, finance, glass, quarrying, furniture.

WEST FLANDERS

Major City: Bruges.
Major Newspaper: *De Gazet van Antwerpen* (West Flanders edition).
Chamber of Commerce: Ezelstraat 25, 8000 Brugge; ☎050 33 36 96; fax 050 34 22 97; emial kamer@ccibrugge.be.
Industry/Other Comments: West Flanders can boast the lowest unemployment in Belgium. In earlier times this was a mainly agricultural area without much heavy industry. Fishing and tourism are also important activities, although they have declined somewhat in the last few decades. The synthetic textiles and carpets industry, mainly close to the French border, is the major employer; the shortage of workers in this area is so acute that some companies are moving their production facilities into northern France. The other major industrial employers are the coach-assembly plants Mol and De Jonckheere in Roeselare. New industries are coming into the area, in particular chemicals and biotechnology. Major activities: tourism, agriculture, textiles, automotive, chemicals, food-processing, fishing.

DIRECTORY OF MAJOR EMPLOYERS

Accountancy

Arthur Andersen & Co: Montagne du Parc 4, 1000 Brussels; ☎02 545 31 00.
Arthur D. Little: Bvd de la Woluwe 2, 1150 Brussels; ☎02 761 72 00.
Ernst & Young SC: Av. Marcel Thiry 204, 1200 Brussels; ☎02 774 91 11.
Moores Rowland Europe: Av. Louise 109, 1050 Brussels; ☎02 541 07 50.
KPMG SC: Av. Bourget 40, 1030 Brussels; ☎02 708 43 00.
PriceWaterhouse Coopers SA: Av. de Cortenbergh 75, 1200 Brussels; ☎02 741 08 11.

Automotive

DAF Trucks: Luxemburgstraat 17, 9140 Temse; ☎03 710 14 11.
Ford Motor Company (Belgium): Groenenborgerlaan 16, 2610 Wilrijk; ☎03 821 20 00.

Jonckheere BVBA: Schoolstraat 50, 8800 Roeselare; ☎051 23 26 11.
Michelin SA: Quai de Willebroeck 33, 1210 Brussels; ☎02 274 42 11.
Pirelli Tyres SA: Rue de Namur 73D, 1000 Brussels; ☎02 514 00 27.
Van Hool NV: Bernard Van Hoolstraat 58, 2500 Koningshooikt; ☎03 420 20 20.
Volkswagen Bruxelles: Bvd de la 2ème Armée Britannique 201, 1190 Brussels; ☎02-348 21 11.
Volvo Cars NV: Kennedylaan 25 bus 273, 9000 Gent; ☎09 250 21 11.

Banks

Bank of America: Av. E. Van Nieuwenhuyse 6, 1160 Brussels; ☎02 663 21 00.
Byblos Bank Belgium: Rue Montoyer 10 b3, 1000 Brussels; ☎02 551 00 20.
Citibank Belgium: Bvd Général Jacques,

1050 Brussels; ☏ 02 626 51 11.
Deutsche Bank SA: Av. Marnix 17, 1000 Brussels; ☏ 02 551 99 40.
European Investment Corporation: Rue des Colonies 18 b7, 1000 Brussels; ☏ 02 511 02 06.
ING Bank: Rue de Ligne 1, 1000 Brussels; ☏ 02 229 87 11.
Lloyds Bank (Belgium) SA: Av. de Tervueren 2, 1040 Brussels; ☏ 02 739 58 11.
Merrill Lynch Pierce Fenner & Smith: Av. Louise 221, 1050 Brussels; ☏ 02 640 00 05.
Morgan Guaranty Trust: Bvd Roi Albert II, 1210 Brussels; ☏ 02 224 12 11.
Sumitomo Benelux: Av. des Arts 58 b6, 1000 Brussels; ☏ 02 509 78 11.

Chemical and Pharmaceutical Companies

3M NV: Hermeslaan 7, 1831 Diegem; ☏ 02 722 51 11.
Agfa-Gevaert NV: Septestraat 27, 2640 Mortsel; ☏ 03 444 21 11.
BASF Belgium: Av. Hamoir 14, 1180 Brussels; ☏ 02 373 21 11.
Belgian Shell: Cantersteen 47, 1000 Brussels; ☏ 02 508 91 11.
BOC Gases NV, Excelsiorlaan 41, 1930 Zaventem; ☏ 02 719 71 11.
BP Belgium NV: Nieuwe Weg 1, 2070 Zwijndrecht; ☏ 03 250 21 11.
Dow Corning Europe: Rue Gén. de Gaulle 62, 1310 La Hulpe; ☏ 02 655 21 11.
Du Pont de Nemours: Antoon Spinoystraat 6, 2800 Mechelen; ☏ 015 44 1411.
Exxon Chemical Belgium NV: Polderdijk 3, Antwerpen; 03 543 31 11.
Floridienne SA: Chaussée de Tervueren 198F, 1410 Waterloo; ☏ 02 353 00 28.
Glaxo Wellcome Belgium NV: Industrielaan 1, 9320 Aalst; ☏ 053 85 25 18.
Hoechst Celanese NV: Chaussée de Charleroi 111, 1060 Brussels; 02 542 08 11.
ICI Belgium NV/ICI Europe Headquarters: Everslaan 45, 3078 Everberg; ☏ 02 758 92 11.
Janssen Pharmaceutica NV: Turnhoutsewег 30, 2340 Beerse; ☏ 014 60 21 11.
Johnson Matthey SA: Av. de Bâle 8, 1140 Brussels; ☏ 02 729 07 11.
Monsanto Europe SA: Av. de Tervueren 270-272, 1150 Brussels; ☏ 02 776 41 11.
Norsk Hydro SA: Av. M. Thiry 83, 1200 Brussels; ☏ 02 773 52 11.
Phillips Petroleum SA: Brusselsesteenweg 355, 3090 Overijse; ☏ 02 689 12 11.
Smithkline Beecham Pharma SA: Rue du Tilleul 13, 1332 Genval; ☏ 02 656 21 11.
Socomer NV: Nieuwbrugstraat 73, 1830 Machelen; ☏ 02 255 76 11.
Solvay & Cie SA: Rue du Prince Albert 33, 1050 Brussels; ☏ 02 509 61 11.
UCB SA: Allée de la Recherche 60, 1070 Brussels; ☏ 02 559 99 99.

Computers

Barco NV: Kennedypark 35, 8500 Kortrijk; ☏ 056 26 22 62.
GE Information Services: Bvd du Souverain 165, 1160 Brussels; ☏ 02 679 01 00.
GEAC: Rue de Genève 10, 1140 Brussels; ☏ 02 727 78 11.
Getronics Belgium SA: Place Madou 1 b8, 1210 Brussels; 02 229 91 11.
Hewlett-Packard Belgium SA: Bvd de la Woluwe 100-102, 1200 Brussels; ☏ 02 778 31 11.
Honeywell SA: Av. de Schiphol 3, 1140 Brussels; ☏ 02 728 27 11.
IBM Belgium SA: Sq. Victoria Regina 1, 1210 Brussels; ☏ 02 225 33 33.
ICL Belgium: E. Mommaertslaan 16A, 1831 Diegem; ☏ 02 712 77 11.
Oracle Belgium: Vuurberg 80, 1831 Diegem; ☏ 02 719 12 11.
Rank Xerox SA: Wezembeek Straat 5, 1930 Zaventem; ☏ 02 761 60 00.

Siemens NV: Chaussée de Charleroi 116, 1060 Brussels; ☎ 02 536 21 11.
Unisys Belgium SA, Av. du Bourget 20, 1130 Brussels; ☎ 02 728 07 11.

EC Consultants

Adamson BSMG: Rue Wiertz 50, 1050 Brussels; ☎ 02 230 07 75.
Belmont SA: Bvd Charlemagne 42, 1000 Brussels; ☎ 02 280 15 95.
Berkley Associates SC: Rue de la Presse 4, 1000 Brussels; ☎ 02 219 04 98.
Cabinet Stewart: Rue d'Arlon 40, 1040 Brussels; ☎ 02 230 70 20.
European Communication Strategies: Ch. de la Hulpe 189, 1170 Watermael Boitsfort; ☎ 02 674 22 50.
GPC Market Access Europe SA: Rue d'Arlon 50, 1000 Brussels; ☎ 02 230 05 45.
Nicholas Phillips Associates SA: Rue Joseph II 36 bte 6, 1040 Brussels; ☎ 02 218 13 70.
Single Market Ventures SPRL: Av. J. Sobieski 15, 1020 Brussels; ☎ 02 479 12 00.

Food and Drink

Callebaut NV: Aalstersestraat 122, 9280 Lebbeke; ☎ 053 73 02 11.
Kraft-Jacobs-Suchard NV: Bilkensveld 1, 1500 Halle; ☎ 02 362 31 11.
Heinz Belgium NV: Guldensporenlei 88, Turnhout, Antwerpen; ☎ 014 40 23 11.
Nestlé Belgilux SA: Rue Birmingham 221 bte 7, 1070 Brussels; ☎ 02 529 52 52.
Spadel SA: Rue Colonel Bourg 103, 1030 Brussels; ☎ 02 702 38 11.
Schweppes Belgium SA: Rue du Cerf 127, 1332 Genval; ☎ 02 656 52 11.
United Distillers Belgium NV: Doornveld 1 bte 19, 1731 Zellik; ☎ 02 466 70 00.
Vandemoortele NV: Kuhlmannlaan 36, 9042 Sint-Kruis-Winkel; ☎ 09 344 88 21.
Warner Lambert Belgium: Oordegemstraat 87, 9520 Sint-Lievens-Houtem; ☎ 053 60 80 97.

Insurance

Boels & Begault Re SA: Rue Colonel Bourg 153, 1140 Brussels; ☎ 02 730 95 00.
Commercial Union Assurance (Belgium) Ltd: Av. Hermann Debroux 54, 1160 Brussels; ☎ 02 676 61 11.
General Accident Plc: Brusselstr. 59, 2018 Antwerp; ☎ 03 221 57 11.
Philip Knight & Co.: Korte Klarenstraat 9, 2000 Antwerp; ☎ 03 233 78 06.
Royal Sun Alliance NV: Bvd de Woluwe 64 bte 1; 1200 Brussels; ☎ 02 773 03 11.

Legal

Berwin Leighton: Av. de Tervueren 13B, 1040 Brussels; ☎ 02 732 31 44.
Cleary Gottlieb Steen & Hamilton: Rue de la Loi 23, 1040 Brussels; ☎ 02 287 20 00.
Clifford Chance: Av. Louise 65 bte 2, 1050 Brussels; ☎ 02 533 59 11.
Denton Hall: Rue du Marteau 15, 1040 Brussels; ☎ 02 223 06 21.
Eversheds: Av. de Cortenbergh 75, 1000 Brussels; ☎ 02 737 93 40..
Freshfields Deringer: Place du Champ de Mars 5, 1050 Brussels; ☎ 02 504 70 00.
Hammond Suddards: Av. Louise 250, 1050 Brussels; ☎ 02 627 76 76.
Herbert Smith SA: Rue Guimard 15, 1040 Brussels; ☎ 02 511 74 50.
Leboeuf Lamb Greene & MacRae: Av. des Arts 19H, 1000 Brussels; ☎ 02 227 09 00.
Linklaters & Alliance: Rue Brederode 13A, 1000 Brussels; ☎ 02 505 02 11.
Lovell White Durrant: Av. Louise 523 bte 24, 1050 Brussels; ☎ 02 647 06 60.

EMPLOYMENT

Norton Rose: Rue Montoyer 40, 1040 Brussels; ☎02 237 61 11.
Price and Partners: Av. Louise 106, 1050 Brussels; ☎02 629 69 11.
Slaughter & May: Av. de Cortenbergh 118, 1000 Brussels; ☎02 737 94 00.
Squire Sanders & Dempsey: Av. Louise 165 bte 15, 1050 Brussels; ☎02 627 11 11.
Stanbrook & Hooper: Rue du Taciturne 42, 1040 Brussels; ☎02 230 50 59.
Stephenson De Berti Barbé: Av. du Diamant 139, 1040 Brussels; ☎02 735 35 20.
Taylor Joynson Garrett: Rue Montoyer 14 b5, 1000 Brussels; ☎02 514 04 02.

Management Consultants

Berkley Associates SC: Rue de la Presse 11, 1000 Brussels; ☎02 219 04 98.
Deloitte & Touche Consultants: Berkenlaan 6, 183142 Diegem; ☎02 718 92 11.
Egon Zehnder International SA: Av. F.D. Roosevelt 14, 1050 Brussels; ☎02 648 00 83.
Hastings McKay Associates: Akkerstraat 26, 2970 Schilde; ☎03 385 15 21.
PA Consulting Group NV: Av. M. Thiry 79, 1020 Brussels; ☎02 761 79 00.
Towers Perrin: Gulledelle 94, 1170 Brussels; ☎02 775 84 11.

Property Management

Brixton Zaventem SA: Av. Louise 250, 1050 Brussels; ☎02 649 52 07.
DTZ Winssinger Tie Leung: Av. Louise 380, 1050 Brussels; ☎02 629 02 00.
Grimley SA: Bvd A. Reyers 110, 1030 Brussels; ☎02 737 70 70.
Healey & Baker: Av. des Arts 58, 1000 Brussels; ☎02 514 40 00.
Jones Lang Wootton SA: Rue Montoyer 10, 1000 Brussels; ☎02 550 25 25.
King & Co SA: Rue de la Loi 26, 1040 Brussels; ☎02 286 91 31.
Knight Frank SA: Rue du Luxembourg 14A, 1040 Brussels; ☎02 548 05 48.
Richard Ellis SA: Av. Louise 240, 1050 Brussels; ☎02 643 33 33.

Steel and Metallurgy

Union Minière: Rue du Marais 37, 1000 Brussels; ☎02 227 71 11.
ALZ NV: Genk-Zuid, Zone 6A, 3600 Genk; ☎089 30 19 00.
Bekaert NV: Bekaertstraat 2, 8550 Zwevegem; ☎056 76 61 11.
Boliden Cuivre et Zinc: Rue du Fourneau 43, 4030 Grivegnée; ☎04 349 98 98.
Cockerill Sambre SA: Chaussée de la Hulpe 187, 1170 Brussels; ☎02 679 92 11.
Corus Aluminium: A. Stocletlaan 87, 2570 Duffel; 015 32 29 15.
Fabrique de Fer: Rue Vital Francoisse 315, 6030 Charleroi; ☎071 47 28 70.
Sidmar NV: John Kennedylaan 51, 9042 Sint-Kruis-Winkel; ☎09 347 31 11.
Usines Gustave Boël: Rue des Rivaux 2, 7100 La Louvière; ☎064 27 27 11.

Textiles

Balta Industries: Wakkensteenweg 2, 8710 Sint-Baafs-Vijve; ☎056 62 22 11.
Bekaert NV: Industriezone De Bruwaan 2, 9700 Oudenaarde; 055 33 30 11.
De Poortere SA: Rue de la Royenne 45, 7700 Mouscron; ☎056 39 31 11.
Depraetere Industries: Heirbaan 73, 8570 Ingooigem; ☎056 77 95 10.
De Witte-Lietaer: Astridlaan 48, 8930 Lauwe; ☎056 43 02 11.
Lano NV: Zuidstraat 44, 8530 Harelbeke; ☎056 73 73 11.
Santens NV: Galgestraat 157, 9700 Oudenaarde; ☎055 31 22 91.
UCO Technical Fabrics: Weverslaan 15, 9160 Lokeren; ☎09 340 98 11.

Miscellaneous

Arjo Wiggins: Rue des Heures Claires 46, 1400 Nivelles; ☎067 28 12 11.
Alcatel Bell: Francis Wellesplein 1, 2018 Antwerpen; ☎03 240 40 11.
BP Belgium: Nieuwe Weg 1, 2070 Zwijndrecht; ☎03 250 21 11.
BT Worldwide Ltd: Excelsiorlaan 48-50, 1930 Zaventem; ☎02 718 22 11.
Castrol Belgium NV: Helmstraat 107, 2140 Antwerpen; ☎03 217 20 11.
Pilkington-Continental Autoglass SA: Heiveldekens 9/B, 2550 Kontich; ☎03 457 36 26.
Reuters Ltd: Rue de Trèves 61, 1040 Brussels; ☎02 287 66 11.
Shell SA: Cantersteen 47, 1000 Brussels; ☎02 508 91 11.

AMERICAN COMPANIES

THE AMERICAN CHAMBER of Commerce in Brussels publishes a yearly list of its 1,700 members and all American firms operating in Belgium at €123.95 (surface mail within Benelux); additional postage is payable outside Belgium. From: American Chamber of Commerce, Av. des Arts 50 bte 5, 1040 Brussels; ☎02 513 67 70; www.amcham.be. A detailed list of businesses in Belgium can be found in the Kompass Register Belgium/Luxembourg at public libraries in the UK.

Further information

The Belgian Employers' Federation issues a free list of member organisations. Obtainable from: Verbond van Belgische Ondernemingen-Fédération des Entreprises Belges, Ravensteinstraat 4, 1000 Brussels; ☎02 515 08 11; fax 02 515 09 99. The VBO-FEB website (www.vbo-feb.be) gives Internet addresses of member organisations.

Starting a Business

WITH THE INAUGURATION of the Single Market in 1993, Europeans from the EU are more aware than ever that starting a business in another Community country can be a rewarding experience both professionally and financially for those who have the skills and energy. In the case of Belgium, support in the form of advice and business loans is readily available. Belgium does not have the reputation of being an entrepreneurial society; the average Belgian is less likely to start a business than almost anyone else in Europe, because of the perception that there is simply too much red tape to be dealt with, or a general reluctance to take risks. While there is plenty of assistance on offer, one should be aware of the particular problems that entrepreneurs face in this country, in particular the labour laws, which are heavily weighted towards the employee. If you have properly understood your market and have a product or service that customers want then there is every likelihood that you will succeed. Managerial ability of some kind or another is also crucial; you may not even be allowed to start your business unless you can show evidence that you can administer a business properly.

Many Britons who move to Belgium start out by working for someone else and then use the knowledge they have gained to become independent. Those who plan to run their own business there will most probably already have a successful business or professional career in the UK and hope to take advantage of greater access to the European market or of a perceived gap in the market in Belgium itself. In certain professions, the target market is other expatriates or foreign companies in Belgium. Having English as one's first language then gives one an advantage over Belgian competitors. Once you have been through the whole process of settling down yourself, your knowledge of local conditions becomes a major selling point.

The prospective entrepreneur in Belgium should be aware of the major differences between Belgium and its neighbours, the Netherlands and France. The Belgians are more cautious about new business ideas than the French and Dutch and you may feel that you are up against excessive red tape (known as *chasse-papier* in French and *rompslomp* in Dutch). As long as you have a well worked-out plan, however, and know whom to address your questions to, there should not be any insurmountable problems. As with any bureaucracy, a great deal of time can be wasted in talking to the wrong people. In a country with five levels of government this problem is particularly acute. There are British-trained lawyers and accountants on hand to ease the process of settling in.

PROCEDURES INVOLVED IN STARTING A NEW BUSINESS

ONE QUESTION which arises is whether one should take over an existing business or start entirely from scratch. Although it could be argued that taking over an existing business avoids a great deal of bureaucracy, the other side of the coin is that it is difficult to know the exact financial state of the package that one is acquiring. If the package includes employing staff, then Belgium's strict labour laws can make a shake-up or dismissal of staff very costly.

Preparation from Scratch

Exhaustive research is essential before launching oneself into the actual process of setting up a business in Belgium. Information about Belgium is easy enough to obtain from the regional and federal authorities. The Belgian Embassy in the USA maintains a website with a general overview on how to set up a company at www.cais.com/usa/business.

Because of Belgium's size and lack of highly developed institutions there are definite gaps in the market to be exploited. Lawyers, chartered accountants and property companies from the UK are moving into Belgium in considerable numbers because there is a demand for their services which is not being filled by their Belgian counterparts.

Preparation is not only about spotting a gap in the market. You also need to know how you would relate to the Belgians on a daily basis. The best way to find out is to spend as much time in Belgium as possible, building up a network of advisers and allies who can support you when you finally take the plunge. Many successful newcomers say that, initially, the advice of the British Chamber of Commerce in Brussels and the Trade Section of the British Consulate has been invaluable.

Other sources of information in Belgium are the numerous Euro-Info centres, usually at the same address as the Chambers of Commerce (see Regional Guide, *Employment* chapter), the regional and provincial investment bodies and the Ministry of Economics library. The National Institute of Statistics has a vast amount of information on the BLEU (Belgian-Luxembourg Economic Union). The documentation centres of the Banque Générale and Banque Bruxelles Lambert in Brussels keep data bases on foreign and Belgian companies which can be consulted by prior appointment.

The Brussels Chamber of Commerce will, for a small fee, go through your business plan with you and explain the procedures for setting up a company. The national Federation of Small & Medium Industries of Belgium (Fédération des PME's/Verbond van KMO's) can also help in this regard.

For those who are already in Brussels there is Focus, a self-help group originally set up for the spouses of expatriates who want to develop their careers or start a business. Membership is open to both male and female, single and married people. Members help each other by exchanging their professional expertise. Focus runs seminars from time to time which deal with starting up a business. Contact Focus, Rue Lesbroussart 23, 1050 Brussels; ☎02 646 65 30; e-mail focus@focusbelgium.org; www.focusbelgium.org.

Useful Addresses

American Chamber of Commerce in Belgium: Av. des Arts 50 bte 5, 1040 Brussels; ☎02 513 67 70; fax 513 35 90; www.amcham.be.

Banque Bruxelles Lambert Documentation Centre: Av. Marnix 24, 1050 Brussels; ☎02 547 39 93.

Belgian-American Chamber of Commerce: 575 Madison Avenue, 24th floor, New York, NY 10022; ☎212-319 7080; www.belcham.org.

Belgo-Luxembourg Chamber of Commerce in Great Britain: Berkeley House, 73 Upper Richmond Rd, Putney, London SW15 2SZ; ☎020-8877 3025; fax 020-8877 3961; www.blcc.co.uk.

British Chamber of Commerce of Belgium and Luxembourg: Rue d'Egmont 15, 1050 Brussels; ☎02 540 90 30; www.britcham.be.

Brussels Chamber of Commerce: Av. Louise 500, 1050 Bruxelles; ☎02 648 50 02; www.ccibrussels.be.

Commercial Section – British Embassy: Rue d'Arlon 85, 1040 Brussels; ☎02 287 62 11.

Commercial Section – Embassy of the United States in Belgium: Bvd du Régent 27, 1000 Brussels; ☎02 508 21 11.

Confederation of British Industry: Rue Joseph II 40, 1000 Brussels; ☎02 231 04 65.

Direction Générale des Etudes et de la Documentation: Ministry of Economic Affairs, Rue de l'Industrie 6, 1040 Brussels; ☎02 506 62 11.

Fédération des PME's: Rue de Stalle 90, 1180 Brussels; ☎02 376 85 57.

Fortis Banque Business Information Services: Montagne du Parc 3, 1000 Brussels; ☎02 565 11 11.

Institut National de Statistique/Nationaal Instituut voor de Statistiek: Rue de Louvain 44, 1000 Brussels; ☎02 548 62 11.

Vlaams Instituut voor het Zelfstandig Ondernemen (Flemish Institute for Independent Entrepreneurs): Kanselarijstraat 19, 1000 Brussel; ☎02 227 63 93; fax 02 217 46 12; e-mail info@vizo.be; www.vizo.be, www.kmoloket.be.

Accountants

Anyone planning to set up a business in Belgium would be well advised to talk to a British accountancy firm with a branch in Belgium. Ernst & Young publish a range of books on Belgium, including *Doing Business in Belgium* (2001). This can be downloaded from the Internet on: www.ey.com. A list of international accountants can be found in the section *Major Employers*. Further names of accountants can be found in the Directory of the British Chamber of Commerce in Brussels.

CHOOSING AN AREA

THE AREA YOU DECIDE to live and work in will depend to a large degree on what kind of business you want to carry out. If other expatriates or foreign companies are your intended market, then you are almost inevitably going to work in Brussels or Antwerp. Incentives to foreign businesses do not vary greatly throughout Belgium. There are certain special employment or development zones ('T-zones') which offer additional incentives if you are thinking of employing Belgian workers. Apart from this it is generally true to say that Dutch-speaking Flanders is more prosperous than French-speaking Wallonia, although unemployment blackspots are not restricted to the latter by any means. Land is in short supply in Flanders, apart from Limburg; Wallonia has more space. Another important consideration is language; most English-speakers find it takes a long time to gain a satisfactory level of French, while in Flanders it seems that English is far more widely used.

Useful Publications

Books and Information Packs
Belgium A Central Location in Europe: 1996. From the Ministry of Economic Affairs, Sq. De Meeûs 23, 1040 Brussels; ☎ 02 506 54 14.
Legal Guide to Establishing a Business in Flanders; Setting Up a Company in Flanders; Tax System and Investment Incentives, Flanders Multimedia Valley, A Dynamic Past – A Dynamic Future: Flanders Automotive Valley etc.: Free from Flanders Foreign Investment Office (FFIO), Leuvenseplein 4, 1000 Brussels; ☎ 02 507 38 52; fax 507 38 51; e-mail flanders@ffio.be; www.ffio.be.

Periodicals
AmCham: Monthly magazine from the American Chamber of Commerce. Free to members.
BCC Newsletter: Monthly newsletter of the British Chamber of Commerce. Can be downloaded from the website: www.britcham.be.
Entreprendre: (French). Brussels Chamber of Commerce monthly. Free of charge. Dutch version called *Dynamiek*.
Le Marché/De Markt: Weekly magazine for managers.
Trends-Tendances: (French). Weekly business magazine. Dutch version *Trends*.

RAISING FINANCE

THOSE CONTEMPLATING starting a business in Belgium should be aware that UK banks will not be able to provide start-up loans where the prospective proprietor intends to be resident abroad. Belgian credit institutions are willing to finance foreign investment to a considerable extent. Smaller entrepreneurs will need to rely on their own resources in the beginning, but once they are established in Belgium the whole range of credit facilities will be open to them. The obvious way to raise money is by selling one's UK home. If this proves insufficient it should be possible to raise a mortgage on a Belgian property. Mortgages are available in Belgium on up to 125% of the value of the property.

An unemployed person in Belgium can apply for a loan of up to €17,350 (£10,410) known as a *prêt subordonné chômeur* in French, with only interest payable for the first five years, in order to start up a new business. The borrower must be able to put up the equivalent of 50% of the loan, which is payed back over 10 to 20 years. Such a loan is in principle available to any EU national who is established in Belgium if they can convince the authorities that their business is likely to succeed.

As an alternative it is well worth looking at regional investment schemes in Belgium.

INVESTMENT INCENTIVES

GENEROUS INCENTIVES and subsidies are available to foreign investors in Belgium. The amount of investment incentives depends very much on the size of the company, its location, the nature of its activities, and its proposed sources of finance. For example, within EU-recognised development regions there are eight so-called Tax-free zones (T-zones) where a high-technology enterprise is exempt from income tax and many other taxes for 10 years if it employs between 10 and 200 workers within two years of start-up. T-zones are to be found in the Kempen (the eastern part of the province of Antwerp), the Westhoek (in the south of West Flanders) and in the provinces of Liège, Namur and Hainaut (the industrialised parts of Wallonia).

Capital grants and/or interest rebates are available up to a maximum of 18% of investment in most of Belgium, and up to 21% in development regions. As well as the regions mentioned in the previous paragraph, Limburg in Flanders, and parts of the province of Luxembourg in Wallonia, are also official EU development regions. The regional government will pay up to half the interest on a loan from a Belgian credit institution for up to five years. Where the enterprise is self-financing, capital grants will be paid out at six-monthly intervals over a five-year period. These and other incentives are usually dependent on a certain number of new jobs being created over a specified period of time. The government will not subsidise any enterprise whose production processes involve the release of hazardous substances and so on into the environment.

SMALL AND MEDIUM ENTERPRISES (SMES)

BELGIUM IS VERY much a land of SMEs, known as KMOs (*Kleine en Middelgrote Ondernemingen*) in Dutch, and PMEs (*Petites et Moyennes Entreprises*) in French. A business is considered to be an SME for bookkeeping purposes if it employs fewer than 50 workers and has a turnover of less than €5 million per year. The definition of an SME varies considerably in different sectors of the economy and between the three regions. Only 2% of industrial and 0.5% of non-industrial enterprises employ more than 50 workers; over half of Belgian businesses are one-person operations.

Precise details of support offered to SMEs are available in the publications given below. It should be noted that support for small businesses is now the responsibility of the regional governments and not of the central government.

Useful Publications

Comment s'installer à son compte?: Obtainable from Ministère des classes Moyennes et de l'Agriculture, WTC III, Bvd Simon Bolivar 30, 1000 Brussels; www.cmlag.fgov.be.

Zich Vestigen als Zelfstandige etc. A range of publications available in French and Dutch from: Ministère de l'Agriculture et des Classes Moyennes, Tour Sablon, Rue J. Steven 7, 1000 Brussels; www.cmlag.fgov.be.

Economische Expansiewet 4 Augustus 1978. Richtlijnen VL7.2: Kleine Ondernemingen: (Dutch). From: Ministerie van de Vlaamse Gemeenschap, Administratie Economie, Dienst Economische Expansie Middenstand, Markiesstraat 1, 1000 Brussel; ☎02 507 31 11; www.vlaanderen.be.

REGIONAL INVESTMENT OFFICES

AS WELL AS THE three regional investment offices given below, there are provincial investment offices, whose addresses can be obtained from Chambers of Commerce or Euro Info Centres. Investment offices are usually a good source of documentation.

Economic, Foreign Trade and Investment Office: Rue du Champs de Mars 25, 1050 Brussels; ☎02 513 97 00.

Flanders Investment Office: Markiesstraat 1, 1000 Brussels, 02 507 38 52; www.ffio.be.

Office for Foreign Investors: Av. Bourgmestre Jean Materne 115-117, 5100 Jambes; ☎081 33 28 50; www.ofisa.be.

RELOCATION AGENCIES AND BUSINESS SERVICES

NEWCOMERS WHO ARE deterred by the practical difficulties involved in setting up a new business can turn to a business relocation agency for assistance. These are always separate from relocation offices for individuals moving to Belgium. Relocation agencies are particularly useful in helping to find office space and equipment at a reasonable price. Other services, such as lawyers, accountants, translators and interpreters can be found in the Directory of the British Chamber of Commerce and the Yellow Pages.

Useful Addresses

Analysts International SPRL: Abstraat 39, 3090 Overijse; ☎02 687 27 28. Consultants in multinational/Belgian financial management accounting. Provide temporary financial management, accounting and word processing staff.

Hastings McKay Associates: Akkerstraat 26, 2970 Schilde; ☎03

> **SETTLER** Settler International Belgium
> **International** your relocation partner
>
> We combine the experience and professionalism of a world-wide operating assistance group with the flexibility and personalized service of a local Relocation Company. Our services include: housing, schooling, administration, legal matters, cultural integration, car imports, 24 hour help line outsourcing.Whatever need you may have, Settler International will find solutions to guarantee a smooth landing and immediate start-up.
>
> Settler International Belgium-Triomflaan, 172, Bld du Triomphe-1160-Brussels
> Phone: 02/533.78.11 Fax: 02/533.77.69 E-mail: info@settler.be www.settler.be

385 15 21; fax 03 383 27 46; e-mail hastings@skynet.be; http://sites.netscape.net/hastingsmckay. Company reorganisation; staff sourcing; management consultancy.

Jordans International: 20-22 Bedford Row, London WC1R 4JS; ☎020-7400 3333; fax 020-7400 3366; www.jordans.co.uk and www.jordans-international.com. Specialises in company formation in the EU, and offshore company formation. Conducts searches on existing companies in Belgium.

Settler International Belgium bvba/sprl: Triomflaan, 172 Boulevard du Triomphe, 1160 Brussels, Belgium: tel 02 533 78 11; fax 02 533 77 69; e-mail : info@settler.be; www.settler.be. The market leader in global reloca-

tion; through its carefully selected and specially-trained network of companies and agents Settler services transferees worldwide. Settler has an experienced and committed staff, a worldwide reputation and commitment to quality and ethics, 12 years of experience in relocation, superior service capability in over 80 countries, a prestigious global database and 800 consultants worldwide, many of whom are expats themselves. Part of the Generali and Europ Assistance group.

Wood Appleton Oliver & Co: Av. Louise 251, 1050 Brussels; ☎02 639 45 30. Tax, accounting and general financial advice for companies and individuals in Belgium.

BUSINESS STRUCTURES

IN ORDER TO OPERATE commercially in Belgium, an individual or company must have a recognised Belgian business structure. It is quite possible to start one's business as a self-employed person and then change to one of the forms of company given below. The procedures involved in changing over from self-employed to limited company status are explained in great detail in the publications listed above.

Most foreigners choose a limited liability company: either an SA/NV (*Société Anonyme/Naamloze Vennootschap*) or the simpler SPRL/BVBA (*Société Privée à Responsabilité Limitée/Besloten Vennootschap met Beperkte Aansprakelijkheid*).

Partnerships and co-operatives are also sometimes used by foreigners.
The formalities of setting up a company are usually entrusted to a fiscal or legal adviser. The British Chamber of Commerce in Brussels will be happy to suggest suitable advisers.
The different business entities and the steps required to form them are as follows:

SA/NV: An SA/NV must have at least two shareholders, and three directors. The subscribed capital must be seen to be sufficient for the planned activity and cannot be less than €61,973.38. At least one quarter of subscribed capital, with a minimum of €61,973.38, must be paid into a bank in Belgium at the time of incorporation. The statutes of the company are drawn up by a notary and signed in his/her presence. The statutes are then filed with the Commercial Court (*Greffe du Tribunal de Commerce/Griffie van de Handelsrechtbank*) and an application made to be put on the Register of Commerce (*Registre de Commerce/Handelsregister*). Extracts of the statutes will appear in the Belgian Official Gazette (*Moniteur Belge/Belgisch Staatsblad*). If the business involves the sale of goods or services under the VAT Code, then the company must obtain a VAT number from the VAT administration. The fee for setting up an SA/NV with the minimum capital requirement of is likely to come to €1,500, including capital duty at 0.5%, notarial fees, stamp duty and publication costs.
The SA is the favoured form for large enterprises which need to raise capital.

SPRL: The SPRL is a private limited liability company and is the preferred form for family enterprises. There are at least two shareholders, and one director. The running of the company is entrusted to one or more managers (*gérants/zaakvoerders*), who need not be shareholders. The subscribed capital requirement is €18,592. At least 20% of the subscribed capital, with a minimum of €6,197, must be paid up at the time of incorporation. There is also a form of SPRL with only one shareholder – an SPRLU/EBVBA (*SPRL Unipersonelle/Eenpersoons BVBA*).
The formalities for incorporating an SPRL are similar to those for an SA, but the fees can be as little as €800. Publication requirements for balance sheets and articles of incorporation are not as strict as for an SA.

SCRL/CVBA: This is a co-operative known as a *Société Coopérative à Responsabilité Limité/Cooperatieve Vennootschap met Beperkte Aansprakelijkheid* and is favoured by groups of professionals, such as lawyers, accountants, and so on, who want a loose business association. The minimum capital requirement is €18,592, of which €6,197 must be lodged in a bank.

Partnerships: The only type of limited partnership much used by foreigners is the SCA/CVA (*Société en Commandité par Actions/Commanditaire Vennootschap op Aandelen*), a company with share capital, where liability is limited to the amount of shares subscribed.

Another business entity one frequently comes across is the ASBL/VZW (*Association Sans But Lucratif/Vereniging Zonder Winstoogmerk*), a non-profit making association.
It is also possible to set up a branch (*succursale/bijhuis*) of an existing foreign company. The main requirement for this is the publication of the articles of

association of the parent company in the state gazette. The company then operates under the same name as in its home country. Total costs for translation of documents, registration etc. are likely to come to at least €1,500.

All companies must prepare accounts and file them with the Commercial Court within 30 days of their approval by the shareholders. An audit must be carried out by a statutory auditor (*réviseur d'entreprises/bedrijfsrevisor*) if two of three conditions apply: the turnover exceeds €4,215,000, the balance sheet exceeds €2,107,500 or there are more than 50 employees. An auditor can be chosen from the members of the Institute of Auditors (*Institut des Réviseurs d'Entreprises/Instituut der Bedrijfsrevisoren*). Where an auditor is not required, the services of a member of the Institute of Accountants (*Institut des Experts-Comptables/Instituut der Accountants*) may be used.

IDEAS FOR NEW BUSINESSES

ENGLISH-SPEAKING EXPATRIATES in Belgium are largely concentrated in cities such as Brussels, Antwerp, Ghent and Mons, and, to some extent, on the coast. It is quite feasible to start up a bar, restaurant or shop which relies on expatriate customers. At the same time one must be aware of the high expectations of Belgian consumers with respect to quality, and think about how one can compete with local enterprises. For this reason newcomers may feel happier about taking over an established and profitable business, through which new products can be introduced on a trial-run basis. Small businesses for sale are frequently advertised in the Belgian press.

Chartered Accountants

Belgian accountants do not have the same high profile or prestige as British chartered accountants. Their services are in many cases limited to checking the company books at the end of the year rather than giving advice on financial management. There is therefore a need for cost and management accountants who have some knowledge of business in other EU countries to advise foreign companies and expatriates setting up businesses in Belgium.

Estate Agents

At the moment a number of British commercial property agents have established themselves in Belgium, but the residential property market is still wide open to newcomers. While Belgian estate agents are not an endangered species, it should be noted that anyone can become an estate agent. The profession is more or less unregulated and there is no special training required. British estate agents are better trained than their Belgian counterparts and could sell not only to expatriates but also to Belgians.

Food

Belgium is rightly famous for its food, and standards are high even in fast food restaurants. While Belgian food is very good, it tends to be high in cholesterol. Interest in health foods is growing and there are opportunities in setting up restaurants or retail outlets for this kind of product. Health food is usually overpriced in Belgium, and there is certainly scope for more efficient operators in this field.

Graphic and Industrial Design

These are areas where Belgium has traditionally lagged behind its neighbours, partly because of a lack of specialised training. Good designers can make their mark here without having to deal with the same level of competition as in Britain.

Publishing

There are considerable opportunities for journalists and writers who can write reports, advertising copy, in-house newsletters and so on for multinationals and local companies. With the use of DTP (Desk-Top Publishing) equipment, it is possible for individuals to design publicity materials and even entire books to a high standard. If you have skills in designing Web pages for the Internet these could be turned into a viable way of making a living. Internet use is developing quickly, and graphic design skills are always in demand.

Other

Other foreign professionals who have found a demand for their services include lawyers, public relations consultants, architects and landscape gardeners.

Exporters

The Trade Partners UK Information Centre may be worth a visit; the Centre has useful information on Belgium, including trade and telephone directories. The Centre's address is Kingsgate House, 66-74 Victoria Street, London SW1E 6SW. It is open from 09.00 to 20.00 Monday to Thursday (last admission 19.30) and 09.00 to 17.30 on Fridays (last admission 17.00). Further information on the Centre's resources is available on the Trade Partners UK website at www.tradepartners.gov.uk, by telephone on 020-7215 5444/5; fax 020-7215 4231 or by e-mail; use the e-mail option on the website. The website also has a useful report on Belgium.

RUNNING A BUSINESS

Employing Staff

EMPLOYER AND EMPLOYEE relations in Belgium are controlled by a mass of social and labour legislation, parts of which vary according to the type of industry involved and the status of the employee. The main categories of staff are higher management (*direction/directie*), low/middle management (*cadres/kaderleden*), white-collar staff (*employés/bedienden*) and workmen/women (*ouvriers/arbeiders*). The level of social security payments, holiday allowance, notice of dismissal and so on will vary depending on the category of worker.

Over the years Belgian labour legislation has aimed to increase job security for workers, but employers still have the absolute right to dismiss workers if they respect the terms of notice. Where a worker is dismissed without good reason, the employer can be made to pay an indemnity by a labour court equivalent to at least six months' salary, or the amount of salary that the worker would have earned during the statutory period of notice. There is no such thing as obligatory reinstatement in Belgium.

Belgian employment law is clearly explained in English in *Labour Law in Belgium*, by Roger Blanpain (Kluwer Law Publishers, 1996).

Trade Unions

Apart from the three major trade union federations (see Chapter Six, *Employment*) which are based on the three main political parties, there are trade unions in specific work sectors almost all of which belong to one of the three federations. Although trade unions have considerable power in Belgium, strikes are not very frequent, because of the well-established procedures for consultation between management and workers. Companies which employ more than 100 workers must institute a company council (*conseil d'entreprise/ondernemingsraad*), where representatives of employers and employees meet once a month to discuss work practices and other matters. Workers have the right to detailed information about the company's affairs and can appoint their own accountant to look at the books. There is no requirement for workers to be represented on the board of directors.

Employers' Organisations

The main employers' organisation is the Fédération des Entreprises Belges (FEB)/Verbond van Belgische Ondernemingen (VBO), Rue Ravenstein 4, 1000 Brussels; ☎ 02 515 08 11; 515 09 99; www.vbo-feb.be. There are also three regional federations of employers whose addresses are given below.

Union des Entreprises de Bruxelles/Verbond van Ondernemingen te Brussel: Rue Botanique 75, 1210 Brussels; ☎ 02 219 32 23.
Union Wallonne des Entreprises: Chemin du Stocquoy 1, 1300 Wavre; ☎ 010 45 11 41.
Vlaams Economisch Verbond: Brouwersvliet 5 b4, 2000 Antwerpen; ☎ 03 231 16 60.

Categories of Underemployment. There is no shortage of well-trained workers in Belgium, many of whom speak English. Unemployment tends to be concentrated in the declining industrial regions of Flanders and Wallonia, so that there are considerable numbers of former miners, metal-workers, textile-workers and so on. One area where workers are hard to find is in computer programming. It is also hard to find workers who have completely mastered several languages. Part-time work is not as popular as it is in Britain, at around the EU average of 11% of employment.

Employee Training

Employers pay 0.04% of gross salary towards 'educational leave' (*congé education payé*), as part of their social security contributions. Employees can take up to 120 hours leave a year for professional training, or 80 hours for general education, during working hours. The employer pays their salary up to €1,908 a month during the period of leave, which is then reimbursed to the employer by the employment ministry. Employers have the right to stop too many employees taking educational leave at the same time.

Wages and Salaries

For each Belgian industry there is a national minimum wage and salary scale. Further details of pay levels and bonuses are given in Chapter Six, *Employment*.

Social Security

Employers and employees are obliged to pay social security contributions, which cover health insurance, unemployment benefit, pensions, family allowances, holidays, industrial accidents, and so on, even when there is only one employee. Fines for non-compliance are severe; in principle no one can do any kind of work for you (even unpaid) without being treated as an employee. The employer's contribution in the case of white-collar workers stands at between 33.33% and 35.11% of gross salary, and in the case of manual workers at 39.13% to 40.91%, depending on the size of the company. The employee's contribution is always 13.07% of gross salary. The precise amounts of social security payments and taxes are normally computed on the employer's behalf by the local social security institution, the *Secretariat Social* or *Sociaal Secretariat*. A self-employed person pays about 22% of their gross income in social security contributions and receives smaller benefits than employees. In the case of a limited company such as an SPRL, social security contributions are only payable on the director's salary, not on the company's income. It is therefore highly advantageous to form an SPRL if you become successful as a self-employed person.

Paid Holidays

The subject of holidays is dealt with in the Aspects of Employment section of Chapter Six, *Employment*.

Taxation

Belgians and foreigners alike find Belgian taxation laws difficult to understand. For this reason companies have their tax returns prepared by tax accountants (*experts-comptable*). The status of the self-employed and small companies has recently become somewhat similar in that taxes have to be paid in advance based on an estimate of projected income in both cases. Above a certain income level trading as an SPRL becomes fiscally advantageous. However, many self-employed Belgians prefer to work in the black economy or to do several jobs at once, thus making the formation of a company irrelevant.

The starting point for determining corporation tax is gross income reported in the financial statements of the company. The reporting period may be either a financial year, or a fiscal year ending any day except 31 December.

Impôt des sociétés/Vennootschapsbelasting: Corporate income tax. Where income exceeds €322,261.58 the total income is taxed at 39%. Below this threshold income may be taxed at rates varying between 28% and 41%, subject to certain conditions. Corporate taxes are payable in advance on April 10, July 10, October 10 and December 20. If payment is not made in advance, a 24% surcharge is added to the tax bill at the end of the year. Self-employed people and companies frequently borrow money from their banks in order to make these advance payments (*versements anticipés/voorafbetalingen*). The interest on these loans is tax-deductible.

Précompte immobilier/Onroerende voorheffing: Real estate tax. The basic rate of this tax is 1.25% of a hypothetical rental value, the *revenu cadastral/kadastraal inkomen*, but the effective rate is 18% to 40% after municipal surcharges.

Précompte mobilier/Roerende voorheffing: Withholding tax. Levied on dividends at 15% or 25% and interests at 15%. Will change to 20% with EU tax harmonisation in 2006.

Plus values/Meerwaarde: Capital gains. These are in many cases exempt from taxation, in particular where they are reinvested in Belgium. Otherwise they are taxed at half the standard corporation tax rate, i.e. 19.5%.

TVA/BTW: VAT is charged at four different rates in Belgium. The standard rate is now 21%. For businesses, each month's VAT is payable on the 15th of the following month, and is calculated on the basis of one-third of the previous quarter's payment. Adjustments are made every quarter in case of under- or over-payment. VAT is administered by the *TVA Enregistrement et Domaines/BTW Registratie en Domeinen*, Tour des Finances, Bvd du Jardin Botanique 50 bte 37, 1010 Brussels; ☎ 02 210 26 11.

Computer tax: In 1996 the central Brussels commune imposed an annual tax of €25 on every office computer, a move which outraged the business community, and which generates about €62 million per year.

The Netherlands

SECTION I

LIVING IN THE NETHERLANDS

GENERAL INTRODUCTION

RESIDENCE AND ENTRY REGULATIONS

SETTING UP HOME

DAILY LIFE

RETIREMENT

GENERAL INTRODUCTION

CHAPTER SUMMARY

- The Netherlands welcomes English speakers: there are currently nearly 40,000 British and 14,000 Americans living there.
- English is widely understood and used in business and daily life.
- There is a high standard of living, but there are also high levels of taxation.
- The Netherlands has a highly modern technical economy and welcomes foreigners with skills who can make a contribution to it.
- The Dutch economy is one of the most stable in the world, with low inflation and healthy trade surpluses.
- Despite their informality the Dutch are hard-working and expect the same of others.
- **Politics.** The system of government is similar to the British one, with an upper and lower house.
  - Most Dutch governments since the war have been coalitions; the current ruling 'purple coalition' has the socialist Wim Kok as prime minister.
- **Geography.** The Netherlands is approximately half the size of Scotland, or twice the size of New Jersey.
  - With a population of 15,800,000 the Netherlands has the highest population density in the world.
  - The climate is temperate but unsettled, with an average of only 23 cloud-free days per year.

DESTINATION THE NETHERLANDS

NOW THAT THE BARRIERS to free movement of people and goods have fallen in the EU, more and more British and Irish citizens are looking to the Continent for professional and business opportunities, in the knowledge that success is just as likely, or even more likely, abroad as it is in their own countries. The attraction of the Netherlands for English-speakers is borne out by the population statistics: in 2001 there were some 39,000 British and nearly 13,500 US citizens living there. Professional and entrepreneurial skills are greatly respected and highly rewarded by the Dutch; there has in the past been something of a brain drain in the direction of the Netherlands from other European countries. Because of the close cultural and linguistic links with the English-speaking world (most Dutch people born after 1945 speak good English), adjusting to life in the Netherlands could not be easier.

Many outsiders have a somewhat romantic image of the Netherlands as a land of windmills and tulips, whose inhabitants wear clogs and make cheese when they are not fighting off the encroaching North Sea. This kind of image is useful in promoting tourism but does not give much insight into the country. A closer look at the Netherlands reveals a highly organised, ultra-modern industrialised society, which has been able to overcome its internal divisions in the pursuit of physical survival and a high standard of living. Anyone who spends more than a short holiday in the Netherlands will also become aware of the peculiar combination of deep-seated conservatism and somewhat superficial liberalism which characterises the people.

The main forces that have moulded the Dutch character are undoubtedly the immense national effort needed to prevent a large part of the country from being flooded by the North Sea, and the desire for freedom of thought and religion, which almost led to the annihilation of the country by the Spanish in the 16th century. The Dutch have had to be tough and self-disciplined in order to create a prosperous country out of a very unpromising physical environment. Without many natural resources of their own, they were obliged to become traders and middlemen, thus accounting for their highly-developed commercial sense.

The Dutch are self-confident people, and they expect others to be self-confident as well. They do not like to waste time when there is work to be done and they expect to be able to rely on their fellow workers. The Protestant work ethic rules everyone, be they Calvinists, Catholics or atheists. The influence of Protestantism is also apparent in an almost religious reverence for reason and tolerance. The true religion of the Dutch might be better characterised as Utilitarianism, which accounts for the common bond with the British. There is also a distinct similarity with the USA, without the inequalities and more extreme social problems.

The Netherlands: Provinces, Main Towns and Water Barriers

Noordzee

GRONINGEN
- Eemshaven
- Delfzijl
- Groningen

FRIESLAND
- Waddenzee
- Leeuwarden
- Harlingen
- Sneek
- Drachten
- Heerenveen

DRENTHE
- Stadskanaal
- Assen
- Emmen
- Hoogeveen
- Coevorden

- Den Helder
- IJsselmeer
- Emmeloord
- Steenwijk
- Meppel

NOORD-HOLLAND
- Alkmaar
- Enkhuizen
- Hoorn
- Zaanstad
- Haarlem
- Amstelveen
- Amsterdam
- Bussum
- Hilversum

FLEVOLAND
- Kampen
- Lelystad
- Almere
- Harderwijk
- Nijkerk

OVERIJSSEL
- Zwolle
- Nijverdal
- Almelo
- Deventer
- Hengelo
- Apeldoorn
- Enschede

ZUID-HOLLAND
- Leiden
- Den Haag
- Utrecht
- Amersfoort
- Zeist
- Gouda
- Delft
- Rotterdam
- Nieuwegein
- Schiedam
- Europoort
- Gorinchem
- Culemborg
- Dordrecht
- Tiel

GELDERLAND
- Zutphen
- Rijn
- Arnhem
- Wageningen
- Doetinchem
- Winterswijk
- Waal
- Nijmegen
- Maas

ZEELAND
- Veerse Gat
- Oosterschelde
- Middelburg
- Vlissingen
- Bergen op Zoom
- Terneuzen
- Roosendaal

NOORD-BRABANT
- Waalwijk
- Breda
- 's-Hertogenbosch
- Tilburg
- Veghel
- Helmond
- Eindhoven
- Veldhoven
- Geldrop
- Valkenswaard

LIMBURG
- Venlo
- Weert
- Maastricht
- Kerkrade

GERMANY

BELGIUM

Legend:
- International borders
- Provincial boundaries
- Randstad conurbation
- Areas flooded in February 1953
- ZEELAND Province
- Haarlem Provincial capitals
- Dam
- Storm surge barrier
- Secondary dike

0 — 50 Miles
0 — 50 Kms

PROS AND CONS OF MOVING TO THE NETHERLANDS

FOR SEVERAL HUNDRED years the Dutch have enjoyed one of Europe's highest standards of living, thanks to their commercial abilities and dedication to hard work. The Netherlands has traditionally welcomed immigrants with useful skills, as well as absorbing large numbers of citizens from its former colonies. Nevertheless, only 5% of its population hold foreign passports, a much smaller proportion than in neighbouring Belgium and Germany. The Dutch authorities do not encourage asylum-seekers or economic refugees, which is understandable given that the Netherlands is already overpopulated and that the population is growing faster than in neighbouring countries.

During the 1960s and 1970s, the Netherlands acquired the reputation of being a haven for anarchists and hippies, and it still has a lively counterculture. Unfortunately, the liberalisation of the 1960s brought a serious drugs and vice problem in its wake, which in turn has given Amsterdam one of the highest crime-rates in the EU. Amsterdam is not at all typical, however, and most of the Dutch are still basically conservative and middle class in their outlook.

The Dutch are hard workers. Business people start work at 8.30am or even 8.00am in some offices, and may carry on after 5.00pm. It would be reasonable to expect to work more hours than are stipulated by your contract. Lunch-breaks are short and the main meal of the day is in the early evening between six and seven. The Dutch prefer an informal atmosphere at work. Clothing is casual but always smart, and colleagues use each other's first names. The emphasis is on efficiency and getting things done quickly. This sometimes leads to a certain lack of attention to details.

Initial contacts with the Dutch can be unnerving, since they can be very direct and even brusque with strangers. It is just as well to stand one's ground and try to be equally direct, or at the very least not to take offence. If you live in the Netherlands, you will come to appreciate the advantages of speaking your mind and knowing where you stand with other people. It is also worth knowing that the Dutch, by their own admission, are given to impatience and this is something which one has to get used to. Once initial communication problems have been overcome, you will find the Dutch are generally helpful and good-natured, as well as having a great deal of good sense.

English-speakers usually have a good social life in the Netherlands, and ample opportunities to pursue the same interests as at home. English-language books, films, music and newspapers all have a wide distribution, and the local people are very aware of what is happening in the English-speaking world. Dutch people enjoy outdoor pursuits and there are excellent sports facilities of every kind. Except during the summer, however, the climate does not encourage sitting around outdoors. The Dutch spend a lot of time in their homes, which are tidy and comfortable.

Pros:
- ○ Strong economy with constant employment prospects.
- ○ English widely used in business and elsewhere.
- ○ Favourable treatment of EU citizens.
- ○ High standard of living.
- ○ Excellent social security system.
- ○ Dutch people are receptive to foreigners.
- ○ Lively cultural scene.

Cons:
- ○ Good-quality rented accommodation is expensive.
- ○ Often wet and windy.
- ○ Flat landscape.
- ○ High personal income taxes.
- ○ Densely populated.
- ○ Very materialistic culture.

POLITICAL AND ECONOMIC STRUCTURE

THE EARLIEST KNOWN inhabitants of the Netherlands were a mixture of Germanic tribes and others, who built mounds known as *terpen* linked by causeways to escape from the sea. These are still visible today in the provinces of Groningen and Friesland. The area south of the Rhine delta, corresponding to the modern provinces of Zeeland, North Brabant and Limburg, was part of the Roman provinces of Gallia Belgica and Germania Inferior from 55 BC, while the north remained unsubdued.

The Dutch are not purely Germanic people, even though many of them are tall and blond. The national language, Dutch, is closely related to English. In the north-east there are also about 250,000 speakers of another Germanic language, Frisian, a language which is even more closely related to English. This connection is accounted for by the fact that the Anglo-Saxons remained in the area of Friesland for some time prior to their invasion of England in the fifth century AD.

While the official name of the country is the Netherlands, most Dutch people call it Holland (meaning 'wooded land') even though, strictly speaking, this only refers to the modern provinces of South and North Holland, the historical centre of the independent Netherlands. It is highly unlikely that anyone will object to your using the term Holland, but one should be aware that this is not the precise name for the country. The Dutch term for the indigenous language is Nederlands; the word Dutch originally meant any Germanic-sounding language spoken in Germany, Flanders or the Netherlands.

During the Middle Ages, the Netherlands was an assortment of duchies and principalities which acknowledged their allegiance to the Holy Roman Empire. The two major powers were the Counts of Holland and the Bishops of Utrecht. The northern provinces of Groningen and Friesland did not even have dukes or counts, but rather councils of leading merchants who dealt with the all-important problem of organising the coastal defences. Even at the dawn of the Middle Ages, the Dutch had already built up a great deal of expertise in draining low-lying land and were much in demand in northern France and Flanders for this type of work. They also established an intermediary role in the trade between the Baltic and the rest of Europe, thus laying the basis for their future commercial success.

Centralised authority was weak. The national decision-making body, the States General, was made up of representatives of the state councils, and could only make decisions with the unanimous support of all the Dutch states. One or other of the local rulers was appointed as the *stadhouder* or 'ruler by proxy', as a nominal representative of the Holy Roman Emperor.

During the 15th century, the Netherlands (a term which included the future kingdom of Belgium) came under Burgundian control, and then under the Habsburgs, with the result that it found itself ruled by the fiercely Catholic King Philip II of Spain from 1555. The Reformation had already taken a strong hold in the Netherlands and a confrontation was inevitable. The struggle for independence lasted from 1568 to 1648 (the Eighty Years' War). The future shape of the Netherlands was more or less determined in 1579, when the seven southern provinces of the Spanish Netherlands (corresponding to what was to become Belgium) reconciled themselves to Spanish domination, while the more Protestant-minded north continued to fight for independence. The great hero of the day was William the Silent, Prince of Orange (1533-1582). The Princes of Orange were not rulers of the Netherlands, but rather continued to be *stadhouders* appointed by the States General who could be dismissed if necessary.

Once the Spanish threat had receded, the Netherlands entered its Golden Age. Thanks to their sea power, the Dutch were able to acquire a number of former Spanish and Portuguese colonies in the East and West Indies, and thus establish a solid base for future economic expansion. At home, the arts and sciences flourished as never before. Dutch painters such as Rembrandt, Vermeer, Frans Hals and others, built up an unrivalled reputation. During the 17th century, the Dutch became powerful enough to challenge the British for commercial supremacy in many parts of the world. The relationship was not always antagonistic, however, and one of the Princes of Orange, Willem III, even became King of England as William III (from 1688 to 1702). During the Napoleonic Wars the Dutch found themselves in the French camp, and consequently lost many of their most valuable colonies to the British, in particular South Africa and much of Guyana. Their only North American colony, New Amsterdam (now New York), had been exchanged for Surinam (Dutch Guyana) in 1667 after a similarly unsuccessful war against the British.

After 1700 Dutch dominance of European trade diminished rapidly and the country found itself drawn more and more into the power struggle between Austria and France. The Batavian Revolution of 1780 saw Napoleon's brother, Louis Bonaparte appointed King of the Netherlands. His popularity was such that, following the battle of Waterloo, the Dutch opted to go over to a hereditary monarchy, and thus Prince Willem VI of Orange became King Willem I of the Netherlands in 1815. From 1815 until 1830, Belgium and Luxembourg also came under the Dutch crown, but the Belgians soon rebelled against Dutch rule and set up their own Catholic state in 1831. Luxembourg continued to owe allegiance to the Dutch crown until 1890 when it became an independent Grand Duchy.

The Netherlands remained neutral during World War I. In spite of its declared neutrality, it was invaded and brutally occupied by the Germans during the Second World War. As a result of its inability to react quickly to the post-war independence movement in Indonesia, the Netherlands lost all its East Indies possessions in 1949, except for New Guinea, which was taken over by Indonesia in 1963. Dutch Guyana also became independent under the name of Surinam in 1975. About 250,000 Surinamese then emigrated to the Netherlands, leading to considerable social problems. The only colonies left to the Dutch now are some West Indian islands, known as the Antilles, which have an equal status to the Netherlands itself in a loose commonwealth.

ECONOMY

THE INDUSTRIAL REVOLUTION began late in the Netherlands. The Dutch were used to living from trade rather than from agriculture and industry, so that when the industrialised provinces of Belgium seceded in 1830 it took some time to catch up. In the beginning Dutch industry centred on shipbuilding and the processing of imports from the East Indies, in particular cotton. In 1866, the coal-mining region of Limburg became a full member of the Dutch State, and in the 1880s large quantities of oil were discovered in Sumatra, laying the foundation for the present-day petroleum industry. Dairy product exports and the commercialisation of margarine also became major activities, still carried on by the Anglo-Dutch multinational Unilever. In the wake of plentiful electricity supplies becoming available in 1886, the Philips brothers were able to start the mass manufacture of light bulbs in Eindhoven. Philips Gloeilampen is now one of the largest electronics and telecommunications companies in the world. The Dutch also took care to develop their own steel and chemicals industry, lest they should become entirely dependent on Germany for these products. Aviation developed early in the Netherlands, and the Fokker company maintained Dutch interest in the world aviation market until it went into liquidation in 1996. After 1945, the Dutch also developed their own car industry in the form of the DAF company (Doorne Auto Fabrieken).

Huge harbour-building and land-reclamation projects gave a constant impetus to the Dutch economy in the early years of the 20th century, as well as helping to develop new technologies. In 1932 the Zuiderzee was sealed off by the 19-mile long Afsluitdijk which joined North Holland to the formerly remote province of Friesland. Plans were also made to reclaim large areas of land from the former Zuiderzee (now called the IJsselmeer). These were interrupted by World War II, but eventually the new province of Flevoland was created almost entirely from reclaimed land (known as *polders*). Plans to reclaim a further area of the IJsselmeer, to be known as Markerwaard, were shelved because of the prohibitive cost. After the catastrophic floods of 1953, huge sums of money had to be invested in building dykes and sea-defences in Zeeland (the Delta Project). Land reclamation has now been more or less abandoned since it has become apparent that it causes the land to sink further in some areas as well as destroying wetland habitats.

The Dutch economy emerged from World War II in an impoverished state, and many economists predicted disaster would follow the loss of the East Indies. The Dutch now had to look to their European trading partners. The Netherlands, Belgium and Luxembourg established a free trade area in 1948, the Benelux Economic Union. The Netherlands was also a founder member of the EC at its inauguration in 1957. The Dutch economy entered a period of rapid expansion in the 1950s, along with its partners, which was only brought to a halt in 1973 by the first oil shock. The 1980s were again years of expansion, followed by a short period of contraction during the 1993 recession. Still, the Dutch economy is still one of the most stable in the world, with consistently low inflation and healthy trade surpluses. In recent years, it has been buoyed up by the discovery of vast natural gas reserves as well as oil. The Netherlands is now the world's second largest exporter of natural gas, after Russia. Since 1997 growth has averaged over 3.5% annually. The economy has been so successful that overheating is a real concern; inflation was 3.6% in 2001. Unemployment stood at 2% at the end of 2001 – although many of the unemployed are not registered as such – and there is now a labour shortage in many sectors.

As with most North European countries, the Netherlands is grappling with the twin evils of mounting social security payments and a shrinking number of young people, as well as increasingly militant pensioners, but given their past successes in overcoming threats to their national survival, the Dutch should be able to maintain their current prosperity.

GOVERNMENT

THE TRADITION OF FINDING a consensus between different parties before taking action is deeply engrained in the Dutch. Different groupings in the Netherlands are traditionally labelled *zuilen*, or pillars of the state. Since the last century the four main pillars of Dutch society have been seen as the Catholics, Protestants, Socialists and the 'neutral' pillar, and the state has attempted to ensure that they have equal representation in national institutions.

Estimates of the numbers of Christians in the Netherlands vary considerably, but it is evident that their numbers are declining steadily. At the moment about 31% of the people are Catholics, 14% belong to the Dutch Reform Church (Nederlandse Hervormde Kerk), 8% to other Protestant groupings, 5% are Muslims; of the remainder 40% profess no religion, and the rest belong to other religions. Catholics are largely concentrated in the provinces of North Brabant and Limburg. Dutch Catholics have a reputation for being very liberal, and have often found themselves in conflict with papal authority.

The present system of government is to some extent modelled on the British one. The Parliament (Staten Generaal) has an Upper House (Eerste Kamer – First Chamber) and a Lower House (Tweede Kamer – Second Chamber). Only the Lower House can propose or amend bills. The Upper House, like the British House of Lords, debates bills and can delay them, but has very limited powers otherwise. The Lower House has 150 members, who are directly elected every four years. The voting system is based on proportional representation. The number of votes is divided by the number of seats, and parties are then allotted seats on the basis of their percentage of votes. The 75 members of the Upper House are elected indirectly by the provincial assemblies. Although Members of Parliament are paid, they are also expected to continue to practise an outside profession.

The Netherlands is divided into 625 municipalities (*gemeenten*), which are governed by councils (*gemeenteraden*) whose members are elected every four years, except for the mayor (*burgemeester*) who is appointed by the Crown. Between the local and national government are the provincial assemblies (*Provinciale Staten*), whose members are also elected every four years.

Until World War II, Dutch governments were formed either by the Protestant Anti-Revolutionary Party and Christian Historical Union, or by the Liberals, with the Catholic People's Party more often in coalition with the Liberals than with the Protestants. During the 1950s, the socialist Willem Drees was the dominant political figure and he did much to establish the Dutch welfare state. Most Dutch governments after the war were coalitions between the Christian parties, who joined together as the Christian Democrat Appeal in 1977, and the Partij van de Arbeid (Labour Party), until the major shift in Dutch politics which occurred after the 1994 general election.

In the 1960s there were frequent riots over inadequate housing and other issues. Some rioters were classified as *nozems* (rowdies) and others as *provocateurs* or *provos* (political activists). Eventually the *provos* formed a political party, the Kabouters (Gnomes) and managed to exert some influence on the Amsterdam City Council in the early 1970s, for example by instituting a free bicycle scheme in the city. Squatters (*krakers*) led popular protests against the building of the Amsterdam metro and the demolition of cheap inner-city housing but their influence has now diminished.

From 1982 to 1994, the country was led by Ruud Lubbers, a Christian Democrat, who had to deal with contentious issues such as the stationing of Cruise missiles on Dutch territory and cutting back the welfare state. In the 1989 elections Lubbers' plan to reduce environmental pollution by 70% at a projected cost of 7 billion euros by the year 2010 found widespread support. With the 1994 general elections, widespread hostility towards proposed social security cuts led to a slump in the fortunes of the ruling coalition, made up of the Christian Democrats and the Labour Party (Partij van de Arbeid), with the result that the Christians were excluded from the government for the first time since universal suffrage was introduced in 1917. A three-party coalition made up of the PvdA, VVD (Liberals) and the progressive D66, the so-called 'purple coalition' came to power, with the socialist Wim Kok as Prime Minister. The same coalition retained power in the May 1998 election, with the two main partners increasing their share of the vote, while the D66 party lost seats. The unexpectedly strong performance of the economy has given the government room to pay off some of the national debt as well as maintain public services; the same coalition can be expected to continue after the May 2002 election.

Political Parties

In the 1998 elections, 10 political parties, or groupings, gained representation in the Lower House. In some cases smaller parties which would have no hope of representation in the national Parliament band together under one name in order to obtain a large enough percentage of the vote to gain seats. Parties (especially left-wing parties) tend to split and regroup quite frequently. At the present time the largest party is the Labour Party (Partij van de Arbeid – PvdA), which was formed out of several socialist, Christian and liberal groupings in 1946. The Volkspartij voor Vrijheid en Democratie (Liberal Party) was formed at the same time and is now a right-wing pro-business party. The third partner in the present coalition are the Democraten '66, usually known as D66, a more radical offshoot of the PvdA, formed in 1966, which is mainly famous for its advocacy of legalised euthanasia. The other major and historically dominant party, the Christen Democraten Appel (CDA – Christian Democratic Appeal) is actually made up of three older Christian parties, the Katholieke Volkspartij (Catholic People's Party), the Anti-Revolutionaire Partij (Anti-Revolutionary Party – a Protestant anti-secular party), and the Christelijk-Historische Unie (Christian Historical Union – more moderate Protestants). In addition there are the Groen Links grouping (Green Left), the Socialistische Partij (SP), and a Calvinist fundamentalist grouping the SGP/GPV/RPF. A new party, Leefbaar Nederland, with anti-immigrant overtones, made up of right-wing elements of the VVD, appeared in 2000 and is likely to lead to a general shift to the right in Dutch politics.

GEOGRAPHICAL INFORMATION

Area

THE NETHERLANDS takes up 15,770 sq miles/40,844 sq km, about half the size of Scotland, or twice the size of New Jersey. It is bounded to the east by Germany and to the south by Belgium. The average distance from north to south is about 188 miles/300 km and from east to west about 125 miles/200 km. The River Rhine flows through the centre of the country where it divides into the Waal, Lek, IJssel and Neder Rijn and is joined by the Maas before it reaches the sea. In the southwest much of the Scheldt delta has been reclaimed from the sea. Over half of the country is below sea level and is protected from inundation by 1,500 miles/2,400 km of dykes. The threat of flooding from rivers is equally serious, and a vast system of canals and drainage ditches has also been constructed. There are 3,100 miles/5,000 km of navigable rivers and canals, which provide a useful means of transport and link up with the waterways of neighbouring countries.

The Netherlands is mostly flat, except for the hilly area of Limburg in the southeast. The highest point is the Vaalserberg near Maastricht at 1,035 ft/310 m. The lowest is at Nieuwekerk aan de IJssel, at minus 6.7 metres. The Netherlands is the least wooded country in the EU with only 8% forests; 54% of the land is used for agriculture.

Regional divisions and main towns

There are 12 provinces:
Zeeland, North Brabant, Limburg, South Holland, North Holland, Utrecht, Gelderland, Flevoland, Overijssel, Drenthe, Friesland and Groningen.

Population

The present population of The Netherlands is approximately 15,800,000, with an annual rate of increase of about 0.5%. A third of this is made up of the surplus of immigration over emigration. The Netherlands has the highest population density in the world at 457 per sq km (compared to 232 per sq km in the UK). Almost half of the population is concentrated in the Randstad (rim city) area, a circle of towns which includes Amsterdam, Haarlem, Leiden, The Hague, Rotterdam, Dordrecht and Utrecht. At the current rate of growth, the country's population could reach 17,200,000 by the year 2030; on the other hand, the falling birth rate will probably lead to a rapid decline thereafter.

Out of a total foreign population of 725,400, most are from the EU. There are also a significant number of Turkish and North African guest workers. Large numbers of Indonesians and Surinamese have also settled in The Netherlands and most have Dutch citizenship. During the 1950s more than 500,000 Dutch citizens emigrated, with the encouragement of the Dutch government, mainly to New Zealand, Australia, Canada, the United States and South Africa.

Climate

The Netherlands has a temperate maritime climate with mainly southerly and westerly winds. The weather is unsettled much of the time because of the collision of high and low pressure systems coming from the south and north. It is frequently wet and windy; it is estimated that there are only 25 days in the year when the sky is free of clouds. Summers can be pleasantly warm, but sudden squalls are always possible. On average there are 820 mm/33 inches of rain, 65 days of frost and 26 days where the temperature reaches 25°. Table 7 shows average maximum temperatures in Amsterdam.

TABLE 7 AVERAGE MAXIMUM TEMPERATURES (°C/°F)

Jan.	Feb.	Mar.	Apr.	May	June
5/41	5/41	8/46	11/52	16/60	18/65

July	Aug.	Sept.	Oct.	Nov.	Dec.
21/69	20/68	18/64	13/56	8/46	5/41

REGIONAL GUIDE

ENGLISH-SPEAKING FOREIGNERS looking for an exciting social and cultural life are generally attracted towards the Randstad cities, and most of all towards Amsterdam. Every city has something to offer, however, and there are few areas of the country which could be described as remote, except perhaps for the north. In any case, distances between towns are short and the public transport system is superb, so one will never feel isolated from civilisation.

Information Facilities

One first source of information is the Netherlands Board of Tourism Office in your home country, where you can find maps and brochures on different areas of the country. In the Netherlands itself, all tourist offices go under the name VVV (Vereniging Vreemdelingen Verkeer) and they will usually have brochures, for which there is a small charge, and information on places to visit and how to get around. Some VVVs now have special rate numbers, beginning 0900. You can no longer call these from abroad. You will probably be asked to press one of the buttons on your telephone (in Dutch!).

There are 350 VVV offices; they will also book a hotel room for you for a small fee and can usually supply information on neighbouring towns. It is worth knowing that hotels in the Netherlands are often full at the weekends in the major cities, and that cheap hotels are always heavily booked, so it is worth booking well in advance, otherwise you may have stay some distance away from where you would prefer to be.

Useful addresses

Netherlands Board of Tourism: PO Box 523, London SW1E 6NT; ☎0906-871 7777; fax 020-7828 7941; e-mail information@nbt.org.uk; www.holland.com/uk.
Netherlands Board of Tourism: 355 Lexington Avenue, 19th Floor, New York, NY 10017; ☎1-888-464-6552; 1-888-GO-HOLLAND; www.holland.com/us.
Holland Rail: Chase House, Gilbert Street, Ropley, Hampshire SO24 0BY; ☎01962-773646; fax 773625; www.hollandrail.com.

The Netherlands Online

As one might expect in a country with strong traditions of participatory democracy and open government, the Netherlands is one of the most switched-on countries in the world as regards the Internet. A useful starting point is to go to www.track.nl, and then enter the name of the place in the Netherlands that you are interested in. This site is essentially a search engine for Dutch websites and can be used to access any kind of information you could want.

Inevitably, a certain amount of 'erotic' material is advertised under the Entertainment sections, but one can also find such esoteric groups as the Didgeridoo Society of the Netherlands or the Society Against Fold-up Bicycles on Trains. For telephone numbers consult www.detelefoongids.nl (White pages) and www.goudengids.nl (Yellow pages). For the various Dutch ministries click on 'Overheid'.

ZEELAND

VVV: Nieuwe Burg 40, 4331 AH Middelburg; ☎0118-659900; e-mail vvvmid@zeelandnet.nl.
Main towns: Middelburg, Goes, Terneuzen, Oost-Souburg, Vlissingen (Flushing), Zierikzee.

Zeeland (Land of the Sea), with a population of only 368,000, is one of the Netherlands' smaller provinces. Many Afrikaner settlers in South Africa have their roots here and their language originated from the local dialect. The main activities are farming, fishing and tourism. The landscape of Zeeland has changed constantly over the centuries because of the activity of the sea and the shifting delta of the River Scheldt originating in neighbouring Belgium. In 1953 the area was inundated by a combined storm and tidal surge which killed nearly 2,000 people. As a result, the Delta Project was started, and by 1986 a vast system of movable barriers had been put in place between the islands of Noord Beveland and Schouwen Duiveland, at a price of some £3.3 billion.

Middelburg, Sluis and Zierikzee on the island of Schouwen Duiveland are all picturesque and well-preserved and worth a visit. Middelburg, the provincial capital, was renowned as a seaport serving the Dutch East and West India Companies during the 17th century. It was badly damaged in 1945 but has been carefully restored to some of its former glory. The main leisure attractions in the area are sailing, surfing and scuba-diving (in particular Grevelingen Lake). The area is also renowned for its seafood, most of all its mussels and oysters.

Vlissingen (Flushing in English) is joined by motorway to Antwerp and all areas of the Netherlands. The islands and peninsulas of Zeeland are joined by impressive bridges. Train services are limited to the Vlissingen-Roosendaal line, hence it is much easier to get around by bus or car. There is a car and passenger ferry service from Vlissingen to Breskens in the southern part of Zeeland, Zeeuws Vlaanderen (contact 0118-46 09 00 for times). Otherwise this area is only accessible from Belgium, of which it was a part until 1815. Zeebrugge in Belgium is a half-hour drive from Breskens. Although a very attractive place to live (apart from the polluted water), job opportunities are somewhat limited in this area. The most likely employment is in tourism or in the shipping industry.

NORTH BRABANT (NOORD-BRABANT)

VVV: De Moriaan, Markt 77, 5211 JX 's Hertogenbosch; ☎0900-112 23 34; informatie@vvvs-hertogenbosch.nl.
Main towns: 's Hertogenbosch, Eindhoven, Breda, Tilburg, Bergen-op-Zoom.

North Brabant is the second largest province in the Netherlands in land area, stretching from the North Sea to the border with Germany, and has 2.3 million inhabitants. Until the Eighty Years' War against the Spanish, the area was part of the Duchy of Brabant. It became part of the Netherlands in 1648, while South Brabant remained in the what later became Belgium. The countryside of North Brabant consists of a variety of moorlands, fens, creeks and woods which attract large numbers of birds and bird-watchers.

The provincial capital, 's Hertogenbosch ('Dukes' Wood') is alternatively known as Den Bosch. Colloquially it comes out as 's Bos. It has a renowned Gothic cathedral built between 1380 and 1530, the St. Janskathedraal and was the home of the painter Hieronymus Bosch (1450-1516). The other towns of North Brabant are mostly industrial, with the electronics industry playing a large role in the region's prosperity. The area has also attracted a number of IT-related companies. In general, North Brabant has a low rate of unemployment; housing is relatively expensive.

Eindhoven, the 'City of Light' (www.dse.nl) is famous as the headquarters of the multinational Philips. Without Philips it would probably be no more than a village. Philips also sponsor the local football team, PSV Eindhoven, who have at times dominated Dutch football. Eindhoven's airport serves London, Birmingham, Manchester, Paris, Zurich, Hamburg, Strasbourg, Amsterdam and Rotterdam. There are regular train services to all parts of the country.

LIMBURG

VVV: Th. Dorrenplein 5, 6301 DV Valkenburg; ☎043-609 86 00; e-mail vvv@valkenburg-mergelland.nl.
Main towns: Maastricht, Kerkrade, Sittard, Roermond, Venlo.

The province of Limburg is a long wedge of land between Belgium and Germany with 1,340,000 inhabitants. It was captured in 1839 by King Willem I in a last-ditch attempt to profit from the weakness of newly independent Belgium. Dutch Limburg continued to have close ties with the German Confederation until 1866, when it finally became a full province of the Netherlands. The local dialect bears some resemblance to that of Aachen.

Limburg is rather different from the rest of the Netherlands, both because of the hilly landscape and as the most strongly Catholic part of the country. The towns bear more resemblance to Belgian and German towns than to the squeeky-clean, chocolate-box image of most Dutch tourist towns.

The capital, Maastricht, derives its name from the Latin Mosae Trajectum, meaning 'Meuse crossing'. It gained new fame as the setting of the EC's Maastricht Conference in December 1991. South Limburg is famous for castles, some of them dating back to the 10th century. The hills around here, which reach the dizzying height of 300 metres in places, are humorously referred to as the Dutch Alps.

Limburg is a prosperous area. House prices are around the Dutch average. Maastricht has attracted 200 foreign companies, many of whom require English-speaking staff. The proximity of French-speaking Belgium and of Germany is a further attraction. Maastricht has an international airport with flights to Schiphol and Stansted; other flights are holiday charters. There is an hourly train service to Liège, Brussels and Ostend.

SOUTH HOLLAND (ZUID-HOLLAND)

VVV: Kon. Julianaplein 30, 2508 CE The Hague; ☎070-361 8888; e-mail info@denhaag.com; www.denhaag.com.
Main towns: The Hague (Den Haag/'s Gravenhage), Rotterdam, Leiden, Dordrecht, Delft.

South and North Holland constitute the historical centre of the Netherlands, and continue to lead the country politically and economically. The capital of the Netherlands is Amsterdam, but the Parliament and administration are based in The Hague. The official name of The Hague is ''s Gravenhage (Counts' Hedge). It was originally a village called Haag, until one of the Counts of Holland built a hunting lodge there in the early thirteenth century. In conversation Dutch people refer to it simply as Den Haag; it is generally listed under G for 's Gravenhage.

The Hague is now a very expensive city, full of foreign embassies and multinational company headquarters, and houses the International Court of Justice. The leafy suburb of Wassenaar is where the better-off prefer to live, and house-prices are the highest in the country. Although it is not a place to stay for most tourists (the hotels in the down-market sea resort of Scheveningen are much cheaper), the city's art museums are essential viewing. The annual North Sea Jazz Festival also brings in large numbers of foreigners.

Just south of The Hague is Rotterdam (www.MediaPort.nl), whose port – the Europoort – is the largest in the world. The entire conurbation of Rotterdam has a population of 1,054,000, virtually the same as Amsterdam's; South Holland is the country's most densely populated province (1,166 per sq. km), with 3.3 million people. After being completely flattened during the war, it now has some of the country's most adventurous modern architecture; its art museums are some of the best in the world. Between Rotterdam and The Hague there is the town of Delft, which gave its name to the blue and white Delftware pottery (originally an imitation of Chinese pottery found on captured Portuguese merchant vessels). The old university town of Leiden (www.leiden.nl) is a few miles to the north.

Rotterdam has many job opportunities for English-speakers, particularly in the temporary work field. To Americans Rotterdam is reminiscent of New York; the local nickname is 'Manhattan-on-the-Maas'. The Hague offers work for au pairs and secretaries; otherwise it is a city for the more well-off expatriate. There are frequent trains to all parts of the country, as well as to Brussels, Antwerp and Paris. Amsterdam Schiphol airport is not far away, but you can fly directly from Rotterdam to London. The downside to this area is the very high population density; you should definitely enjoy urban living if you want to come here.

NORTH HOLLAND (NOORD-HOLLAND)

VVV: Stationsplein 10, 1012 AB Amsterdam; ☎020-551 25 25, 020-700 0888; e-mail info@amsterdamtourist.nl; www.visitamsterdam.nl; www.ampro.nl.
Main towns: Amsterdam, Haarlem, Alkmaar, Amstelveen, Hilversum.

The second most densely populated province with 930 inhabitants per sq. km and 2.47 million people, North Holland also attracts the largest number of foreigners. Amsterdam is the official capital of the Netherlands, but only in name. It attracts large numbers of foreign tourists, drawn by its world-class museums and reputation as one of the world's liveliest cities.

The rest of North Holland is rather more sedate than Amsterdam. To the north there are the tourist towns of Volendam and Alkmaar, with their carefully preserved traditions. On the eastern edge of North Holland is Hilversum, the home of Dutch TV and radio. To the west of Amsterdam is the ancient town of Haarlem with its superb Frans Hals Museum. To the south of Haarlem lie the vast bulb fields of Heemstede and Haarlemmermeer. Nearby is Aalsmeer, the site of the world's largest flower auction house, which is itself a stone's throw from the Netherlands' main international airport, Schiphol. It is estimated that over half of the world's cut flowers are distributed from here.

Many foreigners would like to work in Amsterdam, but are very soon confronted by the fact that rented accommodation here is extremely expensive and difficult to find. For locals this is less of a problem because they have access to housing association accommodation. The better-off tend to live in the area known as Het Gooi, around Hilversum and in Utrecht province, and commute into work. Many foreigners do manage to establish themselves here, nevertheless, if only temporarily. The work opportunities are as varied as Amsterdam itself. Those who are interested in horticulture will be attracted towards Aalsmeer; the north of the province has far less to offer job-seekers, except for summer jobs on the tourist island of Texel.

Almost everywhere in the Netherlands is accessible by train from Amsterdam in less than three hours. The Thalys semi-high speed train connects the city with Antwerp, Brussels and Paris. There are also trains to Lille, Strasbourg, Marseilles, Berlin, Innsbruck, Salzburg, Hamburg, Munich, Zurich, Prague and Milan amongst other places. Schiphol airport, just south of Amsterdam, is one of the world's largest, with daily flights to 15 destinations in the UK.

UTRECHT

VVV: Vredenburg 90, Utrecht; ☎030-233 1544; e-mail vvvutrecht@tref.nl.
Main towns: Utrecht, Zeist, Amersfoort, Soest, Veenendaal.

Utrecht is the Netherlands' smallest province in land area, but is one of the most densely populated with 1,072,000 inhabitants. Of these about 250,000 live in the provincial capital, Utrecht, one of the most significant historical cities in the country. The Treaty of Utrecht was signed here in 1579, whereby the seven United Provinces (Holland, Utrecht, Gelderland, Zeeland, Overijssel, Friesland and Groningen) finally constituted themselves into a Protestant republic free from Spanish domination. The Romans constructed a fort here and later the Bishops of Utrecht exercised both spiritual and temporal power on behalf of the Holy Roman Empire and the Pope. Utrecht has a 365-foot cathedral tower, the Dom. The rest of the cathedral fell down in a storm in 1674.

The other major medieval city in the province is Amersfoort, a mere 10 miles/17 km to the northeast of Utrecht. To the north of Utrecht is the region of lakes and woods known as 't Gooi (properly Het Gooi), part of which is in North Holland, particularly favoured by better-off commuters working in Amsterdam.

Utrecht is notable as the student capital of the Netherlands. The province has the highest per capita income as well as the most burglaries in the country (outside of Amsterdam). Rented accommodation is expensive and going up in price rapidly. Air quality is worse than average.

Utrecht is conveniently located in the centre of the Netherlands, with frequent trains to the Randstad and elsewhere. There is no airport.

GELDERLAND

VVV: Stationsplein 45, 6811 KL Arnhem; ☎026-442 6767; e-mail info@vvvarnhem.nl.

Main towns: Arnhem, Nijmegen, Apeldoorn, Doetinchem, Zutphen.

Gelderland is the largest Dutch province in land area. In terms of population, it is ranked fourth, with 1,784,000 inhabitants. During the Middle Ages, Gelderland enjoyed a large degree of independence under the Dukes of Gelre until the sixteenth century, when it was first taken over by the Habsburgs and then incorporated into the new Dutch Republic. The province is divided into four by the Rhine, the Waal, the Nederrijn and the IJssel. The River Maas (or Meuse) forms the southern border. The northern half of the province is known as the Veluwe, an area of heathland and woods, the only real wilderness in the country. Within the Veluwe is the world-famous art museum, the Kröller-Müller Museum at Otterlo, one of the main tourist sites in the country. Between the IJssel and the German border is the Achterhoek (back corner), a region of farmland and castles.

The provincial capital of Arnhem is famed as the furthest bridgehead of 'Operation Market Garden', the failed Allied attempt to invade Germany via Holland in September 1944. The other city associated with the campaign, Nijmegen, suffered considerable damage to its old buildings, although many have been restored. The city was founded on the River Waal by the Roman Emperor Trajan in 105 AD. The Emperor Charlemagne built a castle here, the Valkhof, and used it as an administrative centre between 800 and 814 AD. Unfortunately it was thoroughly obliterated in the 18th century.

While the local economy has been traditionally based on farming and fruit-growing, with Europe's leading agricultural university at Wageningen, more and more firms are moving to Gelderland thanks to easier availability of land and the healthier environment. Consequently, there is a net annual population movement away from the Randstad and the North into the area. Rental prices are rising faster here than anywhere else.

Train services are excellent; there are hourly trains to Cologne in Germany.

FLEVOLAND

VVV: Stationsplein 186, 8232 VT Lelystad; ☎ 0320-24 34 44.
Main towns: Lelystad, Almere, Urk, Emmeloord.
 Flevoland is made up entirely of land reclaimed from the sea since World War I. The land is completely flat and mostly given over to agriculture and new housing estates. Flevoland is a popular area for recreation and has some of the finest water sports facilities in the Netherlands. The population of the new towns of Lelystad and Almere is expanding rapidly as they are now within commuting distance of Amsterdam. They are not very attractive places to live and largely inhabited by lower-paid workers from Amsterdam.
 Flevoland is a young province with a mere 273,000 inhabitants and is still trying to build up its infrastructure. It has managed to attract a number of well-known electronic and light industrial firms; much of the industry is centred around yachting and outboard motors. The Noordoost Polder is still almost entirely agricultural and not readily accessible from the Randstad. Much of the province's wealth derives from the fact that so many commuters live there. Rental prices are higher than the average since most of the housing is new. There are frequent train services from Almere and Lelystad to the Randstad; there are plans to extend the railway from Lelystad to Zwolle and Friesland.

OVERIJSSEL

VVV: Grote Kerkplein 14, 8011 PK Zwolle; ☎ 038-421 6798.
Main towns: Zwolle, Deventer, Almelo, Hengelo, Enschede.
 Overijssel, home to 1,060,000 people, north of Gelderland on the German border, did not play a major role in Dutch history and is not much frequented by tourists. The province has its fair share of interesting medieval towns, in particular the capital, Zwolle, where the writer Thomas à Kempis made his home for a few years from 1399 and Oldenzaal, where mechanised textile production first took off in the 19th century with British help. The former Hanseatic league port of Elburg (now cut off from the sea) is popular with day-trippers.
 As one moves into the eastern part of Overijssel, the landscape becomes more wooded and hilly. Close by the German border is the region known as Twente, which at one time had a flourishing textile industry. The main town, Enschede (pronounced Enscheday) is worth a visit for its art galleries and festivals. Enschede hit the headlines in May 2000 when an explosion in a fireworks factory destroyed a large part of the town centre.
 Overijssel became something of a backwater with the rise of Amsterdam in the late 16th century. These days there is a steady trickle of firms away from the Randstad looking for a more spacious and peaceful location, bringing with a net shift in population away from the West and North of the Netherlands. Even so, per capita incomes in Overijssel are the third lowest in the country after Groningen and Friesland; unemployment is lower than average. House rentals are on the cheap side.
 Zwolle has a half-hourly train service to Amsterdam. There are trains from

Hengelo and Oldenzaal to Osnabrück and Hannover in Germany. There are no longer direct trains from Enschede to Germany. For Cologne, go via Arnhem.

DRENTHE

VVV: Markstraat 8-10, 9401 JH Assen; ☎0592-314324; e-mail vvvassen@wxs.nl.

Main towns: Assen, Hoogeveen, Emmen, Meppel, Coevorden.

Drenthe was another backwater in medieval times because of its poor agricultural land. The province was ruled by the Bishops of Utrecht until it came into the Habsburg Empire in 1538 and it then joined the Revolt against the Spanish in 1568. The marshlands and peat-bogs of the area were reclaimed for agriculture in the nineteenth century. The most famous feature of the landscape are the *hunebeds*, megalithic tombs dating from 5,000 BC. These days Drenthe is attracting more and more industry looking for greenfield sites close to the German border (Drenthe is exactly equidistant between Brussels and Hamburg). Coevorden and Schoonebeek, in the southeast corner of the province produce enough natural gas for the entire country as well as enough oil to supply about 7% of the Netherlands' needs.

Drenthe is the most thinly populated province in the Netherlands: about 172 inhabitants and 70 houses per square kilometre; total population 460,000. It is also the least urbanised. Drenthe has managed to shake off its image as part of the impoverished North; incomes are now only just below the national average. The area enjoys stable prosperity rather than spectacular growth, thanks to its oil and gas reserves. Housing is cheaper than average, and rents have risen less than the rate of inflation in the late 1990s. The crime rate is low by Dutch standards.

While the road network is perfectly adequate, rail services are limited. One has to go through Zwolle to get to the Randstad. There are no direct train services to Germany. Groningen is easily accessible from Assen by train.

FRIESLAND

VVV: Stationsplein 1, 2011 LR Leeuwarden; ☎058-213 13 43; e-mail vvvleeuwarden@chello.nl.

Main towns: Leeuwarden, Sneek, Heerenveen, Drachten, Dokkum.

Friesland is one of the Netherlands' least populated provinces with about 613,000 souls, and is third largest in size. It includes the West Frisian islands of Terschelling, Ameland and Schiermonnikoog, but not Texel, which is part of North Holland, and some small islands close to Germany which are part of Groningen. These islands are extremely popular in the summer when their population rises about ten-fold.

In medieval times, the Frisians maintained their independence against all-comers until they joined the United Provinces at the Treaty of Utrecht in 1578. Even now the Frisians like to think of themselves as different from the Dutch, and try hard to keep up their own language, Frisian, while having to resort to Dutch for many words. In 1955, the Dutch government introduced Frisian classes in schools, as it was found that younger children had difficulty understanding Dutch.

The capital, Leeuwarden was built on three *terpen* (mounds) when the surrounding area was under water. Apart from its medieval buildings, it is also famous as the birthplace of Mata Hari, spy and *femme fatale*. Friesland's other natives of international renown are Pieter Stuyvesant, founder of New York, and Maurits Escher the graphic artist.

Friesland is generally known for ice-skating, in particular the Elfstedentocht, a notoriously difficult annual circuit of 11 Frisian towns (weather permitting). Doing the Elfstedentocht by bicycle is becoming more and more popular. Friesland has produced a number of champion ice-skaters, notably Sjoukje Dijkstra.

Agriculture is the main industry here, and this also happens to be the Netherlands' main export earner. Many tourists are attracted by the picturesque villages and old trading ports. There is a certain degree of tension between Frisian and non-Frisian speakers, and there are those who would like road signs to be in Frisian. This is not by any means an obvious place for foreigners to look for work, on the other hand, the environment here is the cleanest in the Netherlands and housing is cheap. The tourist islands of Terschelling, Ameland and Schiermonnikoog do offer work in the summer, if you like crowded beaches.

Leeuwarden is connected by frequent trains to the Randstad. By road you can drive across the Aflsuitdijk, or you can take the ferry from Stavoren to Enkhuizen in North Holland.

GRONINGEN

VVV: Gedempte Kattendiep 6, 9711 PN Groningen; ☎050-313 97 74; e-mail info@vvvgroningen.nl.
Main towns: Groningen, Veendam, Winschoten, Sappemeer, Delfzijl.

Groningen (population 560,000), the so-called 'top of Holland', first developed as a trading post on the way from the Baltic to the rest of Europe. Nowadays its prosperity is based on its large reserves of natural gas, first discovered at Slochteren in the 1960s. Groningen used to have 1,400 windmills, of which only 80 remain in working order.

The most famous native of Groningen is undoubtedly Abel Tasman, who was the first white man to discover New Zealand and gave his name to Tasmania and the Tasman Sea. In general, the province of Groningen is not all that rich in historical monuments. It does have special appeal to sailing and wind-surfing enthusiasts, although it is by no means unique in this respect.

Groningen's wealth is very unevenly spread. Even with all its oil and gas production per capita incomes are some 12% below the average; unemployment is the highest in the Netherlands at around 10%. House prices and rentals are consequently cheap. The city of Groningen houses the headquarters of the oil and gas industry, although much of it is located in Drenthe, and hence attracts a number of foreign workers.

Groningen is the remotest province in relation to the Randstad. Amsterdam is about 2½ hours away by train. There is a train service to Oldenburg in Germany. The airport at Eelde is mainly used for holiday charter flights; there are 5-7 flights a day to Schiphol if you want to take a connecting flight. There are no direct flights to London.

GETTING TO THE NETHERLANDS

THE QUICKEST WAY of getting to the Netherlands remains by air. The high speed train (HST – Hoge Snelheids Trein) which will link Brussels with Amsterdam some time after the year 2002, will cut the journey time by rail from London to Amsterdam to under 4 hours and provide a serious competitor to airline travel. At the moment it is still necessary to change at Brussels Midi. There is also the conventional train and ferry via Harwich and the Hook of Holland.

There are a number of options as far as ferry services go, depending on which part of the UK you are travelling from. The most popular is the Harwich-Hook of Holland route, which lands you conveniently close to the centre of the Netherlands, run by Stena Line. Their high-speed ferry service, which has cut the crossing time from 7 hours to 3 hours 40 minutes makes this an attractive option.

By far the cheapest way to reach the Netherlands is by coach. Eurolines runs daily departures from London, with reductions for under-26s and the over-60s.

Flights to Schiphol (on the outskirts of Amsterdam) cost from under £100 from the UK and take about 45 minutes. Ryanair are starting flights from London Stansted to Eindhoven in 2002, which may even undercut coach travel. Other airlines fly to Rotterdam, Maastricht and Eindhoven (see below). Note that routes that are subject to change. Availability can be checked on the website: www.ebookers.com. From North America, there are direct flights to Schiphol run by KLM/Northwest Airlines, Martinair, Delta Air Lines and United Airlines.

Train Services
Eurostar: 08705-186186; www.eurostar.com.
Le Shuttle: ☎08705-353535 (bookings); 08000 969 992 (inquiries); www.eurotunnel.com.
Holland Rail: Chase House, Gilbert Street, Ropley, Hampshire SO24 0BY; ☎01962-773646; fax 01962-773625; www.hollandrail.com.

Ferry Services
Hoverspeed: International Hoverport, Dover CT17 9TG; ☎08705-240241; 076-522 3399 (Netherlands) www.hoverspeed.com. Dover to Ostend.

P&O North Sea Ferries: King George Dock, Hedon Road, Hull HU9 5QA; ☎0870-129 6002; fax 01482-706438; www.ponsf.com. Hull to Zeebrugge/Rotterdam.

P & O Stena Line: Channel House, Channel View Road, Dover CT17 9TJ; ☎08705-455 455; www.amsterdamexpress.co.uk; Harwich to Hook of Holland.

DFDS Seaways: Tyne Commission Quay, North Shields, NE29 6EA; ☎08705-333666; www.dfdsseaways.co.uk; Newcastle to IJmuiden.

Air Services
British Airways: ☎0845-77 333 77; www.britishairways.com; Heathrow/ Gatwick/Manchester/Birmingham to Amsterdam; Gatwick to Rotterdam.
bmi British Midland: Donington Hall, Castle Donington, Derby, E. Midlands DE74 2SB; ☎0870-60 70 555; www.flybmi.com; Heathrow to Amsterdam; East Midlands Airport to Amsterdam.
KLM Royal Dutch Airlines: ☎0870-507 4074; www.klm.com; London Heathrow/Gatwick to Amsterdam; London Heathrow to Rotterdam.
KLM uk: Endeavour House, Stansted Airport, Stansted, Essex CM24 1RS; ☎08705 074 074; www.klmuk.com; Stansted/London City/Aberdeen/ Belfast/Birmingham/Edinburgh/ Glasgow/Humberside/Leeds-Bradford/Manchester/Newcastle/ Norwich/Teesside to Amsterdam; London City to Rotterdam; London Stansted to Maastricht.
Ryanair: 08701-569 569; www.ryanair.com. Stansted to Eindhoven.
Scotairways: ☎0870-606 0707; www.scotairways.co.uk; Cambridge and Southampton to Amsterdam.
VLM: London City Airport, Royal Docks, London E16 2PX; ☎020-7476 6677; www.vlm-airlines.com; London City to Rotterdam; Manchester to Rotterdam.

Bus Services
Eurolines: ☎08705-143219 (UK), 020-560 87 87 (Amsterdam); www.eurolines.co.uk; London to Amsterdam.

Useful Guides

Amsterdam, Rotterdam, Leiden and The Hague: Cadogan Guides. Guide to places to stay, what to do, history and practical information.
Fodor's Holland: The Guide for all Budgets: Fodor Publications. General guidebook.
Get Lost! The Cool Guide to Amsterdam: Get Lost Publishing, 8th ed. For those interested in the seedier side of life.
Holland: The Rough Guide: Rough Guides 2nd ed. Down-to-earth traveller's information.
Time Out Guide to Amsterdam: Penguin, 6th ed. Also website www.timeout.com/amsterdam.
Virago Woman's Guide to Amsterdam: Virago. Things to do as well as everything you might want to know about women in Amsterdam.
Walking Amsterdam: New Holland pub.

RESIDENCE & ENTRY REGULATIONS

THE CURRENT POSITION

THE DUTCH HAVE TWO GOOD REASONS for wanting to restrict entry and residence into the Netherlands. Firstly, the country has one of the highest population densities in the world, 1,040 persons per square mile (or 434 per sq km), and is quite literally bursting at the seams. Secondly, the benevolent social security system, on which the Dutch pride themselves, has been subject to abuse by visitors who, having obtained a residence permit, contrive to live off the state. In recent years the immigration authorities have become more and more zealous in pursuing illegal immigrants and the number of asylum seekers has dropped dramatically. That said, the Netherlands is a member of the European Union and as such UK citizens have the right to live and work there for as long as they wish. A visa is not required for visits of up to three months but to remain longer it is necessary to obtain a residence permit (*verblijfsvergunning*). To qualify for this it is up to you to prove your stay is bona fide. In the case of non-EU citizens the situation is much more difficult. In the majority of cases they will be sent to the Netherlands by their employers who will deal with their applications for a residence permit.

ENTRY AND RESIDENCE FOR EU NATIONALS

EU NATIONALS DO NOT REQUIRE a visa to enter the Netherlands with a view to looking for work. You may enter as a tourist and then change your status to a resident. If you wish to do voluntary work with a recognised institution for less than three months there is no need to register with the authorities.

British citizens entering the Netherlands to look for work are advised to register with the aliens police (*vreemdelingenpolitie*) within eight days of arrival. The local police station is the place to find the aliens police, with the exception of Amsterdam (see address below); in smaller communities they are often to be found at the local town hall (*stadhuis*). Look under *politie* in the phone book. In theory, you need only take your passport along at this point, but there is no harm in having your birth certificate, marriage/divorce certificate, health insurance papers etc. with you in case you are asked. The police will then put the necessary sticker in your passport; note that this is a country where passport stamps are of great significance. Since the aliens police are very overworked, it is as well to find out in advance when the best time is to go along; you may have to queue up early in the morning.

Once you have registered with the police they will send you to the local town hall (*stadhuis* or *gemeentehuis*) to put yourself on the population register (*bevolkingsregister*), even if you do not have a fixed address. There are in total some 625 municipalities (*gemeente*) in the country. At this point you must have all the necessary identity papers as well as two passport photographs; in particular you must have your birth certificate, and your marriage/divorce certificate, which for British citizens have to be validated with the *apostille* (apply to the Legalisation Office, Foreign and Commonwealth Office, Old Admiralty Building, The Mall, London SW1A 2LG; ☎ 020-7008 1111; www.fco.gov.uk). Not all local authorities will ask for the apostille, but it is still necessary to have it, to be on the safe side. In order to apply for a job you will require proof of your registration with the town hall in the form of an extract from the population register (*uittreksel van de burgerlijke stand*).

Your next move before you can apply for a job is to obtain a Dutch national insurance number, or social-fiscal number, known as a *SOFI nummer*, from the nearest tax office (*belastingkantoor*). At this point you can legally look for work. It is also possible to find work with just the SOFI number. You can apply for a SOFI number from abroad; send a copy of your passport (if you are an EU citizen) or your residence or work permit (if non-EU) to the International Tax Office in Heerlen (see below).

Note that if the aliens police do not like the look of you they can make unreasonable requests such as asking to see the stamp in your passport from the border police to prove when you entered the country, something which you are not likely to have. If you are sleeping on someone's floor then they could inform the municipality who could impose a higher council tax on your host. It therefore pays to look smart and to anticipate awkward questions.

Once you have successfully found work and you are paying into a health insurance scheme (*ziekenfonds*), which your employer will deal with unless you are earning more than €30,700 per year, you can then go back to the aliens police with all your papers and more passport photos in order to start the process of applying for an EU residence permit (*E-document*). This now takes the form of a plastic card and is valid for five years. It is also issued to spouses and children of EU citizens in paid employment resident in the country. If you plan to stay for less than a year you will receive a stamp in your passport. If you decide to leave the country permanently, then you are obliged to inform the aliens police and town hall.

There are a number of helplines for foreigners who are in difficulties with the immigration authorities. If you want to make an anonymous enquiry in English then you can call the aliens police on 0900-8844. The Dutch Ministry of Justice will answer queries concerning the red tape involved in applying for residence in the Netherlands on 070-370 31 24. If your problem is more serious and you need legal advice then you can make an appointment to go to the Bureau voor

Rechtshulp at Spuistraat 10, Amsterdam; ☎020-626 44 77. The Bureau voor Rechtshulp does not answer questions over the phone, and is mainly concerned with helping citizens from the Third World and Eastern Europe. The voluntary organisation, ACCESS, in The Hague, can also put you in touch with sources of help.

The Immigratie- en Naturalisatiedienst (Immigration and Naturalisation Service) publishes a variety of helpful booklets such as: *Visa for Short Stay in the Netherlands*, *The Admission of EU Citizens to the Netherlands*, *Working as a Self-Employed Person*, *Au Pair in the Netherlands* and *Practical Training and Courses of Study in the Netherlands for non-EU/EEA Subjects*. The EU also produces a leaflet on residence rights in the Netherlands; order on 0800-581591 in the UK, or look at the website: http://citizens.eu.int.

Entry On A Self-Employed Basis

EU citizens have the right to self-employed status in the Netherlands. Many professions are regulated by law; a list is given in the *Employment* chapter in Section II. In most cases you will need to contact your own professional organisation in the UK before you can consider moving to the Netherlands. The Royal Netherlands Embassy in London can also give advice.

Many employment contracts in the construction industry are issued on a self-employed basis. The Overseas Placing Unit of the British Employment Service warns prospective self-employed workers to take specialist advice before going to the Netherlands, for the simple reason that you may not be covered by Dutch sickness benefit should you be injured or become ill. If you wish to become self-employed you can continue to pay UK National Insurance contributions for up to 12 months by completing form E101, and you will then be exempt from paying Dutch social security contributions for that time. This form is available from the Overseas Branch of the Department of Work and Pensions. They can also offer advice on self-employment. Form E111 will give you emergency health cover for up to a year in the Netherlands if you are self-employed.

Dutch employers are very strict about having the right paperwork, and may refuse to employ you if you do not have the right forms with you. You must also complete form CF11 declaring the intention to become self-employed. This can be done at any DWP office in the UK. A Dutch employer may insist on seeing this document before the work contract is signed.

Useful Addresses

Pensions and Overseas Benefits Directorate: Department for Work and Pensions, Tyneview Park, Whitley Rd., Benton, Newcastle-upon-Tyne NE98 1BA; ☎0191-218 7777; www.inlandrevenue.gov.uk/nic/intserv/osc.htm.

Immigratie- en Naturalisatiedienst, afdeling Communicatie: Postbus 30125, 2500 GC Den Haag; ☎070-370 31 24; fax 370 31 34; e-mail voorlichting@ind.minjus.nl.

NON-EU NATIONALS

US, CANADIAN, AUSTRALIAN and New Zealand nationals can enter the Netherlands for up to three months without a visa. Other non-EU citizens require permission to enter either in the form of a 90-day Schengen visa or an *Authorisation for Provisional Sojourn* (*Machtiging voor voorlopig verblijf/MVV*) from the Dutch Consulate General in their country of residence if they wish to stay for more than three months. An application must include details of means of support and accommodation.

If you did not require a visa to enter the Netherlands then you may work for up to three months, provided you have registered with the aliens police within three days of arrival and that your employer can obtain a *tewerkstellingsvergunning* (permission to employ a foreign national) from the local Employment Ministry (Centraal Bestuur Arbeidsvoorziening). For very short-term jobs even a *tewerkstellingsvergunning* may not be required, if the work you are doing is considered to be in the public interest; this particularly applies to the IT sector. Because of the current shortage of qualified staff, IT personnel from non-EU countries who earn over €36,000 per annum may be exempted from the usual work permit regulations.

Other workers who want to stay for more than three months need to obtain the MVV (see above) from a Dutch Consulate in your country of origin before your prospective employer can apply for a work permit. The employer has to prove that there is no EU citizen available who could the job in question. This means the vacancy should have been reported to the local employment office for at least five weeks, and be advertised in the press. These rules do not apply to high-level executives working for multi-nationals, visiting lecturers, clergy and trainees.

The regulations are somewhat more lenient for US citizens, in that they can go to the Netherlands for three months to look for work, provided they register with the aliens police within three days of arrival. In most cases US citizens will apply for a work permit through their employer from outside the Netherlands, followed by an application to enter the country. Once permission is granted the applicant can travel to the Netherlands. He or she then reports to the aliens police within 48 hours of arrival. The police will check the work permit and stamp the passport to show they are in the country legally. They can then go through the process of obtaining an annually renewable residence permit, known as a *D-document*. After five years they can apply for the five-year *Vergunning tot vestiging* (Permission to remain).

Non-EU citizens to work in the Netherlands with self-employed status will have to show that their work in the Netherlands is in the public interest. They will have to go through rigorous medical and legal vetting which can easily take up to a year or more.

All non-EU citizens, whether they require a visa or not, are required to register with the aliens police within 48 hours of arrival if they are not staying in a hotel. Your hotel deals with this formality otherwise. A further crucial point to note is that the Dutch authorities require you to have a passport which is valid for three months beyond the date on which you intend to leave the Netherlands.

SUMMARY

WHILE THE RULES GOVERNING EU residents in the Netherlands have become more relaxed since the introduction of the Single Market in 1993, local town halls have a considerable degree of freedom in how they apply the rules. Fortunately, there will always be English-speaking staff on hand to help you.

Once resident in the Netherlands, it is essential to register with your local Consulate. This enables the authorities in your country to trace you in the event of an emergency and to keep you up to date with new information. You are also required to register births, marriages and deaths with your Consulate. Consulates cannot help you to find work and are not a source of general information and advice, although they will supply some basic handouts on settling down in the Netherlands. The British Consulate can supply the leaflet *Living & Working in the Netherlands*. For US citizens, the American Consulate General issues the *General Information Guide for American Citizens Residing in the Netherlands*.

Embassies

Royal Netherlands Embassy: 38 Hyde Park Gate, London SW7 5DP; ☎020-7590 3200; fax 020-7581 3458; e-mail london@netherlandsembassy.org.uk; www.netherlandsembassy.org.uk.

Netherlands Consulate: 3 Annandale Terrace, Dalnottar Av., Old Kilpatrick, Glasgow G60 5DJ; ☎01389-875 744.

Netherlands Vice-Consulate: Kings Court, 12 King Street, Leeds LS1 2HL; ☎0113-234 0795.

British Embassy: Lange Voorhout 10, 2514 ED Den Haag; ☎070-427 04 27; e-mail library@britain.nl; www.britain.nl.

British Consulate-General: Koningslaan 44, 1075 AE Amsterdam; ☎020-676 43 43.

US Embassy: Lange Voorhout 102, 2514 EJ Den Haag; ☎070-310 92 09; www.usemb.nl.

US Consulate: Museumplein 19, 1071 DJ Amsterdam; ☎020-575 53 09.

Royal Netherlands Embassy: 4200 Linnean Avenue, NW Washington DC 20008-3896, USA; ☎202-244 5300; fax 202-364 2410; www.netherlandsembassy.org.

Aliens Police

Johan Huizingalaan 757, Amsterdam; ☎020-559 62 14.

Burgemeester Patijnlaan 35, 2585 BG Den Haag; ☎070-360 98 79.

Doelwater 5, 3011 AH Rotterdam; 010-424 25 88.

Other

ACCESS: Sociëteit de Witte, Plein 24, 2511 CS Den Haag; ☎070-346 25 25; www.access-nl.org.

Bureau voor Rechtshulp: Spuistraat 10, Amsterdam; ☎020-520 51 00 (for free legal advice).

Immigration and Naturalisation Service: Postbus 30125, 2500 GC Den Haag; ☎070-370 31 24; e-mail voorlichting@ind.minjus.nl.

International Tax Office: PO Box 2865, 6401 DJ Heerlen; ☎045-573 66 66.

SETTING UP HOME

THE GOLDEN RULE to remember when renting or buying property in the Netherlands is: if in doubt keep quiet. An oral agreement is legally binding under Dutch law. Do not even say that you think the house looks nice as this simple statement can be interpreted as an acceptance of the contract being discussed at the time. It is easier and safer to sit back and let your representative do the talking. With that in mind this chapter aims to unravel some of the ins and outs of the Dutch property market. There are no restrictions on foreign nationals owning property in the Netherlands but it is an expensive business, especially in the more fashionable areas of Amsterdam and The Hague. The majority of UK citizens have traditionally settled in and around the major cities. However, more and more Britons are finding work in the east and south of the country. Deciding where to stay has often had as much to do with the education of one's children as it has to do with the environment. The choice of schools is dealt with in Chapter Four, *Daily Life*.

HOW DO THE DUTCH LIVE?

THE STANDARD OF LIVING and quality of accommodation in the Netherlands are high; at the same time there is a serious housing shortage. Prices have risen rapidly during the recent economic boom, but the annual increase had slowed to 5% in 2002. In order to meet the needs of the growing population it is estimated that 100,000 new units have to be built every year; in 2001 this was only 55,000. The greatest obstacles are the lack of land and the shortage of government funding.

At the start of 2002 the average price of a house was €220,000 (£107,000), an apartment €145,000 (£68,000). Most new houses being built now are in the expensive category, the average price being €250,000 (£117,000). Prices vary widely between different areas; Groningen and the north have the cheapest accommodation, with prices almost half the national average. In the exclusive area of het Gooi, and the suburbs of The Hague, prices are twice the national average.

Less well-off Dutch people are protected by a complex set of regulations which reserve the sale of cheap accommodation for those who need it, and by a comprehensive system of rent subsidies. The most startling statistic is that out of 6,500,000 housing units, 2,400,000 are in the hands of housing corporations and other organisations working with the Ministry of Housing; 900,000 households receive rent subsidies. The bad news for foreigners is that they do not qualify to go onto a waiting list for cheap housing until they have been in the country for two years, and even then there is a four- to eight-year wait for a cheap home.

Three-quarters of the population live in one-family houses and a further 20% live in apartments. Shared houses are not all that common. Half of dwellings are owner-occupied, the rest are rented. Following the boom in prices between 1975 and 1979, values hit a historical low in 1985. Since 1998 prices have been rising at between 10 and 20% a year, thanks to the booming economy and low interest rates. Government policy is now to encourage home ownership by selling off rented accommodation or building more homes for sale.

As in Britain, more and more households are made up of one person; still, families are important in the Netherlands and relatives are usually not far away. The Dutch are on the whole considerate and polite; if you are a noisy neighbour they will be quick to tell you. The average Dutch home is quite small in keeping with the thrifty nature of the people. Even in the countryside houses are small and often surrounded by trees to keep out the biting wind.

ESTATE AGENTS

IN THE NETHERLANDS the majority of reputable estate agents (*makelaars*) belong to the largest national association: the Nederlandse Vereniging van Makelaars in Onroerende Goederen (NVM). There are also two smaller organisations, the LMV and the VBO (see below). The NVM has more than 3,000 members; choosing to use their services has a number of benefits. Each member has passed rigorous examinations in subjects such as property valuation, law, finance and insurance; all members adhere to a strict code of conduct and have sworn an oath of good conduct with the local chamber of commerce. Probably the most useful service the NVM operates is a national multi-listing register in which members have at their fingertips all properties offered by both themselves and colleagues via a constantly updated computer network. This reduces much of the legwork associated with buying a home in the UK when clients often have to trudge from one estate agent's office to another. The association also publishes the useful booklet *You and Your NVM broker*.

Dutch law prevents a conflict of interests by stipulating that a *makelaar* can act only for one client: either the seller (or lessor) or the buyer (or lessee). Fees are negotiable, but the NVM recommends a commission of 1.85% of the transaction price in the case of sale or purchase of property. If your agent finds you rented accommodation you can expect to pay a month's rent as a commission. The NVM will provide help in finding an estate agent and publishes a list of its members. There is no UK-based estate agent affiliated to the National Association of Estate Agents that deals specifically with the Netherlands. However, the NAEA is one of nine members of the Confédération Européenne d'Immobiliers (which includes the

NVM) and it can offer advice to individuals planning to move to the Netherlands.

Useful Addresses

Estata Makelaars: Badhuisweg 234, 2597 JS Den Haag; ☎070-350 70 50; fax 070-350 31 21.

Nassauhuis Makelaardij: Nassaulaan 19, 2514 JT Den Haag; ☎070-324 50 50; e-mail info@nassauhuismakelaardij.nl.

Landelijke Makelaars Vereniging (LMV): Postbus 108, 2870 AC Schoonhoven; ☎0182-380096; fax 0182-387643; www.lmv.nl.

Makelaars Associatie: Stevinstraat 201, 2587 EG Den Haag; ☎070-352 68 00; fax 070-352 22 61; www.makass.nl.

Nederlandse Vereniging van Makelaars in

Onroerende Goederen (NVM): Fakkelstede 1, PO Box 2222, 3430 DC, Nieuwegein; ☎030-608 51 85; fax 030-603 40 03; e-mail Consumentenzaken@nvmorg.nl; www.nvm.nl.

Vereniging Bemiddeling Onroerend Goed (VBO): Postbus 17330, 2502 CH Den Haag; ☎070-345 87 03; www.vbo.nl.

National Association of Estate Agents (NAEA): Arbon House, 21 Jury Street, Warwick CV34 4EH; ☎01926-496800; fax 01926-400953; e-mail info@naea.co.uk; www.naea.co.uk.

WHERE TO LOOK FOR ACCOMMODATION

THE TWO MAIN publications for property sales are *De Woningcourant* and *Huis Aanbod* which cover all areas, price ranges and include some rented accommodation. Newspapers also have property adverts. The two largest circulation newspapers, the Amsterdam-based *De Telegraaf* and *Algemeen Dagblad* in Rotterdam, as well as *De Haagsche Courant* in The Hague, carry daily listings. The classified ads magazine *Via-Via* is one of the best sources for rented accommodation; the free weekly *De Echo* in Amsterdam is also popular. It is also common practice to advertise properties in shop windows and on supermarket notice boards. Advertisements for rented property carry the title *Te Huur Aangeboden*. There is a website run by the NVM with listings for property: www.funda.nl. Other groups within the NVM have useful websites for example www.era.nl and www.garantiemakelaar.nl. See also the VBO and LMV websites. The expat website www.elynx.nl carries adverts for all kinds of accommodation including sublets. For specific areas search for 'makelaar' or 'onroerend goed' with the search engine www.track.nl.

RELOCATION AGENCIES

A NUMBER OF RELOCATION agencies exist to take the hassle out of moving. These companies will do practically everything for new residents, from finding accommodation to securing a place at a local school. Clients are asked to answer a questionnaire about themselves and how they want to live in the

Netherlands. The agency will then draw up a tailor-made moving schedule which will usually require just one fact-finding trip to the Netherlands. A client will be shown 10 to 15 properties suitable for his or her needs (i.e. size, location, price) and given guidance on the practical and legal procedures involved in buying or renting accommodation. As a rule, relocators are engaged by companies moving executives and other highly-paid staff over to the Netherlands. Charges start from around £500.

The London-based relocator, T.W.G. Estates, can arrange for the purchase, management or letting of a property in London and the Home Counties, for investment purposes, or if you need a property for when you move back to the UK. They can also manage your property for you while you are abroad.

Useful Addresses

T.W.G. Estates Ltd: 36/37 Maiden Lane, Covent Garden, London WC2E 7LJ; ☎020-7420 0300; fax 020-7836 1500; twg.estates@virgin.net.

Dutch Relocation: Willem Alexanderplantsoen 12, 2911 ND Barendrecht; ☎0180-62 02 21; fax 0180-62 02 60; www.dutchrelocation.nl.

Formula Two Relocations: Stadionweg 131, 1077 SL Amsterdam; ☎020-672 25 90; fax 020-672 30 23; www.formula2.com.

Link'O: Dorpsstraat 227, 1531 HE Wormer; ☎075-642 67 00 or 0620 95 53 26.

Relocation Advisers: Joh. Verhulststraat 14, 1071 NC Amsterdam; ☎020-664 7470; fax 020-664 7469; www.relocationadvisers.nl.

Relocation Services: Postbus 95953, 2509 CZ Den Haag; ☎070-387 17 15; fax 070-387 77 41; www.relocationholland.nl.

MORTGAGES

Dutch Mortgages

IN THE NETHERLANDS there are no UK-style building societies and all mortgages (*hypotheken*) are taken out through one of the five *hypotheekbanken*. The conditions relating to Dutch mortgages differ in many ways from those in Britain. One of the important factors favouring guilder mortgages at the moment is that Dutch interest rates are currently 3% or more below the UK rate. Banks in the Netherlands offer home loans of up to 125% of the value of the property and the repayment period is fixed by agreement for between five to 30 years. It is common practice that lenders send a future borrower a letter outlining the conditions of the loan. The borrower has the right to cancel a loan agreement before it is signed. Once the contract has been signed it may be cancelled only after the loan has been redeemed in full, otherwise the lender is entitled to compensation of up to 3% of the loan.

The main difference between Dutch and British mortgages is the fact that interest payments are completely tax-deductible. For this reason interest-only or endowment mortgages (*spaar-hypotheek* or *levenhypotheek*) work out cheaper in the long run than a simple repayment mortgage and are now the most popular. Evidently, those who are in the highest tax bracket benefit the most from taking out an endowment or investment-related mortgage. In the case of repayment mortgages, there is the possibility of taking out a mortgage where the payment of the capital is heavily weighted towards the beginning of the repayment term (*lineaire hypotheek*), recommended for the over-50s. Those who expect their income to go up over the years should look at the opposite type of mortgage, an *annuiteitenhypotheek*, although these work out more expensive in the long run. As in Britain there are various types of fixed and revised rate mortgages, and penalties for early repayment. Foreigners will inevitably have to pay mortgage protection insurance (*risicoverzekering*).

A mortgage will only be given to UK citizens resident in the Netherlands. To assess an applicant's suitability for a home loan the bank will require proof of salary and it may also contact the applicant's current employer for a personal reference. A mortgage arrangement fee of 1% is charged by the bank. The Nationale Vereniging van Makelaars runs 27 Hypotheekshops throughout the country where you can arrange a mortgage.

Vereniging Eigenhuis (Own Home Association) publishes a useful booklet on how to calculate the best mortgage deal, the *Hypothekengids*, also available on CD-Rom. They will also offer advice on house purchase by appointment for a moderate fee. Vereniging Eigenhuis also publishes a monthly magazine *De Wooneonsument*.

Useful Addresses

Nederlandse Vereniging van Makelaars in Onroerende Goederen (NVM): Fakkelstede 1, PO Box 2222, 3430 DC, Nieuwegein; ☎030-608 51 85; fax 030-603 40 03; e-mail Consumentenzaken@nvmorg.nl; www.nvm.nl.

Vereniging Eigenhuis: Postbus 735, 3800 AS Amersfoort; ☎033-450 77 50; e-mail veh@veh.nl; www.eigenhuis.nl.

UK Mortgages

Until the UK joins Euroland there will always be some fluctuation in exchange rates. It is useful to bear in mind that if the value of the euro rises against sterling, the mortgage repayments for a purchaser financing his or her loan with a UK bank or building society will increase correspondingly. The majority of mortgages for Dutch properties are taken out with Dutch banks but it is possible to use a UK mortgage. Mortgage lenders in the UK do not usually make loans outside their area of jurisdiction. Unless you are a well-established customer with an offshore bank then your choice will be limited. Two UK companies who may be able to help are Conti Financial Services (www.conti-financial.com) and Oryen International (ww.oryen.co.uk).

TABLE 8 MORTGAGE COMPARISON TABLE

	UK Mortgage	Dutch Mortgage
Types available:	Repayment, endowment, pension mortgages etc.	Interest only endowment, repayment
Maximum % of value:	95%	up to 125%
Maximum compared to income	2.5 x joint, or 3.5 x 1	up to 4 x 1, related to property value
Interest rate	approx 9%	5% to 9%

Offshore Mortgages

The principle of offshore mortgages involves turning a property into a company, the shares of which are held in a tax haven such as the Channel Islands, as collateral against a mortgage of up to 75% for the repayment term of up to 20 years. The property owner's name is strictly confidential and the company is administered on his or her behalf by the offshore trustee. The advantage in the past of using an offshore loan was that it reduced tax liability in the country of purchase, and when the property was resold it merely became a question of transferring the shares to a new owner. The Dutch authorities take a dim view of tax evasion and it is strongly recommended that anyone considering an offshore mortgage should take professional advice. Such schemes may also become more difficult if banking secrecy in the European Union is abolished. For suitable companies see *FT Expat*, published by the *Financial Times*; see www.ft.com on how to subscribe.

THE PURCHASING AND OWNERSHIP OF PROPERTY

TO BUY A PROPERTY in the Netherlands a UK citizen requires: a residence permit, the deposit and approval from the *Gemeentelijke Dienst Volkshuisvesting* (Department of Housing) at your local town hall. In certain areas it is necessary to show that you have a good reason for being there, i.e. your work requires it. The national ministry responsible for housing policy is the Ministerie van Volkshuisvesting Ruimtelijke Ordening en Milieu (VROM), who can give information on whether you need a permit (*woonvergunning*) to live in a particular area.

Your *makelaar* will guide you through the Department of Housing approval, which basically requires proof of good character and adequate finances. The sticking point is likely to be the downpayment which can be anything between 30% to 40% of the house price. In addition, the buyer will have to pay 10% of the property value in fees; 2% to the estate agent, an appraisal charge, loan initiation fee, a 0.15% recording fee and a 6% registration tax (*overdrachtsbelasting*). All legal transactions go through a solicitor specialising in property (*notaris*) who will charge an additional 2% of the cost of the house for drawing up the agreement. A mortgage can be obtained from any reputable bank and the contract will include a get-out clause, should a mortgage application be unsuccessful. Whenever you move you must notify the town hall.

The Koop

Buying property in the Netherlands is divided into two parts: the purchase (*koop*) and the transfer of property ownership (*transport*). The price of a property is usually negotiable. The agent will estimate what he believes is a fair price and the first bid can go in (as with most types of haggling it is expected that you bid lower than the amount you are prepared to spend). After bidding and counter-bidding the price is verbally agreed. This deal is legally binding and if the agreement is broken the prospective buyer can be held liable. The contract is subsequently put into writing and signed by both the buyer and seller. The buyer is expected to immediately deposit a down payment at the *notaris*' office and within three weeks pay the outstanding amount. This completes the purchase part (*koop*) of buying a Dutch property, but you are not yet the legal owner.

The Notaris and the Transport

The transfer of the property into the buyer's name (*transport*) can be completed only by a notary public. Both the buyer and the seller must attend a meeting in which the notary will examine the property deeds to determine whether the house is free of claims (*onbezwaard*). If all sides are satisfied the transfer of ownership will take place and the buyer's name will be placed on the public register (*kadaster*). It is strongly recommended that your representative attends the meeting to ensure the process is handled correctly.

Property-Related Taxes

Every property in the Netherlands is assigned a value by the municipality for the purposes of tax assessment. This valuation, known as the *WOZ-waarde*, currently runs for four years from 1 January 2001 to 1 January 2005 and remains uniform unless you make extensive improvements to your property. You are required to add 0.8% of the *WOZ-waarde* onto your taxable income when you make your tax return. This amount is payable on your principal residence, and is therefore known as the *eigenwoningforfait*. Other properties you own are taxed under 'box 3' in the new tax system (see below).

On the basis of the *WOZ-waarde* the municipality calculates a property tax (*onroerende zaak belasting*), which is then split between the owner and the user of the property. This may be included in your utilities bill. The rates are shown on municipality websites; they come out at roughly 0.2% of the value of the property. Finally, there is a small tax for sea defences and dike-maintenance, the *waterschapsheffing* which is rarely more than €50 annually.

Useful Addresses

Koninklijke Notariële Beroepsorganisatie: (Notaries Organisation) Spui 184, 2511 BW Den Haag; ☎ 070-330 71 11; fax 070-360 28 61; www.knb.nl.

Ministerie van Volkshuisvesting Ruimtelijke Ordening en Milieu: Rijnstraat 8, 2515 XP Den Haag; ☎ 070-339 37 50; 070-339 38 46; e-mail bibliotheek@minvrom.nl; www.minvrom.nl.

RENTING PROPERTY

THE COST OF RENTED accommodation is high, and as a foreigner you can expect to pay the highest rates. More than nine out of ten British citizens moving to the Netherlands rent property. An assortment of Dutch homes are listed by rental departments of estate agents and rental agencies (*woningbureaux*). Some estate agents specialise in dealing with foreigners, while others generally only deal with Dutch nationals. The basic rental contract is one of unlimited duration, and it is extremely difficult for owners to eject tenants once they are established. Cheaper accommodation is reserved for those on low incomes. The Dutch government keeps a close eye on the rentals of cheaper unfurnished (*ongemeubileerd*) living quarters and rents are annually indexed. Since 1994 the rents of more expensive properties, roughly speaking those with a monthly rental of €550 or more, have been liberalised; landlords also have considerably more freedom to raise rents. The most important thing to remember is that everything is negotiable in advance. Another point to look out for are service charges in apartment blocks; there are definite risks involved here. Again, it pays to look very carefully at the contract that you are signing. Appealing later on is expensive and time-consuming. One consolation for foreigners is that it is very hard for landlords to evict tenants. The Tenants' Association (Woonbond) provides a range of model contracts and booklets in Dutch, available from: Woonbond, Nieuwe Achtergracht 17, 1018XV Amsterdam; ☎ 020-551 77 00; www.woonbond.nl.

Rental costs can be divided into two residential areas: the Randstad (the urban area including Amsterdam, The Hague, Rotterdam and Utrecht) and the less urbanised area to the east. Most foreigners do not want to buy all the fittings for their property and so they rent a partially-furnished (*gestoffeerd*) or fully furnished (*gemeubileerd*) property. In the Randstad, a partially furnished small studio on the unregulated market will cost you at least €700 a month (£100 a week). Three-bedroom houses in Amsterdam start at around €2,500 monthly. Prices in the north and east of the country are around half those in the Randstad, but one-bed apartments are much less common.

Expect an unfurnished house to be just that. Such properties do not have furniture, light fittings, curtains, water heaters or floor coverings. *Gestoffeerd*, or partly furnished properties, will have light fittings, and floor and window coverings but furniture and appliances may disappear after viewing so make sure that what you see is what you get. *Gemeubileerd*, furnished homes, will have just about the lot, including furniture, fixtures and fittings, pots and pans, linen, cutlery and crockery, but not always an oven. A deposit will be charged which can

---

Inter Agency Holland

Apartment Service

(Semi) furnished apartments, houses, villas, long and short term in and around Amsterdam. No cure, no pay.

Telephone +31 (0)20 - 624 84 44   Fax +31 (0)20 - 626 54 52
Weteringschams 53 - 1017 RW Amsterdam
www.interagency.nl   –   info@interagency.nl

LICENSED BY THE CITY OF AMSTERDAM

---

be anything from one to three months' rent.

Electricity and gas bills are usually charged separately from the rent. It is advisable to keep receipts for utility payments to enable your rental agency to accurately calculate your bills. An extra service charge is often necessary for apartments. This covers maintenance and sometimes the central heating bill. Heating costs tend to be high as insulation and double glazing are not common. To keep out the cold the Dutch traditionally hang heavy curtains in front of doors and windows.

The Rental Contract

The final written contract simply puts down on paper the verbally agreed deal. Contracts for foreigners are generally for a fixed period of time. The standard terms of the majority of contracts are as follows:

- Rent is payable on the first day of every month.
- A deposit, or bank guarantee, along with proof of your monthly income, and a letter from your employer are required.
- Minor repairs are the responsibility of the lessee; major repairs of the lessor.
- Rent increases in line with the rate of inflation or as specified.

If you are likely to have to move out at short notice it is strongly advisable to ensure the contract has the so-called diplomatic clause allowing you to leave with two months' notice. Before agreeing to anything make sure an inventory (*inventarislijst*) lists all items in the property to your satisfaction. Also, make a record of the condition of furniture, walls, doors etc. (*staat van onderhoud*) in the presence of the owner or representative. Complaints, giving notice, and so on, are always done by registered letter (*aangetekend schrijven*).

Useful Addresses

Eigen Haard: Rental Department, Geversstraat 63, 2341 GC Oegstgeest; ☎071-519 19 10; fax 071-519 19 29; e-mail rentals@eigenhaard.nl.

Estata Makelaars: Badhuisweg 234, 2597 JS Den Haag; ☎070-350 70 50; fax 070-350 31 21.

GIS Apartments: Prinsengracht 201, 1015 DT Amsterdam; ☎020-625 00 71; fax 020-638 04 75; www.gisapartments.nl.

I.D.A. Housing Services: den Texstraat 30, 1017 ZB Amsterdam (PO Box 843, 1000 AV Amsterdam); ☎020-624 83 01; fax 020-623 38 44.

INTER AGENCY HOLLAND – Apartment Service Weteringschans 53, 1017 RW Amsterdam; ☎020-624 84 44; fax 020-626 54 52; e-mail info@interagency.nl; www.interagency.nl.

Nassauhuis Makelaardij: Nassaulaan 19, 2514 JT Den Haag; ☎070-324 50 50; e-mail info@nassauhuismakelaardij.nl.

Renthouse International BV: Nederhoven 19, 1083 AM Amsterdam; ☎020-644 87 51; fax 020-646 59 09; www.renthouse.nl.

Unique Housing Service: Keizersgracht 520, 1017 EK Amsterdam; ☎020-625 90 95/620 87 97.

TABLE 9   USEFUL DUTCH WORDS

kosten koper/k.k.: registration and legal fees paid by the buyer
vrij op naam: registration and legal fees paid by the seller
vraagprijs/vr.pr.: asking price
te koop: for sale
te huur: for rent
voorlopig koopcontract: offer to buy
makelaar onroerend goed: estate agent
hypotheek: mortgage
vrijstaand: detached
villa: large detached house with garden
halfvrijstaand/tweekapper/twee-onder-een-kap: semi-detached
hoekhuis: end terraced house
gestoffeerd: partly furnished
gemeubileerd: fully furnished
ongemeubileerd: unfurnished
onderhouden: well-maintained, in good repair
inbouwapparatuur: built-in appliances
centrale verwarming/c.v.: central heating
kamer: room
badkamer: bathroom
woonkamer: living room
slaapkamer: bedroom
keuken: kitchen

Renting Out Property

In order to rent out your property you will first need permission from the local town hall housing department. Under the Dutch system, tenants enjoy a high level of protection. The law protecting tenants against eviction (*huurbeschermingswet*) does not operate in cases where the house is standing empty and waiting to be sold, or if the rental period is very short, such as holiday homes. In other cases, it is essential to draw up a contract which specifies that you will move back into the property at the end of the rental period. Such an agreement can run for six to 24 months, with a possible extension of 12 months. The period of notice from the tenant's side is one month, from the owner's three to six months.

There is no direct tax on rental income; instead you pay a tax based on the notional income from your assets (see Box 3 under 'Taxation'). If you rent a room out in your house, then the tenant can be made to leave after one year. Making an informal agreement to rent out your property is risky; the tenant could refuse to leave. Serving notice or complaints about rent arrears must be done by registered letter (*aangetekend schrijving*, or by a summons (*deurwaardersexploit*).

Several organisations produce model rental contracts, including the Tenants Association (Woonbond), the Consumers Association (Consumentenbond) and the Owners Association (Vereniging van Huis- en Grondeigenaren). In practice, most expatriates renting out a property will want to engage an estate agent to deal with the process, from putting the house on the market to supervising maintenance and collecting rent. The cost of this management can be anything up to 6.5% of the yearly rent and comes on top of the agent's commission.

Useful Addresses

Consumentenbond: Leeghwaterplein 26, Postbus 2800, 2502 KA Den Haag; ☎ 070-384 74 00; www.consumentenbond.nl.

Woonbond: Nieuwe Achtergracht 17, 1018 XV Amsterdam; ☎ 020-551 77 00; www.woonbond.nl.

UTILITIES

THE *GEMEENTE ENERGIEBEDRIJF* (Municipal Energy Company) supplies both gas and electricity in the Netherlands, and usually charges both together on one bill. When you move into a dwelling you are expected to read the meters yourself and send the readings to the energy company. Otherwise you will receive a card once a year, asking you to give your reading. Advance payments are made every month or two (except in July), any discrepancies in the account are corrected at the end of the year. Your rental company will do the initial reading before you move in. The *Gemeente Energiebedrijf* will carry out a free check on pipes and wiring and the cost of any repairs must be met by the owner of the property.

The domestic electricity supply is 220 volts. Fifty-cycle appliances must be fitted with two-pin round plugs and light fittings are screw-type. Equipment designed to run on 110 volts and 60 cycles will be damaged by a higher voltage.

Some equipment can be converted to run on European voltages, but if it has a timer or motor it may not work properly. If you are coming from North America you will need transformers and adapters if you decide to bring your own electrical equipment.

The local municipality charges a separate, monthly utility bill, which includes: refuse removal, sewerage, water, an environmental tax and in some areas cable television charges. In some cases the bill may include your annual property tax. The levy varies in different parts of the country; it is charged according to the size of the house; the amount starts from €80 per month for an apartment.

The Dutch set a great deal of store by recycling and other environmental measures. You will be asked to separate organic from non-organic rubbish; metal and plastic are put out in special yellow bags or containers. Glass you should take to a bottle bank and dispose of yourself. Paper will be collected from your door, as long as you tie it up neatly with bio-degradable string. It is illegal to dispose of batteries, used oil and other hazardous materials along with your household waste, on pain of a fine. Supermarkets, filling stations and some municipal buildings have facilities for disposing of such waste. The municipality will also collect hazardous waste four times a year. For the collection of large items (*grof vuil*) contact the town hall in advance.

INSURANCE AND WILLS

Insurance

DUTCH LAW REQUIRES a minimum of third party insurance, and it is advisable to have at least a multi-risk policy that covers theft and damage by fire. Insurance is widely available but it is strongly recommended that you seek the help of an insurance advisor (*verzekeringsadviseur*). The Netherlands Organisation of Insurance Advisors (*Nederlandse Vereniging van Assurantie Adviseurs, NVA*) can offer help and advice.

Useful Addresses

Lobbes Insurance: Bronkhorststraat 16, 1071 WR Amsterdam; ☎020-679 13 36; www.lobbes-insurance.com; U.S. representative: 188 Fenimore St, Brooklyn NY 11225; ☎718-856-6927.

NVA: Koningin Wilhelminalaan 12, Postbus 235, 3800 AE Amersfoort; ☎033-464 34 64; fax 462 20 75; e-mail info@nva.nl; www.nva.nl.

Wills

One of the first tasks to carry out after the completion of a property purchase is to draw up a Dutch will. This has to be done by a notary public (*notaris*) and can either cover just property and belongings in the Netherlands, or also include possessions in the UK and elsewhere. The drawing up of a new will automatically renders all previous wills void under international law. However, the *notaris* can state in the new document whether parts of the old will still apply. Death duties are payable where the deceased is deemed to have had his or her principal place of residence (see the section on Wills in Chapter Five *Retirement*).

REMOVALS

MOVING HOME is not easy at the best of times – moving overseas can present even more obstacles. In general, for a longer stay people will want to take a number of personal possessions, but because the cost of transportation is high it is advisable to pack only what is essential. When choosing a removals company contact an experienced international remover, preferably with an office in the Netherlands. As regards the cost of moving, one can realistically expect to pay at least £100 per cubic metre, and there will be a minimum fee of around £500. If you wish to check on the reliability of removers, there is the Dutch Association of Removers, SAVAM, as well as the British Association of Removers, whose members must post a bond as a guarantee against sudden bankruptcy. Members of SAVAM use the logo Erkende Verhuizer (Recognised Remover).

Useful Addresses

British Association of Removers: 3 Churchill Court, 58 Station Road, North Harrow HA2 7SA; ☎020-8861 3331; fax 020-8861 3332; e-mail info@bar.co.uk; www.barmovers.com.

Capital Worldwide: Kent House, Lower Stone Street, Maidstone ME15 6LH; ☎01622-766380 (UK) *or* 02 535 74 30 (Belgium); e-mail moving@capital-worldwide.com; www.capital-worldwide.com.

SAVAM: Postbus 3008, 2700 KS Zoetermeer; ☎079-363 62 28; e-mail savam@tln.nl; www.erkende-verhuizers.nl.

Allied Pickfords: Heritage House, 345 Southbury Road, Enfield, Middlesex EN1 1UP; ☎020-8219 8000; www.allied-pickfords.co.uk.

Crown Worldwide Movers: Security House, Abbey Wharf Industrial Estate, Kingsbridge Road, Barking Essex IG11 0BT; ☎020-8591 3388; fax 020-8594 4571; www.crownww.com.

General Import Conditions

Whether you are an EU subject or not, household effects and tools needed for your work can be imported duty-free into the Netherlands as long as you have registered with the local authorities. EU residents will have to make an application in advance if they wish to import a car or motorcycle without paying tax (see below). There are also restrictions on the import of alcohol, tobacco, firearms and medicines. The Dutch Customs and Excise issue a free booklet, *Moving to the Netherlands*, which you can order on the free helpline 0800-0143 or +31 455 74 30 31 from outside the country. British Customs and Excise or the Royal Netherlands Embassy will also be able to help.

Import Procedures (non-EU citizens)

To apply to import personal effects into the Netherlands contact the Royal Netherlands Embassy in your country, or ask your removals company to take care of the procedure. The leaflet *Moving to the Netherlands*, mentioned above, details the conditions you need to meet. Items to be imported should be at least six months old or show signs of wear and tear, and you are not allowed to sell them again for six months. The Dutch authorities will require the following documents:

- Proof that your principal place of residence is being transferred to the Netherlands; a residence permit or an employment contract are sufficient.
- Three signed inventories of the goods to be imported.
- A Single Administrative Document (SAD) – this is required if the move is arranged through a professional company. It is issued by the Dutch Customs authority.

Useful Addresses

HM *Customs and Excise Helpline*: ☎0845 010 9000; www.hmce.gov.uk.
Belastingdienst Douane (Dutch Customs Helpline): 0800-0143; +31 455 74 30 31 (from abroad); e-mail douanetelefoon@douane.nl; www.douane.nl.

IMPORTING A CAR

THE DUTCH AUTHORITIES do not charge duty on cars (and motorbikes) imported into the Netherlands providing the person importing the vehicle is moving his or her principal place of residence to the Netherlands and the car has been registered in his or her name for at least six months prior to the date of entry. A residence permit or employment contract and the car's registration document are sufficient proof. The vehicle cannot be sold or lent out for a period of 12 months after importation. No distinction is made between EU and non-EU residents, except that your car goes onto your SAD document for the latter; you must apply for a permit, otherwise you will be liable for the Car and Motorcycle Tax (BPM) regardless of whether you have already paid VAT in your own country. A vehicle must be registered and issued with Dutch registration plates as soon as possible after arrival. You are not allowed on the road until you have paid road tax. (For details see the section entitled Car Registration in Chapter Four *Daily Life*.)

A complex levy is charged on the importation of cars and motorbikes that have been in the owner's possession for less than six months. A comprehensive guide to the charges is available from Dutch Customs and Excise.

Buying a Car

There are no restrictions on EU nationals buying a car in the Netherlands.

Dutch car prices are comparable to those in the UK but unlike the British motor trade special offers and finance deals are not generally available. It must also be remembered that a car bought in the Netherlands is subject to UK import restrictions if the purchaser returns it to Britain.

IMPORTING PETS

DOGS AND CATS can now be admitted to the Netherlands from the UK (not from other EU countries) without a certificate of inoculation against rabies, but the Dutch veterinary authorities do require a health certificate. To issue the certificate a veterinary surgeon will need to examine the animal seven days before it travels to the Netherlands. Other animals, such as horses and birds need an import permit prior to export. The permit is issued by the Dutch Ministry of Agriculture and applications should include the following details:

- Age, breed, colour, sex and name of the animal.
- The country of export and place of import.
- Intended address in the Netherlands and date of arrival.

Initial enquiries should be made to the Department of the Environment, Food and Rural Affairs in the UK, or to your vet. The relevant department in the Netherlands is the Rijksdienst Keuring Vee en Vlees (Livestock and Meat Certification Service), part of the Ministerie van Landbouw, Natuurbeheer en Visserijen (Ministry of Agriculture, Conservation and Fisheries).

Pets can now be brought back into the UK without having to undergo quarantine. Call DEFRA for further information. Note that preparations should be made a long time in advance if you are thinking of taking your pet abroad and then bringing it back again. It can take up to seven months from the rabies vaccination to receiving the all-clear and a PETS 1 re-entry certificate from the vet.

The Dutch take good care of their pets. There is a small annual tax on dogs (*hondenbelasting*) payable at the town hall, dependent on the size of the beast. Dogs pay up to €5 to travel on trains; on trams and buses they travel on a child's *strippenkaart*. Cats and budgies travel free. Since the pavements in the Netherlands are clean enough to eat your lunch off, the locals understandably become upset if your pooch uses them as a lavatory. The notice *hond in de goot!* (usually printed on the pavement) means *dog in the gutter!* If your pet falls ill then look for a vet (*dierenarts*) or animal ambulance (*dierenambulance*) in the phone book.

Useful Addresses

Department of the Environment, Fisheries and Rural Affairs: Pets Helpline; ☎0870 241 1710; www.defra.gov.uk.

Par Air Services: Warren Lane, Stanway, Colchester, Essex CO3 5LN; ☎01206-330332; e-mail parair@btinternet.com; www.parair.co.uk. Specialise in the transportation and quarantine of pet animals.

Rijksdienst Keuring van Vee en Vlees: RVV, PO Box 3000, 2270 JA, Voorburg; www.minlnv.nl/rvv/intrl.htm.
Nederlandse Vereniging tot Bescherming van Dieren (Dutch Society for the Protection of Animals) : Zeilstraat 37, 1075 SB Amsterdam; ☎020-470 50 00; in The Hague: 070-314 27 00.
Dieren Ambulance: 020-626 21 21 (Amsterdam); 070-328 28 28 (The Hague); 010-476 87 50 (Rotterdam); 040-252 31 88 (Eindhoven); 043-352 0454 (Maastricht).
Animal Crematorium and Cemetery: Orionstraat 8, 2516 AS Den Haag; ☎070-335 0222.

DAILY LIFE

CHAPTER SUMMARY

- Although all Dutch students expect to be fluent in English by the time they leave school foreigners intending to stay in the Netherlands should try to learn Dutch.

- **Education.** Education is a top priority in the Netherlands, and 24% of the population has taken higher education.
  - Full time education is compulsory up to the age of 16, and part-time education up to 18.
  - There are many international schools catering for the children of foreigners working in the Netherlands, but fees are not cheap.

- **The media.** With cable tv you can access BBC1 and BBC2 plus stations from other European countries.

- **Transport.** Towns in the Netherlands are linked by an excellent network of roads and toll-free motorways.
  - The state-owned railway system and urban public transport are amongst the most efficient in Europe.

- Health care is funded by a number of insurance funds; private health insurance is recommended for foreigners.

- Social security benefits in the Netherlands are comparatively generous, but funded by large deductions from wages.

- **The people.** The Dutch are open, tolerant and generally friendly, but can seem unusually direct to foreigners.
  - Workplaces are generally more informal than in the UK and use of first names is the norm.

CERTAIN ASPECTS OF LIFE which often constitute the more mundane side of existence in the UK can take on a nightmarish quality when encountered in conjunction with a new home and a different culture. Opening a bank account, going to the doctor and using public transport can cause panic attacks. This chapter deals with all such dilemmas and will serve to smooth your way into Dutch society.

THE LANGUAGE

THE DUTCH PLACE great emphasis on ensuring that all students are fluent in English by the time they go to university. In addition many Dutch people also have a good command of German and French, making them the best linguists in the EU after the Flemish. If you intend to stay in the Netherlands for a long period of time it is essential to try to learn the language. Dutch grammar is straightforward; most of the difficulties stem from the rather unusual sounds, and many unfamiliar words. Many English words, such as deck, landscape, hops, brandy, mannikin and sketch have their origins in Dutch, while these days more and more English expressions are accepted Dutch, in particular *sorry, privacy, happy ending, last but not least* and *een must* (a must). For German speakers Dutch is very easy because of the shared vocabulary, but the languages are not as closely related as one might think. Telling the Dutch that their language is a dialect of German is a sure-fire way of losing friends.

The standard Dutch language of today, General Civilised Dutch (*Algemeen Beschaafd Nederlands*), came into being in the 17th century. Dutch is part of the same language family as English, German and Danish, but closest to English and Low German. Seafarers and colonists took the language around the world. Most notably it provided the basis for Afrikaans – the language now spoken by the former Dutch settlers in South Africa. Modern Afrikaans can be understood by the Dutch (and vice versa), especially by speakers of the Zeeland dialect. Dutch also survives in Surinam and the Dutch Antilles, in a pidgin form, but it has died out in the former colonies of Indonesia and Sri Lanka.

Dutch spoken in the Netherlands is not the same all over the country; that spoken south of the Rhine and Maas has something more in common with Flemish or Dutch as spoken in Belgium. The north of the country also has its own distinctive pronunciation. Further information can be found in Bruce Donaldson's *A Comprehensive Grammar of Dutch* (Routledge, 1997).

Language Courses

A number of colleges and educational establishments in Britain offer Dutch language courses. The Berlitz School of Languages (9-13 Grosvenor Street, London W1A 3BZ; ☎ 020-7915 0909), Inlingua School of Languages (Rodney Lodge, Rodney Road, Cheltenham GL50 1JF; ☎ 01242-250493) and Linguarama (Oceanic House, 89 High Street, Alton, Hants GU34 1LG; ☎ 01420-80899) all offer courses, taught by native speakers, catering for a wide range of standards and abilities. For those who are unable to attend formal classes a number of self-study courses and texts are also available. Linguaphone (head office: 111 Upper Richmond Rd, London SW15 2TJ; ☎020-8333 4898; www.linguaphone.co.uk, www.linguaphone.com/usa) provides self-study courses in the form of books, cassettes and compact discs. *In-Flight Dutch*, published by Living Language, is an inexpensive CD for self-study. In the US the specialist retailer All Things Dutch sells self-study cassettes (and a lot of other Dutch items): PO Box 419, Accord MA 02018-04119; www.allthingsdutch.com. There are also on-line Dutch courses at: www.learndutch.org, and dictionaries at: www.yourdictionary.com.

Courses in the Netherlands. As one would expect, there are numerous language schools offering courses both in Dutch language and in Dutch culture. Depending on how much individual attention you require, prices can vary from €15 to €50 per hour; private schools can offer tailor-made courses in business Dutch or other kinds of specialised Dutch, but these are inevitably the most expensive courses on offer. Success depends a great deal on how well the student understands learning strategies, and on how much practice you can get outside the classroom. Access to a language laboratory should also be a consideration in booking a course. Dutch universities and local authorities in the larger cities run language classes, in larger groups and therefore more cheaply. Some of these are listed below; the first four schools are private.

If you feel that you would like to take an examination in Dutch then the NT2 (*Nederlands als Tweede Taal* – Dutch as a Second Language) is for you. Your school will advise on when they are held. For further information on Dutch language training the Foreign Student Service (Oranje Nassaulaan 5, 1075 AH Amsterdam; ☎020-671 59 15) will supply a comprehensive list of names and addresses of schools and institutions.

Useful Addresses

ABC Talenpraktikum Rotterdam: Villapark 4, 3051 BP Rotterdam; ☎010-422 40 11.

Direct Dutch: Piet Heinplein 1A, 2518 CA Den Haag; ☎070-365 46 77; fax 356 11 40; www.directdutch.com.

Eerste Nederlandse Talenpraktikum: Kalverstraat 112.1, 1012 PK Amsterdam; ☎020-622 93 76.

Elsevier Talen: Entrada 151, 1096 EC Amsterdam; ☎020-695 24 96.

Regionale Opleidingen Centrum (Community College): Meer en Vaart 290, 1068 LE Amsterdam; 020-410 63 10, 020-556 78 00; www.rocva.nl.

Universiteit van Amsterdam: Instituut Nederlands Als Tweede Taal, Spuistraat 134, 1012 VB Amsterdam; ☎020-525 46 42; www.uva.nl.

Volksuniversiteit Amsterdam: Rapenburgstraat 73, 1011 VK Amsterdam; ☎020-626 16 26.

Vrije Universiteit Taalcentrum: De Boelenlaan 1105, 1081 HV Amsterdam; ☎020-444 50 50; www.vu.nl.

SCHOOLS AND EDUCATION

THE DUTCH PLACE education at the top of their priorities, and can rightly claim to be one of the world's best educated people. This in spite of the fact that the Netherlands spends less than the European Union average on education (5.1% of GDP as opposed to 6.1%). About 24% of Dutch people have completed a course of higher education, and many continue to go to evening classes in their spare time. The Ministry of Education, Culture and Science (Ministerie van Onderwijs, Cultuur en Wetenschappen) spends more than 21 billion euros (£12 billion) a year on education. This sum is 15.7% of the national budget – the highest single budget of any Dutch ministry – and means education is for the most part free. (Some schools do ask parents for a small contribution, usually for classroom materials.) In 1848 a 'Freedom of Education' clause was written into the Dutch constitution, which passed the running of schools from the government to the municipal authorities. Nearly 80 years later the government also voted to grant state and private schools equal rights. Seventy per cent of schools are private institutions, half of them religious. Confessional schools are very popular and encouraged by the state.

Full-time education is compulsory from the age of five to 16; part-time education is compulsory up to 18. The Dutch education system uses a multiplicity of acronyms, such as HAVO and MAVO, some of which are explained below. The Ministry of Education, Culture and Science issues a free Dutch/English brochure *Going to School in the Netherlands* which you can order from: DOP, Postbus 11594, 2502 AN Den Haag. Some of the information is also available on the Ministry's website: www.minocw.nl. The Foundation for International Education issues a detailed list of international schools in the Netherlands, *International Education in the Netherlands* on its website www.sio.nl. The British-based COBISEC (Council of British Independent Schools in the European Communities) and ECIS (European Council of International Schools) and the volunteer organisation ACCESS in The Hague can also supply information (see below for addresses).

In general, there are three options regarding schooling for your children. The first is to choose a school following a British or American system of education, secondly to opt for a truly international school, or thirdly to go into the Dutch education system itself. The major considerations are the age of the child and the length of one's stay. While younger children might be able to master Dutch if they start young enough, if you feel this is unrealistic then there are also Dutch schools which have an English stream (ES), most of them with quite reasonable fees (see below for list).

The Structure of the Education System

Primary Schools: Primary education caters for children aged four to 12 years old. It is compulsory as soon as your child reaches the age of five and the curriculum includes reading, writing, history, science, English language and social studies. There are both publicly run schools (*openbare scholen*) which are financed by the state as long as they follow the statutory regulations, and privately run schools (*bijzondere scholen*) which are either religiously based, or which follow some special educational philosophy, e.g. Montessori or Rudolf Steiner. In the last year many (but not all) pupils sit a leaving exam; their placement into secondary education will be influenced by these results and a teacher's report. In any case it is up to parents to think well in advance about which secondary school they want for their offspring.

Secondary Education: Secondary schools offer four-, five- and six-year courses of several types, depending on whether the student wishes to go into the vocational, professional or university education. Larger schools may offer all three types of courses, so that it is possible to move from one to the other if the student cannot keep up. The advantage of the larger schools is that they will have more equipment and specialised teachers.

The MAVO stream (*Middelbaar algemeen voortgezet onderwijs/Middle general continued education*) leads to the MAVO diploma, from where the student can go into the last year of the HAVO course or opt for vocational training. A MAVO diploma is not in itself a qualification for a job. The HAVO course (*Hoger algemeen voortgezet onderwijs/Higher general continued education*) may lead on to university or to a professional training college (HBO) (*Hoger beroepsonderwijs*) and lasts five years. Those who are aiming for university from the outset follow the VWO (*Voorbereidend wetenschappelijk onderwijs/Pre-university education*), but it is quite possible for MAVO and HAVO students to go into this stream if they have the aptitude.

Students who wish to follow a vocational training go into the VBO stream (*Voorbereidend beroepsonderwijs/Pre-vocational training*), followed by an apprenticeship or short course in senior vocational education (MBO) (*Middelbaar beroepsonderwijs*). Students with learning difficulties can go into Individualised pre-vocational training (IVBO) (*Individueel voorbereidend beroepsonderwijs*).

The *atheneum* and the *gymnasium* are regarded as pre-university schools and both offer six-year courses. Gymnasium students study Latin and Greek in addition to other subjects. Where a Gymnasium is combined with an Atheneum it is generally known as a Lyceum.

All secondary education culminates in written state examinations. Pupils who leave school at the age of 16 are required by Dutch law to attend a one-year course of continued training for two days a week during their 17th year and a one-day course for their 18th year. Education ceases to be free after the age of 16; small grants are available for over-16s living away from home who are still obliged to attend school by law.

Useful Addresses

ACCESS: Sociëteit De Witte, Plein 24, 2511 CS Den Haag; ☎070-346 25 25; fax 356 13 32; www.access-nl.org.

The Council of British Independent Schools in the European Communities: Lucy's, Lucy's Hill, Hythe, Kent CT21 5ES; tel/fax 01303-260857.

The European Council of International Schools: 21B Lavant Street, Petersfield, Hants GU32 3EL; ☎01730-268244; fax 01730-267914; e-mail ecis@ecis.org; www.ecis.org.

Foundation for International Education

(Stichting Internationale Onderwijs): Prinses Irenelaan 11, 2341 TP Oegstgeest; tel/fax 071-515 32 00; www.sio.nl.

Ministerie Onderwijs, Cultuur en Wetenschappen, Secretariaat VBI: PO Box 25000, 2700 LZ, Zoetermeer; ☎ 079-323 23 23; www.minocw.nl.

HIGHER EDUCATION

LEIDEN UNIVERSITY IS THE OLDEST in the Netherlands, founded in 1575 by William of Orange. Utrecht has the second-oldest university and is also the city with the highest concentration of students. Amsterdam has two universities, the Universiteit van Amsterdam and the newer Vrije Universiteit or Free University. The Netherlands can also boast the most prestigious agricultural university in Europe at Wageningen. A major advantage for foreigners who wish to study in the Netherlands is that many university courses are now taught in English, and there are those who think that all courses should be in English. NUFFIC and ACCESS can advise on which courses are in English.

There are three types of higher education in the Netherlands: the university-level education (WO), higher professional education (HBO) and the Open Universiteit. University education is divided into four-year *doctoraal* (undergraduate) courses and *doctoraat* (postgraduate) research or study. The first year of university is a preparatory year known by the extraordinary-sounding Greek term *propedeuse.* Someone who has successfully passed the first university degree is known as a *doctorandus,* abbreviated Drs., a source of great confusion to foreigners. The Drs. title is roughly comparable to a Masters degree: it is a preparation for starting a doctorate, and requires one to write a dissertation. One-year Masters courses are also becoming more common. At some point in the not too far-off future Dutch universities will go over to the British system of B.A. and M.A. courses. The title *meester* or Mr. is only awarded to law graduates. Engineers receive the title *ingenieur* or Ir. If you gain a doctorate then you receive the title *dokter,* shortened to Dr.

Higher professional schools (*hogescholen*) offer courses in varied subjects such as social work, agriculture, health care and teacher training. They do not award titles, only degrees. All higher education establishments are financed entirely from government funds. There are also seven theological colleges, which are partly funded by the state.

The Open Universiteit (www.ou.nl) is based in Heerlen, and has 18 study centres throughout the Netherlands, as well as another six in the Dutch-speaking area of Belgium. Most degrees can be studied for and charges are quite moderate. For more information on higher education and recognition of qualifications, the Netherlands Organisation for International Cooperation in Higher Education (NUFFIC) is the most useful organisation (see below).

Foreign Students

Nobody knows how many foreign students there are in the Netherlands. NUFFIC registers about 7,000 per year, but the real figure could be anything up to 15,000. The most popular subjects are business and agricultural studies. The Dutch government is in any case keen to increase the number of foreign students, and has various grants available for long-term foreign residents and those from developing countries. Many EU students are now catching on to the fact that they can obtain grants via the EU-subsidised Socrates scheme to study in the Netherlands for 3 to 12 months, after which they return home to complete their degrees. The Netherlands is also a popular destination for Americans wanting to study physiotherapy, since the courses here are less demanding than in the US. The NUFFIC publication *Study in the Netherlands* lists over 500 courses taught in English.

International Universities

As well as a number of foreign business schools, such as the European University in The Hague, which can offer BAs and Masters in Business Administration, there is also the Dutch branch of Webster University in Leiden. The latter has seminars and workshops which are open to the general public. The British Open University is also active.

Useful Addresses

Amsterdam-Maastricht Summer University: Postbus 53066, 1007 RB Amsterdam; ☎020-620 02 25; www.amsu.edu.

University of Amsterdam: O.Z. Achterburgwal 237, 1012 DL Amsterdam; ☎020-525 80 80; www.uva.nl.

British Open University: The Coordinator, Postbus 91496, 2509 EB Den Haag; ☎070-322 23 35.

International Training Centre for Women (ITW): Postbus 3611, 1001 AK Amsterdam; ☎020-420 52 43; e-mail itw@euronet.nl.

NUFFIC: Kortenaerkade 11, Postbus 29777, 2502 LT Den Haag; ☎070-426 02 60; fax 426 03 99; e-mail nuffic@nuffic.nl; www.nuffic.nl.

Netherlands America Committee for Educational Exchange: Herengracht 430,
1017 BZ Amsterdam; ☎020-627 5421; fax 020-627 54 26; e-mail nacee@nacee.nl; www.nacee.nl.

Rotterdam School of Management: Burg. Oudlaan 50, Postbus 1738, 3000 DR Rotterdam; 010-408 19 36; www.rsm.nl.

Universiteit Nyenrode, The Netherlands Business School: MBA Office, Straatweg 25, 3621 BG Breukelen; 0346 29 1211; www.nyenrode.nl.

Wageningen University: Postbus 9101, 6700 HB Wageningen; ☎031 748 36 18; www.wau.nl.

Webster University: Boommarkt 1, 2311 EA Leiden; ☎071-514 43 41; www.webster.nl.

INTERNATIONAL EDUCATION

A CONSIDERABLE NUMBER of English-speaking schools and classes exist to cater for children whose parents are living in the Netherlands. The British schools cater for the GCSE curriculum; the American ones will equip students to leave with a High School Diploma. International schools tend to follow a broadly American-based education, and will prepare for the International Baccalaureate or International General Certificate in Secondary Education. Some Dutch schools run an English stream which is taught along the lines of the European

International Baccalaureate curriculum. International schools overcome any language or cultural problems and do offer qualifications better known to British and American universities or employers. Fees are not cheap, and there is always an enrolment fee of €500 or more.

Useful Addresses for Primary Education

Den Haag
The British School in the Netherlands: Vlaskamp 19, 2592 AA Den Haag (070-333 81 11; fax 333 81 00; www.britishschool.nl) 3-11.
Elckerlyc Montessori: Klimopzoom 41, 2353 RE Leiderdorp (071-589 29 45) 4-11.
Haagsche Schoolvereniging: (International Stream) Nassaulaan 26, 2514 JT Den Haag (070-363 85 31; fax 346 33 78; e-mail hsvnass@worldonline.nl) 4-11. Part Dutch medium.
The American School of The Hague: Rijksstraatweg 200, 2241 BX Wassenaar (070-512 10 60; fax 511 24 00; www.ash.nl) 4-11.

Amsterdam
The British Primary School of Amsterdam: Anthonie van Dijckstraat 1, 1077 ME Amsterdam (020-679 78 40; fax 675 83 96; e-mail britams@xs4all.nl) 3-11.
The International School of Amsterdam: Sportlaan 45, 1185 TB Amstelveen (020-347 11 11; fax 347 12 22; www.isa.nl) 2-11.

Rotterdam
Basisschool De Blijberg: (ES) Postbus 27518, 3003 MA Rotterdam (010-466 96 29; www.blijberg.nl) 4-12.
American International School of Rotterdam: Verhulstlaan 21, 3055 WJ Rotterdam (010-422 53 51; fax 422 40 75; www.aisr.nl) 3-11.

Other
European School: Molenweidtje 5, Postbus 99, 1860 AB Bergen N.H. (072-589 01 09; 589 68 62) 3-11.
Groningse Schoolvereniging: (ES) Sweelincklaan 4, 9722 JV Groningen (050-527 08 18; fax 526 53 71; www.g-s-v.nl) 4-12.
The Helen Sharman British School: Lottingstraat 17, 9406 LX Assen (0592-344 590; fax 370 998; e-mail hsschool@bart.nl) 3-11.
International School Eerde: Kasteellaan 1, 7731 PJ Ommen (0529-451 452; fax 456 377; www.eerde.nl) 5-11.
Dr Aletta Jacobsschool: (ES) Slochterenweg 27, 6835 CD Arnhem (026-323 07 29; fax 327 10 38; e-mail primary@arnheminternationalschool.nl) 4-12.
Regional International School: Humperdincklaan 4, 5654 PA Eindhoven (040-251 94 37; fax 252 76 75; e-mail rischool@iae.nl; www.rischool.nl) 4-12.
Basisschool Joppenhof International Department: Kelvinstraat 3, 6227 VA Maastricht (043-367 13 35; fax 367 24 40; e-mail joppenhof.6227@hetnet.nl; www.joppenhof.nl) 2-11.
Violenschool International Department: (ES) Rembrandtlaan 30, 1213 BH Hilversum (035-621 60 53; fax 624 68 78; www.violenschoolintdept.nl) 4-12.

Secondary Education

Den Haag
British School in the Netherlands: Vlaskamp 19, 2592 AA Den Haag (070-333 81 11; fax 333 81 00; www.britishschool.nl) 11-18.
British School in the Netherlands: Jan van Hooflaan 3, 2252 BG Voorschoten (071-560 22 22; fax 560 22 00; www.britishschool.nl) 11-18.

The American School of The Hague: Rijksstraatweg 200, 2241 BX Wassenaar (070-512 10 60; fax 511 24 00; www.ash.nl) 11-19.
The International School of The Hague: (ES) Theo Mann-Bouwmeesterlaan 75, 2501 Den Haag (070-328 14 50; fax 328 20 49; e-mail ishstaff@knoware.nl; www.ishthehague.nl) 11-18.

Amsterdam
British School of Amsterdam: Anthonie van Dijckstraat 1, 1077 ME Amsterdam (020-679 78 40; fax 675 83 96; e-mail britams@xs4all.nl) 11-18.
The International School of Amsterdam: Sportlaan 45, 1185 TB Amstelveen (020-347 11 11; fax 347 12 22; www.isa.nl) 11-19.

Rotterdam
American International School of Rotterdam: Verhulstlaan 21, 3055 WJ Rotterdam (010-422 53 51; fax 422 40 75; www.aisr.nl) 11-18.
Rotterdam International Secondary School – Wolfert van Borselen: (ES) Bentincklaan 280, 3039 KK Rotterdam (010-467 35 22; fax 467 50 22; e-mail info.riss@wolfert.nl; www.wolfert.nl) 12-19.

Other
Arnhem International School: Groningensingel 1245, 6835 HZ Arnhem (026-320 01 10; www.arnhemintern ationalschool.nl) 12-19.
European School: Molenweidtje 5, Postbus 99, 1860 AB Bergen N.H. (072-589 01 09; 589 68 62) 11-18.
Gemeentelijke Scholengemeenschap Woensel: International Secondary School, Henegouwen Laan 2A, 5628 WK Eindhoven; ☏040-241 36 00) 11-22.
International Boarding School Eerde: Kasteellaan 1, 7731 PJ Ommen (0529-451 452; fax 456 377) 11-18.
International School 'Alberdingk Thijm': Emmastraat 58, 1213 AL Hilversum (035-672 99 31; fax 672 99 39; www.klg.nl) 11-18.
International School Maartens College: Postbus 6105, 9702 HC Groningen (050-534 00 84; fax 534 00 56; www.maartenscollege.nl/internat/) 11-19.
Het Rijnlands Lyceum Oegstgeest International School: Apollolaan 1, 2341 BA Oegstgeest (071-519 35 55; fax 519 35 50; e-mail admissions@rijnland s.ros.nl; www.rijnlandslyceum.nl/ oegstgeest) 11-18.
Jeanne d'Arc College International Department: Oude Molenweg 130, 6228 XW Maastricht (043-356 58 56; fax 361 91 52; e-mail admin.ID@jeanne-d-arc-college.nl) 11-18.

MEDIA AND COMMUNICATIONS

Newspapers

THE DUTCH DO NOT read newspapers as much as the British, even though there are many good national and regional newspapers available. The situation is such that newspaper companies are calling on the government to provide subsidies for the press. The majority of newspaper readers appear to be interested in the more serious aspects of news coverage. The quality newspapers generally have the highest circulations: *De Telegraaf* (756,000), the *Algemeen Dagblad* (400,000) and *De Volkskrant* (360,000). The main business newspaper, *NRC/Handelsblad* has a circulation of 270,000. The Dutch tabloid press is more serious in nature than

its UK counterparts and much of the gossip news is covered by magazines. The average price of a newspaper is €1.00; a yearly subscription is about €200.
The majority of national British newspapers appear on the day of publication on newsstands in the main cities.

Algemeen Dagblad: Centrist. The Dutch *Independent.* Amsterdam.
De Haagsche Courant: Local paper in The Hague.
Parool: Independent. Underground resistance paper during World War II. Amsterdam (www.parool.nl).
Trouw: Christian, right-leaning. Amsterdam.
De Telegraaf: Right-wing and sensational. (www.telegraaf.nl).
De Volkskrant: Socialist. Same company as *Trouw* and *Parool* (www.volkskrant.nl).
Het Financieele Dagblad: Business daily. Amsterdam.
NRC/Handelsblad: High-brow business daily. Rotterdam (www.nrc.nl).

Magazines

The range is vast. In terms of numbers, the most widely-read is *Kampioen*, a free motoring monthly, with 3.15 million copies. *Libelle* and *Margriet* are the most popular women's weeklies, with 700,000 and 500,000 each. There are dozens of TV weeklies, such as *Veronica*, *Avrobode/TeleVizier*, *TrosKompas* and *Vara TV Magazine*, which enjoy vast sales. The main news weeklies are: *Elsevier* (130,000), *Vrij Nederland* (100,000), *HP/De Tijd* (42,000), *De Groene Amsterdammer* (18,000) and *Hervormd Nederland* (15,000).

For foreigners, there are two publications which are essential reading: *Roundabout* with listings of meetings and events, and *Day by Day*, with listings for Amsterdam. *TimeOut* Amsterdam is now only available on the Internet: www.timeout.com/amsterdam. If you want to keep up with the news in English, there is the *Dutch News Digest* which appears daily and weekly, and on the internet. Finally, the Dutch Ministry of Foreign Affairs publishes an excellent quarterly, *Holland Horizon*, available free to anyone who is interested.

Dutch News Digest: Roerstraat 113/2, 1078 LM Amsterdam; ☎020-664 22 27; www.dnd.nl.
Holland Horizon: Ministry of Foreign Affairs, Foreign Information Division (DVL/VB), Postbus 20061, 2500 EB Den Haag; www.minbuza.nl.
Roundabout Magazine: Postbus 96813, 2509 JE Den Haag; ☎070-324 16 11; fax 070-328 47 00; e-mail info@roundabout.nl; www.roundabout.nl.
Day by Day: c/o VVV, Postbus 3901, 1001 AS Amsterdam; ☎020-551 25 12; fax 020-625 28 69; www.amsterdamtourist.nl.

Foreign Language Bookshops

The choice is limited. All good Dutch bookshops stock English books; specialised books are rarely translated into Dutch. The full range of books about the Netherlands for foreigners listed in the *Bibliography* is available from the following:

American Book Center: Kalverstraat 185, 1012 XC Amsterdam; ☏ 020-625 55 37; fax 020-624 80 42; e-mail info@abc.nl; www.abc.nl.
American Book Center: Lange Poten 23, 2511 CM Den Haag; ☏ 070-364 27 42; fax 070-365 65 57; e-mail dh@abc.nl; www.abc.nl.
Waterstone's: Kalverstraat 152, 1012 XE Amsterdam; ☏ 020-638 38 21; fax 020-638 43 79.

Television and Radio

The Dutch can tune in to enough channels to suit even the most fanatical TV addict. They watch far less television than the British, and change channels far more often. There are three national television stations, Nederland 1, 2 and 3, which roughly correspond to BBC1, BBC2 and ITV. Some programmes are broadcast in Frisian under the title Omrop Fryslân. Amsterdam has its own local station, AT 5. Other channels include RTL 4, RTL 5, Veronica, SBS 6 and TV 10, all of which show a huge amount of subtitled American programming. Hilversum is the home of Dutch broadcasting; the international section, Wereldomroep, broadcasts daily in English. For further details write to: Radio Netherlands, Postbus 222, 1200 JG Hilversum; ☏ 035-672 43 33; e-mail wereldomroep@rnw.nl; www.wereldomroep.nl.

Users are required to buy a yearly TV and radio licence *Kijk en Luister Geld*, available from post offices. The cost depends upon the number of televisions and radios in a household. Watching without a licence can incur a fine of €2,270, as well as having to pay up to five years' licence fees.

Almost all television owners subscribe to cable TV; the price per month is generally less than €10. With cable TV you can have access to BBC1 and BBC2, BSkyB, MTV, CNN, Eurosport as well as German, Belgian, French and Italian stations. The main cable companies also provide Internet access and other services:

Casema: 0800-0692; www.casema.nl.
Essentkabelcom: 0800-0330; www.essentkabelcom.nl.
Multikabel: 072-518 67 00; www.multikabel.nl.
UPC TV: 020-770 07 00; www.upctv.nl.

The Postal System

The postal service is run by the PTT, with internal letters almost always arriving the next day. Stamps can be bought from post offices (*postkantoren*), vending machines and sub-post offices in the larger department stores, as well as stationery shops, newsagents and some petrol stations. The main post offices are open 8.30am to 6pm on weekdays, and 9am to 12 noon on Saturdays. When using the post offices you need to take a number and wait your turn. A whole range of transactions can be carried out, including giro payments. Main post offices keep sets of telephone books behind the counter, and you ask to have a look. The basic cost of a letter within the country is 39 cents. A postcard or letter to the UK is 45 cents. Post boxes are red and rectangular. It is important to note that there are often two post boxes side by side, one for local mail, labelled *streekpost* with a list of destinations, and the other for all other post, labelled *overige bestemmingen*. Most boxes are emptied on Sunday evening, but not on Saturdays.

Telephones

Up until deregulation Dutch consumers paid slightly more for their telephone calls than the British. Since 1997 several new companies have come into the market, including cable companies. The main competitor to the privatised KPN Telecom is Telfort, a joint enterprise run by British Telecom and the Dutch railways. Whichever company you use, you will still have to your subscription to KPN Telecom every two months.

To have your telephone installed, enquire at a post office, go to a KPN Primafoon shop or call the customer services number 0800-0402. Your telephone should be installed within three weeks. A new line costs a basic €100 to install. Most subscribers take their number with them to their new address, so you have little chance of avoiding the installation charge. Non-EU citizens may be asked to pay a hefty deposit before they can have a phone installed; once you have paid your bills on time for six months the deposit will be returned to you.

Bills are issued every two months. It is advisable to pay up quickly; your telephone can be cut off without warning after just one reminder. A daytime call to a number in the same dialling code area costs a basic 2.80 cents per minute; cheap rate calls (after 7pm) are charged 1.50 cents a minute. The equivalent charges outside your zone, are 2.80 and 4.25 cents. An international call costs a minimum of 10 cents. To telephone the UK dial 00-44 followed by the number, omitting the first zero. To call the Netherlands from the UK dial 00-31 and the Dutch number, again omitting the first number of the provincial code. To make an internal call dial the area code (*netnummer*), followed by the subscriber's number (*abonneenummer*). Each town or area has its own commercial directory (*Gouden Gids* – Yellow Pages) as well as white pages (*Telefoon Gids*). These are available on the Internet: (www.detelefoongids.nl; www.goudengids.nl). In directories the diphthong IJ is treated the same as Y.

Payphones are usually in working order and have instructions in English. The minimum call charge is 10c for two minutes. It is useful to remember that unless the phone has a credit counter there is no advance warning when your money runs out. The most irritating aspect of using a public telephone is that the phones in railway stations only take Telfort cards, while the rest take KPN cards, so you are obliged to have both.

Many Dutch organisations now use sophisticated call queueing. A common message is *Er zijn [drie, twee, een] wachtenden voor u* meaning 'There are [three, two, one] callers waiting before you'. Another is *U bent verbonden met de* ..., 'You have reached the ...'. *Al onze medewerkers zijn in gesprek* means 'All our colleagues are busy'. You will often be asked to type a number on the keypad, thus: *Toets een, twee, drie, vier, vijf, zes, zeven, acht, negen, nul*, 'Type one, two, three, four, five, six, seven, eight, nine, nought'. If you do not understand what is being said, hit the last figure mentioned and hope to be connected with a human voice.

Most Dutch telephone numbers now have 10 figures; free and special rate numbers begin with 08 or 09. At one time 09 numbers were available from abroad, but this loophole has now been plugged. Directory enquiries within the country are still free, international enquiries are not. 0800 numbers are always free. The national emergency number is now 112.

TABLE 9	USEFUL NUMBERS
Directory enquiries	0900-8008
International directory enquiries	0900-8418
Emergency	112
Customer Services	0800-0402
Business enquiries	0800-0403
Account queries	0800-0404
Telephone repairs	0800-0407
Telegrams	0800-0409
Operator-assisted calls	0800-0410
International collect calls	0800-0410
Speaking clock	0900-8002
Traffic information	0900-9622
Public transport information	0900-9292

CARS & MOTORING

Roads

THE NETHERLANDS has an excellent network of roads and toll-free motorways which link all the main cities and towns. The motorway network covers over 2,180 km. Dutch roads are among the safest in Europe; only the UK, Norway and Sweden have fewer road deaths per head of population. There has been a gradual fall in the number of fatalities; in 1997 there were 1,163 fatalities, and 11,718 casualties needed hospital treatment. Every year over 200 cyclists are killed on the roads. Cyclists are the major traffic hazard in towns, although cycle paths are usually well-defined and their use is compulsory. Apart from having to drive on the right, the other unfamiliar feature of driving in the Netherlands are the trams, which have absolute priority.

Breakdowns and Accidents

Members of British motoring organisations will receive a free accident and breakdown service if they pay for extra cover in Europe. The RAC operates Reflex and the AA runs Five Star Service. In the Netherlands two motoring organisations, the ANWB and the Koninklijke Nederlandse Automobile Club (KNAC), operate 24-hour breakdown services on main roads and motorways. They will give assistance to AA and RAC members with the appropriate cover if you are unable to contact a garage. Temporary membership of the ANWB can be paid for at a breakdown, at around €100 for a three-month membership. The usual membership fee varies according to your age.

Useful Addresses

Automobile Association (AA): Overseas Department, PO Box 2AA, Newcastle-upon-Tyne, NE99 2AA; ☎0191-235 5733; www.theaa.com.

RAC Motoring Services: Travel Services, PO Box 1500, Bristol BS99 1LH; ☎0800-550055; www.rac.co.uk/going-away.

ANWB: Wassenaarseweg 220, 2596 EC Den Haag; ☎0800 0503 (freephone), 070-314 71 47; fax 314 65 05. Breakdown service: 0800-0888; e-mail asv@anwb.nl; www.anwb.nl.

Koninklijke Nederlandse Automobile Club (KNAC): Postbus 446, 2260 AK Liedschendam; ☎070-383 16 12. Breakdown service: 0800-099 44 02; www.knac.nl.

Driving Regulations

Dutch motorists are limited to a speed of 30 kph (18 mph) or 50 kph (31 mph) in built-up areas, 80 kph (50 mph) on single and dual carriageways and 100 kph (62 mph) or 120 kph (75 mph) on motorways. Road signs in a red warning triangle are obligatory and through routes are indicated by the sign *doorgaand verkeer,* or by rectangular blue signs with a slender white arrow. In built-up areas a blue sign bearing a white house means traffic must proceed at walking pace (10 kph). The practice of flashing car headlights should not be taken to mean 'please go ahead' but rather 'get out of my way'. If both cars are stationary, then flashing your headlights can be taken to mean 'go ahead'. Military convoys, funerals and trams have absolute priority.

The main rule to be aware of is that traffic coming from the right has priority (*voorrang van rechts*). On the other hand, if you come to an intersection and there is a row of white shark's teeth in front of you, or a stop sign, or a triangular yield sign (white bordered with red) then you must give priority to oncoming traffic. The only other exception is in built-up areas where a square orange sign with a white border indicates that you are on a priority road. The same sign with a black line through it indicates the end of the priority road. Traffic entering a roundabout (*rotonde*) always has priority and you may see a sign *rotondeverkeer heeft voorrang*, meaning just that. The status of cyclists coming onto a roundabout is less clear and a subject of intense debate. In most cases they do not have priority, but some cyclists will take their priority regardless, so watch out.

There are laws against leaving your car unlocked, and parking against the direction of the traffic, amongst other things. If you have foglamps fitted, then you may only use them outside of built-up areas where visibility is less than 50 metres. Misuse of foglamps can lead to a fine.

Seat belts must be worn at all times by drivers and front seat passengers. Back seat belts are compulsory and must be worn where fitted (except for children under three years). Where a child seat is fitted it must be used. Children under 12 are banned from the front seat. Since 2002 it has been illegal to use a mobile phone while driving.

Drink-Driving: Dutch drink-driving limit are strictly enforced. The limit is currently 50 milligrams of alcohol per 100 millilitres of blood (0.5 promille); or less than one pint of beer. The Dutch police carry out spot checks and by law drivers are required to take a breath test if asked. The penalties for drink driving are tough; they increase according to the alcohol level and the number of offences. Anyone who registers an alcohol level above 2.1 promille will receive an automatic prison sentence.

Contrary to some reports, drink-driving does not necessarily lead to immediate incarceration. On the other hand, the police will make you leave your car where it is while you accompany them to the police station if they are in any doubt about your fitness to drive. In recent years, convictions for drink driving have gone up to as many as 30,000 per year, thanks to the greater vigilance of the police. New measures are being taken to reduce drink-driving further: from the summer of 2002 new drivers will have a penalty point put on their license if they are caught with over 20 milligrams of alcohol per 100 millilitres of blood. Anyone found to have over 80 milligrams of alcohol will be obliged to take an alcohol education course (EMA-cursus).

There are two useful books in English for foreign drivers:

Traffic Manual B and *Pre-Exam Test Driving License B* published by Verjo BV, Bedrijvenweg 6, 5272 PB Sint Michielsgestel; ☎073-551 47 26; fax 073-551 23 85; e-mail info@verjo.nl.

Driving Licences

EU citizens who hold an EU driving licence can drive in the Netherlands with no alteration to it for as long as they wish. You will have to register your licence with the authorities, however, within one year. Licences older than 10 years will not be registered. You also have the option of exchanging your licence for a Dutch one. You only need to provide proof of residency, two passport photographs and your old licence. This will not necessarily be returned unless you make a specific request when you hand it over. You should start the procedure for exchanging your licence well in advance.

Non-EU citizens are deemed to hold non-exchangeable licences. If you belong to a country which has a reciprocal tax agreement with the Netherlands, then it is possible to exchange your licence (*rijbewijs*) within six months. This applies in particular to US citizens. To complete this procedure you will need not only the application form, a medical certificate and proof that you have registered your car, but also proof from the tax authorities that you come under the 30% tax ruling (see *Taxation*). If you do not qualify, then you have to take the 'Special Extra Quick Driving Test'. The authority which deals with the exchange of foreign driving licences is the Rijksdienst voor het Wegverkeer, Onderafdeling Rijbewijzen; ☎0900-0739; www.rdw.nl/eng.

If you have to take a Dutch driving test then you should look at the Centraal Bureau Rijvaardigheidsbewijzen website: www.cbr.nl. The 'quick' test is administered by the BNOR or Special Exams Division of the CBR: ☎070-413 03 00; fax 070-413 03 99.

Car Registration

At the same time as receiving your certificate exempting you from paying car tax on your vehicle you will receive a form telling you the amount of car owner tax (*houderschapsbelasting*) you have to pay; this is proportional to the size of your vehicle. These forms are also available from any post office.

To register an imported car it must conform to Dutch standards. The Rijksdienst voor het Wegverkeer will inform you about the place and time of the inspection (*keuring*), once you have sent in the application form for registration, which can obtained from their head office (see below). Assuming that your vehicle passes the inspection you will then fill in a declaration stating that you have been exempted from paying car and motor cycle tax, known as BPM (see above: 'Importing a Car'. The registration papers consist of three parts: *Deel I* (the title and description of the car), *Deel II* (details of the owner) and *Deel III* (registration disc). The first two parts, or copies of them, must be kept in your vehicle while driving, ready for inspection, and *Deel III* must be displayed in the car's windscreen. It is essential to keep the copy of *Deel III* in a safe place, in case you need to sell your car.

Having paid your *houderschapsbelasting*, you can buy your number plate from any car dealer. Once you have negotiated all of the above steps, you should let the road tax office know your new registration number.

Useful Addresses

Rijksdienst voor het Wegverkeer (Traffic Authority): Skager Rak 10, Postbus 30000, 9640 RA Veendam; ☎ 0598-62 42 40; www.rdw.nl.

Centraal Bureau Motorrijtuigenbelasting (Central Road Tax Office): Postbus 9047, 7300 GJ Apeldoorn; ☎ 0800 0749; fax 055-528 36 33.

Insurance

For the moment, British drivers are advised to obtain a Green Card when going abroad, even though the EU regulations do not strictly require it. You should also have a Green Card if you are covered by Dutch car insurance and want to drive abroad.

You are legally obliged to take out a minimum of third-party cover (*WA verzekering*). To cover yourself for damage to your car or injury to passengers, you will require all-risk insurance (*WA plus CASCO*). If you want coverage against all conceivable risks then you require the *WA plus mini-CASCO* or *WA Extra*.

Insurance cover is expensive; the ANWB and KNAC will give you further information on what is available. Insurance contracts run for one year and are automatically renewed. Dutch insurance companies will usually accept up to 70% of no-claims bonuses accrued in the UK.

TRANSPORT

Waterways

THE DUTCH WERE AMONG the pioneers of waterway travel and established an extensive inland waterway system long before a road network was developed. Vast stretches of canals had to be created to drain the land on which many cities are built; just about every tourist who goes to Amsterdam will have been for a trip on one. In other parts of the country, large areas have been cut off from the open sea by huge dikes. The IJsselmeer is the largest man-made lake in the world and the *Afsluitdijk* (the 32km dam separating the IJsselmeer from the sea) is the only man-made object on earth, besides the Great Wall of China, visible to the naked eye from outer space. Rotterdam stands at the head of three great rivers: the Maas (Meuse), the Rijn (Rhine) and the Scheldt. From here some 5,500 inland vessels transport 116 million tons of cargo a year throughout Europe. About 51% of all traffic on the Rhine and Meuse originates from the Netherlands.

Rail

THE STATE-OWNED NV Nederlandse Spoorwegen (NS) operates one of the most efficient railway systems in Europe and an estimated 750,000 customers use their trains every day. As in the UK there are two classes of travel and first class seating costs 50% more than second. Fares are uniform throughout the country and slightly cheaper than in Britain. For example, a single to The Hague from Amsterdam (64km) costs €8.00 (about £5.00 or $7.30); a day return ticket costs €14.10. The same tickets between Rotterdam and Groningen will cost €28.30 and €35.50. Children under four years old can travel free and children aged four to 11 receive a 40% discount. Timetables (*spoorboekje*) are updated annually in May and are on sale at stations, bookshops and some post offices. There is also the website www.ns.nl.

If you are just visiting the Netherlands, or already living there, then the Euro Domino ticket is a convenient way of exploring the country. It is somewhat cheaper to buy it in the Netherlands. Anyone with a foreign passport is eligible, as long as they are not permanently resident (i.e. there is no residence stamp in your passport). It can be bought in advance in the UK from the office below; prices start from £39 for three days.

Useful Addresses
Holland Rail: Chase House, Gilbert Street, Ropley, Hampshire SO24 0BY; ☎ 01962-773646; fax 773625; www.ns.nl.
Public transport enquiry line: 0900-9292. Will tell you the most efficient way to get from anywhere to everywhere. Can only be accessed within the Netherlands.

Air

The Dutch do not use internal air travel much, except to make a connecting flight at Schiphol when going abraod. Domestic flights are expensive; the principal services link Amsterdam with Enschede and Groningen in the north, and with Eindhoven and Maastricht in the south. Schiphol is the nearest airport to Amsterdam and acts as the hub of all Dutch air travel as well as being a stopping-off point for flights to other parts of Europe: in 2000 it handled 40 million passengers. Sixty airlines operate from it including the national carrier KLM (Royal Dutch Airlines), which has services to 160 cities in 80 countries. Two Dutch charter companies, Martinair Holland and Transavia, also carry international passenger traffic. Schiphol is situated 19km from Amsterdam and is easily accessible from all over the country. Trains operate every 15 minutes to Amsterdam and Leiden/Rotterdam. Buses run regular services to The Hague, Utrecht, Delft and Eindhoven.

Useful addresses

KLM: Kon. Wilhelminaplein 29, 1062 HJ Amsterdam; ☎ 020-474 77 47.
British Airways: Neptunusstraat 33, 2132 JA, Hoofddorp; ☎ 020-346 95 59.
British Midland Airways Ltd: World Trade Centre, Strawinskylaan 721, 1077 XX Amsterdam; ☎ 020-662 22 11; fax 675 23 01.

Public Transport

The Dutch public transport system (excluding trains) carries an estimated three-quarters of a billion passengers every year. Buses and trams operate an ultra-modern network of regional and municipal services and reach virtually every town and village in the country. Villages with less than 2,000 inhabitants are normally served by a community minibus service manned by volunteer drivers and financed by the state. The bus and tram services have a unified fare system which divides the Netherlands into zones of 4½ kilometres. The price per zone is the same nationwide and the same tickets can be used on both urban and regional transport. The cities of Amsterdam and Rotterdam also have their own underground metro systems.

Strippenkaart: This is a multiple ride card which is valid all over the country on buses, metros and trams. The rectangular boxes printed on the card are *strippen*. Each *strip* represents one zone, and a fixed amount of time during which you can travel. The most basic *strippenkaart*, the *stadskaart*, has three strips and allows you to travel for one hour in two zones. This can only be bought from the tram conductor; the same applies to the eight-strip card, which allows you to travel all day within the cities of Amsterdam, Rotterdam and The Hague, or alternatively to cross seven zones within a period of two hours. If you intend to use your eight-strip card as an all-day card then you must tell the conductor at the time of purchase. For a whole day's travel throughout the country, buy two eight-strip cards. Cheaper are the 15- and 45-strip cards, which you can buy from ticket machines at stations, post offices, newsagents, etc. but not from the conductor. You can also buy a 12-journey card if you find the business of strips too intellectually challenging.

The *strippenkaarten* must be stamped at the beginning of the journey; the stamp shows the zone in which you are travelling and the time you are allowed to travel. The procedures for stamping the card vary depending on the means of transport. In Amsterdam many trams have a *conducteur* at the back sitting in a booth, who stamps your *strippenkaart*. It is compulsory to get on at the back of the tram (there are notices *niet instappen*, 'do not get on', at the front), where there is a conductor. With other trams you can get on where you like, as long as you have a ticket. Otherwise you must ask the driver to sell you one. You must also show your ticket if you change trams/buses etc.

Trams have several orange stamping machines. The main thing to remember is that you always stamp one more strip than the number of zones you are planning to travel. You only stamp the last strip you need to use, by folding the card over and inserting at the relevant strip. Tram doors do not open automatically. When getting on and off you need to press the button marked *deur open*.

In the case of buses, the driver will stamp your ticket, or sell you one. You get on at the front, and leave by the back. You only need to state the number of zones you want to travel, or your destination. Metro trains do not have stamping machines; you stamp your ticket before you get onto the platform. The penalties for not stamping your ticket start with an on-the-spot €29.30 fine, plus the full single price of the ticket you should have bought. Being foreign is not an acceptable excuse.

As well as the *strippenkaart* there are also weekly, monthly and annual season tickets (*abonnementen*) for use on trams, metros and buses. These are assigned a star-value (*sterwaarde*) according to the number of zones you wish to travel in. They can only be used by the person they are issued to, and before you can use one you will need an identity card (*stamkaart*) with your photo to go with it.

Bicycles

The flatness of the landscape makes the Netherlands an ideal country for two-wheelers. The bicycle (*fiets* or *rijwiel*) became a powerful symbol of Dutch identity after the Germans confiscated all cycles during the occupation. These days 16 million cycles cover 16 billion kilometres a year. The Dutch have built an extensive network (6,200 miles/9,920 km) of cycle paths (*fietspaden*), which are marked by a round blue sign with a white bicycle superimposed. Hiring bicycles is popular: they are available from cycle dealers and at railway stations. Renting a bicycle costs around €5 (£3.00) for a day or €20 per week. If you are in the country for any length of time then it is far more economical to buy your own. It is essential to invest in a strong lock as an estimated 500,000 are stolen every year. Throwing them into canals is a favoured pastime in Amsterdam. You cannot leave your cycle where the sign *geen rijwielen* or *geen fietsen plaatsen* is displayed.

The police expect bicycles to be kept in working order. In particular you should have the following equipment: reflectors on the rear mudguard, wheels and pedals; front and rear lights; a bell; brakes in working order. There is no rule governing the use of helmets.

Every year over 200 cyclists are killed and more than 2,000 end up in hospital following accidents. While Dutch cycling organisations would like cyclists to have the same rights as cars as regards priority from the right, not giving way to traffic can have fatal consequences. Crossing points for cyclists are indicated by the sign *fietsers oversteken* or *fietsers daar*. Take great care at roundabouts, and use the cycle lanes wherever possible.

BANKS AND FINANCE

Opening an Account

THERE ARE NO LEGAL restrictions for UK nationals who wish to bank in the Netherlands and it is a relatively simple process to open an account. The bank will only require to see some form of identification (a passport will suffice) and an initial deposit to open an account. However, should you wish to borrow money, either in the form of an overdraft or a loan, the bank will want evidence of adequate means. This can take the form of either a letter from your employer or your bank in the UK. It is very difficult to open an account in the Netherlands from the UK as most Dutch banks insist on a personal visit to finalise the details.

Choosing a Bank

The banking system is dominated by the big four Dutch banks: Rabobank, ABN-AMRO, Internationale Nederlanden Groep (ING and Postbank) and Mees Pierson. A number of smaller banks, such as Staal and Van Lanschot Bankiers, offer very good services. The main banks operate networks throughout the country and, as with the major UK banks, there is probably little to choose between them. The Internationale Nederlanden Groep (ING) became famous when it took over the bankrupt Barings Brothers in 1995. ING Barings deals with corporate banking, however, not with private banking.

Useful Addresses

ABN-AMRO Bank: 250 Bishopsgate, London EC2M 4AA; ☎020-7678 8000; www.abnamro.nl.
Postbank: No London office; ☎0800-0400 (Netherlands); www.postbank.nl.
Rabobank: 108 Cannon Street, London EC4N 6RN; ☎020-7280 3000; www.rabobank.nl.

Using a Dutch Bank Account

Dutch banks offer every conceivable service: the catch is that this does not come cheaply, and bank charges are higher than in the UK. To avoid a nasty letter (and a charge) it is advisable to ask for an overdraft facility before going into the red. You will not be able to withdraw more than you are allowed when using cashpoints or a debit card.

Official opening hours are from 9am to 4pm (or 5pm) and 7pm on late shopping nights. Branches are closed at weekends with the exception of special banks on the border, at the main train stations and airports. The Postbank is open at post offices on Saturday mornings between 9am and 12pm.

The Dutch still like payment in cash whenever possible and to accommodate this the number of cashpoints has grown rapidly; the use of credit cards and personal cheques is not as widespread as in the UK. One of the surprising features of this money-obsessed society is that the Netherlands has the smallest number of bank accounts in the European Union per head of population.

Bank Accounts: On opening an account, you will be given some transfer forms (*overschrijvingsformulieren*) with which you can put money into other accounts and pay for bills. You will also get some cheques (*betaalcheques*) and a guarantee card (*bankpas*). The bank guarantee card has a number on it which you write on the back of the cheque. You must always keep the cheques and card separate, since the card guarantees payment of the cheque. If you should lose your card, then call 0800-0313 immediately (or whatever number you are given by your bank). You will also be given a secret PIN number along with your card. With this you can withdraw money from a cashpoint (*betaalautomaat*) and pay bills in numerous shops, garages and restaurants. Your account is debited instantaneously as soon as you pass the card through the machine.

Bank statements (*dagafschriften*) are issued far more frequently than in the UK, but you do have to pay charges for these. The balance of account is known as the *saldo* in Dutch. You can also arrange to pay bills by standing order (*opdracht voor automatische betaling*).

Postbank: The Dutch Post Office (KPN) runs Postbank, although it is actually owned by the ING Groep, and offers banking services at 2,500 branches. The Postbank's cheques (*girocheques*) can be used for purchases of up to €136 and the *giromaatpas* to withdraw up to €226 from cashpoints (*giromaten*). The *giromaatpas* can also be used as a direct debit card in conjunction with a *pincode* (PIN number). A transfer form is known as an *overschrijvingskaart* in the Postbank, and a cheque is a *girobetaalkaart*. A giro account is a *girorekening*. The emergency number for lost cards is 058-212 60 00.

Acceptgiros: These are very convenient preprinted invoices for goods or services, such as from the telephone or electric company. They have the look of a computer printout and state how much is owed. Simply sign the card (if the amount is correct), add your bank account number and send it to your bank for handling.

Chippen en Pinnen: Since 1997, a rechargeable debit card known as a *chipper* or *chipknip* has come into use. It can be loaded wherever you see the *chipknip* logo, usually next to a cash point, with up to €450 per day. You can also load at telephone boxes with a *Chipper* sign. Most account-holders have a Europas with a *pinpas* and *chipknip* included, but it is possible to have a separate *chipknip*. When paying at a shop with the sign *chippen en pinnen*, or with a portable machine, you only need to confirm that you agree to the amount being deducted from your account when the card is 'swiped' through the machine. With the *pinpas* it is necessary to key in your PIN number. The *chipknip* can also be used to pay for smaller amounts than the *pinpas*. The disadvantage is that the *chipknip* is no different from cash; anyone can use the balance if you lose it.

The Currency

The monetary unit is the euro: the Dutch guilder or florin ceased to be legal tender in February 2002. Old banknotes and coins can still be exchanged at banks, but there may be a charge. One euro (€) is made up of 100 cents. 1, 2, 5, 10, 20 and 50 cent euro coins are in use. Banknotes come in 5, 10, 20, 50, 100, 200 and 500 euro denominations. Note that banks outside Euroland are reluctant to exchange 200 and 500 euro notes; it is advisable to change them into smaller denominations first.

Transferring Funds to the Netherlands

For non-residents there are no restrictions on the import or export of currency. The international Swift system, by which funds can be sent direct to the local branch of your bank, is one of the most efficient ways to transfer money to the Netherlands. Most Dutch banks will accept money through the Swift system and all transactions are logged with the precise time and date of transfer. The arrival of funds is guaranteed within two days.

Offshore Banking

One of the financial advantages of being an expatriate is that money can be invested in tax-free offshore savings accounts. Many familiar names have established branches in tax havens such as the Isle of Man, the Channel Islands and Gibraltar. The facilities are as flexible as UK high street banking and range from current accounts to long-term, high interest earning deposits. When banking secrecy is abolished in the EU (probably from 2003) such tax-havens may be closed down. Further information can be found on the FT Expat website www.ft.com. The magazine is only available to subscribers with a foreign address.

Useful Addresses

FT Expat Magazine: see www.ft.com.

Bradford and Bingley (Isle of Man) Ltd: 30 Ridgeway Street, Douglas, Isle of Man IM1 1TA; ☎01624-695000.

Brewin Dolphin Bell Lawrie Ltd: 5 Giltspur Street, London EC1A 9BD; ☎020-7248 4400; fax 020-7236 2034. For investment fund management and financial planning.

Nationwide International Ltd: 45-51 Athol Street, Douglas, Isle of Man IM99 1RN; ☎01624-696000.

TAXATION

FOREIGNERS COMING FROM the UK and USA find the level of taxation in the Netherlands extremely high. One crumb of comfort is that resident taxpayers never have to pay more than 68% of their income in taxes; any amount over this will be refunded. Some of these taxes are quite unfamiliar, such as the principal residence tax and the environmental taxes. All taxes are administered by the Rijksbelastingdienst, a department of the Ministry of Finance. They are divided into direct payments (on income) and indirect tax (such as VAT, wealth tax or inheritance tax). In the case of direct taxes the burden of proof lies with the taxpayer. The tax year runs from January to December and all tax returns (*aangiftebiljet*) must be made by April 1. Failure to pay tax can result in fines equal to 5% of the amount due up to €500. An incorrect tax return can incur a 100% penalty, and a deliberate attempt to mislead the tax authorities can lead to imprisonment.

The Dutch taxation authority supplies a detailed guide to Dutch taxes, in English, *Taxation in the Netherlands* (see below). Further information sources are listed in Chapter Six *Starting a Business*.

Income Tax

Anyone moving to the Netherlands to work should contact their local tax authority to determine whether they will be liable for tax in their home country while they are abroad. For British citizens the rule is that you will not be taxed on your foreign income if you are abroad for an entire tax year, as long as you do not spend more than 183 days in a year, or 91 days a year averaged out over a four-year period in the UK. The British Inland Revenue produces several useful leaflets on working abroad, such as IR138 *Living or Retiring Abroad* and IR20 *Residents and Non-residents* which are essential reading. They are available from your local tax office or from the address given below.

US citizens are required to file tax returns unless they have entirely severed their connection with the USA. Full details can be found in *Tax Guide for US Citizens and Resident Aliens Abroad*, known as Publication 54, which can be downloaded from the internet on www.irs.gov. See also the 'Taxation' section under *Daily Life*, Belgium, in this book.

The Netherlands has double taxation agreements with a number of non-EU countries, including the USA. US and other non-EU citizens working for a Dutch-based employer or a foreign employer in the Netherlands subject to Dutch taxation law, can benefit from the '30 per cent rule', in which case your employer can pay you a tax-free allowance of up to 30% of your salary and allowances and benefits in kind. The 30% allowance is intended to cover extra-territorial expenses, i.e. the cost to the worker of coming to work in the Netherlands, and can be extended for up to 10 years. The 30% rule applies to 'experts' coming from abroad, i.e. where there is no one in the Netherlands available with your expertise, or where such persons are very hard to find. It can also apply to Dutch citizens who have done their training abroad. Enquiries about the 30% rules should be made to the Belastingdienst Particulieren en Ondernemingen Buitenland (Foreign Taxation Office) in Heerlen (see below).

The Dutch Tax System

The taxation system was completely overhauled at the start of 2001. Taxes have been made more transparent, and a greater emphasis has been placed on rewarding environmentally friendly activities. Instead of personal allowances, there are now 'levy rebates' (*heffingskortingen*).

Foreign taxpayers are classified as either residents or non-residents (with some variations). Resident taxpayers are subject to tax on their worldwide income, while non-residents pay tax only on sources of income in the Netherlands. Residence is determined in accordance with an individual's principal place of residence and what the tax courts call 'durable ties of a personal nature'. Durable in this case means the closeness of the tie rather than the length of the stay.

Dutch employers are obliged to deduct tax at source and pay it to the Belastingdienst. If the amount deducted corresponds to your final liability, then you do not necessarily have to file a tax return. If your income exceeds €40,000 per annum, or your tax affairs are more complex, then you will need to contact your local tax office.

Taxable income is now divided up under three 'boxes' (*boxen*). Most foreigners will only have to concern themselves with 'Box 1'.

- **Box 1:** Wages, salaries, pensions and social security benefits. Taxed on a sliding scale, after deduction of 'levy rebates'. Also includes business profits and capital gains.
- **Box 2:** Substantial shareholdings. Only applies if you own 5% or more of shares in a Dutch company (BV or NV).
- **Box 3:** Your net total worth is calculated and then a tax of 30% is levied on a notional income of 4% derived from your assets in excess of €17,600. You are not required to declare the actual income. This includes savings, second homes, stocks and shares and certain insurance policies. This replaces the former 'wealth tax' (*vermogensbelasting*).

Before your levy rebates are calculated a number of items can be deducted from your taxable income: e.g. travel deduction (*reisaftrek*): if you use public transport to go to work; bicycle deduction (*fietsaftrek*): if you cycle more than 10km to work; childcare deduction (*uitgaven voor kinderopvang*); deduction for losses on investments, etc.

- There are a number of levy rebates; these are just the most common ones:
- **General levy rebate** (*algemene heffingskorting*): For all under-65s, up to €1,576.
- **Work rebate** (*arbeidskorting*): applies to salaries, wages, business profits and freelance work. For under-65s: maximum €920.
- **Child rebate** (*kinderkorting*): there are several kinds of *kinderkorting* depending on income and age. No more than €192.
- **Single parent rebate** (*alleenstaandeouderkorting*): worth up to €1,261. Double if you go out to work.

A significant feature of the new tax system is that partners are taxed separately as far as possible, although a few deductions can still be divided up between the two. Partners can mean married persons (of whatever sex), a couple who have registered themselves as partners with the town hall, or anyone who lives with another person for at least six months of the year at the same address. You should contact the tax authorities in advance if you wish to declare that you are partners.

While levels of taxation have come down, certain sections of the population may be worse off. If you own a company car, which you also use privately, a percentage of the car's value will be added to your taxable income. Nor is it any longer possible to deduct professional costs of any sort, apart from the travel deductions above.

TABLE 10   TAXATION IN THE NETHERLANDS

Tax rate	Taxable Income
32.35% (2.95% tax + 29.40% national insurance)	the first €14,870
37.60% (8.20% tax + 29.40% national insurance)	€27,010-27,009
42%	€27,010-46,309
52%	over €46,310

Self-employment

To be considered as self-employed you must be a Dutch resident who spends over 1,225 hours per annum running a business. Self-employed EU nationals are entitled to a special €6,135 deduction if their net profit is less than €45,000. This deduction goes down as your profit goes up, to a minimum of €4,085 if the net profit is more than €50,745. An extra deduction of €1,795 will also be made to an individual for the first three years of a new business.

The self-employed must make pension contributions and pay social security.

Other taxes

Inheritance and Gift Tax: Both gifts and inherited items are taxed at rates between five and 63 per cent depending on the relationship between the donor and recipient, and the amount. The inheritance tax (*successierecht*) applies only to individuals who have died while a resident of the Netherlands. For a gift it is the responsibilty of the donor and donee to make a declaration to the local Inspector of Registration and Succession (Inspecteur der Registratie en Successie). Non-residents are subject only to gift tax (*schenkingsrecht*) on property (for a detailed account of inheritance tax see Chapter Five, *Retirement*).

Capital Gains Tax: Profits from the sale of assets, including property acquired for the purpose of selling at a profit, are taxed at the same rate as regular income.

Dividend Withholding Tax: Companies are obliged to withhold 25% in tax on dividends (*dividendbelasting*).

Indirect Taxes

VAT: Value added tax (*belasting op toegevoegde waarde – BTW*) is a general tax on goods and services. The standard rate is levied at 17.5%. A reduced rate of 6% is charged on essential items such as food, medicine, newspapers, passenger transport and non-alcoholic drinks. A special 0% applies to the export of goods from the Netherlands. Insurance premiums are taxed at 7%.

Local Taxes: These include a property tax (*onroerende zaak belasting*) related to the value of your property, and various small taxes for garbage disposal, sewerage and environmental protection, as well as a new 'archaeology tax', to pay for the excavation of building sites (see under *Utilities* above).

Useful Addresses

Non-Resident Claims: Fitz Roy House, PO Box 46, Nottingham NG2 1BD; ☎0115-974 1919; fax 0115-974 1919; www.inlandrevenue.gov.uk.
Centre for Non-Residents (CNR), Residence Advice & Liabilities Unit 355: St. John's House, Bootle, Merseyside L69 9BB; ☎0151-472 6202; fax 0151-472 6003.
Ministerie van Financiën (Ministry of Finance): Central Information Directorate, Postbus 20201, 2500 EE Den Haag; ☎070-342 75 42; www.minfin.nl or www.belastingdienst.nl.
Team GWO (Overseas Taxation Office): Postbus 2865, 6401 DH Heerlen; ☎045-573 66 66; www.belastingdienst.nl.

HEALTH INSURANCE AND HOSPITALS

THE NETHERLANDS has a two-tier health care service comprising curative and preventative care, under the overall control of the Ministry of Health, Welfare and Sport (Ministerie van Volksgezondheid, Welzijn en Sport). The interface between the ministry and the health care providers is the College voor Zorgverzekering. Most health care provision comes from private organisations and is funded through insurance schemes. The Dutch health service has been under increasing pressure in the last few years, with longer waiting lists, shortages of hospital beds and staff, and the other ills one has become used to in the UK. A complete reform of the health care system is under consideration.

The E111

Anyone intending to move permanently to the Netherlands must register their change of address with the Overseas Branch of the Department of Work and Pensions in Newcastle. You will be sent the paperwork required to obtain an E111 (allow one month for processing) which entitles all EU nationals to subsidised medical treatment in any Member State. The E111 covers emergencies, but will only cover part of your costs. It is advisable to take out private medical insurance for temporary visits to cover treatment not regarded as an emergency. The E111 is only valid for three months in any one country. It is available from any post office or from the Inland Revenue if you are already abroad. For further information, ask for leaflet SA29 *Your social security, benefits and health care rights in the European Community* from: International Services, Inland Revenue, National Insurance

Contributions, Longbenton, Newcastle upon Tyne NE98 1ZZ; ☎08459 154811 or +44 191 225 4811 from abroad; fax 084591 57800 or +44 191 225 7800 from abroad. Details are also available on the website: www.inlandrevenue.gov.uk/nic/intserv/osc.htm.

Medical Insurance

Health care in the Netherlands is funded through a number of insurance schemes. People with an annual income of less than €30,700 (£18,000) or €100 per day, pay a monthly contribution to the state's Health Insurance Fund (*ziekenfonds*) in return for which they receive medical, pharmaceutical and dental treatment, and hospitalisation, but not entirely free of charge (see below). If your income exceeds €30,700 then you have to take out private insurance (*particuliere verzekering*). These figures are indexed and go up annually. Individuals paying into the *ziekenfonds* usually take out a subsidiary insurance (*aanvullende verzekering*) which covers health expenses abroad and ante/post-natal services. A state-run scheme also exists that covers what are termed exceptional medical expenses (*Algemene Wet Bijzondere Ziektekosten* – AWBZ). The AWBZ provides treatment in recognised nursing homes, medical children's homes and institutions for the deaf, blind, handicapped and mentally ill.

UK organisations such as Expacare and BUPA offer a variety of international health insurance schemes: see under *Private Medical Insurance* in the *Daily Life* chapter of Belgium for their details. The advantage of taking out a UK policy is that it will cover the claimant for treatment costs incurred anywhere in Europe and not just in the Netherlands.

Anyone intending to use the Dutch health service must be able to prove they are paying into either the Health Insurance Fund or a private medical insurance scheme. Therefore, it is advisable to have several copies made of your insurance certificate and hand out copies where necessary.

Since 1997 additional charges have been levied on certain medical services, notably a 20% contribution to the cost of medicines, visits to a specialist, ambulance and paramedical help. There is also a charge for hospital stays, or if you need regular hospital services, depending on your income. Visits to a GP, a dentist, and obstetric services are still free. There is an annual limit on what you have to pay.

Useful Addresses

Public Relations Department, Ministry of Health: Postbus 5406, 2280 HK Rijswijk: ☎070-340 78 92; www.minvws.nl.
College voor Zorgverzekering (Health Insurance Council): Postbus 396, 1180 BD Amstelveen; ☎020-347 55 55; fax 020-647 34 94; www.cvz.nl.
BUPA: Russell Mews, Brighton BN1 2NR; ☎01273-208181; fax 01273-866583; www.bupa-intl.com.
Expacare: email info@expacare.net or visit www.expacare.net.

Using the Dutch Health Service

The Dutch health service operates through *huisartsen* or general practitioners. To use the system (except in the case of extreme emergencies) it is essential to register with a GP as they sanction the use of ambulances and specialists, and authorise hospital admittance. A list of English-speaking GPs is available from Access (see below) or look in the telephone book under *artsen – huisartsen*. It is very important to note that hospitals are entitled to refuse to treat patients in a non-life threatening situation unless they are referred by a *huisarts*. GPs hold surgeries (*spreekuur*), and carry out both house and hospital calls.

Mothers-to-be can choose either a midwife service (*verloskundige*) or a gynaecologist (*gynaecoloog*). The midwife service operates both at home and in hospitals, whereas gynaecologists work solely in hospitals. Hospital deliveries fall into two categories: at an out-patient hospital (*polikliniek*), which means just 24 hours in hospital; or a maternity bed, which is provided for as long as is necessary. All new mothers are offered a mother and baby home carer (*kraamverzorgster*).

As well as the regular health care system, there are also the Kruisverenigingen (Medical Service Associations), which offer ante-natal clinics and exercise classes, as well as paediatric services in return for a moderate membership fee. Other services include the loan of medical equipment and home nursing help.

ACCESS: Offers free medical advice (including mental health problems) as well as help on most everyday problems, in English. It is staffed by volunteers from the international community and runs a telephone information line (weekdays, 9.30am to 3.30pm), workshops and counselling.

USEFUL NUMBERS

ACCESS: ☎ 070-346 25 25.
AIDS Infolijn: ☎ 020-022 22 20.
Alcoholics Anonymous: ☎ 020-625 60 57.
Cancer Information Line: ☎ 020-570 05 00.
Drugs Advice: ☎ 020-570 23 35.

Emergencies

If you are involved in or are a witness to a serious accident call an ambulance (*ziekenwagen*) on 112. In the event of a non life-threatening emergency such as a broken bone call your *huisarts*. He or she will make a house call and if necessary arrange for the patient to be taken to hospital. All Dutch hospitals have a casualty department (*Eerste Hulp Bij Ongelukken – EHBO*) for first aid and emergencies. To be admitted to a hospital you will require both your insurance card and doctor's notes. Your details will be recorded on an identity card (*ponsplaatje*) and used for reference if further visits are necessary. For minor ailments Dutch pharmacists are highly qualified and will probably be able to prescribe something for you. In the Netherlands two types of chemist exist. The *apotheek* supplies prescriptions and over-the-counter medicines, whereas the *drogisterij* sells toiletries, baby products and non-prescription medicines.

SOCIAL SECURITY AND UNEMPLOYMENT BENEFIT

Social Security

THE DUTCH SOCIAL security system is one of the more benevolent in the EU and taxpayers are required to make no fewer than eight contributions. These total nearly 40% of their salary and are mostly withheld at source by employers. The different types of social security are known by their various abbreviations and appear in this form on your wages slip.

Since 2002 five different social security agencies have come together under one organisation: the Uitvoering Werknemersverzekering (UWV) or Employees Social Security Agency. Information about social security is given out by 2ZW (Zorg, Zekerheid en Welzijn).

If you go to work in the Netherlands you are generally required to pay social security contributions in the Netherlands. The USA does, however, have a totalisation agreement with the Netherlands, whereby, if you are sent by a US employer to work in the Netherlands you may continue to be covered by US social security for up to five years, and be exempted from paying contributions in the Netherlands.

Sickness Benefits Act (ZW): People unable to work as a result of sickness, disablement or an accident are entitled to 70% of their basic wage for up to 52 weeks. The maximum amount in 2002 was €41,575 in one year or €159.99 daily. The amount must be at least equal to the minimum wage; it may be more than 70% if there is an industry-wide agreement. After a year you go on to the WAO scheme.

Where the worker has fallen sick during the first year of employment, or for some reason there is no employer to pay for them, e.g. temporary workers, the state will pay the benefit at 70% of wages. Benefit is also payable for maternity leave of up to 16 weeks. Contact the UVW if you are having a baby.

Disablement Benefits Act (WAO): If you have not been able to work because of sickness for more than a year, you become eligible for WAO benefit. The length of time for which it is payable depends on your age; it is not payable at all to anyone under the age of 32. The amount depends on to what extent you are unfit for work and is a percentage of your last wage; it cannot fall lower than the minimum wage. You have to be assessed as being at least 15% unfit for work to receive the WAO benefit. A person assessed as over 80% unfit to work is entitled to up to 70% of their former wage.

The WAO scheme has become notorious as a malingerers' charter; some nine per cent of the working population receive WAO benefits, one-third of them suffering from stress and other ill-defined psychological problems, which perhaps reflects the difficulties some have in keeping up with the hectic pace of life here. Plans to reform the WAO are under way. To begin with employees will be obliged to take alternative work if they are only slightly disabled; employers may be obliged to offer work to employees who are assessed as up to 80% disabled. This measure is seen as essential in order to bring more working-age people back to the labour market.

General Child Benefits Act (AKW): Families are entitled to family allowance (*kinderbijslag*). It is a quarterly payment and is payable for economic dependants up to the age of 17. Further payments are also made for students up to the age of 27. The allowance is calculated on the number and ages of the dependants. For example a family with two children, aged 8 and 10, would receive about €90 per month for each child. Benefits have been cut for children born after October 1994.

General Old Age Pensions (AOW): Anyone who reaches the age of 65 is entitled to draw a state pension. The state pension contribution is 17.90% of the employee's salary, up to about €3,500 annually. Entitlement to AOW is accumulated at the rate of 2% for each year of insurance. The amount is calculated on the basis of 50% of the minimum wage for each married partner and 70% for single people. A married couple received a fixed sum of €1,122 per month in 2001 and a single person €810). Very few Dutch people rely entirely on the state pension provision; over 85% take out additional pension provision. Under EU rules state pension contributions in separate Member States can be combined. For further details see Chapter Five, *Retirement*.

Health Insurance Act (ZFW): Applies to those earning under €30,700 per annum. The employee pays a contribution of 1.75% of their wage, the employer 6.35%. Your partner and children are also insured if you are the sole breadwinner. If you earn over the €30,700, then your employer should pay for your health insurance. If one partner earns more than €30,700 per year, then you must both take out private insurance.

Unemployment Benefit

In general, the Dutch unemployment benefit system is open only to UK citizens who are made unemployed in the Netherlands. The benefit amounts to 70% of the claimant's most recent wage and is payable for at least six months. To qualify an individual must have worked for at least 26 weeks in the 39 weeks preceding unemployment. It is also a condtion that the claimant has received a salary for over 52 days during four out of the last five year. The income-related WW benefit continues for a minimum of six months if you satisfy the conditions. If you do not fall into this category you will receive only 70% of the minimum wage, or 70% of your last wage, whichever is less. The income of the claimant's partner, if any, is not taken into account. To apply for benefit it is necessary to register with the local employment centre, or *Centrum voor Werk en Inkomen*.

If you have left a job of your own accord, or you refuse to accept work that is offered to you without a good reason, then you will not receive income-related benefit. After a year of unemployment, the CWI will work out a plan of action with you, which may include training, and interviews for work, which you are obliged to accept. If you do not qualify for income-related benefit, then you have to apply under the National Assistance Act (ABW), a sort of safety-net for the destitute.

Transferring UK Benefit

If you have received UK unemployment benefit for at least four weeks it is possible to receive up to three months' payments in the Netherlands. You will also need to have paid full Class 1 contributions during the two tax years previous to the one you are claiming in. You should contact your usual benefit office who will in turn contact the DWP Overseas Branch. In order to receive the medical care you are entitled to you should also ask for the form E119 at the same time. For general information about benefits and social security in EU countries, you should ask for forms SA29 and JSAL22, either from your Jobcentre or from the DWP.

Useful Addresses

Social Insurance Information Centre: 2ZW, Postbus 19260, 3501 DG Utrecht; ☎030-230 67 55; fax 030-230 67 41; e-mail info@2zw.nl; www.2zw.nl.
Pensions and Overseas Benefits Directorate, DWP: Tyneview Park, Whitley Rd., Benton, Newcastle-upon-Tyne NE98 1BA; ☎0191-218 7777; fax 0191-218 7293.

LOCAL GOVERNMENT

RUNNING PARALLEL to the central government are two levels of local government: a provincial council/assembly (*provinciale staten*) and a municipal council (*gemeenteraad*). The Netherlands is divided into 12 provinces and 625 municipalities (*gemeenten*). Each province has its own *provinciale staten* and the members are directly elected every four years; the number is proportional to the province's population. Each council appoints a six-strong executive committee which is responsible for the day-to-day running of the province. The council also elects members to the Upper House of Parliament (De Eerste Kamer – First Chamber). A Commissioner (Commissaris van de Koningin) is appointed by the monarch and presides over the council.

The administration of each municipality is conducted by a municipal council, a municipal executive and a mayor (*burgemeester*). The council is largely independent and responsible for local administration, law and order, the fire service and civil defence; it is required to prepare and implement central government and provincial council decisions. The Crown appoints the mayor, for a six-year term, to preside over the executive and the council. Council members are elected every four years and foreigners legally resident for five years or more are entitled to vote. Municipal councils are increasingly joining forces into unofficial regional authorities to tackle matters such as the location of industry, environmental issues, housing and transport.

CRIME AND THE POLICE

THE NETHERLANDS has the second highest crime rate in Europe (the UK has the highest). Much of the crime is petty theft (24%) and to a large degree drug-related. Serious assault and rape are rare. On the other hand, muggings are quite common in Amsterdam and other inner cities; it is not advisable to hang around in unlit areas after dark, even in the centre of the city. You should also be very careful about withdrawing money from cash machines at night. If you are in the habit of throwing away litter, it is best to make sure that no one is watching: you could be fined €100 or more.

The authorities have tried to increase the number of officers on the beat, but are hampered by a shortage of suitable candidates. In Amsterdam some of the police are now equipped with roller-skates; a typically original Dutch idea. The clear-up rate stands at about one-fifth of all reported crimes; a figure comparable with the UK. The Dutch authorities claim that crime is falling, but the statistics are by no means convincing. There is information in English on the police website: www.politie.nl.

In the event of an emergency, for the most urgent calls use the national emergency number 112. If your call is less urgent then call the police (*politie*) on one of the following numbers. Emergency numbers are given on the back of telephone directories under *alarmnummers*.

Amsterdam: 020-559 91 11.
Rotterdam: 010-274 99 11.
Den Haag: 070-310 49 11.
Wassenaar: 070-515 73 11.

Drugs: Possession of any kind of drugs is illegal, however, the police tend to turn a blind eye to the buying and selling of small quantities of cannabis, and these are openly available in coffee-bars which specialise in their sale. Possession of more than 30g will be treated as an offence. The Dutch authorities point out that the rate of hard drug addiction in the Netherlands is lower than in neighbouring countries. Authorities in neighbouring countries, on the other hand, point out that liberal Dutch drug policies create a major law enforcement problem in the rest of Europe. The number of 'coffee shops' or drugs cafés has decreased in recent years.

The Judiciary

The legal system in the Netherlands is based upon Roman Law and there is no trial by jury. The justice organisation is administered by a four-tier court system. The highest court in the land is the Supreme Court of the Netherlands (*Hoge Raad*). This heads a pyramidal court structure consisting of five Courts of Appeal (*Gerechtshof*), 19 District Courts (*Arrondissementsrechtbank*) and 62 Sub-district Courts (*Kantongerecht*).

RELIGION

THE DUTCH CONSTITUTION guarantees freedom of religion and more than half of the population claim to belong to a recognised church. One-third are Roman Catholics (mostly concentrated in the provinces of Noord-Brabant and Limburg), one fifth belong to the Dutch Reformed Church (Nederlandse Hervormde Kerk), and 7% to other Protestant groups. Dutch Catholics are regarded as among the most liberal in the world and as a result have often found themselves in conflict with the papal authorities.

Useful Addresses

The following English-speaking churches in the Netherlands are Anglican unless otherwise indicated.

The Hague
Trinity Baptist Church: Bloemcamplaan 54, 2240 EE Wassenaar; ☎070-517 80 24.
The Church of St John and St Philip: Riouwstraat 2C, 2585 HA Den Haag; ☎070-355 53 59; www.stjohnstphilip.org.
The American Protestant Church: Esther de Boer van Rijklaan 20, 2597 TJ Den Haag; ☎070-324 44 90.
International Roman Catholic Parish of The Hague (The Church of Our Saviour): Parish House, Ruychrocklaan 126, 2598 ES Den Haag; ☎070-328 08 16.
First Church of Christ Scientist: Andries Bickerweg 1B, 2517 JP Den Haag; ☎070-363 66 52.
Orthodox Synagogue: Cornelis Houtmanstraat 11, 2593 RD, Den Haag; ☎070-347 32 01.
Liberal Jewish Congregation: Prinsessegracht 26, 2514 AP Den Haag; ☎070-365 68 93.

Amsterdam
English Reformed Church: Begijnhof 48, 1012 WV Amsterdam; ☎020-624 96 65.
Christ Church: Groenburgwal 42, 1011 HW Amsterdam; ☎020-624 88 77.
Church of St John & St Ursula: Begijnhof 29/35C, 1012 WV Amsterdam; ☎020-627 02 60.
Jewish Community: Van der Boechhorststraat 26, 1081 BT Buitenveldert; ☎020-646 00 46.
Liberal Jewish Community: Jacob Soetendorpstraat 8, 1079 RM Amsterdam; 020-642 35 62.

Rotterdam
St Mary's Church of England: Pieter de Hoochweg 133, 3024 BG Rotterdam; ☎010-220 24 74.
The Scots Church Rotterdam: Schiedamsevest 119, 3012 BH Rotterdam; ☎010-412 47 79.
Roman Catholic Church: Pieter de Hooghweg 133, 3024 BG Rotterdam; ☎010-414 45 77.

Other
Protestant Services in Arnhem, Nijmegen, Twente, Haarlem: ☎026-495 38 00.
Het Pensionaat Eikenburg Chapel: Aalsterweg 289, 5644 RE Eindhoven; 040-242 42 77.
International Families Association Chapel: 38 Wetroude van Caldenbourgh Laan, Maastricht; ☎045-526 28 04.
Holy Trinity: Van Limburg Stirum Plein, Utrecht; ☎030-251 34 24.
Chapel of St Nicholas: Scheldepoort, Vlissingen; ☎011-847 49 37.

SOCIAL LIFE

The Dutch

THE DUTCH are neither the clog-wearing windmill-dwellers of popular folklore, nor the drug-dealing pornographers which they have been made out to be in recent times. Few Dutch people would recognise themselves in such stereotypes. They are certainly a unique people and this begins with the fact that they have quite literally had to create their own country in the face of overwhelming natural adversity. To do this they have had to be both ingenious and courageous, two traits that are as common today as they have ever been.

They are a commercially-minded people. Experience has shown that tolerance and openness are good for business. They have also had to be tolerant in order to integrate the large numbers of refugees and immigrants who have traditionally found a safe haven in their country. The Dutch are not by any means an idealistic people. Nonetheless, they feel that anything that might disturb social harmony needs to be addressed, and they are willing to try unconventional solutions to problems. In particular, there is the idea that it is best to organise activities which most people would classify as vices, rather than trying to drive them underground.

Also basic to the Dutch view of life is the belief in the equality of all members of society and their acceptance of outsiders who are prepared to work hard and conduct themselves as upstanding citizens. For some, Dutch tolerance goes too far, and there is always the suspicion that the necessity of making a fast buck outweighs other considerations, but at the end of day, many a foreigner has come round to the view that the rest of the world could learn a great deal from the way the Dutch run their country.

Dutch tolerance has its limits: outside of the Randstad attitudes are much more conservative, in particular in the more Catholic south and areas with a lot of fundamentalist Calvinists. The rather paradoxical nature of Dutch liberalism is well illustrated by the many posters warning against the evils of blaspheming, put up by the Union Against Swearing. Unconventional dress or behaviour attract the same kind of disapproval you might expect in France or Germany from certain locals.

One area where the Dutch appear to forget their tolerance is in their well-known prejudice against the Germans. While this seems to be diminishing as the last war recedes into memory, it is in any case not advisable to tell the Dutch how similar their country is to Germany, or how much their language resembles German.

Manners and Customs

The Dutch are generally friendly and helpful but they do not believe in wasting time on trivialities. They tend to be very direct in their attitude which means they can come across as rude and abrupt (the Dutch word is *bot*). You will soon learn to distinguish between those who are genuinely rude and the rest of the population, who are genuinely friendly. Speaking one's mind is a trait that is bred into the people from childhood. No doubt the toughness of the environment has had a great deal to do with this.

The workplace is much less formal than UK counterparts and it is common practice for employees to be on first name terms. Older people can be rather formal and expect to be treated with respect. If you learn Dutch, you will quickly realise that there are two words for 'you', the formal *U* and the informal *je*. The way you are addressed will tell you quite a lot about how people see you. Once you are over a certain age, say 45, most people will address you as *U* in the first instance. Amongst young people, the use of *je* is almost universal, unless you are in a very formal situation. Sometimes, as in French and German you may find that the changeover from *U* to *je* is the cause of some embarrassment, but these are nuances which English-speakers will take time to appreciate.

Keeping Your Head Down

There is a well-known saying in Dutch, which goes: 'Act normal and you'll be weird enough'. The apparent meaning of this cryptic statement is that it is best not to draw attention to yourself. Dutch multi-nationals succesfully operate with this principle in mind, so that no one knows just what they are getting up to.

In general, the Dutch tend towards a minimalist view of life. One French writer called the Netherlands 'le pays du petit bonheur' – taking pleasure in small things. The Dutch generally dislike arrogant or snobbish behaviour, while still having a high opinion of themselves and their country. Other unacceptable forms of behaviour are laziness (most of all), lack of punctuality and extravagance with money. In general, the Dutch avoid doing anything that might disturb social harmony, and they will be quick to tell you if you are in danger of falling out of line.

Making Friends

The well-known Dutch culture of openness and directness has its paradoxical aspect as well. It is considered good form not to draw your curtains, so that people can look inside your house and see what you are up to. On the other hand, the Dutch tend to avoid physical contact with strangers (or even people they know), which may have something to do with living in such a small country.

In reality the Dutch guard their privacy as much as anyone and many a foreigner has wondered if they are ever going to make close friends.

The answer lies in understanding the culture and being prepared to change one's expectations. The key concept is the difference between *vrienden* (friends) and *kennissen* (acquaintances) and the point where you graduate from one to the other. To begin with one should be aware of the idea of *gezelligheid*, the feeling of being at ease and of warmth in the company of others, something which exists within the family and which you can find in your local café if you are lucky. The opposite is *ongezellig*, which means anything anti-social. Fortunately, one great advantage of being here is that almost any topic of conversation is acceptable in the right company, with the exception of one's financial affairs, so one does not necessarily have to feel isolated.

The expatriate population in the Netherlands has established a large number of English-speaking clubs and societies in most major towns. They can often provide a friendly face and guidance on how to settle into your new Dutch way of life. A comprehensive list of expatriate social clubs is listed in the Chapter Five, *Retirement*.

Hospitality: When entertaining business colleagues it is usual to take them out to a restaurant in the first instance. If you are invited to someone's home, then it is always acceptable to offer flowers or chocolates to the hostess, in proportion to the occasion. You can also offer flowers to men. Chrysanthemums are strictly for funerals. Dress up rather than down for dinner invitations, and don't take your jacket off unless you host does. Make sure to shake hands with everyone and introduce yourself. Don't help yourself to food or drink without asking first.

If friends drop by during the daytime, then offer them coffee and biscuits (*koekjes*) or fruit juice. Tea is generally an afternoon drink. Evaporated milk (*koffiemelk*) is used rather than ordinary milk. The Dutch like spicy cakes, like the well-known breakfast cake (*ontbijtkoek*). Male visitors after work may be offered a *borrel*, a small glass of gin (*jenever*). This moment of the day is the famed *borreluur*.

Entertainment and Culture

There is a saying in the Netherlands that one works in Rotterdam, plays in Amsterdam and sleeps in The Hague. Anyone deciding where to locate would be well advised to bear this in mind. The Hague does have some nightlife and Amsterdam has its quieter moments, but on the whole it is not far from the truth!

Art and Museums: It is virtually impossible to discuss the world of paint and canvas without mentioning at least one of the great Dutch artists. The names of Rembrandt, Hals, Vermeer and Van Gogh enjoy a huge international reputation. The Netherlands has one of the highest numbers of museums and art galleries in proportion to its population in the world. They are generally superbly organised, with special displays for children, the blind, etc. Top of the list are the Rijksmuseum in Amsterdam which is home to Rembrandt's 'The Night Watch' and the Van Gogh Museum. Only the bigger museums have explanations in English, but there are usually guided tours in English. Anyone planning to visit more than seven or eight museums a year should buy the Museumjaarkaart, which allows unlimited access to most of the major museums and art galleries for a year, and costs about €32 (see www.museumjaarkaart.nl).

Nightlife: Dutch nightlife can be divided into two distinct areas: Amsterdam/ Rotterdam and the rest. The country's two largest cities offer everything from all-night bars to casinos, and nightclubs to live sex shows. The rest of the Netherlands does not have quite the same diversity and the nightlife is generally much quieter. The Dutch are happy to spend an evening at a restaurant or live music bar, or even entertain at home, rather than live it up at a disco.

Theatre: The theatre scene in the Netherlands is very active and an estimated 4,500 performances are staged every year. There are a number of repertory companies staging both classical and modern works. However, the government has been trying to promote more experimental companies which deal with subjects such as sexuality, drugs and women's rights.

Music: The Dutch have the largest number of stereo systems per head in the EU, hence one can conclude that they like music. Traditionally, classical music has centred around the Dutch symphony orchestras, the two opera companies and three dance troupes which seem to be constantly in action. A number of major music competitions are held annually including the International Organ Competition in the St Bavo Cathedral in Haarlem, where Mozart once played. The Dutch are jazz fanatics and there are hundreds of bars catering for live music throughout the country. Jazz festivals are common to several towns and each specialises in a particular style. The largest is the North Sea Jazz Festival held every year in The Hague. Bluegrass music is also extraordinarily popular.

Films and the Cinema: The Dutch were among the first to pioneer cinemas at the turn of the century and going to the pictures is still a popular pastime. The majority of films are foreign and are subtitled. However, the Dutch film industry has had some international successes; *De Aanslag* (The Assassination) won an Oscar in 1987. A number of film festivals are held each year. The Rotterdam festival is held in February and Utrecht's takes place in September. All films are rated by the Dutch board of censors. The minimum age certificate (either 12 or 16) is always shown with the advert for a film and strictly enforced at the cinema. The letters AL (*alle leeftijden* – all ages) mean the film has no age restriction. KNT (*kinderen niet toegestaan*) means absolutely no admittance for children.

Sport

Sport is an extremely important part of Dutch life. One-third of the population belongs to an official club and and the same number again take part in sport purely for recreational purposes. Sixty separate sports have national organisations. Cycling and angling are reckoned to be the two most popular pastimes, and tennis is second only to football in the number of official participants, especially since Richard Krajicek, a Dutchman of Czech descent, won Wimbledon in 1996. The Dutch have always excelled at hockey as well.

Football: Dutch football has the unenviable record of being regarded as producing the finest national teams never to have won the World Cup. In 1974 and in 1978 the national side lost in the final. However, in 1988 the Netherlands did win its first international title, the European Championship. The Royal Netherlands Football Association has more than one million members and is by far the largest sporting organisation in the country. The Dutch league is one of the most competitive in the world and its leading clubs, Ajax (Amsterdam), Feyenoord (Rotterdam) and PSV Eindhoven rank among the best in Europe. For more on Dutch football, read *Brilliant Orange* by David Winner (Bloomsbury).

Ice Skating: Seventeen thousand competitors take part in the Netherlands' greatest sporting event – the Elfstedentocht (Circuit of the Eleven Towns). The race is organised annually if the weather allows (the last time was in 1997) and participants skate 200 km along frozen canals between 11 towns in Friesland. The overall popularity of skating has risen dramatically in recent years. To meet the rising demand new rinks have been built in many major towns. Most of these have both a 400 metre track for speed skating and a separate area for ice hockey and figure skating.

Water Sports: The Dutch love the water and an amazing 600,000 sailing and motor yachts ply the country's waterways and canals. The use of fast sailboats (*speeljachten*) for sport was pioneered by the Dutch aristocracy in the 17th century. The Netherlands is well equipped to cope with the demand and has an abundance of facilities. This includes more than 1,000 marinas nationwide. For further information contact the national watersports association: Koninklijke Nederlandse Watersport Verbond, Postbus 87, 3980 CD Bunnik; ☏ 030-656 65 50; www.knwv.nl.

Fierljeppen: In Friesland, the locals have turned an unusual way of crossing canals into a bizarre type of sport. *Fierljeppen* has its origins in local traditions and is similar in principle to the pole vault in field athletics. However, rather than leaping over a bar and landing on a soft mat competitors use a long pole to vault over a wide ditch.

Wadlopen: Off the north coast of the Netherlands a fringe of islands marks the old coastline before the last Ice Age. At low tide, some of the old land reappears, and at this time some hardy souls indulge in the highly dangerous sport of *wadlopen* or 'mud-walking', which consists of wading from the mainland to one of the offshore islands without disappearing into the sand. Only to be atttempted with a trained guide.

SHOPPING

THE DUTCH ARE BY NO MEANS EXTRAVAGANT, nor do they have much space in their homes for junk. However, this does not mean fashion is ignored and they have a knack for combining it with quality. Shopping in the Netherlands is an easy and enjoyable pastime. The majority of city centres have extensive shopping facilities ranging from supermarkets and department stores, to street traders and small speciality shops (*speciaalzaak*). Food stores are generally open between 8.00am and 6.00pm on weekdays and Saturdays. While the regulations prohibit most shops from opening at other times, there are some which open in the evenings and on Sundays, but they may well charge higher prices. The number of shops allowed to open outside ordinary hours is calculated on the basis of the population of the place, at the rate of one to 10,000 inhabitants. Most town centres also hold weekly markets, which will probably have some of the more competitive prices, especially for fresh produce.

You will soon notice the large number of special offers. If a shop is closing down then there will be a sign in the window saying *uitverkoop* or *opruiming*. Bargains are not always what they seem and it is as well to be on your guard against shoddy goods at a suspiciously cheap price.

Environmental awareness has also penetrated into Dutch supermarkets. Plastic bags have been replaced by small paper bags without handles, so it is best to take your own. You will also have to pay 25 cents deposit (*statiegeld*) on large plastic bottles; each supermarket has a machine which will swallow up your bottle in exchange for a ticket (*bon* or the diminutive *bonnetje*). You do not need the receipt for your bottle, only the correct brand. When weighing your own purchases, you will need to press the button marked *bon* in order to get the necessary ticket. Receipts are also called *bonnetjes*.

Dutch Food and Drink

Dutch food and drink are well-known around the world, even if Dutch cuisine is not. The number of Dutch cookery books written in English is, nonetheless, remarkable. Almost everyone has come across Dutch cheeses, of which there are about 450, and you will almost certainly have eaten Dutch chocolate. The Netherlands is the world's largest chocolate exporter, and Veghel is home to the world's largest chocolate factory. Indeed, the Dutch invented the chocolate bar during the last century, for the convenience of soldiers on manoeuvres, according to the original publicity.

Dutch pancakes (*pannekoeken*) have become well-known abroad. In the Netherlands, the small variety known as *poffertjes* are most popular. Another popular type of Dutch fast food is the *uitsmijter* (literally 'chucker-out'), a large open sandwich with meat or cheese.

The most common kinds of non-Dutch restaurants are the ubiquitous Indonesian-Chinese types which serve cheap but often tasteless fare dripping with monosodium glutamate, and kebab houses, which go under the name of *shoarma* and often have Egyptian names. Genuine Indonesian or Surinamese food is worth looking out for.

The Dutch have a taste for both brewing and drinking beer. Not just Heineken, but Grolsch and Skol, are renowned for refreshing the parts others cannot reach. But these are just the more famous exports. Each town and even village produces its own special beer. The Dutch on average drink 90 litres of beer each and consume an estimated 100 million litres of distilled drinks every year. The most popular spirit is the colourless *jenever* which accounts for more than half of Dutch sales.

METRICATION AND TIME

For details see *Metrication* and *Time* at the end of the *Daily Life* chapter in the section on Belgium.

PUBLIC HOLIDAYS

APART FROM THE PUBLIC HOLIDAYS listed below, there are a number of other days in the year which are of special significance. One of these is the famed *Pakjesdag* when presents are handed out, actually on December 5, St. Nicholas Day. Christmas Day is strictly a family affair with a strongly religious connotation. New Year's Eve, *Oudejaarsavond*, is also very much for families.

PUBLIC HOLIDAYS

1 January	New Year's Day (*Nieuwjaar*)
March/April	Good Friday (*Pasen*)
March/April	Easter Monday
30 April	Queen Beatrix's Official Birthday
5 May	Liberation Day (*Bevrijdingsdag*)
May	Ascension Day (*Hemelvaart*)
June	Whit Monday (*Pinksteren*)
25 December	Christmas Day (*Eerste Kerstdag*)
26 December	Christmas Holiday (*Tweede Kerstdag*)

Retirement

NO FEWER THAN 10,000 UK citizens retire from work every week. Many may dream of a cottage by the sea or a villa in Spain, but unless they have some prior link few would contemplate moving to the Netherlands. The standard of living in the Netherlands is high, but so is the cost and it would be prudent to work out whether your budget would cover this. The health provision and public transport networks are excellent. There are also several well-established communities of working and retired Britons in and around The Hague and Amsterdam, so you won't be short of company.

Despite its many attractions, the Netherlands is very different from the UK, so anyone contemplating a move must have a clear idea of what they are letting themselves in for. A successful relocation will require not just enthusiasm but a certain degree of adaptability.

RESIDENCE REQUIREMENTS

SINCE 1 JANUARY 1992 pensioners from EU Member States have been free to live wherever they wish in the European Community, providing they have adequate means of financial support. Anyone who intends to retire to the Netherlands will have to obtain a residence permit (*verblijfsvergunning* – see Chapter Two, *Residence and Entry*). The application will have to provide pension details, prove adequate health insurance and supply proof that individuals can support themselves. The residence permit (*verblijfsvergunning*) entitles the holder to live and work in the Netherlands and will need to be renewed every five years. The most important criterion for being allowed to stay in the Netherlands is likely to be money. If you cannot show you have sufficient funds to support your stay, the authorities can ask you to leave.

CHOOSING AND BUYING A RETIREMENT HOME

THE OBVIOUS POINT to remember about selecting a retirement property in the Netherlands is to choose something which is within one's financial scope.

The majority of people will need to draw up a financial assessment based on their experience of the country to see if they can afford the expense involved in both moving abroad and the running and upkeep of a Dutch property. Also anyone reliant on public transport (which in the Netherlands is first class) will need to bear in mind the proximity of shops, friends and health care amenities. Once you have decided on your new home you will need to follow all the procedures regarding the purchase of a property which are outlined in Chapter Three, *Setting up Home*.

HOBBIES AND INTERESTS

ONCE YOU HAVE SETTLED into your new home, your thoughts will undoubtedly turn to socialising and the pursuit of interests you never quite had time for in the past. The Netherlands boasts many opportunities in this department. Gardening is very popular, but gardeners used to the inclement British weather will find a similar hardiness required. For lovers of art and history the Dutch have spent a lot of time and energy saving and displaying their rich heritage. There are anywhere up to 1,000 museums to help you while away the time.

For those looking for a more active retirement cycling is a national pastime and cyclists have the use of several thousand miles of cycle tracks. The Dutch are also keen anglers and there is plenty of opportunity for both sea and coarse fishing throughout the country. For the dedicated walker the Netherlands may prove a disappointment as the country has very few hills, and the lowest percentage of woodland in the EU. But for gentle rambling both the coastline and acres of famous Dutch flower fields are areas well worth exploring. If all that sounds a little too strenuous what could be more relaxing than guiding a barge along the extensive Dutch canal network. There are also plenty of spectator events on offer, from football to *fierljeppen*.

Work.

Unemployment in the Netherlands is very low (2%), but, unlike in the UK, older people generally do not go out to work. Only 30% of people in the 55 to 64 age range are in paid employment, most of them male. Over-65s who do work benefit from a more generous tax regime, since the authorities quite reasonably do not expect them to contribute to the social security system at the same rate as younger people. Tax is levied at about half the usual rate up to a threshold of €27,009; you also benefit from additional 'levy rebates' if your income does not exceed this level.

If you feel that you could still be doing useful work, then there is considerable scope for doing voluntary work, and the following two organisations will be happy to give you further information.

Useful Addresses

ACCESS: Sociëteit de Witte, Plein 24, 2511 CS Den Haag; 070-346 25 25; www.access-nl.org.

De Nederlandse Organisatie Vrijwilligerswerk (NOV): Information and Documentation Department, Postbus 2877, 3500 GW Utrecht; ☎0900-899 86 00; www.vrijwilligerscentrale.nl or www.freeflex.nl.

NOV: Hartenstraat 16, 1016 CB Amsterdam Binnenstad; ☎020-530 12 20; 020-638 79 10; amsterdam@vrijwilligerscentrale.nl.

ENTERTAINMENT

THE BBC WORLD SERVICE is without doubt in a class of its own and is an easy way of keeping in touch with home. The information you need can be found at: www.bbc.co.uk/worldservice. Should you prefer to watch rather than listen the advent of satellite and cable TV means that BBC1 and BBC2 can be easily (and relatively cheaply) received in the Netherlands. Dutch television stations show a vast amount of subtitled English-language programmes. Cultural activities come in all shapes and sizes. It would be hard to be bored.

ENGLISH-LANGUAGE CLUBS

BEING RESIDENT in a country where both the language and the people are unfamiliar can make the company of fellow expatriates very alluring. The Netherlands has a wealth of English-speaking, expatriate social and activity clubs. Whether you want to cultivate a dormant artistic ability or simply share a pot of tea and a gossip with fellow Brits the following list should provide a good starting point. The British Consulate in The Hague can also provide a list.

Amsterdam

American Women's Club of Amsterdam; ☎020-644 35 31; www.awca.org.

Americans in Holland Association; http://aiha.dyndns.org.

British Society of Amsterdam: PO Box 7429, 1007 JK Amsterdam; ☎020-624 86 29; www.britishsocietyofamsterdam.org.

Royal British Legion: (Amsterdam Branch) In de Papiermolen 23, 1115 GS Duivendrecht; ☎020-699 19 63.

Breda

International Women's Club: Cafe Brauwers, Ginnekenmarkt, Breda; ☎016 847 33 00.

Den Haag

American Baseball Foundation: c/o Postbus 133, Deylerweg 155, 2240 AC Wassenaar; ☎070-511 90 67; www.abfsport.nl.

American Women's Club: Nieuwe Duinweg 25, 2587 AB Den Haag; ☎070-350 60 07; www.fawco.org.

Anglo-American Theatre Group; PostApart 2003, 2280 LA Rijswijk;

www.aatg.nl.
British Women's Club: Clubhouse de Sociëteit de Witte, Plein 24, 2511 CS Den Haag; ☎070-346 19 73 (10.30am to 2.30pm Tues-Fri); www.bwclubthehague.demon.nl.
Commonwealth Club: ☎070-354 70 44.
The Decorative and Fine Art Society of the Hague (DFAS): ☎070-387 26 06.
English Speaking Club: Scholeksterstraat 3, 2352 ED Leiderdorp; ☎071-541 87 30.
International Art Club: Postbus 717, 2501 CS Den Haag.
International Contact: Postbus 91405, 2509 EA Den Haag; ☎070-382 08 58.
Genootschap Engeland Nederland/ Netherlands England Society: e-mail bridgewater@wanadoo.nl.

Dordrecht
English Language Bond of Women (ELBOW): ☎078-618 36 81.

Leiden
Leiden English Speaking Theatre Group Lest: www.feats.org.

Nijmegen
Foreign Exchange: Kraayenburg 94-15, 6601 PE Wijchen; ☎08894-11335.

Rotterdam
American-Netherlands Club of Rotterdam (ANCOR): Postbus 34025, 3005 GA Rotterdam.
Commonwealth Club: ☎010-414 51 09.
Pickwick Club of Rotterdam: Central Hotel, Kruiskade, Rotterdam; ☎010-422 70 70.

Utrecht
International Women's Contact: Cultureel Centrum Oog in Al, Corner Pijperlaan & Handelstraat; c/o Rootstraat 28, Oudewater.

PENSIONS

IF YOU BECAME entitled to a state pension before leaving the UK there is no reason why it cannot be paid to you in the Netherlands. The important point to remember is that a UK pension will always be pegged at UK levels. Should European Monetary Union become a reality then this will no longer pose a problem, but until then there is always the chance of devaluation.

People who move to the Netherlands before reaching retirement age can continue paying national insurance contributions in the UK, in order to qualify for a British state pension, or pay into the Dutch social security to qualify for a combined pension. To claim a solely British state pension after retiring one must apply to the Pensions and Overseas Benefits Directorate of the DWP (Tyneview Park, Whitley Rd, Benton, Newcastle-upon-Tyne NE98 1BA; ☎0191-218 7777; fax 0191-218 7293) and ensure that your pension is delivered to a designated bank account each month. The normal procedure to claim a combined pension is for the British and Dutch authorities to exchange social security records and calculate the amount of pension payable by each country. Further details are given in the DWP leaflet SA29 – *Your Social Security, Health Care and Pension Rights in the European Community.*

The basic Dutch pension provision amounts to 70% (for single people) and 50% (for married couples) of the minimum wage. The monthly pension payment currently stands at €810 for a single person and €561 each for a married couple.

Taxation

The DSS will not deduct tax from your UK state pension provided that you can prove you are resident in the Netherlands. In such a case payments must be transferred into a Dutch bank account and will be subsequently liable for Dutch income tax. A more complex situation arises if one spends time in both the UK and the Netherlands and for this it is essential to get professional advice. In particular you cannot completely escape UK taxes if you spend more than 183 days in Britain in the first year of obtaining residence abroad. People who intend to maintain connections with the UK must get professional taxation advice. Investments already established in the UK do not need to be altered and in most cases interest will be paid on deposits without any deduction of tax where one is non-resident. The Dutch tax year runs from January to December, whereas the UK tax year runs from April to March. The date of moving could affect one's tax liability. You can find further information in the leaflet IR138 *Living or Retiring Abroad? A Guide to UK Tax on Your UK Income and Pension* from the British Inland Revenue (see below for address).

Inheritance Tax

As far as the Dutch authorities are concerned, if you died in the Netherlands then you will be liable for inheritance taxes (*successierechten*) which are far higher in the Netherlands than in Great Britain. Wherever you end up paying death duties it will include worldwide assets. The heirs are required to file an inheritance tax return within five months of death and pay the tax within two months of the assessment.

Taxes are levied on a sliding scale with certain exemptions depending on the relationship to the deceased. The maximum rate paid by a spouse and children is 27%; for distant relatives or unrelated persons it rises to 63%. The wife receives a tax-free allowance up to about €270,000. Children receive allowances depending on their age. Similar rates are paid on gifts within one's lifetime, the gift tax (*schenkingsrecht*), and on the transfer of property and other assets (*recht van overgang*).

In view of the very high inheritance taxes in the Netherlands, it is highly advisable to find out how to protect one's heirs. The British Inland Revenue publishes the leaflet IHT18 *Inheritance tax. Foreign aspects*. The booklet *Taxation in the Netherlands* also has some information; the Dutch tax authority website www.belastingdienst.nl has more.

Useful Addresses

Ministry of Finance, Central Information Directorate: Postbus 20201, 2500 EE Den Haag; ☎070-342 75 42; www.belastingdienst.nl.

HEALTH

ONE OF THE DRAWBACKS of retiring in the Netherlands is that there is no free National Health Service. Dutch hospitals and doctors provide excellent health care, but to receive medical treatment in the Netherlands you must have adequate health insurance. Unless you have paid into the Dutch Sickness Fund (*ziekenfonds*) this will have to take the form of a private policy. It will be necessary to prove you have medical insurance not only to receive treatment but also to be issued with a residence permit (*verblijfsvergunning*).

As part of a general cost-cutting drive, the Dutch government has decided that persons who have been privately insured will have to remain in the same health insurance scheme when they reach 65, and will not be allowed to switch to the state scheme, unless their taxable household income is less than €20,000 per annum. This is likely to prove very expensive to those retiring in the Netherlands. There is no restriction on over-65s moving from the state scheme to a private scheme, assuming they can find someone willing to insure them.

WILLS

MAKING A WILL CAN SEEM only one step removed from arranging one's own funeral. However, should you die intestate – without having made a will – in a foreign country the question of inheritance can become extremely complicated. Assets in the UK and the Netherlands (and elsewhere) will be treated differently. This will mean a minefield of inheritance laws for relatives to sort out and the legal costs will almost certainly mount up. If you have not made a will then take the advice of a UK solicitor with experience of both the UK and Dutch legal systems. If a UK will has already been made it may be necessary for it to be reviewed. In the Netherlands a will must be drawn up by a notary public (*notaris*). A new will automatically renders all previous wills void under international law. However, a new will can still incorporate parts of the previous will if you wish. If you have assets in both countries it is necessary to draw up a will for both countries.

The rules concerning who you can leave money to in the Netherlands are complex. It is possible to disinherit your spouse or partner, although they will still have some claim on any profits generated by your assets, as well as the right to remain in the marital home. Partners who have been together for more than five years are treated the same as married couples; it is best to register a partnership contract at the town hall. Homosexual marriages are legal in the Netherlands and have the same validity as traditional marriages, except in matters of adoption. It is possible to disinherit the rest of your family in favour of your partner, but not your children. Children can disinherit their parents.

DEATH

DYING ABROAD CAN COMPLICATE matters in that one's relatives are not always on the spot to deal with the necessary formalities. It is therefore advisable to make your funeral wishes known in advance and preferably written down in a will. It is very expensive to have one's body shipped home for burial, so it might be worth considering making arrangements in the Netherlands itself. A death must be certified by a doctor and registered within 24 hours at the town hall (*gemeentehuis*) of the municipal council, with a valid death certificate and identity papers. The British Embassy can help with the arrangements.

Section II

Working in the Netherlands

EMPLOYMENT

BUSINESS AND INDUSTRY REPORTS

TEMPORARY WORK

STARTING A BUSINESS

EMPLOYMENT

CHAPTER SUMMARY

○ The Dutch economy is in an enviable state of low inflation with steady growth.

○ There is a high demand for skilled foreigners, and thanks to EU regulations most British professional qualifications are acceptable in the Netherlands.

○ **Finding work.** There are large numbers of private employment agencies; other sources of information about jobs include the pan-European job information network EURES, professional organizations and online job resources.

○ The Netherlands has at 37.9 hours per week the shortest working week in the EU.

○ Fields offering good possibilities for permanent work include the petrochemicals, engineering and information technology industries, medicine and architecture.

○ Temporary work may be found teaching English, as an au pair, or in seasonal agricultural jobs including bulb picking and packing.

○ The northern provinces of Groningen and Friesland have not benefitted fully from the prosperity enjoyed by the rest of the country but their potential for development should attract greater investment in future.

THE EMPLOYMENT SCENE

FOLLOWING AN EXPORT-LED period of growth and investment in the mid-80s the Dutch economy was only temporarily knocked off course during the 1993 recession. The new government elected in 1994 (and again in 1998) pushed through imaginative policies, cutting taxation and social security expenditure and encouraging the creation of more and more part-time and temporary jobs. Revenues from natural gas production and a strong investment programme guarantee the nation's prosperity. For a while, the Dutch appeared to have achieved that nirvana of low inflation and steady growth which they had sought for so long. In 2001 growth was less spectacular, and a serious labour shortage threatens to lead to higher inflation.

Cynics point out that many of the new jobs created recently are not full-time, but there is no mistaking the envious tone of the Germans and Belgians, who would dearly like to find the same degree of flexibility as the Dutch in tackling their economic problems. One of the secrets of Dutch success is good labour relations. Wages are negotiated on a national basis and strikes are almost unheard of. Companies are scrupulously careful about consulting their employees about their plans, and keeping up an appearance of democracy in the workplace.

A striking feature of the Dutch employment scene is the degree of pride which even the humblest worker takes in doing their job. In this egalitarian society, there should be no such thing as an unimportant or demeaning job, but, in practice, there are jobs that Dutch people would rather not do, and some of them are inevitably taken by foreigners.

As in the UK, the job for life is becoming less common. Many contracts are now for one or two years, and the practice of outsourcing (*detachering*) is becoming all the rage. A recent survey by the Dutch Federation of Trade Unions suggests that 25% of employees would like to go part-time, but many believe that this will damage their promotion prospects. For this reason the Dutch parliament passed a bill in 1997 obliging employers to allow employees to work part-time, against the wishes of both the trade unions and employers' organisation.

Headline unemployment has fallen gradually from 8% in 1993 to 6% in 1998, to as little as 2% in 2002. Dutch unemployment figures are notoriously misleading, and some have estimated that the true figure is over 15%. Only 65% of the population who are of working age actually work. On top of this, the Netherlands has the highest rate of part-time working in Europe, with one-third of employees doing less than a full week. Some 40% of workers are on contracts.

The number of people employed in agriculture and the manufacturing industry is in decline, while the demand for workers in the service industries (administration, tourism and catering) has steadily increased. Presently, 69% of the Dutch workforce is employed in the service sector, 26% in manufacturing and 4% in agriculture. A national survey revealed that 10% of the working population aged 18 years or older did shift work, 25% complained of high noise levels at work and 8% felt their working conditions were potentially dangerous. However, two-thirds of the workforce felt they had an opportunity to develop their skills in their job, 74% considered their job secure, 63% were content with the wage they received and one-third were satisfied with their promotion prospects. Almost 80% of the working Dutch population said that they enjoyed their work. Amongst office-workers the figure is as high as 93%.

The overall prospects for the Dutch economy are bright. It is modern, efficient and leads the world in certain areas of agriculture and engineering. The demand for skilled foreigners is high. English is used to a large extent in everyday life, so language need not be a barrier. Whether you intend to be an employee or an employer the Dutch economy looks certain to offer a wealth of opportunity.

RESIDENCE AND WORK REGULATIONS

EUROPEAN UNION REGULATIONS allow for the free movement of labour within the EU, and UK citizens do not require a work permit to work in the Netherlands. British nationals looking for employment can enter the country on a valid passport, but must apply for a residence permit (*verblijfsvergunning*) within eight days of arrival if they intend to stay and work for more than three months. The application must include a letter from your prospective employer stating the terms of the contract, salary level and proof that the company will pay your health insurance contributions. See Chapter Two, *Residence and Entry Regulations*.

SKILLS AND QUALIFICATIONS

MANY EU DIRECTIVES have appeared over the years concerning mutual recognition of professional qualifications in all EU countries. Such directives give every Community national certain rights to have their qualifications and experience recognised or taken into account in another member state where entry to particular jobs is regulated by law. Where there are significant differences in the training required to exercise a profession the directives provide for the need to take an aptitude test or for an assessed period of supervised practice.

There are two main directives concerning mutual recognition of education and training (89/48/EEC and 92/51/EEC). The first concerns higher education, the second qualifications gained through any post-secondary course of more than one year or work experience. This means that National and Scottish Vocational Qualifications (NVQs/SVQs) and their equivalents are now recognised by the EU. The UK organisation responsible for providing information on the comparability of all academic qualifications is the National Academic Recognition Information Centre (NARIC), which can be contacted at UK NARIC, ECCTIS Ltd, Oriel House, Oriel Road, Cheltenham, Glos GL50 1XP; ☎01242-260010; fax 01242-258611; e-mail naric@ecctis.co.uk; www.naric.org.uk. You should first ask the jobcentre in the UK, or in the Netherlands, if you are already there, to approach NARIC on your behalf. You can also approach NARIC directly, but there will be a charge for the service.

If you have experience but no formal qualifications, it is possible to obtain a European Community Certificate of Experience. For EU citizens in the UK this is issued by the DTI. Since the Certificate costs £80 to process, you should first make sure that your type of work experience is covered by an EC directive by asking the authorities in the Netherlands or the DTI, who will try to send you a copy of the relevant directive, together with an application form and any available literature. There is an enquiry line on 020-7215 4004 (fax 020-7215 4489) or you can write to: Certificates of Experience Unit, Department of Trade & Industry, Kingsgate House, 66-74 Victoria Street, London SW1E 6SW.

If your qualifications are vocational or in hotel and catering, the motor trade, travel and tourism or office work and you want to know how your qualifications stand up against the Dutch equivalent, you can consult the Comparability Co-ordinator through your local job centre or direct: Comparability Coordinator, Employment Dept., Qualifications and Standards Branch (QSI), Room E454, Moorfoot, Sheffield SP1 4PQ; ☎ 0114-2594144.

A considerable amount of information on professional bodies and EC directives can be found on the EU website http://citizens.eu.int. The European Commission will send their booklets *Working in Another Country* and *Studying, Training and Doing Research in Another Country*; call 0800-581591 in the UK. They will also send one factsheet per applicant on one of the regulated professions.

Regulated Professions

A useful starting point to research opportunities is to contact the International Trade Team at your local Business Link. You can find out their address by calling 0845-606 4466. Apart from the professions regulated by professional bodies, there are a considerable number of non-salaried or independent trades which are subject to statutory conditions in the Netherlands. To become self-employed in one of these areas you will be expected to show managerial as well as work experience, and that you have the capital to start a business. You will have to register your qualifications with a local Chamber of Commerce (Kamer van Koophandel) whose address can be found in the Yellow Pages.

Enquiries in the Netherlands: In the Netherlands two bodies act as contact points for information on the first and second directives mentioned above. For a direct comparison between UK qualifications obtained through higher education and those recognised in the Netherlands, contact IRAS (*Informatiecentrum Richtlijn Algemeen Stelsel*) which is located in the NUFFIC building in The Hague (NUFFIC being the National Academic Recognition Information Centre). You can contact them directly or ask any Dutch job centre (*centrum voor werk en inkomen*) and ask them to contact IRAS on your behalf. Alternatively, your own professional association should be able to provide this and other useful information on transferring your skills to the Netherlands.

In the case of the second directive, dealing with advanced vocational training, the contact point is COLO in Zoetermeer. COLO (*Vereniging landelijke organen beroepsonderwijs*) is an association of 21 national bodies for vocational training and training. A number of vocational qualifications are acceptable in the Netherlands. COLO and IRAS will supply a new booklet which contains a list of all the regulatory bodies in the Netherlands for the various professions, as well as an explanation of your rights in the field of comparability of qualifications. For information, contact the department for international credential evaluation (IDW) within Colo.

Useful Addresses

IRAS: Postbus 29777, 2502 LT Den Haag; 070-426 03 90; fax 070-426 03 95.
COLO: PO Box 7259, 2701 AG Zoetermeer; 079-352 30 00; fax 079-351 54 78; e-mail idw@colo.nl; www.colo.nl.

SOURCES OF JOBS

THE MEDIA

Newspapers

VACANCIES IN THE NETHERLANDS do not appear all that frequently in the British press. *The Guardian* has a European Appointments page on Fridays. *The Independent* and *The Times* also occasionally advertise jobs. These include adverts for executives, lawyers, financial analysts and academic staff.

International newspapers circulate editions across several national boundaries and carry a number of job advertisements for different countries. The following are the names and addresses of four newspapers in this category.

Financial Times: www.ft.com.
International Herald Tribune: 00 800 4448 7827; www.iht.com.
Wall Street Journal: 00 800 9753 2000; www.dowjones.com.

Magazines, Journals and Directories

Financial weeklies like *The Economist* occasionally carry advertisements for jobs in the Netherlands. If you want to work as a schoolteacher you may sometimes find advertisements in the *Times Educational Supplement* published on Fridays. The specialist fortnightly publication, *Overseas Jobs Express* (available only by subscription from *Overseas Jobs Express*, 20 New Road, Brighton, East Sussex BN1 1UF; ☎01273-699611; www.overseasjobsexpress.com) usually has a few Dutch-based jobs: accountancy, banking, computer programmers, engineers, hotels and catering, agriculture, agribusiness, secretarial work, nannies, au pairs, and so on.

Many professional journals are available at public libraries, and some will carry Dutch job ads, for instance, *Computer Weekly*, *Oil and Gas Journal* and *Caterer and Hotel Keeper*. Some journals and trade magazines are more obscure, so it is worth looking through a media directory, such as *Benn's Media* or the *European Media Directory*, to see what is available.

Advertising in Newspapers

Those wishing to place advertisements in several daily Dutch newspapers, including *Algemeen Dagblad*, *NRC Handelsblad* and *De Telegraaf*, can contact Powers Turner Group (100 Rochester Row, London SW1P 1JP; ☎020-7630 9966; www.publicitas.com). For a list of Dutch newspapers see Chapter Four, *Daily Life*.

Specialist Job Publications and the Internet

Job magazines include *Intermediair, Via Via, Vacant, Toekomst Magazine, Jobster, De Sollicitatiekrant* (for graduates), *Vraag en Aanbod* and *Vacature Informatie*. Of these *Intermediair* (www.intermediair.com) is the most substantial; it appears weekly on Thursdays. Higher-level positions are usually handled by executive recruitment agencies. Adverts usually specify the level of education required; see the section on *Education* in Chapter Four, *Daily Life* for an explanation of the abbreviations. University graduates are called *academicus/academici* in adverts; those with the HBO degree are HBOers, etc. Advertisements sometimes appear for English native speakers, particularly for secretaries and commercial representatives. For many jobs English is a prerequisite (*Engels een pré*); a knowledge of French or German is also sometimes required.

There are numerous websites with job ads. Searching on the word *vacatures* on the search engine www.zoek.nl will turn up thousands of sites. In order to find your way about this the website http://banen.vinden.nl offers useful lists of sites. http://werk.net and www.jobs.nl are good general sites, as is www.jobpartners.com. Under the local websites, click on *banenmarkt* (job market) or *zakelijk* (business). Most major employers maintain Internet sites and sometimes jobs are advertised on them. The Talentendatabank offers a specialised Internet service linking job-seekers (*sollicitanten*) with employers (*werkgevers*). After filling in a specially designed CV form, your requirements will be passed on to potential employers. The Talentendatabank operates with the approval of the Dutch Ministry of Employment and has had considerable success in helping job-seekers. See www.tdb.nl.

The JoHo organisation (*Jobs and Holidays*) offers careers advice services to job-seekers with a degree, as well as information on travel and study. They have offices in Amsterdam, Rotterdam, Leiden and Groningen. The head office is at Stille Rijn 8, Leiden; ☎071-513 13 57; e-mail info@joho.nl; www.carrierebank.nl.

EMPLOYMENT ORGANISATIONS

THE RECRUITMENT AND EMPLOYMENT CONFEDERATION (36-38 Mortimer Street, London W1N 7RB; ☎020-7462 3260; www.rec.uk.com) issues a list of employment agencies who are members; some offer work in the Netherlands. The state-run Centra voor Werk en Inkomen co-ordinate short-term summer jobs. A similar service is also offered by the UK-based Employment Service Overseas Placing Unit. Both accept applications for a number of summer vacancies in the Netherlands, but stress that individuals must not travel to the Netherlands prior to confirmation of a job placement.

Job agencies (*uitzendbureaux*) are a good starting point. A temporary job often leads to a full-time job. They are listed in the telephone book (*Gouden Gids*) and often have Internet sites. There are more than 125 in Amsterdam alone – and among the largest are Randstad, Vedior, ASB and Manpower. There is one agency in The Hague which specialises in English-speaking staff, the Job-In Uitzendbureau (see below). The Undutchables agency has branches in Amsterdam, Eindhoven, Rotterdam and Utrecht. You can ask for a list of job agencies from the national federation, the Algemene Bond Uitzendondernemingen. Other recruitment agencies are listed under specific professions.

Useful Addresses

Centra voor Werk en Inkomen *(Centres for Work and Income):* see www.cwi.nl.

Employment Service Overseas Placing Unit: Rockingham House, 123 West St, Sheffield, S1 4ER; ☎0114-259 6190; afx 0114-259 6040.

Algemene Bond Uitzendondernemingen: Prins Mauritslaan 29-39, 1171 LP Badhoevedorp, Amsterdam; ☎020-658 01 01; fax 020-659 24 25.

ASB: P. Potterstr. 10, 1071 CZ Amsterdam; ☎020-470 58 28.

Job-In Uitzendbureau: Javastraat 35a, 2585 Den Haag; ☎070-363 51 20; fax 070-363 38 51; www.jobin.nl.

Manpower BV: Gebouw Athena, Diemerhof 16-18, 1112 XN Diemen; ☎020-600 14 46; www.manpower.nl.

Randstad Uitzendbureau: Postbus 12600, 1100 AP Amsterdam-Zuidoost; ☎0900-726 378 23; e-mail vacaturemanager@randstad.nl; www.randstad.nl.

Undutchables Agency: Burgemeester Haspelslaan 21 1181 NB Amstelveen; ☎020-345 51 04 (head office).

Vedior: Europaboulevard 2a, Amsterdam; ☎020-549 19 40; www.vedior.nl.

EURES

THE EMPLOYMENT SERVICES of the 15 EU countries are linked together by a computer network known as EURES (European Employment Services), by which information on specialist vacancies notified to the employment service in one country can be made available to the employment services in the others. At any one time there are over 5,000 vacancies on the system, including jobs for graduates and professionals. In addition the EU has trained 450 Euro-advisers, including six at British universities.

The British branch of EURES is based at the Overseas Placing Unit (OPU) of the Employment Service in Sheffield (see above). Most UK Employment Service offices have computer access to the vacancies held at Sheffield. Some of the vacancies available through the Overseas Placing Unit are published in the fortnightly newspaper *Overseas Jobs Express* (see above). They can be viewed online at: http://europa.eu.int/jobs/eures.

The Employment Service produces a useful booklet, *Working in the Netherlands*, available from their offices nationwide or from the OPU.

JOB CENTRES

AT THE START OF 2002 Dutch job centres (*arbeidsbureaux*) were renamed Centra voor Werk en Inkomen; the reorganisation of the employment service aims to create a closer link between social security provision and the employment service. CWIs offer job placement services, advice on employment in the Netherlands and help to prospective entrepreneurs. You can go to the CWI to apply for social security benefits; your enquiry will be passed through to the UWV for evaluation. Under EU law these centres are obliged to assist foreigners, but do not expect them to bend over backwards to help. A full list of addresses of CWIs is available on their website: www.cwi.nl. The CWIs in the major cities are located as follows:

Amsterdam: Westeinde 26, 1017 ZP Amsterdam; ☎020-553 34 44.
Arnhem: Groningensingel 1, 6835 EA Arnhem; ☎026-324 44 00.
Deventer: Smedenstraat 280, 7411 RM Deventer; ☎0570-690700.
Eindhoven: Begijnenhof 8, 5611 EL Eindhoven; ☎040-238 57 93.
Groningen: Gedempte Zuiderdiep 31, 9711 HB Groningen; ☎050-368 75 55.
Haarlem: Jansweg 15, 2011 KL Haarlem; ☎023-553 24 44.
The Hague: Amsterdamse Veerkade 66, 2512 AJ Den Haag; ☎070-311 15 00.
Maastricht: Het Bat 12a, 6211 EX Maastricht; ☎043-329 12 12.
Middelburg: St. Sebastiaanstraat 12, 4331 PL Middelburg; ☎0118-683400.
Rotterdam: Eudokiaplein 15, 3037 BT Rotterdam; ☎010-403 95 50.
Utrecht: W. Dreeslaan 113, 3515 GB Utrecht; ☎030-273 79 11.

THE APPLICATION PROCEDURE

AS A GENERAL RULE, Dutch companies do not respond to vague enquiries. If you decide the best way to sound out the Dutch job scene is to send a speculative enquiry, make sure that you have the skills and experience that the employer is looking for; you are more likely to get a response if you can send an e-mail message. It is advisable to send a one- or at most two-page CV, whether the letter is speculative or in response to an advertised vacancy. Including a photo and something about your interests will go down well.

Dutch employers almost always have an excellent knowledge of written English, but if for some reason you feel your application would be more effective in Dutch then you can have it professionally translated. The Institute of Translation and Interpreting (Exchange House, 494 Midsummer Boulevard, Central Milton Keynes MK9 2EA; ☎01908-255905; email info@iti.org.uk) can put you in touch with a qualified translator, whose charges may range from £60 for one thousand words. It is also worth contacting a college of further education for this purpose. The list *Directory of Employers* at the end of this chapter is a good source from which to base a speculative job hunt.

Dutch business people are less formal than their UK counterparts. In many cases smart casual wear will be more appropriate than a suit. You will definitely shake hands both on arrival and departure. Potential employers will be anxious to find out how much background reading you have done on their business, so it is vital to do as much research as possible before going for interview.

ASPECTS OF EMPLOYMENT

SALARIES

SINCE 1982 THE GOVERNMENT has left the negotiation of pay levels to the employers' organisations and the trade unions. Although only a minority of workers belong to trade unions, the agreements (called CAOs) arrived at are usually accepted throughout the entire industry. The Foundation of Labour (Stichting van de Arbeid) is responsible for maintaining good relations between employers and employees. The Minister of Social Affairs and Employment is empowered to disallow agreements that are deemed contrary to the national interest and freeze wages if necessary. The Dutch unions pride themselves on being realistic about wage demands. There is a legal minimum wage for all workers aged 23-65; during 2001 this stood at €1,122 per month. All wage contracts are reviewed at six-monthly intervals, and adjusted in accordance with the cost of living index.

Salaries for executives are similar to those in the UK, but somewhat less than in Belgium, France and Germany. A lower-level manager can expect to start at €35,000 (£23,400) per annum; personnel managers make upwards of €40,000 (£24,000), a sales director €70,000 (£42,000) and a top manager at least €100,000 (£60,000).

In technical fields, an engineer can expect at least €40,000 (£24,000), and a computer programmer starts on about €25,000 (£15,000); an IT project leader can earn €60,000 or more (£36,000). If you are interested in comparing the available salaries, the executive jobsearch magazine *Intermediair* keeps a database on the Internet at www.intermediair.nl, under the heading 'Salariskompas'.

A number of fringe benefits are used by Dutch firms to attract and retain staff. These include subsidised canteens and social clubs, a company car, and full wages for the first year of sickness (but not the first two days). A number of employers also pay a 13th month bonus at Christmas. A holiday allowance of 8% of annual salary is mandatory for monthly salaries of up to €3,000.

WORKING CONDITIONS

THE AVERAGE working week in the Netherlands is the shortest in the EU, at 37.9 hours per week. Maximum working hours are restricted by law to eight and a half hours per day or 48 hours per week. Employers must obtain permits for overtime from the Labour Inspection Board and overtime is restricted for employees under the age of 18. The minimum holiday entitlement is 20 working days, although, the more usual figure is 23 days, during which salary is fully paid, on top of the 13th month paid at the end of the year. The working day commonly starts at 8am, and official business hours are 8.30am to 5pm.

ETIQUETTE IN THE WORKPLACE

THE DUTCH LIKE to foster an egalitarian atmosphere in the workplace. There is a strong emphasis on discussion and consensus; the Dutch for this is *overleg*. Members of a company are seen as a team; overtly dictatorial behaviour is not considered acceptable. Meetings are held more frequently than in the UK, but they rarely last longer than 45 minutes. If you want to have your opinion listened to, then you will have to do your research beforehand. Being well-informed is an absolute must, but being pedantic will soon make you unpopular. It is also well known that Dutch employers do not much like shy, introverted employees; on the whole, shy people do not fit in well in Dutch society, to the extent that they have formed their own organisation to defend their interests.

While being well-organised is a typical Dutch trait, the Dutch workplace will seem less hierarchical and more relaxed than in the UK. Nonetheless, the Dutch are very aware of their position in their particular organisation and will not do things without the approval of their superiors. Quibbling over minor details is not considered good practice. There are the inevitable meetings if you want to put your point of view over.

If you have an appointment then make sure you are punctual and get straight to the point. The local chamber of commerce will often act as a go-between, but once a name is given, it is quite acceptable to telephone a contact. Appointments should be confirmed in writing, but remember to communicate with the person by name; not to do so is considered rude. If a potential Dutch client agrees to see you it means he or she is interested in what you have to offer. If they invite you to lunch then the deal is clinched.

It is a common British trait to understate one's achievements. The Dutch are self-effacing in private but they will tend to take self-criticism literally. As negotiators the Dutch are tough and shrewd; they will drive a hard bargain but once a deal is struck they make good business partners. Finally, always try to say a few pleasantries in Dutch, have some knowledge of the Dutch Royal Family (but never make jokes about them) and avoid calling their country Holland, as this in fact refers to just two provinces in the Netherlands.

For further details about Dutch business culture, consult *Going Dutch* by Dick Pappenheim, published by International Books, and *Minding your Manners: A Guide to Dutch Business and Social Etiquette* by Magda Berman, published by Tirion.

TRADE UNIONS

TRADE UNION MEMBERSHIP is compulsory only in the printing industry, but approximately 29% of the Dutch workforce, some 1,865,000 workers, still belong to a recognised organisation. The three main unions are the Federation of Dutch Trade Unions (FNV-NCW; www.fnv-ncw.nl) – an amalgamation of non-denominational and Catholic associations, the (Protestant) National Federation of Christian Trade Unions (CNV) and, the Trade Union Federation for Staff and Managerial Personnel (MHP) – an association for executive and middle grade civil servants. A number of organisations also cover agricultural and retail trades.

The Joint Industrial Labour Council (Stichting van de Arbeid) was set up in 1945 by employers and employees to maintain good relations and acts as an arbitrator in industrial disputes. Another major organisation, the Social and Economic Council (Stichting Economische Raad), is made up of equal numbers of representatives from the government, employers and employees. The government is required by law to seek the council's advice on all major economic and social issues. Dutch trade unions are not regarded as militant and do not normally strike to achieve their goals. The number of working days lost through strikes in recent decades has been small.

WOMEN IN WORK

OUTSIDERS ARE ALWAYS surprised to learn that women in the Netherlands are still far from enjoying the same professional prospects as men. Only 41% of the workforce is made up of women (the same percentage as in Belgium). The reason for this is the lack of nursery facilities as much as anything else. The main agitation for equal rights emanates from Amsterdam; the rest of the country is far more conservative.

Women earn 25% less than men taking the country as a whole, although they have virtual parity in government jobs. Self-employed women earn 20% less. In spite of government policy and progressive social policies, women managers are still much more of a rarity than in the UK or the USA.

PERMANENT WORK

PETROCHEMICALS AND ENGINEERING

THE ENGINEERING PROFESSION is not regulated in the Netherlands. You do not need to apply for recognition of your foreign diploma. The professional body is ONRI (Orde van Nederlandse Raadgevende Ingenieurs, Koninginnegracht 22, 2514 AB Den Haag; ☎ 070-314 18 68; fax 070-314 18 78;

e-mail onri@onri.nl; www.onri.nl). The Netherlands is one of the world's largest producers of natural gas. Engineering has also developed in conjunction with the need for sophisticated sea defences. If you have suitable experience, then one of the following agencies may be able to find you a posting in the Netherlands.

Useful Addresses

Anthony Moss and Associates: 173-175 Drummond St, London NW1 3JD; ☎020-7388 0918; fax 020-7387 4973.
CCL: 162-164 Upper Richmond Road, London SW15 2SL; ☎020-8333 4141; fax 020-8333 4151.
Hunterskil Howard: Postbus 155, 5600 AD Eindhoven; 040-294 86 86; fax 040-212 02 60; www.hunterskilhoward.com.
Search Consultants International: 4545 Post Oak Place 208, Houston, TX 77027; ☎713-622-9188; fax 713-622-9186; e-mail info@searchconsultants.com.

INFORMATION TECHNOLOGY

WHILE THERE ARE NO PRECISE REGULATIONS about the comparability of qualifications in the area of IT, you are unlikely to find employment without some kind of training and experience. Advertisements are easy enough to interpret, since English terminology is used so much. The area around Den Bosch and Eindhoven, as well as Utrecht, has large numbers of new software firms. The following are some recruitment agencies which may find you work in the Netherlands. The job websites mentioned above have vacancies in IT.

Useful Addresses

Computer Futures: 2 Fouberts Place, Regent Street, London W1V 2AD; ☎020-7446 6644; fax 020-7446 0099; www.computerfutures.com.
Comtex Solutions: Kingswood House, Woburn Road, Leighton Buzzard, Beds LU7 0AP; ☎01525-379111; www.comtexsolutions.com.
Elan IT: Frankemaheerd 12, 1102 AN Amsterdam Z-O; ☎020-311 6500; e-mail info@elanit.nl.
James Baker Associates: 46 Queens Road, Reading, Berks RG1 4BD; ☎01734-505022; fax 01734-505056; www.jba.clara.net.
Octagon Support BV: Jan van Nassaustraat 87, 2596 BR The Hague; 070-324 93 00; fax 070-326 47 12.

MEDICINE AND NURSING

VIRTUALLY ALL MEDICAL and paramedical professions are regulated by law in the Netherlands. The relevant authority for the recognition of qualifications is the Ministry of Health, Welfare and Sport, Bureau Buitenlandse Diplomahouders, Postbus 20350, 2500 EJ Den Haag; 070-340 78 90; fax 070-340 62 51. The entire list of diplomas in this area recognised in the Netherlands is available on the website: www.bigregister.nl/buitendipl.pdf. It can be sent to you by the Ministry. The Geneeskundige Vereniging tot Bevordering van het Ziekenhuiswezen (Postbus 3140, 3502 GC Utrecht) provides information on vacancies in Dutch hospitals. The website www.medweb.nl lists all the professional organisations, as well as vacancies and a CV-bank.

Worldwide Healthcare Exchange (The Colonnades, Beaconsfield Close, Hatfield, Herts AL10 8YD; ☎01707-259233; fax 01707-259223) recruits nurses for hospitals in the Netherlands. Contracts are for six months, with the possibility of a permanent post. RGNs and ENs must be qualified in either operating theatre or intensive care unit nursing; ODAs and radiographers must have at least one year's experience. For further information see *Health Professionals Abroad*. published by Vacation Work, 9 Park End Street, Oxford OX1 1HJ; see www.vacationwork.co.uk.

ARCHITECTS

THE NETHERLANDS has some of the world's best architecture and is a mecca for trainees and those who want to develop their skills. The Ministry of Housing, Spatial Planning and Environment oversees the architecture profession (write to Ministerie VROM, Rijnstraat 8, 2515 XP Den Haag; ☎070-339 37 99; www.minvrom.nl). According to EU regulations there should be no restrictions on practising as an architect, but in order to use the title architect you will have to be registered with the professional body: Stichting Bureau Architectenregister, Nassau Plein 24, Postbus 85506, 2508 CE Den Haag; ☎070-346 70 20; e-mail info@bni.nl; www.bni.nl/lidmaatschap-sba.nl. Job-ads can be placed on this website.

OTHERS

THE NETHERLANDS IS AN ATTRACTIVE location for many international firms, precisely because multilingual employees are easy to find. While many foreign firms locate their production facilities in the UK or elsewhere, the Netherlands is the top choice for multi-lingual technical support providers and call centres. The European Call Centre, a market research agency, recruits foreign native-speakers to conduct surveys over the telephone. The main requirements are a good telephone manner, computer experience and a willingness to stay for at least four months. The Centre is at: Overtoom 519-521, 1054 LH Amsterdam;

☎ 020-589 66 76; e-mail v.nassi@edcc.emis.nl; www.edcc.nl.

Britons may find the competition tough as far as the number of foreign languages they can work in goes. There are many firms where a knowledge of Dutch is not always a prerequisite, the obvious ones being foreign-owned multinationals. Positions for English-speaking sales representatives are sometimes advertised by job recruitment agencies.

In areas of work where you have to find customers among the local population a commitment to learning Dutch is an absolute necessity. Fortunately, the language is by no means as fearsome as it sounds. Musicians, art restorers, photographers and graphic designers are just a few of the people who have found success here.

TEMPORARY WORK

ANY WORK THAT LASTS less than six months is considered temporary employment. Many short-term jobs are available because the Dutch do not want to do them; therefore, in manual jobs especially, expect poor pay and conditions. The minimum wage is about £160 a week (for over 23's) and employers are obliged to pay holiday pay which can prove a welcome bonus at the end of a contract. Under Dutch employment laws temporary work contracts must have an instant termination clause available to both parties.

TEACHING ENGLISH

THE DUTCH POPULATION has a very high level of competence in the English language. Educated Dutch people are so fluent that the Minister of Education suggested that English should become the main language in Dutch universities. The implication for prospective English teachers is clear – this is not a country in which any old BA (Hons) degree enables you to step into a TEFL job! The best prospects for teaching work are with the *Volksuniversiteit* (People's University), but even these can only offer the possibility of part-time work. What demand there is is for teachers with extensive experience of teaching business English or other types of English for Special Purposes (ESP). For the rest, most of the work has been sewn up by long-established spouses of expatriates. The British Council in the Netherlands (Keizersgracht 343, 1016 EH Amsterdam; ☎ 020-622 36 44) can provide a list of schools. These are also easily found under *taalscholen* in the Yellow Pages.

Language Schools
The Hague
The Hague Language Centre: Prinsengracht 31, 2501 CH Den Haag; ☎ 070-365 49 36.

Amsterdam
Berlitz: Rokin 87-89 IV, 1012 KL Amsterdam; ☎020-622 13 75.
English Language Institute: Prins Hendrikkade 136, 1011 AR Amsterdam; ☎020-623 13 02.
International Language Consultants: PC Hooftstraat 57 II, 1071 BN Amsterdam; ☎020-671 00 51.

AU PAIR WORK

IT WAS NOT UNTIL 1986 that the Dutch employment laws officially recognised the au pair arrangement. The business is now above board and au pairs in the Netherlands enjoy good working conditions and a comparatively high rate of pocket money. The concept of au pair is still somewhat foreign to the Dutch, and may be seen as too much of an invasion of privacy. There are plenty of wealthy foreign families in the big cities who will consider au pairs especially in Amsterdam, Rotterdam, The Hague and Utrecht. Positions are open to women and men aged between 18 and 25, and applicants must be able to commit themselves for at least six months.

A standard contract stipulates that time must be given for the au pair to attend a Dutch language course (although a knowledge of Dutch is not necessary, except in more rural areas) and health insurance contributions must be paid by the host family. EU nationals do not require a visa, but will be required to sign an undertaking that they will leave the country within one year when registering with the local police (see Chapter Two, *Entry and Residence Regulations*). The application must include a hand-written letter of invitation from the host family setting out the au pair's rights and obligations, an undertaking to take out full health insurance and that the applicant has no criminal record.

Only a few agencies in the Netherlands deal with au pair placements. A few agencies in the UK and USA send au pairs to the Netherlands. The standard fee for placement by a Dutch agency is about €150-€250. For further information on au pairs, see *The Au Pair and Nanny's Guide to Working Abroad* (£12.95) published by Vacation Work (www.vacationwork.co.uk).

Useful Addresses

Activity International: Postbus 7097, 9701 JB Groningen; ☎050-313 06 66; www.activity.aupair.nl.
Academy Au Pair & Nanny Agency: 42 Milsted Rd, Rainham ME8 6SU; ☎01634-310808; www.academyagency.co.uk.
InterExchange: 161 Sixth Ave, New York, NY 10013; ☎212-924-0446; fax 212-924 0575; e-mail aupairinfo@interexchange.org; www.interexchange.org.

Childcare International Ltd: Trafalgar House, Grenville Place, London NW7 3SA; ☎020-8959 3611; www.childint.co.uk.
Global Au Pairs: Moorlands House, Oldfield Rd, Bromley, Kent BR1 2LE; ☎020-8467 6092; 020-8467 6121; e-mail aupairs@dial.pipex.com.
House o Orange Au Pairs: Noordeinde 134, 2514 GN The Hague; ☎070-324 59 03.

Travel Active: Postbus 107, 5800 AC Venray; ☎0478-551 900; fax 0478-551911; e-mail info@travelactive.nl; www.travelactive.nl.

SEASONAL WORK

Farming

WHILE DUTCH AGRICULTURE is highly mechanised, there is still seasonal farming work available starting from February onwards. A limited number of short-term placements (three months to one year) are available through Agriventure (National Agricultural Centre, Stoneleigh Park, Warwickshire CV6 2LG; ☎01203-696578). Applicants to the scheme must have at least two years' training or practical experience in agriculture or horticulture.

Biologica (Postbus 12048, 3512 LC Utrecht; ☎030-233 99 70; www.platformbiologica.nl), the organisation for ecological agriculture, may be able to help with information and contacts. Stichting de Kleine Aarde (Het Klaverblad 1, Postbus 151, 5280 AD Boxtel; ☎0411-68 49 21; fax 0411-68 34 07; www.dekleineaarde.nl) is an environmental education and information centre. It has an intensive ecological garden and greenhouse and offers the opportunity to work in organic agriculture. The minimum stay is two months.

Bulb Picking. The agricultural industry does provide a wealth of jobs in the bulb fields (from April to October) which traditionally go to foreign workers. The Dutch tourist office (PO Box 523, London SW1E 6NT; ☎0891-200277) produces a free map of the Netherlands showing the bulb growing areas. The centre for bulb picking has shifted from Hillegom to Noordwijk. Essential pieces of equipment are a tent and a bicycle, the latter to tour around the factories. Conditions can be poor, especially in the smaller businesses, but food, accommodation and even beer are often provided free. Two recommended factories are Van Waveren BV (Postbus 10, 2180 AA Hillegom; ☎0252-523112) and Peter Keur BV (Postbus 129, 2180 AC Hillegom; fax 0252-521790). The national association of bulb-growers, the KAVB, will give names of firms looking for workers: Koninklijke Algemene Vereniging voor Bloembollencultuur, Postbus 175, 2180 AD Hillegom; 0252-515 254; fax 0252-519 714; e-mail kavb@bulbgrowing.nl; www.bulbgrowing.nl.

Other Agricultural Work: An alternative to bulbs is tomatoes. The trade is concentrated in Westland, near the villages of Naaldwijk, Westerlee, De Lier and Maasdijk. The season begins in mid-April and the hours are long – 5am to 7pm.

There is plenty of work available in tree and other nurseries around Boskoop, near Gouda. Creyf's Interim (Bootstraat 7, 2771 DL Boskoop; ☎0172-212 424; fax 0172-216 401; www.creyfs.nl) can help jobseekers with relevant experience in this area, from February onwards. Another possibility is fruit- and vegetable-picking in Limburg, near the Belgian border, in the area to the north and south of Roermond. The local paper *De Limburger* is worth consulting.

Hospitality

The Netherlands attracts more than five million visitors every year and as a result the tourist industry employs large numbers of extra workers during the summer months. Jobs tend to be short-term: only a quarter of workers have full-time jobs in the tourist business. The best areas for finding work are Amsterdam and the coastal resorts of Scheveningen, Kijkduin (both near The Hague) and Zandvoort. The islands of Texel, Terschelling, Ameland and Schiermonnikoog also need extra staff in the summer. Vacancies are sometimes advertised on the EURES system (ask your employment centre to look) and *Overseas Jobs Express*. If you are on the spot, contact the nearest Centrum voor Werk en Inkomen (job centre) or *uitzendbureau* or look in the local free newspaper.

Opportunities for tour guides are limited, but if you feel you have the necessary stamina and knowledge of the country, then it could be worth asking a local travel agency or the Netherlands Tourist Board for names of companies operating in the Netherlands. Many British coach operators send parties over to the bulbfields in the spring; they can be found in the Yellow Pages. The companies listed below operate activity holidays for young people. Further details, including advice on training, can be found in *Working in Tourism*, published by Vacation Work (see inside cover).

3D Education and Adventure Ltd: Business Support, Osmington Bay, Weymouth, Dorset DT3 6EG; ☎01305-836226.

Eurocamp: Overseas Recruitment Department (Ref SJ/02); ☎01606-787522.

Conferences and Exhibitions: The numerous conferences and exhibitions held in the Netherlands require hosts/hostesses with foreign languages. The Amsterdam Congress Bureau (Postbus 3901, 1001 AS Amsterdam; ☎020-551 25 70; fax 020-551 25 75; www.amsterdam.congress.nl) can give details of organisers of forthcoming conferences and conventions. For exhibitions contact Amsterdam RAI, Europlein 8, Amsterdam; ☎020-549 12 12; fax 020-646 44 69; www.rai.nl. Further information can be found in *Working in Tourism*, published by Vacation Work.

SECRETARIAL WORK

THE OPPORTUNITIES FOR bilingual secretaries in the Netherlands are not overwhelming. The first obstacle is the ability of Dutch employees to speak English and secondly many positions are filled by qualified expatriates already present in the Netherlands. However, good secretaries are always in demand, especially by the business communities of The Hague, Rotterdam and Amsterdam. The Hague is also the seat of the Dutch Parliament and the International Court of Justice. The Job-In Agency and Blue Lynx specialise in placing English-speakers; see above, under *Employment Organisations* for more agencies. The Dutch association of temporary work agencies (ABU) can supply a list of agencies.

Useful addresses

Algemene Bond Uitzendondernemingen *(ABU):* Postbus 302, 1170 AH Badhoevedorp; ☎020-658 01 01.
Blue Lynx Employment: Mauritskade 5, Postbus 85691, 2508 CJ The Hague; 070-376 99 77; e-mail thehague@bluelynx.nl. Siriusdreef 17-27, 2132 WT Hoofddorp; ☎023-568 92 51; e-mail hoofddorp@bluelynx.nl.
Job-In Uitzendbureau: Javastraat 35a, 2585 AD Den Haag; ☎070-363 51 20; fax 070-363 38 51.
Michael Page International: Strawinskylaan 1057, 1077 XX Amsterdam; ☎020-578 94 44; www.michaelpage.nl.

VOLUNTARY WORK

THE MAJORITY OF VOLUNTARY work available to British citizens in the Netherlands is co-ordinated through UK organisations. Dutch organisations will, in general, direct you to the organisation in your own country. If you are already in the country you can make enquiries to the Dutch Organisatie Vrijwilligerswerk (Organisation for Voluntary Work), who will put you in touch with suitable organisations. The head office of Universala Esperanto-Asocio, the organisation for the promotion of Esperanto in Rotterdam requires volunteers who are fluent in Esperanto for six to 12 month periods. The Unrepresented Nations and Peoples Organisation (UNPO) welcomes voluntary help and can offer places for stagiaires and sometimes paid work.

International Voluntary Service (IVS) Britain: Old Hall, East Bergholt, nr. Colchester CO7 6TQ; 01206-298215; www.ivsgbn.demon.co.uk; www.sciint.org.
Nederlandse Organisatie Vrijwilligerswerk: Information and Documentation Department, Postbus 2877, 3500 GW Utrecht; ☎0900-899 86 00;
www.vrijwilligerscentrale.nl or www.freeflex.nl.
UNPO: Javastraat 40A, 2585 AP Den Haag; ☎070-360 33 18; www.unpo.org.
Universala Esperanto-Asocio: Nieuwe Binnenweg 176, 3015 BJ Rotterdam; ☎010-436 10 44; fax 010-436 17 51.

BUSINESS AND INDUSTRY REPORT

THE NETHERLANDS is a far wealthier country than appears at first sight, with huge investments in US and UK industry. The Dutch prefer to keep a low profile, so few of us are aware of how many Dutch products and inventions we use every day. Their nation's wealth has come about through hard work and organisational ability. Most of all the Dutch have succeeded in turning the harshness of their environment, always at risk of inundation, into their greatest asset. As the French traveller Denis Diderot observed with some envy in 1774: 'The Dutch have put the air, water and land in chains; without these three slaves they would not be able to carry out one-twentieth of their work'.

The first Dutch Golden Age was during the 17th century, when they completely dominated European trade. Political events brought about a decline in Dutch fortunes, but by then they had already pioneered the concept of the multinational, with the Dutch East India Company, for 200 years the world's most powerful trading organisation, followed by Unilever, Philips and Royal Dutch Shell. These days, Dutch prosperity is based on a superb integrated transport system, a highly trained multilingual workforce and a strong emphasis on cooperation between all sections of society. Businesses which are natural competitors tend to work together for everyone's benefit. Universities and research institutes are always closely involved in new developments.

The Dutch have always sought to promote free trade; the establishment of the Benelux Customs Union in 1948 set the stage for the establishment of the European Community. These days 79% of Dutch exports go to the EU, which is also the origin of 66% of imports. Since the difficulties of the immediate postwar era, the Dutch economy has grown steadily. The oil shocks of the 1970s had a strongly adverse effect, but the 1980s were again years of expansion. The 1992-1993 recession temporarily pushed up unemployment to as high as 9%, but this had already fallen to 6% by the end of 1997 and in 2001 stood at only 2.2%. The 1994 general election marked a watershed; for the first time the Christian Democrats were excluded from power, and a coalition of socialists and liberals, the so-called 'purple coalition' came into power. At this time, some highly controversial measures were pushed through in order to stimulate economic growth. Social security was cut, along with tax and social security contributions, with the intention of creating 350,000 new jobs. For several years, the Dutch economy prospered with average growth rates of 3% but 2001 has seen as a slowing down.

Economic policy has been so successful that there is more of a danger of the economy overheating than anything else. Some question the wisdom of cutting taxes further when there is already a consumer spending boom. The advent of the euro may bring further growth. To some extent the poor state of the German economy inevitably dampens down optimism in the Netherlands, as 29% of exports go there. The next largest export markets are Belgium and Luxembourg, France and the UK (13%, 11% and 10% each).

Most areas of the economy have been opened up to foreign ownership, with the exception of the national airline, KLM. One result has been that many of the utility companies have sold their assets to US investors, who use them as tax write-offs, and then lease them back, with large savings for Dutch consumers, at the expense of American taxpayers.

The following section provides a guide to the most important Dutch industries. The current prosperity, or otherwise, of each sector is assessed with a view to its business and employment potential to the expatriate.

AEROSPACE

FOKKER AEROSPACE, once ranked fifth among the West's aircraft manufacturers, was one of the crown jewels of Dutch industry until 1996, when its owners, Daimler-Benz, decided it was no longer viable and pulled out. All attempts since then to revive the core business have been fruitless. Fokker still maintains an aircraft servicing business, and its space technology arm, Fokker Space, continues to operate successfully.

A wide range of institutions, both private and public are involved in the business of space technology, co-ordinated by the Netherlands Industrial Space Organisation (NISO). The establishment of the European Space Research and Technology Centre (ESTEC) in Noordwijk, near The Hague, has resulted in a proliferation of space-related businesses, with various commercial spinoffs, such as airbags for cars.

AGRICULTURE

AGRICULTURAL EXPORTS are worth around €26 billion annually and generate about 80% of the entire trade surplus. While fewer than 4% of the population work directly on the land, nearly a quarter of all Dutch workers are in some way involved in the food, fishing, drinks, tobacco and horticulture sectors. The extraordinary development of this branch of Dutch industry has come about through a relentless drive towards increasing mechanisation and innovation which began in the late nineteenth century. Much of this was led by state-run agricultural colleges; the Agricultural University in Wageningen is now a world-leader.

The Netherlands produces three main crops: wheat, sugar-beet and potatoes. The potato accounts for the highest single yield: the average harvest is over 5 million tonnes, most of which is turned into french fries. While most farming is highly mechanised, the fruit and vegetable industry still requires seasonal workers, and many of these are traditionally foreigners (see Section *Temporary Work* above).

An undesirable side-effect of the Dutch agricultural success story has been an increasing level of pollution caused by the excessive use of herbicides and pesticides, as well as enough manure to bury the entire country. As a consequence the Dutch government is working on ways to promote less harmful practices;

environmental technology and know-how are developing rapidly, giving the Dutch another potential world-beating export.

CHEMICALS

THE OUTLOOK for the Dutch chemicals industry is bright, although heavily dependent on economic conditions in Germany. The two major multinationals that dominate the sector, AKZO-Nobel and DSM, are among the most profitable in the world. Close behind are the likes of Shell and Unilever; internal competition alone is likely to keep the Dutch chemical industry at the forefront of worldwide development and production. The industry is centred on a modern base around Europoort, Rotterdam. This provides companies with excellent transport links to worldwide suppliers and markets. The industry exports about three-quarters of production, accounting for 16% of all Dutch exports (about €24 billion a year). The greatest proportion of output comes from bulk chemicals such as fertilisers, caustic soda and plastics. The Dutch are working to expand their share of the specialist chemicals market, in particular pharmaceuticals. Foreign multinationals with a strong presence in the country include ICI and Dupont.

ELECTRONICS

THE DUTCH ELECTRONICS INDUSTRY is dominated by one name, Philips. This multinational company is synonymous with quality electrical goods and pioneering research. Philips invented the audio cassette and the compact disc, and was one of the pioneers in the development of colour television. It employs over 200,000 people in 60 countries, and has a turnover of €40 billion a year. Philips produces 2.5 billion lighbulbs each year, and is the world leader in this field. In recent years, fierce competition from the Far East has made it increasingly difficult for Philips to maintain its position. More and more production is being shifted abroad where costs are lower; Poland is now the site of one of Philips' main production facilities. On top of this, its head office has been moved to the southern edge of Amsterdam, away from its traditional base in Eindhoven. In spite of the upheavals, Philips is still an employer which any electronics graduate would want to work for, and some its higher management have come from the UK and USA.

FOOD AND BEVERAGES

THE FOOD AND DRINK INDUSTRY accounts for nearly one-fifth of the total turnover of Dutch industry. Along with the tobacco industry, food and drinks concerns employ some 152,000 workers. In particular, the Netherlands is the world's leading exporter of cocoa and dairy products. While the domestic market has grown little in recent years, exports are buoyant. The industry works closely with research institutes and universities, in order to maintain its leading-edge position.

Heineken, Amstel, Grolsch and Oranjeboom are some of the more famous names in the brewing world. The beer industry boasts a long history and the Heineken Group can trace its roots back to 1592. Limburg is the brewing capital of the Netherlands and has no less than eight major breweries within its boundaries. Its oldest brewery is Brand which dates back to 1340. In all, the Netherlands exports around 1 billion litres of beer per year.

HORTICULTURE

THE HUMBLE TULIP, which among other things has been described as a peculiar looking onion with an unpleasant taste, is at the heart of a thriving industry that employs 36,000 Dutch workers and has an annual turnover of €3.5 billion. Dutch horticulture traditionally concentrated on salad products such as lettuce, cucumber and tomatoes, however, in recent years these have been increasingly overshadowed by the cultivation and marketing of flowers. To say the Dutch like flowers is an understatement and no shopping trip is complete without a visit to the florist. There is one florist shop for every 1,800 people; in the UK the number is closer to one florist per every 10,000. The Dutch Flower Council estimates that 63% of the world's cut flowers and 51% of pot plants, or seven billion cut flowers and 530 million pot plants, are exported every year. At the centre of the industry is the Verenigde Bloemenveilingen Aalsmeer (VBA). It was founded in 1912 and is the largest flower auction centre in the world. It covers 500,000 square metres and every day 50,000 transactions sell 12 million cut flowers. The European Community accounted for 83% of total flower exports, with Germany alone receiving 43%.

HYDRAULIC ENGINEERING

MORE THAN HALF the Netherlands lies below sea level; without sea and river defences some 65% of the country would be flooded every day. A complex system of barriers and dykes now exists to protect the low-lying areas and pumping stations work day and night to drain the land. Through necessity the Dutch have been at the forefront of water control techniques and their expertise has been used throughout the world, from the Aswan Dam in Egypt to London's Thames barrier. Two projects have led the way in The Netherlands:

The Delta Project: On 1 February 1953 1,835 people lost their lives when large areas of the south-western part of the country were flooded. Today, all but two estuaries can be closed to the sea. (The New Waterway and the Western Scheldt remain open to allow access to Rotterdam and Antwerp.) Across the mouth of the Eastern Scheldt Dutch engineers have constructed a storm-surge barrier that measures 3.2 km long, which can be opened and closed.

The Zuyder Zee Project: Fifty years before the Delta Project a 30 km dam was built across the Zuyder Zee, connecting the provinces of Friesland and Noord-Holland. This transformed the area into an inland, freshwater lake (the IJsselmeer). Four huge polders (areas of reclaimed land) were drained and 165,000 hectares of new land were created for agriculture and housing. There are no plans to create any further polders. In certain places, controlled flooding has been allowed in order to bring the water table up.

The Dutch have an unparalleled degree of expertise in dredging (*baggeren*), and are often called in either to develop new airports and seaports, or to clean up polluted sludge. The main area of expansion has been in Asia; the Hong Kong airport project gave the industry a temporary boom, but there is no shortage of other projects.

INFORMATION TECHNOLOGY

THE DUTCH HAVE TAKEN A LEAD over the rest of continental Europe in information technology, on the basis of their close ties with the English-speaking world and the desire to be involved in the industries of the future. Most of the leading computer companies can be found here, including IBM, Digital, Logica, Hewlett Packard and AT&T. Other major names are R.R. Donnelley, Merisel, Packard Bell, BMC Software and Computervision Corporation.

A whole new industry has taken off in recent years centred on the development of sophisticated industrial automation and integrated software solutions which are now being exported around the world. The main automation companies are Origin, Cap Gemini Ernst & Young and Getronics, each with turnovers in the region of €1 billion. Suppliers of software packages enabling the integration of all the diverse activities of one company, include Exact Software, Baan Company, Unit 4 and Afas. Dutch software companies are now making a major impact in the USA and other foreign markets; job opportunities for English-speaking IT specialists are very good.

THE MOTOR INDUSTRY

TAKEN IN ALL ITS ASPECTS, some 62,000 workers are dependent on the motor industry in the Netherlands. The leading vehicle manufacturer is DAF (Doorne Auto Fabrieken), which concentrates almost entirely on the commercial vehicle sector. The DAF company no longer has links with LDV in the UK, which it part-owned at one time. Vehicles are exported throughout the EU and to many eastern European countries including Russia, Hungary, Czechoslovakia and Poland. Major foreign car manufacturers include Mitsubishi, Ford and Saab Scania.

OIL AND GAS

THE NETHERLANDS' NATURAL reserves of hydrocarbon fuels are an important factor in providing stability for the national economy. The country is the EU's leading producer and exporter of natural gas and the fourth largest producer of natural gas in the world. Gas supplies about half of the total energy needs and of the 80 billion cubic metres of gas annually produced, about 50% is exported. Oil makes up a further 40% of Dutch domestic energy requirements. Dutch oil wells already supply more than 7% of domestic needs and promising new fields have been discovered in the North Sea. Dutch gas reserves are not unlimited, and are expected to run out in 2025. The Dutch have now entered into an agreement with the Russian state gas producer to import gas with the intention of exporting it again. The oil and gas sector employs about 26,000 workers, and there are excellent opportunities for English-speaking staff.

TOURISM

THE NETHERLANDS is the holiday destination for five million foreigners every year, making it one of the most popular countries in Western Europe for tourists. Amsterdam is one of Europe's top attractions and is the centre of the tourist industry. In order to keep bringing in new visitors, new museums and activity centres are constantly being opened; there are over 1,000 of them now. The bulb fields between Haarlem and Leiden are major tourist attractions. For the more hardy traveller they can also prove a useful source of seasonal work.

For the Dutch themselves, the northern provinces of Friesland and Groningen, and the Frisian Islands, with their uncrowded and clean environment have long been popular. For those who do not want to 'get away from it all' a number of west coast beach resorts have developed, including Scheveningen and Zandvoort which offer plenty of entertainment. These resorts provide a large number of seasonal jobs in the hotel and catering trades.

TRANSPORT

THE TRANSPORTATION INDUSTRY generates 8% of GNP and employs some 400,000 workers. Integration of the transport system is one of the keys to Dutch success, but much remains to be done in terms of linking road haulage with the railways. There are some 9,000 road haulage companies in the Netherlands; many of these are one-man operations. It is estimated that there is an over-capacity in the road haulage industry of some 5%. The Dutch own one-third of road transport companies in the UK. 27% of international road transport in Europe originates in the Netherlands. Schiphol Airport, south of Amsterdam, handles over 1 million tonnes of cargo every year, and is used by 80 airlines.

As far as water transportation goes, the inland waterways are of great importance; Dutch carriers transport more than one half of the Rhine's cargo (about 116 million tonnes a year). The greatest superlatives must go to Rotterdam, the world's busiest port, which handles over 300 million tonnes of cargo a year. The second largest seaport, Amsterdam, is growing rapidly as well. Because of congestion at Rotterdam, new facilities have been developed at Eemshaven and Delfzijl in Groningen. The Rotterdam authorities are hoping to build a second port opposite the Hook of Holland, the Maasvlakte 2, and there are definite plans to develop the port at Terneuzen on the Schelde. In total, Dutch seaports handle some 37% of the cargo coming in and out of Europe.

REGIONAL EMPLOYMENT GUIDE

IN THE *GENERAL INTRODUCTION* to the Netherlands, the main cities and regions were discussed with a view to residence. In this section, the regions are covered with a view to employment prospects in each area. The information provided will give some idea of the industries which are dominant and the type of jobs which are most readily available in each area. Enquiries about investment should first go to the Netherlands Foreign Investment Agency (NFIA): www.nfia.nl.

THE NORTH

Groningen, Drenthe and Friesland

THE THREE NORTHERN PROVINCES have traditionally been seen as under-achieving in the race for prosperity. While per capita incomes in Groningen and Friesland are below the national average, Drenthe has virtually caught up. The fact that the three northern provinces still have space for expansion as well as an attractive living environment and lower labour costs inevitably means that more and more investment will come their way as the rest of the country reaches saturation point. The northern region is already the raw materials centre of the Netherlands; now it hopes to attract more high value-added industries which have recently tended to go to the south-east.

The area has to fight against its perceived 'remoteness' from the rest of the country. A common joke told by northerners is that the distance from Amsterdam to Groningen is twice as far as the distance from Groningen to Amsterdam, thus emphasising that the gap between the two is greater psychologically than in reality; it takes only two and a half hours to travel by train between these cities. The local development corporation points out that the area is closer to Germany and Scandinavia than the rest of the country. Groningen province is taking advantage of this by developing the ports of Delfzijl and Eemshaven thus taking traffic away from the overcrowded Rotterdam.

A proposal for strengthening both the image and the power of the north was that the three provinces should join forces and form one 'super province'; this is unlikely to happen. Development is handled by one super-agency, the

Investerings- en Ontwikkelingsmaatschappij voor Noord Nederland, who will be happy to advise on investment possibilities: NV NOM, Postbus 424, 9700 AK Groningen.

Groningen: The 'Top of Holland' is definitely the raw materials capital of the Netherlands. The discovery first of salt in Winschoten in the 1950s and later gas at Slochteren in the 1970s has twice stimulated growth in Groningen City, Slochteren and Delfzijl (which has the country's third largest seaport). More recently rich deposits of magnesium have been discovered and these are currently processed at Veendam. Agriculture is also of great significance, accounting for 13.4% of the economy.

In the wake of the petrochemicals industry and the development of new port facilities, the chemical industry has taken off around Delfzijl and Eemshaven. Major companies include Akzo, FMC, Kemax, Dow Benelux, BF Goodrich and PPG Chemicals. The Japanese firm Kyowa plans to establish a facility at Veendam.

Centred on the University of Groningen, biotechnology and pharmaceuticals are developing fast. Kikkoman has recently set up a soy-sauce factory at Hoogezand. Another great success story has been the revival of shipbuilding at Eemshaven and Delfzijl. Both ports are likely to expand to keep up with demand.

Drenthe: Drenthe has large reserves of both gas and oil. One of the largest inland oilfields in Europe is located in Coevorden. The province provides virtually the entire gas needs of the Netherlands and about 7% of the country's oil. Metal and textile industries have a strong presence in Emmen and throughout the province the construction and chemical industries are two of the leading employers. Main activities include rubber, plastics, glass fibre, packaging and synthetic textiles.

Drenthe has been successful in attracting foreign investment and leading foreign companies to locate in the province include Honeywell Computers, Saab Scania and Yamanouchi. Further information on Drenthe can be obtained from NV NOM (see above).

Friesland: A black and white cow that takes its name from the province gives some idea as to the mainstay of the Friesland economy. The Frisian cow has a reputation for high milk and beef production and is reared worldwide. Friesland is dominated by agriculture and its farmers pioneered the centralisation of dairy produce processing. Now with less than 5% of the Dutch population it claims production of 55% of cheese, 17% of milk and butter, and 75% of cattle exports.

Because of the proximity of suppliers, the processing of food ingredients has become an important activity, the main names being Friesland Dairy Foods and CSK (dairy products), AVEBE (starch derivatives), Chonoblij (chocolate) and Atlanta Dethmers (baking). In order to supply the needs of the food industry, Friesland is also home to many companies involved in food packaging, production lines, storage facilities and refrigeration.

Much of the province is at or below sea level and as a result the area is also a key centre for the development and testing of hydraulic engineering. This includes the pioneering Zuyder Zee project. The cultural theme combined with the coastline and recreational activities are at the centre of a growing tourist industry.

THE SOUTH

Noord-Brabant and Limburg

THE SOUTH OF THE NETHERLANDS has been a remarkable economic success story. Twenty years ago the area was in decline and much of the economy was based on coal. Today the provinces of Limburg and Noord-Brabant consistently outperform the rest of the country in terms of economic growth and are likely to continue to do so.

Noord-Brabant: Noord-Brabant is the most industrialised province in the Netherlands and the centre of the Dutch electronics industry. It has the highest industrial output of any region in the Netherlands and is ideally located in the triangle between the German Ruhr-district, Antwerp and Rotterdam. Noord-Brabant's economy is growing and the area has attracted more than 250 foreign companies including Volvo, Hewlett Packard, ICI and Fuji. Noord-Brabant has been one of the areas to benefit most from the overspill of the main Randstad conurbation. The growth in industry is reflected in the fact that employment levels in the province are rising faster than the national average. The leading light behind the region's growth is the Brabant Development Company (*Brabantse Ontwikkelingsmaatschappij – BOM*). The main objective of BOM has been to strengthen and create businesses, through both investment and know-how.

The city of Eindhoven is the driving force behind the province's economy. It is internationally renowned for its electronics and precision engineering sectors and is home to Philips' international headquarters. It also hosts the World Trade Centre for Electronics and the Centre for Micro-Electronics. Nearby Tilburg was once a thriving woollen/textile centre. This has long gone and the town now relies on a highly developed electronics base and is a leading service industry centre. The province's capital, 's-Hertogenbosch, (Den Bosch – 'the woods') is fast assuming industrial importance with a growing light industry zone. Further information is available from: BOM, PO Box 3240, 5003 SK Tilburg (www.bom.nl).

Limburg: Within two decades Limburg has been transformed from a depressed region to a fully fledged success story. In 1965 one in three of the workforce was dependent on the coal mining industry. The local authorities realised the need for diversification early on. By using the province's favourable location between Belgium and Germany, and investing heavily in research and development, the area has now become one of the most prosperous in the country.

The area's biggest employer is the chemicals giant DSM with a 10,000-strong workforce. It accounts for one quarter of the province's industrial output and invests nearly €500 million annually into its Limburg operations. Rank Xerox and Océ van der Grinten produce office equipment here, and other light industry has followed their lead. Japanese companies have been particularly attracted by the area's excellent transport links, the most prominent being Mitsubishi. Mitsubishi and Volvo, together with the Dutch government have invested almost €1.5 billion in the NedCar plant at Born, although Volvo has since pulled out of the venture. A whole range of automotive components companies have set up here. Perhaps the region's greatest coup was attracting Mobil Plastics to build a €200 million plastic film plant on a greenfield site at Kerkrade. Contact Limburgse Ontwikkelings Maatschappij, PO Box 1310, 6210 BH Maastricht; www.liof.com.

THE WEST

Noord-Holland, Zuid-Holland and Zeeland

TWO CITIES DOMINATE THE WEST of the Netherlands: Amsterdam and Rotterdam. This is the heartland of the Randstad and the number and variety of industries is too large to mention each individually. However, the area as a whole does have certain key industries.

Zuid-Holland: The famous bulb fields dominate the area to the north of Leiden. Millions of flowers are grown every year and provide the basis for one of the Netherlands main export earners, as well as a famous tourist attraction. Delft and Gouda are household names, for china and cheese respectively, but both now rely more upon light industry and service industries than the products for which they became famous. Delft's real claim to fame is Gist Brocades, the world's largest producer of penicillin.

At the turn of the century Rotterdam was a small shipping and fishing community and during the Second World War the port and city were almost completely devastated. Today Europoort is the busiest seaport in the world and handles over 250,000 ships a year. The port complex itself covers more than 5,300 acres of land and a host of associated industries have grown up to service the transport and storage sector. Unilever is based here.

The Hague is the province's second largest city and is the seat of the Dutch government. It houses the offices of numerous foreign companies. To outsiders it is mainly known for its embassies and as the home of the International Court of Justice, as well as various international lobbying groups. A thriving tourist business has grown to meet the demands of the huge urban population. The seaside town of Scheveningen, which also has a large fishing fleet, is the equivalent of Blackpool in the Netherlands. The area to the south of The Hague, the Westland, is notable for its nurseries and horticulture (especially vegetables). Contact: Ontwikkelingsbedrijf Rotterdam, PO Box 6575, 3002 AN Rotterdam; www.obr.rotterdam.nl.

Noord-Holland: There are few areas that can offer as diverse an economic base as that around Amsterdam. Banking, tourism, manufacturing, pharmaceuticals, information technology, telecommunications, farming and horticulture all play a significant part in the economy of Noord-Holland. Aalsmeer has the world's largest auction hall (*Verenigde Bloemenveilingen Aalsmeer*) which acts as the focus to the entire Dutch horticulture business. The Bennebroek-Lisse-Sassenheim area is the heart of the bulb fields that extend from Leiden to the southern limits of Haarlem, the nerve centre of the bulb industry. Amsterdam itself is a mecca to tourists and a thriving tourist industry has developed around the seaside resorts of Zandvoort and Noordwijk. The Dutch broadcasting industry is centred around

Hilversum. Further information on Amsterdam is available from the Amsterdam Promotion Foundation, Postbus 15713, 1001 NE Amsterdam; www.amsterdampromotion.nl.

Zeeland: Zeeland, as its name suggests, is a land of the sea. In the past, Middelburg was a major ports; these days it is the focal point of the local tourism and leisure pursuits industry. Vlissingen, just to the south, is a working fishing and shipbuilding centre, as well as a holiday resort. There are plans to develop a port at Terneuzen, which would take some of the traffic that currently goes to Antwerp and Ghent. A motorway will soon be built from Terneuzen to Ghent.

The Delta project, which centred on Zeeland, is probably the world's greatest engineering feat. Some of the world's main dredging companies are to be found along the Westerschelde, dedicated to keeping this vital artery open. Agriculture is a major industry in this area. Other activities include transportation and petrochemical-related services. Yerseke, on the Oosterschelde, is the oyster capital of Europe producing 30 million Zeeland oysters in a good year.

THE CENTRAL AREA

Utrecht, Gelderland, Overijssel and Flevoland

Utrecht: This is the smallest province in the Netherlands and home to many of its wealthiest people. The province is conveniently close to the country's main cities; consequently a number of governmental and other national organisations have set up around Utrecht, Nieuwegein and Amersfoort. The regional economy is extremely diverse, but is mainly based on service industries, including insurance, banking, logistics centres, call centres and software companies. Thanks to its position between North Holland and Germany, it is also home to many transportation concerns.

Utrecht is known as the academic centre of the Netherlands and has been able to attract numerous foreign companies to set up their European coordination centres here. Computervision Corp., the largest supplier of CAD/CAM software has a call centre near Utrecht. BMC Software is based in Nieuwegein. The US food giant, Sara Lee, operating from Utrecht, is possibly the largest foreign employer in the country, after taking over Douwe Egberts, the coffee producer. The city also claims to be the world leader in holding trade and industrial fairs.

Gelderland: Gelderland is the largest of the Netherlands' 12 provinces and is split by the three great rivers: the Rhine, the Maas and the Ijssel. Both Arnhem and Nijmegen have become important centres for water transport and act as links between Rotterdam and Germany. The area has a reputation for pioneers; in Zaltbommel the Philips brothers first experimented with mass-producing electric light bulbs. These days Nijmegen is part of the Dutch 'silicon triangle', along with Den Bosch and Eindhoven.

Apeldoorn and Wageningen carry on the pioneering tradition. The Dutch have few natural resources and Apeldoorn is the country's leading papermaking and recycling centre. Wageningen is responsible in part for the Netherlands' thriving agricultural industry. It is the seat of Europe's foremost agricultural university with 21 laboratories, 22 independent institutions and 10 associated concerns. Also located in Wageningen are the principal ship-testing laboratories where small-scale boats are tested under simulated trial conditions. A survey of 267 regions in Europe rated Gelderland as the most promising area to establish a business, in terms of workforce, costs, communications and quality of life. Contact: Gelderse Ontwikkelings Maatschappij, PO Box 5215, 6802 EE Arnhem; www.nvgom.nl.

Overijssel: Zwolle is the capital of a province with many contrasts. The old towns of Blokzijl and Vollenhove have been turned from seafaring ports on the Zuyder Zee into specialist recreation and yacht-building centres on the IJsselmeer. The textile industry in Almelo, Enschede and Oldenzaal was at the heart of the Dutch Industrial Revolution; what remains is concentrated on high-tech synthetic fibres. In other respects, the province is mainly known for its precision engineering and tool-making. The two main employers in Enschede are Grolsch beer and the leading tyre manufacturer in Benelux, Vredestein Banden. In Zwolle it is Scania trucks, DSM Resins and Stork-Wärtsilä Diesel.

As far as foreign investment goes, Overijssel and Gelderland are likely to be the next big growth area in the Netherlands. Overijssel is particularly looking for chemical, rubber and plastics firms to set up there, continuing its industrial traditions. In the survey mentioned above, Overijssel came sixth out of 267 European regions. Apart from Scania, the other well-known foreign company is Texas Instruments, based in Almelo. The foreign investment agency is the Overijssel Industrial Development Company, Postbus 5518, 7500 GM Enschede; www.oomnv.nl.

Flevoland: Flevoland was reclaimed from the sea and is the Netherlands' youngest province. Its very existence is testimony to Dutch engineering brilliance and the same innovative spirit pervades the whole Flevoland economy. The idea that Flevoland is a 'test case' has been translated into many areas of research and development. Its economy is growing at a remarkable rate and new industries, especially small concerns in the field of high technology, are setting up every day. The province has given a high priority to agricultural and agriculture-related technological research. It is Europe's most up-to-date farming region with more than 20 research institutes and experimental farms. NLR National Aviation and Aerospace Laboratory (with Europe's largest wind tunnel) at Noordoostpolder and De Voorst Hydrodynamic Laboratory at Kraggenburg. One other important growth industry is that of water sports and recreation. The IJsselmeer is a popular destination for both sailors and fishermen. Government incentives for foreign businesses are generous. Giant, the cycle manufacturer, and Yanmar, the Japanese outboard motors firm, have both set up here. Other well-known foreign names include Pioneer, Samsung and Yakult. Further information can be obtained from Provincie Flevoland, Department of Economic Affairs, Postbus 55, 8200 AB Lelystad.

DIRECTORY OF MAJOR EMPLOYERS

THE NETHERLANDS-British Chamber of Commerce publishes a detailed list of its members, the *Members Register* and *Anglo-Dutch Trade Directory* including British subsidiaries operating in The Netherlands, obtainable from the NBCC (The Dutch House, 307 High Holborn, London WC1V 7LS; ☎020-7242 1064; e-mail nbcc@btinternet.com; www.nbcc.com) for £25 including postage. The Netherlands office is at: Nederlands Britse Kamer van Koophandel Nieuwezijds Voorburgwal 328L, 1012 RW Amsterdam; ☎020-421 70 40.

Also available is *The Netherlands-American Trade Directory* which gives a complete picture of the American presence in the Netherlands and the Dutch presence in the USA, published by the American Chamber of Commerce in the Netherlands, Burg. V. Karnebeeklaan 14, 2585 BB Den Haag; ☎070-365 808; fax 070-364 6992; e-mail office@amcham.nl; www.amcham.nl.

The Dutch equivalent of the CBI, the VNO-NCW, can put you in touch with relevant organisations, and also displays a complete list on the Internet: VNO-NCW, Bezuidenhoutseweg 12, 2594 AV Den Haag; ☎070-349 03 49; fax 070-349 03 00; www.vno-ncw.nl. The site www.abc-d.nl has a convenient list of companies in the Netherlands.

Foreign Banks

Bank of America NA: Herengracht 469, 1017 BS Amsterdam; ☎020-557 18 88.

Barclays Bank plc Business Banking: Strawinskylaan 1353, 1077 XX Amsterdam; ☎020-626 22 09, fax 020-626 65 11.

Citibank NA: Hoogoorddreef 54B, 1101 BE Amsterdam; ☎020-651 42 11.

Lloyds Bank-TSB Bank plc: Gatwickstraat 17-19, 1043 GL Amsterdam; ☎020-626 35 35.

Nomura Bank Nederland NV: De Boelelaan 7, 1083 HJ Amsterdam; ☎020-549 69 69.

Dutch Banks

ABN-Amro Bank: Herengracht 595-597, 1017 CE Amsterdam; ☎020-628 93 93.

Crediet-en Effectenbank NV: Herculesplein 5, Postbus 85100, 3508 AC Utrecht; ☎030-256 09 11.

Mees Pierson NV: Rokin 55, 1012 KK Amsterdam; ☎020-527 11 88.

ING Groep: Strawinskylaan 2631, 1077 ZZ Amsterdam; ☎020-541 54 11, fax 020-541 55 44.

Rabobank Group: Postbus 17100, 3500 HG Utrecht; ☎030-216 00 00.

Van Lanschot Bankiers: Hoge Steenweg 29, 5211 JN 's-Hertogenbosch; ☎073-615 39 11, fax 073-615 30 66.

Insurance Companies

Aegon NV: Postbus 202, 2501 CE Den Haag; ☎070-344 32 10.

Amev Nederland: Archimedeslaan 10, Postbus 2072, 3500 HB Utrecht; ☎030-257 91 11.

Delta Lloyd Levensverzekering: Spaklerweg 4, Postbus 1000, 1000 BA Amsterdam; ☎020-594 91 11.

Kamerbeek Groep BV: Stationsplein 121, 3818

LE Amersfoort; ☎033-464 07 00.
Nationale Nederlanden NV: Prinses Beatrixlaan 35, 2595 AK Den Haag; ☎070-513 03 03.
Sedgwick European Risk Services: Nachtwachtlaan 20, 1058 EA Amsterdam; ☎020-541 71 00.
Sumitomo Marine & Fire Insurance BV: Amsteldijk 166 6E, 1079 LH Amsterdam; ☎020-644 41 01.
The Gouda Insurance Company: Postbus 9, 2800 MA Gouda; 0182-54 49 16.

Breweries

Bols Royal Distilleries: Wattstraaat 61, 2723 RB, Zoetermeer; ☎079-330 53 05.
Grolsche Bierbrouwerij Nederland: Postbus 55, 7500 AB Enschede; ☎053-483 33 33.
Gulpener Bierbrouwerij: Postbus 51, 6270 AB Gulpen; ☎043-450 75 75.
Heineken Nederland BV: Postbus 530, 2380 BD Zoeterwoude; ☎071-545 61 11.
Interbrew Nederland: Ceresstraat 13, Postbus 3212, 4800 MA Breda; ☎076-525 24 24.

Agriculture and Horticulture

Bloemenveiling Holland: Postbus 220, 2670 AE Naaldwijk; ☎0174-633 333.
Coop. Verenigde Bloemenveilingen Aalsmeer: Legmeerdijk 313, 1431 GB Aalsmeer; ☎0297-34 74 18.
Krinkels Beplantings Mij. BV: Plantagebaan 58, Postbus 5, 4724 ZG Wouw; ☎0165-301 851, fax 0165-302 781.
Rijk Zwaan Zaadteelt BV: Burg. Crezeelaan 40, Postbus 40, 2678 ZG De Lier; ☎0174-532 300.

Food Processing

Avebe BA: Postbus 15, 9640 AA Veendam; ☎0548-669 111.
CSK: Postbus 225, 8901 BA Leeuwarden; ☎058-284 42 42.
Friesland Export: Postbus 226, 8901 MA Leeuwarden; ☎058-299 24 91.
Friesland Coberco Dairy Foods: Postbus 124, 7940 AC Meppel; ☎0522-276276.
Heinz BV: Postbus 6, 6660 AA Elst; ☎0481-366 757.
Koninklijke Ahold NV: Postbus 3000, 1070 MX Amsterdam; ☎075-659 91 11.
McCain Foods Holland: Postbus 43, 2130 AA Hoofddorp; ☎020-655 17 00.
Quaker Oats: Postbus 5219, 3008 AE Rotterdam; ☎010-290 68 88.
Sara Lee/DE NV: Vleutensevaart 100, 3532 AD Utrecht; ☎030-292 73 11.
Smiths Foods Group: Postbus 4, 4940 AA Raamsdonksveer; ☎0162-582 800.

Computer Services

AT&T Network Systems: Postbus 1168, 1200 BD Hilversum; ☎035-687 31 11.
Baan Benelux BV: Apeldoornsestraat 131, 3781 PM Voorthuizen; ☎0342-477500.
Centric Informatie Engineering BV: Hogehilweg 8, 1101 CC Amsterdam Z.O.; 020-409 97 50.
Computervision Automatisering: Spoorsingel 1, 7741 JG Coevorden; ☎0524-51 60 60.
Digital Equipment BV: Postbus 9064, 3506 GB Utrecht; ☎030-283 91 11, fax 030-289 06 23.
Getronics: Postbus 652, 1000 AR Amsterdam; ☎020-586 14 12.
Hewlett-Packard Nederland: Postbus 667, 1180 AR Amstelveen; ☎020-547 69 11.
Holland Automation International BV: Binnen Walevest 98, 3311 AB Dordrecht; ☎078-613 56 66.
Honeywell BV: Postbus 12683, 1100 AR Amsterdam Z.O.; 020-565 69 11.
IBM Nederland: Postbus 9999, 1006 CE Amsterdam; ☎020-513 51 51.
ICL Nederland BV: Postbus 4000, 3600

KA Maarssen; ☎0346-598111.
Intel Benelux BV: Luifelstede 54, 3431 JP Nieuwegein; ☎030-600 15 00.
Invensys Systems NV: Postbus 146, 3740 AC Baarn; ☎035-548 42 11.
Koninklijke Philips Electronics NV: Postbus 77900, 1070 MX Amsterdam; ☎020-597 77 77.
Logica BV: Wijnhaven 69, Postbus 22067, 3003 DB Rotterdam; ☎010-433 08 44, fax 010-433 14 47.
Oracle Nederland: Postbus 147, 3454 ZJ De Meern; ☎030-669 90 00.
Pink Roccade Megaplex BV: Fauststraat 1, 7327 BA Apeldoorn; ☎055-577 88 22.
Sema Group Informatica BV: Van Houten Industrial Park 11, Postbus 143, 1380 AC Weesp; ☎0294-239 500.
Sun Microsystems: Postbus 1270, 3800 BG Amersfoort; ☎033-450 12 34.

Chemicals

Acheson Produktie BV: Haven NZ 6, Postbus 1, 9679 ZG Scheemda; ☎0597-591 303.
AFA Polytek BV: Postbus 6140. 5700 EV Helmond; ☎0492-502 600.
AkzoNobel Chemicals: Postbus 247, 3800 AE Amersfoort; ☎033-467 67 67.
Dow Benelux: Herbert Dowweg 5, 4542 NM Hoek; ☎0115-67 12 34.
DSM NV: Postbus 6500, 6401 JH Heerlen; ☎045-578 81 11.
Mainetti Pendy BV: Engelseweg 175, 5705 AD Helmond; ☎0492-538 835.
Exxon Chemical Holland BV: Botlekweg 121, 3197 KA Botlek (RT); ☎010-487 59 11.
Silicones GE Bayer BV: Plasticslaan 1, 4612 PX Bergen-op-Zoom; ☎0164-292 291.
Unilever NV: Postbus 760, 3000 DK Rotterdam; ☎010-217 40 00.

Oil and Petrochemical Companies

Amoco: Postbus 11550, 2502 AN Den Haag; ☎070-333 75 00.
BP Nederland BV: Westblaak 163, 3012 KJ Rotterdam; ☎010-417 51 11.
Esso Nederland: Postbus 1, 4803 AA Breda; ☎076-529 10 00.
Hunting Oilfield Services: Olieweg 10, 1957 NH Velsen-Noord; ☎0251-22 92 19.
Mobil Oil BV: Graaf Engelbertlaan 75, 4837 DS Breda; ☎076-529 19 34.
Nederlandse Aardolie: Postbus 28000, 9400 HH Assen; ☎0592-364 111.
Nederlandse Gasunie: Postbus 19, 9700 MA Groningen; ☎050-521 91 11.
Oil Control Nederland BV: Pieter Goedkoopweg 16, 2031 EL Haarlem; ☎023-542 09 73.
Shell Nederland Raffinaderij BV: Vondelingenweg 601, 3196 KK Rotterdam; ☎010-431 91 11.
Shell Petroleum NV: Carel van Bylandtlaan 30, Postbus 162, 2501 AN Den Haag; ☎070-377 91 11.
Texaco Nederland BV: Weena Zuid 166, 3012 NC Rotterdam; ☎010-403 34 00.
TotalFinaElfNederlandNV: Nieuwe Havenstraat 2, 2272 AD Voorburg Z-H.

Pharmaceutical Products

Brunschwig Chemie BV: Butaanweg 8, Postbus 74213, 1007 BE Amsterdam; ☎020-611 31 33.
Gist Brocades NV: Postbus 1, 2600 MA Delft; ☎015-279 91 11.
Glaxo Smithkline BV: Postbus 780, 3700 AT Zeist; ☎030-693 81 00.
Hoechst Holland NV: Europaweg Zuid 4, 4389 PD Ritthem; 0113-68 92 06.
Pfizer BV: Postbus 37, 2900 Capelle a/d IJssel; ☎010-406 42 50.
Pharmachemie: Postbus 552, 2003 RN Haarlem; ☎023-514 71 47.

Management Consultants

KPMG Management Services BV: Churchillplein 6, 2517 JW Den Haag; ☎070-338 23 38.

Ernst & Young Consulting: Drentestraat 20, 1083 HK Amsterdam; ☎020-549 75 49.

PA Consulting Group: Postbus 1043, 3430 BA Nieuwegein; ☎030-288 40 49.

Price Waterhouse Coopers NV: Prins Bernhardplein 200, 1097 JB Amsterdam; ☎020-568 66 66.

Carriers and Storage

Continentale Scheepsagenturen: Wattweg 11, 3208 KH Spijkenisse; ☎0181-65 93 77.

DFDS Transport BV: Oost Randweg 42A, 4782 PV Moerdijk; ☎010-428 64 00.

Europe Combined Terminals BV: Postbus 7400, 3000 HK Rotterdam; ☎010-491 69 11, fax 010-491 69 99.

Kon. Frans Maas Groep NV: Noorderpoort 15, 5900 AZ Venlo; ☎077-359 76 00, fax 077-351 84 11.

Geest North Sea Line BV: Postbus 54143, 3008 JC Rotterdam; ☎010-491 23 45.

Maersk Benelux BV: Achterdijk 55, 3161 EB Rhoon; ☎010-503 07 00.

Nedlloyd Districenters: Keienbergweg 20, 1101 GB Amsterdam Z-O; ☎020-409 44 89.

Nedlloyd Chemical Logistics: Middenweg 6, Haven M397, 4782 PM Moerdijk; ☎0168-38 48 00.

P&O Transeuropean GTW: Postbus 99, 7040 AB 's-Heerenberg; ☎0314-679 911.

Metal

Bolding Verpakkingen BV: Provincialeweg 200, Postbus 1037, 1500 AA Zaandam; ☎075-612 31 05.

Borstlap BV: Zevenheuvelenweg 44, Postbus 5034, 5004 EA Tilburg; ☎013-594 12 34.

Chubb Lips Nederland BV: Merwedestraat 48, Postbus 59, 3300 AB Dordrecht; ☎078-639 40 41.

Cirex BV: Postbus 81, 7600 AB Almelo; ☎0546-540 400

Corus Staal BV: Kesslerplein 1, 1971 AA IJmuiden; ☎0251-49 82 93.

Corus Tubes BV: Souvereinstraat 35, 4903 RH Oosterhout (NB); ☎0162-48 20 00.

Ferro Techniek: Bremstraat 1, 7011 AT Gaanderen; ☎0315-339 922.

Oostwoud International BV: Harlingerweg 49b, 8801 PA Franeker; ☎0517-399 200.

Uzimet BV: Postbus 19, 2600 AA Delft; ☎070-319 22 21.

Civil Engineering

Blok Groep BV: J.F. Kennedyplantsoen 2, 2912 AD Nieuwerkerk a/d IJssel; ☎0180-313 744.

Hamworthy Marine: Aploniastraat 33, 3084 CC Rotterdam; ☎010-462 47 77.

Hollandsche Beton Groep NV: Generaal Spoorlaan 489, Postbus 81, 2280 AB Rijswijk; ☎070-372 39 11.

Kvaerner John Brown Engineering: Houtsingel 5, 2719 EA Zoetermeer; ☎079-362 46 28.

PRC Bouwkostenmanagement BV: Stationsweg 20, 6861 EH Oosterbeek; ☎026-333 50 78.

Siemens Nederland: Postbus 16068, 2500 BB Den Haag; ☎070-333 22 11.

STARTING A BUSINESS

THE NETHERLANDS has for many years conducted an open-door policy vis-à-vis foreign enterprises and Dutch-registered companies can be formed by foreigners without difficulty. In fact, the Dutch government's policy of non-discrimination has been so successful that one-quarter of business investment in the Netherlands now comes from foreign sources. A number of professional activities are by their nature only open to Dutch nationals, but in general the Dutch economy is extraordinarily open. The status of foreign-owned companies is generally the same as that of purely Dutch-financed enterprises. A number of tax and other investment incentives are offered to foreign companies and it is expected that the favourable attitude towards foreigners moving to the Netherlands will continue. These operate at national, provincial and municipal level.

For anyone considering setting up a business, the Netherlands has a number of further economic attractions. The taxation system is particularly favourable to entrepreneurs, with no withholding tax on royalties and dividends. Dutch membership of the euro must also be counted as an advantage as it makes trading with neighbouring countries much easier. The cost of telecommunications and energy are low by European standards. The workforce is highly skilled and it is not uncommon for people to speak three or four languages, although at the moment there is something of a shortage of skilled workers. The Dutch are not only some of the world's most commercially-minded entrepreneurs, they are also very discriminating consumers. They appreciate a good product; for those with the necessary talent and application the potential rewards are tremendous.

PROCEDURES INVOLVED IN BUYING OR STARTING A NEW BUSINESS

Preparation from Scratch

THE NETHERLANDS FOREIGN INVESTMENT AGENCY (NFIA), a division of the Ministry of Economic Affairs, provides financial and economic information to potential businesses. This includes help with project evaluation, implementation and location. Its services are free of charge, entirely confidential and available from offices in the Netherlands and abroad. Each region of the country has its own investment agency or development authority (the names vary), some of which are listed under the *Regional Employment Guide*. The cities of Amsterdam, Rotterdam and The Hague also have development agencies (see below). These bodies can tell you everything you need to know about subsidies and legal requirements. The local Euro Info Centre can tell you about EU subsidies. You can also use the services of a specialist company to help set up your business, such as those listed below. If you are already in the Netherlands, there are numerous libraries and organisations to help small businesses, but most of what they provide will be in Dutch. See *Small and Medium Enterprises* below.

Once you have decided what kind of business to start, the next step is to go along to the local town hall or municipality to find out which permits are required and how long they will take to process. The relevant office is the Vergunning Informatiepunt, or Permit Information Point.

All new business ventures must be entered in the commercial register (*handelsregister*), which is also known as the trade register and register of companies, at the local chamber of commerce (*kamer van koophandel*) within one week of commencing business. The register is open to public inspection and a prospective company is required to supply the following details: articles of incorporation (name, address and nature of business) which may be in English; a statement of authorised, issued and paid-in share capital; a list of shareholders and directors; a list of partners if the company is a partnership; a statement concerning the authority of each managing director to represent the company in its dealings with third parties, and whether they can act alone or in combination with others. Firms must also register with the tax and social security offices. If an operation has the potential to cause damage or be a nuisance to its surroundings, it is necessary to apply for an environmental licence (*milieuvergunning*) under the Public Nuisance Act (*hinderwet*). The establishment of all companies must be published in the *Official Gazette* (*De Staatscourant*). Until all legal procedures have been completed the directors remain personally liable for any debts incurred by a new business.

Useful Addresses

Deloitte & Touche: (Orlyplein 50, Postbus 58110, 1040 HC Amsterdam; ☎020-582 40 00; fax 020-582 40 22; www.deloitte.nl) provides a range of services to new companies including accounting, tax and legal advice.

Information Service of the Ministry of Economic Affairs: Bezuidenhoutseweg 30, 2594 AV Den Haag; ☎070-379 88 20; e-mail ezinfo@postbus51.nl; www.minez.nl.

Jordans International: (20-22 Bedford Row, London WC1R 4JS; ☎020-7400 3333; fax 020-7400 3366; www.jordans.co.uk and www.jordans-international.com) offers research and administrative help to individuals setting up a business in the Netherlands.

Netherlands Foreign Investment Agency: 38 Hyde Park Gate, London SW7 5DP; ☎020-7584 5040; fax 020-7581 3450; www.nfia.com; or NFIA, 2 Bezuidenhoutseweg, Postbus 20101, 2500 EC Den Haag; 070-379 88 18; www.minez.nl/nfia.

Netherlands Foreign Investment Agency: One Rockefeller Plaza, New York, NY 10020; ☎212-246-1434; fax 212-246-9769; www.nfia.com.

Van Beuningen Advocaten: Lange Houtstraat 37, 2511 CV Den

Haag; ☎070-356 08 50; fax 070-361.50 50; e-mail van.B@wxs.nl, netherlands@avrio.net.

Marketing and Research Companies

Veldkamp Marktonderzoek: Groot Bickersstraat 76, 1013 KS Amsterdam; ☎020-522 59 99.
IBT Marktonderzoek: Keizersgracht 461, 1017 DK Amsterdam; ☎020-428 88 68.

CHAMBERS OF COMMERCE

THERE ARE 30 LOCAL CHAMBERS of commerce (*kamers van koophandel* or *kamers van koophandel en fabrieken*), with 24 sub-offices, covering the country. A list is available from the VVK; they are also to be found in telephone directories. The chambers are statutory bodies and their main role is to promote trade and to supply detailed information about the industrial and commercial situation in a specific area. However, the extent to which groups can undertake research work on behalf of individual companies varies considerably between the chambers. They are generally unwilling to provide information on local employment opportunities. Anyone setting up a business in the Netherlands must register with the local chamber of commerce on arrival.

If you are planning to open a shop, sell crafts or operate as a street trader, you will also need to register with the Central Registry for Retail Trade and Crafts (Centraal Registratie Detailhandelkantoor en Ambacht). Street traders and market stall holders also need a licence from the local Afdeling Ambulante Handel, part of the municipal government.

Useful Addresses

Vereniging van Kamers van Koophandel en Fabrieken in Nederland (VVK): (National Association of Chambers of Commerce), Postbus 265, 3440 AG Woerden; ☎0348-426911; fax 0348-424368; www.kvk.nl.
Amsterdam Chamber of Commerce: De Ruyterkade 5, 1013 AA Amsterdam; ☎020-531 46 13; fax 020-531 46 98; e-mail post@amsterdam.kvk.nl; www.amsterdam.kvk.nl.
The Hague Chamber of Commerce: Koningskade 30, 2596 AA Den Haag; ☎070-328 71 00; fax 070-326 20 10; e-mail info@denhaag.kvk.nl; www.denhaag.kvk.nl.
Rotterdam Chamber of Commerce: Beursplein 37, 3011 AA Rotterdam; ☎010-405 77 77; fax 010-414 57 54; e-mail post@rotterdam.kvk.nl; www.rotterdam.kvk.nl.
Centraal Registratie Detailhandelkantoor en Ambacht: Postbus 90756, 2509 LT Den Haag; 070-338 57 77.

CHOOSING AN AREA

AFTER HAVING A BUSINESS idea and carrying out the necessary market research the next logical step is to decide where to locate. In the *Regional Employment Guide* (in Chapter Six, *Employment*) the general commercial base of the 12 Dutch provinces is discussed. The most dynamic regions are Noord- and Zuid-Holland and Noord-Brabant and to a lesser extent Limburg, Gelderland and Drenthe. There are generous financial incentives for businesses locating in the less commercially developed areas of Groningen, Friesland and Overijssel, and most of all in Flevoland. The Netherlands is a relatively small country and possesses an excellent transport network. As a result no one area can be described as 'remote'. If you are planning to rely on expatriate clientele will almost certainly have to be near Amsterdam, The Hague or Rotterdam, or in the Silicon Triangle between Den Bosch, Eindhoven and Nijmegen.

USEFUL PUBLICATIONS

Business Information: Guide to information sources in the Netherlands: by A. Strek and H. van Herwijnen, publ. NBLC, The Hague, 1995.
Doing Business in the European Union: by Paul Gibbs, publ. Kogan Page Ltd. Useful guide to business culture in the EU.
Doing Business in the Netherlands: HLB Nederland Accountants and Consultants: National Secretariat, Buitenveldertselaan 106, 1081 AB Amsterdam; ☎020-646 32 51.
In Touch: Quarterly Anglo-Dutch Trade magazine published on behalf of the Netherlands-British Chamber of Commerce. c/o The Dutch House, 307 High Holborn, London WC1V 7LS; ☎020-7242 1064; fax 020-7405 1689; e-mail nbcc@btinternet.com; www.nbcc.com). NBCC also publishes the *Anglo-Dutch Trade Bulletin* and *NBNews*.
Investment News: Magazine published three or four times a year by the NFIA, with useful articles on all aspects of investment and business, and up-to-date news on economic trends in the Netherlands; see the website www.nfia.com.
Monitor: Bi-monthly magazine published by SENTER (www.senter.nl) for high-tech entrepreneurs; see below.
Starting a Business: See the National Chamber of Commerce website www.kvk.nl.

RAISING FINANCE

BRITISH BANKS do not lend money to people contemplating setting up a business in the Netherlands, where the prospective proprietor intends to be resident abroad. However, Dutch banks will lend money to foreign businesses, and at a lower interest rate than their UK counterparts. Commercial banks can offer businesses overdraft facilities or cash loans for up to two years. Medium- and long-term loans are also available from the banks and specialist institutions

such as the Nationale Investeringsbank.
The government and local municipalities operate various schemes to help finance new businesses. The government will guarantee a bank loan, provided that the bank provides an equal credit without security. The bank can then call on the government for half the loan if the business cannot meet its obligations. This is known as a 'Small and medium-sized business guarantee instrument'. If you plan to develop new products or services where there is a high degree of risk, you may be able to call on a 'Technical development credit' or you may benefit from the EC Eureka programme; contact SENTER, ☎ 070-361 02 77; www.senter.nl. SENTER, an agency of the Dutch Ministry of Economic Affairs, has nearly €1 billion at its disposal to support the development of new technology products. Proposals from entrepreneurs not yet resident in the Netherlands will also be considered.

Support for Independents Scheme

If you are starting a business, but do not have enough funds to invest, or expect to have difficulty supporting yourself in the early stages, then you may qualify for the BBZ or 'Support for Independents' scheme. To qualify you should work for 1225 hours per year in your own business or as a self-employed person. The hours can be split between two people. You can receive a loan of up to €28,134 to buy equipment and stock, and up to €152,016 for general financing. You may also qualify for a living allowance, depending on your status. Interest is payable on start-up loans. Your businesses will be inspected regularly by the Belastingdienst (Inland Revenue) to see that you meet the required norms for administering a business.

Women starting a business in their own name can receive a three-year loan guaranty, under the amusingly named Mama Cash scheme.

VAT for Small Businesses

Most businesses are required to charge their customers Value Added Tax. The Belastingdienst will give you a VAT registration number. For businesses which have very little VAT to pay, the Kleine Ondernemersregeling (Small Business Allowance) applies. In this case you will pay little or no VAT. To qualify you would normally be liable for a maximum annual amount of €1,883. When you are ready to start your business, you should ask for the *Opgaaf gegevens startende ondernemers* (Statement of Information by a New Business) from the Starters Desk at the Belastingdienst (Tax Office).

Investment Incentives

In recent years the Dutch government has placed an increasing emphasis on balanced regional growth of the economy and to realise this, special incentives have been offered to firms locating in particular areas. The assisted areas broadly comprise Flevoland, the northern provinces of Groningen, Friesland, Drenthe, the northern part of Overijssel and the south of Limburg. Other regions of the Netherlands that experience a specific hardship (e.g. the closure of a factory) can also become eligible for assistance from time to time. The government has a very favourable attitude towards foreign investment and such enterprises are afforded the same rights as Dutch businesses.

Tax Concessions: Taxpayers can apply for a percentage of their investments during the financial year to be deducted when calculating taxable earnings. This is calculated on a sliding scale between 24% and 3%, starting from €1,724 and going up to €252,302. The purchase of land, private houses, boats and fixed assets costing less than €500 is not taken into account.

If their country of origin has a double taxation agreement with the Netherlands, foreign-trained employees can qualify for the '30 per cent rule' which allows the employer to pay 30% of salary as a tax-free allowance. There are also exemptions from dividend withholding tax according to the rates agreed in the reciprocal taxation agreement.

Regional incentives: To attract business investment to the economically weaker areas of the Netherlands the government has set up the Investment Premium Regulation (IPR). The IPR is a financial incentive given to companies that settle in specified areas. Regions and communities designated for this premium include: Groningen, southeast Drenthe, Friesland, south Limburg, Lelystad, Arnhem, Nijmegen and Wijchen. Three types of business development are eligible for a variety of IPR grants. Projects to establish or restructure businesses can obtain a grant of 25% of the capital investment, up to a maximum of €8.2 million. The expansion of an existing business qualifies for 15% of the cost, up to €3.64 million.

Bonded storage: There are no free ports or fixed free zones in the Netherlands. However, the extensive and highly sophisticated transport network means that there are hundreds of bonded storage facilities that escape payment of import or excise duties, VAT, and agricultural levies. Goods stored in bond can undergo transportation, repacking, testing, bottling or mixing without being classified as imports subject to duties. Payment of levies becomes due only when the goods are cleared for use in the Netherlands.

SMALL AND MEDIUM ENTERPRISES (SMES)

THERE ARE NUMEROUS sources of information for SMEs, some of them free. The main organisation is the IMK (Instituut Midden- en Kleinbedrijf Nederland), which has offices all over the country (look under IMK in the telephone book). Their publications and advice services are not free. The Stichting Kleinnood (Kleinnood Foundation) and the Stichting Ondernemersklankbord do offer free advice to SMEs. If the IMK or the local chamber of commerce do not have the information you seek, you can ask the Central Bureau of Statistics (CBS) for one of their starter packs (*starterpakketen*) which cover 75 different types of business. The library of the Economisch Instituut voor het Midden- en Kleinbedrijf (EIM) in Zoetermeer has a comprehensive collection of relevant literature; they sell a list of what they have available for €5.26. Ordering a report on your particular area of business from one of the above organisations will cost you at least €50, according to the IMK. If your business involves some kind of technical innovation, then you should contact the nearest Innovatie Centrum.

Useful Addresses

CBS: Postbus 4000, 2270 JM Voorburg; ☎045-570 70 70; fax 045-570 62 68; www.cbs.nl.

Dutch Management Association (NIVE): Postbus 266, 2270 AG Voorburg; ☎070-300 15 00; fax 070-300 15 99; www.management.nl.

EIM: Communicatie en Informatie, Postbus 7001, 2701 AA Zoetermeer; ☎079-341 36 34; fax 079-341 50 24; e-mail info@eim.nl; www.eim.nl.

EVD Informatiecentrum: (Information Centre of the Ministry of Economic Affairs), Bezuidenhoutseweg 30, Den Haag; ☎070-379 89 11; www.info.minez.nl.

IMK Intermediair: Postbus 93, 3860 AB Nijkerk; ☎033-247 11 80; fax 033-247 11 99; e-mail nijkerk@imk.nl; www.imk.nl.

Raad voor het Zelfstandig Ondernemerschap (Council for Self-employed Entrepreneurs): Badhuisweg 72, PB 84272, 2508 AG Den Haag; ☎070-306 50 20; fax 070-351 26 32; www.rzo.nl.

Stichting Kleinnood: Henri ter Hallsingel 68A, 2284 XD Rijswijk; ☎070-396 09 90; e-mail info@kleinnood.nl; www.kleinnood.nl.

Stichting Ondernemersklankbord: Offers a free mentoring service on all aspects of starting and running a business. Contact 070-396 0990 or 020-531 4404; e-mail info@ondernemerskla nkbord.nl; www.ondernemersklank bord.nl.

BUSINESS STRUCTURES

FOREIGN INVESTORS can operate through a variety of business entities. The types of organisation most commonly used are a private limited liability company *(Besloten Vennootschap met Beperkte Aansprakelijkheid – BV)*, a public corporation *(Naamloze Vennootschap – NV)*, and a branch office. There are about 2,000 NVs, 156,000 BVs, and 360,000 one-person businesses, out of a total of 688,000 businesses.

Naamloze Vennootschap (Public Corporation): To form a public company a minimum of €45,000 (£28,500) is required. In addition at least 20% of the authorised share capital must be issued, of which 25% must be paid for on subscription. There is no limit on the number of shareholders but the corporation cannot purchase more than 10% of its own shares. An NV must have at least two bodies – the general meeting of shareholders and the board of managing directors. A board of directors does not exist in the Netherlands, but an NV usually has a third body, the Board of Supervisory Directors. This oversees the management board. (For companies with a workforce of more than 100, and consolidated share capital and reserves of at least €11.34 million the appointment of a supervisory board is mandatory.)

To form a public corporation one person (either an individual or a legal business entity) participating in the share capital is required to execute a deed before a public notary. The notary will draw up a deed of incorporation (*akte van oprichting*), which includes the articles of association (*statuten*) – the company's details and its aims and objectives. The articles of association must be recorded in the trade register (*handelsregister*) at the local chamber of commerce (*kamer van koophandel*). The deed of incorporation must be submitted to the Ministry of Justice (Ministerie van Justitie) and if approved it will receive a declaration of no objection (*verklaring van geen bezwaar*). The decision will take on average two to three months to come through. If ministerial approval is not given an appeal can be made to the Council of State within one month. Once a declaration of no objection is received, the deed of incorporation is notarised and the details of the NV are published in the *Official Gazette* (*De Staatscourant*).

Besloten Vennootschap met Beperkte Aansprakelijkheid (BV): A BV is usually subject to less stringent requirements than an NV. A sum of €18,000 is required to set up a private company. One or more individuals (or companies) need to sign the articles of association in the presence of a public notary. They must also provide proof that the €18,000 is deposited in a Dutch bank account. (It is useful to note that the money can be immediately withdrawn.) The deed of incorporation must be approved by the Ministry of Justice before the company can be established. The cost of the process for both an NV and a BV will normally include a 1% capital issue tax, and the fees payable to the public notary, the chamber of commerce, the bank receiving the capital and the Ministry of Justice. An NV can be converted to a BV, or vice versa, provided such a change is approved at a shareholder's meeting, the deed of incorporation is modified to accommodate the change and the Ministry of Justice issues a declaration of no objection.

Branches: It is common for foreign companies to begin operations as a branch (*bijkantoor* or *filiaal*). A new branch must be recorded in the register of companies, giving information concerning both itself and its parent company (including the parent's articles of asociation). The foreign parent is held responsible for all liabilities and obligations of its Dutch branch.

Partnerships: Three types of partnership are permitted in the Netherlands: general, professional and limited. A general partnership (*Vennootschap onder Firma – VOF*) must be formed by contract and its details must be registered with the local chamber of commerce. Professional partnerships (such as lawyers and accountants) are known as *Maatschappij*. A limited partnership (*Commanditaire Vennootschap*) is essentially the same as a VOF but has one or more limited partners. No annual accounts need to be published. The three partnerships do not actually exist as legal entities in the eyes of Dutch law and each partner is individually liable.

Co-operative Societies: A co-operative society is an association of persons that allows for the free entry and withdrawal of members. Its name must contain the word *coöperatief* and must give some indication of its objectives, for example buying and selling dairy products. In addition the name must include certain initials to indicate the liability of its members; WA, unlimited liability; BA, limited liability; or UA, no liability. Co-operatives are frequently used in such trades as agriculture and horticulture, and are formed to represent the interests of its members collectively, rather than earn profits for an investor. It is a legal entity and is founded by a notarial deed.

IDEAS FOR NEW BUSINESSES

THE DUTCH ARE NOT only very successful businesspeople, they also speak very good English. This latter consideration makes it harder to set up a business which relies on expatriate clientele. In effect, whatever you do you will have to do as well as or better than the Dutch. On the other hand, anything which is becoming trendy in the USA and the UK is also almost certain to catch on in the Netherlands; it is just a matter of knowing what is going to be popular next.

Teaching English

Despite the fact that the Dutch have a good command of the English language there is always a demand for qualified teachers, especially in the field of Business English and English for Academic Purposes. There is therefore scope for opening a language school or private tutor agency.

Publishing and Translating

Many of the world's most prestigious academic publishers are located in the Netherlands and much of what they publish. There are openings for copy-editors and other publishing professionals at all levels of the publishing industry in a country where so much is published in English.

Many expatriates turn to translating from Dutch into English. If you have a background in Germanic languages you may soon find yourself ahead of the field. Translators with a technical background are also at an advantage.

Sport and Recreation

The majority of the Dutch population lives in urban areas and the Dutch have an increasing amount of leisure time at their disposal. Sports and recreation are therefore playing an increasingly important role in Dutch life. New businesses are being established to cater for the demand especially in the field of water sports. Both instructors and equipment are in short supply around the IJsselmeer and along the west coast. Adventure holidays and golf are two other forms of activity that are expanding rapidly and at the moment much of the expertise comes from abroad.

Tourism

Amsterdam dominates the Dutch tourist industry. However, outside the country's capital city there is tremendous scope for development of small family hotels and restaurants, and other tourist facilities. Friesland and Groningen are becoming increasingly attractive to both Dutch and foreign visitors.

Art and Antiques

The tradition of displaying heritage in museums is as strong as ever and at the last count nearly 1,000 museums were registered in the Netherlands. More affluent Dutch households have always been keen to invest in art and antiques; with the current consumer boom, this is a good time to sell. Dutch tastes are predominantly centred around the history of the Netherlands, but there is also a great deal of interest in items from Britain, France and Belgium which could also have some connection with Dutch history, such as old maps. There is also a certain amount of interest in ethnic arts and crafts, provided they are of good quality.

The Dutch Arts Council (Raad voor Cultuur) offers grants to artists from abroad to work in the Netherlands. See website www.cultuur.nl.

Therapists

The Dutch are well aware of the boom in therapy in the UK and USA. At the same time expatriates generally prefer a therapist from their own country who speaks their language. The Dutch on the other hand are quite open to English-speaking therapists. There is also an obvious market amongst wealthy expatriates for such things as acupuncture, aromatherapy, massage, reflexology and other types of complementary medicine.

Exporters

The Trade Partners UK Information Centre may be worth a visit; the Centre has a large amount of useful information on the Netherlands, including trade and telephone directories. The Centre's address is Kingsgate House, 66-74 Victoria Street, London SW1E 6SW. It is open from 09.00 to 20.00 Monday to Thursday (last admission 19.30) and 09.00 to 17.30 on Fridays (last admission 17.00). Further information on the Centre's resources is available on the Trade Partners UK website at www.tradepartners.gov.uk, by telephone on 020-7215 5444/5; fax 020-7215 4231 or by e-mail; use the e-mail option on the website. The website also has a useful report on the Netherlands.

RUNNING A BUSINESS

Employing Staff

Contracts: Employment contracts must be written and drawn up in accordance with Dutch labour laws. The Civil Code defines a contract as 'an agreement in which the employee undertakes to carry out work in return for wages, during a certain period of time'. Contracts are normally indefinite, although fixed-term contracts are in use. Trial periods can be specified, during which time contracts can be terminated without notice by either side. The minimum notice period is normally one week for each year of service, up to a maximum of 13 weeks. For workers aged 45 or over there is an additional week for each year they have worked beyond 45. The maximum number of weeks is 26. Employers wishing to terminate a contract, other than by mutual agreement, must obtain approval from the Regional Labour Office. Dutch employers are increasingly using casual, external labour on contracts for outwork (work from home), contracts for temporary employment (six months maximum), on-call commitments and freelance agreements. In each of these cases the employer and the employee have the right to terminate the contract at any time or, in the case of on-call contractors, ignore it.

Trade Unions: Although trade union membership is not compulsory about 29% of the Dutch workforce belongs to a labour organisation. There are three trade union federations (FNV, CNV and MHP), one central employers' organisation representing large trade associations and some multinationals (the VNO-NCW), and a central organisation for medium- and small-size enterprises (MKB Nederland). Union leaders do not tend to regard strikes as a means to achieve a goal and the number of days lost through strike action is very small. During the present period of expansion following a long period of wage restraint, the numbers of workers who might resort to strikes is on the increase.

Labour Relations: Companies with more than 35 employees must set up a Works Council (*Ondernemingsraad*) to advise employers on certain labour matters (see below). Structured companies (*structuur vennootschappen*), *NV*s and *BV*s with more than 100 employees or more than €11.34 million capital reserves, must appoint a Supervisory Board (*Raad van Commissarissen*); this supervises the Board of Management on behalf of employees and must have at least three members. In companies with less than 35 staff members, the management is obliged to meet with the whole workforce at least twice a year. Works Councils must be consulted on such matters as mergers, closures, a firm's change of location and important reorganisations. Managements must obtain the consent of a Supervisory Board on decisions regarding pensions, insurance, profit sharing, working time and holidays, work safety, promotions, training, and the handling of complaints. In 1945 the Joint Industrial Labour Council was set up to handle labour agreements at national level. There is also a 45-strong Socio-Economic Council comprising: 15 members appointed by the employers' organisations, 15 by union groups and 15 independent experts appointed by the Dutch government. The government is required by law to seek the advice of the council on all major issues concerning wages, prices and social policy negotiations.

Employee Training: The Dutch government provides financial assistance for the training of labour. For approved training programmes, employers are given grants for wage costs of employees during training, the cost of the training course and travelling expenses.

Wages and Salaries: The statutory minimum wage is currently €1,122 per month for workers aged 23 and over. The minimum wage for younger employees is based on a percentage of the full minimum wage. The band ranges from 30% for 15-year-olds to 85% for 22-year-olds. In common with many other European Community countries, employees are often paid an additional month's salary ('the thirteenth month') in December. Dutch firms also use a number of fringe benefits to attract and retain staff. These include subsidised canteens, pensions and savings plans, company cars and payment of 100% of wages for the first year of sickness. The latter is something that companies have to insure themselves for now, since the state no longer contributes anything to sickness payments.

Social Security Contributions: The social security system is governed by numerous different acts and has developed over several decades; as a consequence it is very complex. In broad terms it can be grouped into two categories – national insurance and employee insurance. The national insurance comprises contributions towards old age pensions, the widows and orphans fund, major medical expenses, disability benefits and child benefits. The premiums are paid solely by employees and are incorporated into income tax payments. The employee insurance programme requires payments from employers as well as employees. This covers sickness benefits, unemployment benefits, disability insurance and compulsory health insurance. Payments are withheld at source and paid in advance each month to the Industrial Insurance Board.

Paid Holidays: The legal minimum holiday is 20 days a year and a minimum holiday allowance of 8% on annual salaries, of up to three times the minimum wage, must be paid. There can also be as many as nine statutory holidays in a year (see Chapter Four *Daily Life*).

TAXATION

THE PRINCIPAL TAXES are corporate income tax, personal income tax and VAT. A tax return (*belastingaangifte*) is due within six months of the end of a company's financial year. The authorities issue a provisional tax assessment in March, based on the average taxable income of the company during the two previous years. A double taxation treaty is currently in force between the Netherlands and the UK.

Corporate Income Tax (vennootschapsbelasting):

A two-tier system of corporate income tax charges 30% on taxable profit up to €22,720 and 34.5% on all taxable profit in excess of €22,720. Reductions in this tax to a uniform rate of 30% are likely in the coming years. Companies controlled in the Netherlands and established under Dutch law are subject to tax on their worldwide income. (This also applies to subsidiaries.) Branches of foreign firms are taxed on profits derived in the Netherlands and income arising from the sale of Dutch real estate.

Individual Income Tax *(inkomstenbelasting)*

Taxable income is the aggregate amount of net income or profit arising from employment and profits. The rate of income tax ranges from 13% to 60%. Foreign nationals can be eligible for the 30 per cent rule, which enables employers to pay a tax-free allowance of 30% of an employee's salary as compensation for the costs involved in coming to work in the Netherlands. Capital gains from the sale of shares representing a substantial interest are taxed at a flat rate of 20%.

Value Added Tax

VAT is referred to as BTW *(Belasting Toegevoegde Waarde)* or OB *(Omzetbelasting)*. The standard rate is 17.5% and business registration can take up to six months. There is a reduced rate of 6% for designated essential goods and services, such as foods, books and water, and a zero rate for exports. Transactions in real estate (including rental and leasing), medical and educational services, banking, and postal services are exempt from BTW. Prostitutes must pay VAT at 17.5% after the Ministry of Finance ruled that they, like other entrepreneurs, were liable not only for income tax but also for sales tax. However, written receipts are not necessary and businessmen who visit prostitutes cannot write-off the extra VAT levy against tax.

Since January 1 1993 all inter-business cross-border trading within the European Community has been subject to VAT in the country of purchase, rather than the country of origin. To aid the process the European Commission has set up an EU-wide computer network – the VAT information exchange system *(Vies)*. A company selling a product to an EU business customer can tap into *Vies* check the customer is VAT registered, and dispatch the goods. The buyer will have to declare the purchase on his or her periodical VAT return.

Property Tax

For property transfers, a transfer tax *(overdrachtsbelasting)* of 6% is levied on the value of commercial and private property. This transfer tax also applies to the movement of shares in real estate companies. In both cases it is the purchaser who is legally responsible for filing a tax return.

Other: Excise taxes are levied on beer, wines, spirits and soft drinks; on tobacco products; on alcohol-containing substances; on sugar and sugar-containing products and on petroleum products. A capital issue tax of 1% is levied on the formation of a company or any increases in share capital. A special consumption tax is applied to personal cars. Wealth tax has been abolished; instead a tax of 30% is levied on a notional income of 4% derived from your assets in excess of €17,600. Gifts and inheritance tax is levied at rates of 5% to 63%, depending on the amount bequeathed and the relationship between the donor and the recipient.

ACCOUNTANCY AND AUDITING ADVICE

Dutch law requires all businesses to keep financial accounts in such a way that the liabilities and assets can be determined at any time. Financial statements should be prepared and signed within five months of a company's year-end for NVs and BVs, or within six months for other business organisations. Under Dutch law the books of account and records, financial statements, and incoming and outgoing correspondence of an enterprise should be retained for at least 10 years. These records can be kept in any form, including on mechanised and electronic systems.

The annual accounts should include:

- Balance sheet
- Directors' report
- Income statement
- Audit report
- A statement detailing the appropriation of profit or loss
- Full accounts of subsidiaries not already included
- A description of any third-party rights to share in the company's profits
- A statement of any events with significant financial consequences that have arisen after the financial year.

Large- and medium-size companies are required to prepare full financial statements whereas small firms are required to file only abridged balance sheets and accompanying notes. A company is defined as medium in size if it conforms to two of the following criteria: 50-249 employees, annual net turnover of €3.63-15.9 million, and assets of €3.63-7.71 million. A small company should conform to two of the following: 49 employees or less, turnover of less than €3.63 million, and assets of no more than €1.81 million. Large companies are those which do not meet these criteria.

Auditing

Audits (the formal examination of accounts) are compulsory only for large- and medium-size companies. They must be carried out by independent qualified Dutch accountants or by individuals recognised by the Ministry of Economic Affairs (Ministerie van Economische Zaken) on the basis of qualifications obtained abroad. The following organisations can provide names of suitably qualified auditors and accountants:

Netherlands Order of Accountants and Administration Consultants (NOVAA): Nieuwe Parklaan 25, Postbus 84921, 2508 AG Den Haag; ☎070-338 36 00; www.novaa.nl.

Royal Netherlands Institute of Registered Accountants (Royal NIVRA): A.J. Ernststraat 55, 1083 GR Amsterdam; ☎020-301 03 01; www.nivra.nl.

Directors' Report

The directors' report should discuss the results of the company's operations and give expectations about the future course of the business, giving special attention to finance, personnel and investment. Information in the directors' report should not conflict with any data given in the annual accounts.

Luxembourg

LIVING AND WORKING IN LUXEMBOURG

GENERAL INTRODUCTION

RESIDENCE AND ENTRY REGULATIONS

SETTING UP HOME

DAILY LIFE

RETIREMENT

EMPLOYMENT

TEMPORARY WORK

BUSINESS AND INDUSTRY REPORT

STARTING A BUSINESS

GENERAL INTRODUCTION

DESTINATION LUXEMBOURG

MENTION LUXEMBOURG to anyone over 40 and probably the first thing they will think of is the radio station of the same name. For younger people Luxembourg perhaps only signifies a national football team that never wins a match. One could say that Luxembourg plays a fairly minor part on the world stage, even if the election of Jacques Santer to the leadership of the EU for a short (and rather ignominious) period in the 1990s raised its profile somewhat. Although one of Europe's smallest countries, Luxembourg's position in the world of banking is similar to that of Switzerland. It is not widely known, for example, that Luxembourg is the world's leading centre for offshore fund management. Luxembourg's Gross Domestic Product per capita was $46,800 per annum in 2000, the highest in the world. The reform of the laws on banking secrecy in the EU may, however, have a detrimental effect on Luxembourg's prosperity within the near future.

Down the years Luxembourg has had an important part in Europe's political and economic development. It became a distinct power during the 10th century based around the impregnable fortress which gives the country its name, with close connections to neighbouring ruling families; four Holy Roman Emperors came from here during the 14th century. Between 1448 and 1815 Luxembourg was ruled in turn by Burgundy, Spain, France and Austria. During a short period of Dutch rule, Luxembourg entered into a customs alliance with Prussia. In 1867 the Congress of London decided that Luxembourg should become an independent state, placed under the collective guarantee of the signatory powers. Despite being neutral Luxembourg was overrun by Germany in both world wars. Following World War I, Luxembourg broke off its economic union with Germany and entered into the Belgium-Luxembourg Economic Union (BLEU). In 1948 it went a step further when it adopted a customs union with Belgium and the Netherlands (the Benelux Union), which can be seen as the forerunner to the creation of the EC. From that moment Luxembourg started to play a central role in European affairs and has been at the forefront of forging peaceful economic unification in Western Europe.

The Grand Duchy is a constitutional monarchy and as a founder member joined the then EEC and EURATOM in 1957. Today its capital Luxembourg-Ville (or Lëtzebuerg) is the home of the Secretariat of the European Parliament, the EU Court of Justice, the European Investment Bank, the European Court of Accounts and for three months of the year it is also the meeting place of the Council of Ministers of the European Communities.

POLITICAL AND ECONOMIC STRUCTURE

LUXEMBOURG'S DEVELOPMENT has been determined by its location and natural resources (iron ore) and by a long tradition of economic co-operation with neighbouring countries. In the past this was imposed from outside. These days Luxembourg enjoys a peaceful coexistence with its larger neighbours; the Grand Duchy's commitment to European unity has given it a leading role in the EU.

Economy

Luxembourg's economy was built on the iron and steel-making industries and for a period in the early 70s it suffered a setback owing to a decline in demand. A radical change of direction has seen the economy steadily break free from a dependence on heavy industry and move towards a lighter industrial base. The result is a diversified manufacturing sector that incorporates plastics, chemicals, textiles, mechanical engineering, electronics and a modern, rationalised iron and steel industry. In the wider economy banking plays a key role. Luxembourg is now best known as a financial centre, and as a base for banking and investment services. A love of money and a favourable fiscal climate have attracted more than 150 foreign banks, including the ill-fated Bank of Credit and Commerce International (BCCI). Although not as famous as its Swiss counterpart, the importance of banking to the Grand Duchy is evident from the fact that the industry employs over 16,000 people – or one out of every 12 of the Luxembourg workforce.

The people are hard-working and strikes are virtually unheard of – values which combined with successful diversification have produced an economic growth rate in recent years above the EU average. Luxembourg now boasts relatively low unemployment (2.6 per cent of the workforce) and low inflation (1.5 per cent per annum) – proof of economic stability.

Government

Luxembourg is a constitutional and hereditary monarchy currently under the watchful eye of HRH Grand Duke Henri (who succeeded his father Grand-Duke Jean in 2000), who exercises executive power through a 12-strong Council of Ministers led by the President of the government (Prime Minister) Jean-Claude Juncker. There is also a Council of State, nominated by the monarch, comprising 21 members, which acts as the supreme administrative tribunal but has limited legislative functions. Primary legislative authority is through the Chamber of Deputies (reduced to 60 in number in 1989).

General elections to this chamber must be held at least every five years using a system of proportional representation, which has tended to produce coalition governments made up of members of two of the three large political parties; the Christian-Social Party (PCS), the Socialist Workers' Party (POSL) and the Democratic Party (PD). The Christian-Social Party has played a key role in all the post-war governments with the exception of 1974-79. The last coalition between the PCS and POSL, under the leadership of Jean-Claude Juncker, came to power in 1984 and continued in power until the most recent elections in 1999, when the POSL's vote fell below that of the PD. Juncker now leads a coalition of the PCS and PD; there are several other small parties including the Green grouping which holds five seats.

GEOGRAPHICAL INFORMATION

THIS TINY NATION measures just 999 square miles and on most maps even a shortened version of its name, LUX, scarcely fits within its borders. Luxembourg is land-locked, lying to the east of Belgium and sandwiched between France and Germany. The population of Luxembourg has increased by over 20% in the last 20 years and currently stands at around 442,000. The rise can be explained in part by the number of non-Luxembourgeois nationals, some 160,000 at the last count. This proportion of aliens is the highest in Europe, and twice the number of second-placed Switzerland. The Portuguese account for the biggest single group (59,000) followed by the Italians (20,300). These two groups, who were largely brought in to supply the iron and steel-making industries, now fill unskilled and manual positions. The British community totals 4,900 and the largest non-EU group are the Yugoslavs at 2,500. Luxembourg-Ville accommodates one-fifth of the population, 81,800, and Esch-sur-Alzette ranks second with 25,400.

Climate

Nobody goes to Luxembourg for the weather – the climate is very similar to the UK's, temperate, with cool summers and mild winters. The average annual rainfall is approximately 32 inches; early winter is the wettest time of the year. Snowfalls are frequent between December and March.

REGIONAL GUIDE

THE GRAND DUCHY has two natural regions, to the north the Oesling (one-third of the country) and the Good Land (two-thirds) to the south, and is split into 12 administrative cantons and 118 municipalities. Information is available from tourist offices (see below). For Internet access, try http://

www.online.lu. Telephone directories are available online at: www.annuaire.lu/ap/ or www.luxcentral.lu.

Useful Addresses

Office National du Tourisme: 1 rue du Fort Thüngen, BP 1001, 1010 Luxembourg; ☎42 82 82-10; fax 42 82 82-38; e-mail info@ont.lu; www.ont.lu.

Luxembourg City Tourist Office: Place d'Armes, Luxembourg-Ville; ☎22 28 09; fax 47 48 18; e-mail touristinfo@luxembourg-city.lu; www.luxembourg-city.lu.

Luxembourg Tourist Office: 122 Regent Street, London W1R 5FE; ☎020-7434 2800; fax 020 7734 1205; e-mail tourism@luxembourg.co.uk; www.luxembourg.co.uk.

Luxembourg Tourist Office: 17 Beekman Place, New York, NY 10022; ☎212-935 8888; fax 212-935 5896; e-mail luxnto@aol.com; www.visitluxembourg.com.

Luxembourg-Ville

The valleys of the Alzette and Pétrusse rivers meet to make the setting of Luxembourg-Ville one of the most dramatic in Europe. The capital is tiny and broadly divides into four distinct sections. The name derives from Luculinburhuc, meaning 'little fortress'. The old centre is situated on the northern side of the Pétrusse, high on the small central plateau of the old fortifications. It is made up of a tight grid of cobbled streets and Gothic houses, and is a lively, pleasant area to live. The new centre is on the opposite side of the river connected by the Pont Adolphe and Pasarelle bridges to the old quarter. It must be said this is a less attractive part of town and home to its seamier side. The third area, the Valleys, covers the land from the river banks up to the old centre. Finally, to the east, the fourth area, situated on the Plateau du Kirchberg, is the home of the European Community Institutions. Most of the medieval city was destroyed in 1554 and much of the older part was rebuilt in the 17th century. The city was renowned for its awesome defences but the once impenetrable barriers were partly dismantled in 1867, giving an open feel today to many areas in the city. In 1995 Luxembourg was the European City of Culture.

TABLE 11   CLIMATE IN LUXEMBOURG CITY

	Jan	April	July	Oct
Temperature celsius/fahrenheit				
– Average	0.8/33.4	8.3/46.9	17.5/63.5	9.5/49.1
– Maximum	9.5/49.1	22.0/71.6	30.7/87.3	20.7/69
– Minimum	–9.5/14.9	–2.2/28	6.9/44.4	–0.4/31
Relative humidity (%)	89.0	74.0	73.0	86.0
Hours of sunshine	38.6	158.7	200.5	94.7
Rainfall(mm)	69.0	50.6	62.9	63.8

The South

The Moselle and Industrial Southwest. The south of Luxembourg is generally regarded as the least picturesque region containing much of the Grand Duchy's industrial base around Esch-sur-Alzette. The area was built on mining and iron/steel production and has the scars to prove it. At nearby Rumelange the old industrial remains have been turned to advantage and the Musée National des Mines operates guided tours 1000m down a disused mine shaft. The one redeeming feature is the Moselle river and 25km of vineyards that constitute Luxembourg's small but famous wine industry.

The Central Area

Echternach, Ettelbruck and Diekirch. North from the capital the undulating countryside gives way to stunning hills and woodland. Much of the area around Ettelbruck and Diekirch suffered heavy damage in late 1944 during the Battle of the Bulge and many monuments mark where those who fell are buried. To the east, towards Germany, Echternach is the main centre of what is known as Little Switzerland.

The North

Esch-sur-Sûre, Clervaux, Vianden and Wiltz. Much of the northern part of Luxembourg lies in the Ardennes region with its fairy-tale castles. Vianden is the main centre through which the booming tourist trade from neighbouring countries reaches the region. In 1871 Victor Hugo exiled himself to this delightful town which has recently seen its eleventh century castle restored to its former glory. Clervaux lies in the far north of the country and the town's castle, dating from the twelfth century, forms part of a centuries-old defence structure. To the west the picturesque towns of Bourscheid, Esch-sur-Sûre and Wiltz nestle in the beautiful wooded scenery.

GETTING THERE

THE EASIEST WAY to get to Luxembourg is by air. The national airline, Luxair, operates two daily flights from Stansted and Heathrow, and flies four times a week from Manchester. British Airways operates daily flights from Heathrow and Gatwick. If you are coming from North America, it is generally cheapest to take a flight to London and change. Alternatively, Icelandair (www.icelandair.com) run flights to Luxembourg via Reykjavík from New York, Boston, Baltimore and Minneapolis, and twice a week from Orlando and Halifax, Nova Scotia. There are discount flights from London available at £100.

The second quickest way to reach Luxembourg is by Eurostar train. It takes about 6½ hours from London to Luxembourg City, including the changeover at Brussels Midi station. The cheapest way to go is by coach; Eurolines operate one scheduled service from London a day.

For car-drivers, if you take the ferry or the Shuttle via Calais, you should head towards Brussels, but turn off towards Charleroi and Namur, after which there will be signs to Luxembourg. Calais is some 258 miles from Luxembourg. Zeebrugge and Ostend in Belgium are less than 200 miles from Luxembourg. The Luxembourg Tourist Office will supply further information about travelling to Luxembourg.

Useful Addresses

British Airways: ☎0845-77 333 77 *or* 0845-606 0747; www.britishairways.com; Heathrow/Gatwick/Manchester/Birmingham/Glasgow to Brussels.
Luxair: ☎020-8745 4254; fax 020-8759 7974; www.luxair.lu.
Eurostar: ☎08705-186186; www.eurostar.com.
Le Shuttle: ☎08705-353535 (bookings); 08000 969 992 (inquiries); www.eurotunnel.com.
Eurolines: ☎08705-143219; e-mail welcome@eurolines.co.uk; www.eurolines.co.uk.

Useful Guides

See Belgian Section, end of Chapter One, *Getting There*.

RESIDENCE AND ENTRY REGULATIONS

THE COSMOPOLITAN nature of Luxembourg's population is a testament to its willingness to accept foreigners. More than 37% of the population are non-Luxembourg nationals and the figure is set to continue rising.

REQUIREMENTS FOR BRITISH CITIZENS

UK CITIZENS need only a full British passport – which must be endorsed with the words 'Holder has the right to abode in the UK' – to stay in Luxembourg for up to three months. If you enter Luxembourg with the intention of staying for more than three months, you are required to apply for a resident permit within three days of arrival; the European Commission considers this to be too short a time. Nonetheless, you can be fined if you do not comply.

Residence Permit

To extend a stay beyond three months, UK citizens must obtain an Identity Card for Foreign Nationals. To apply, contact the Police des Etrangers and provide the following three documents: proof of identity, (usually a passport, but a driving licence is sometimes accepted), a *Déclaration Patronale* (proof of sufficient means of subsistence or employment contract), and a certificate showing proof of residence in Luxembourg. The card is valid for five years and is renewable.

Entering to Work

The Grand Duchy is subject to European Union regulations concerning the free movement of labour. As a result holders of a valid UK passport can freely enter the Grand Duchy to look for employment, a work permit is not required. However, to work continuously for more than three months it is necessary to obtain the Identity Card for Foreign Nationals. The application to the police should include a letter from your employer stating the terms of your contract (such as the salary and the duration). This acts as the *Déclaration Patronale*.

Entering to Start a Business

The Grand Duchy actively promotes business within its borders and treats foreign entrepreneurs in the same positive manner as it does its own. The above terms for entry and residence cover individuals entering the country with the aim of setting up a business. All industrial and commercial activities require a government permit, issued by the Ministry of Small- and Medium-sized Businesses (Ministère des Classes Moyennes). To qualify applicants need to show professional qualifications and experience in the field they wish to trade, and evidence of good standing and solvency. For detailed information on how to start trading see Chapter Seven, *Starting A Business*.

NON-EU NATIONALS

VISAS TO VISIT Luxembourg for less than three months are not required for persons from the United States, Canada, New Zealand, Australia, Israel, Singapore, Japan, Malaysia and nationals from Member States of the European Free Trade Association. Other visitors must obtain an entry visa, which is valid for tourist and business purposes. An Autorisation de Séjour Provisoire (residence/work permit) is required by non-EU nationals intending to work or stay longer than three months in the Grand Duchy. It is issued only if employment has been secured and at least one month should be allowed for processing. An applicant must be in possession of the permit before travelling to Luxembourg. The application for the permit must be made to the Luxembourg Embassy of the applicant's country of residence. It needs to include two completed application forms, two recent passport photos and a Déclaration Patronale.

Useful Addresses

Luxembourg Embassy: 27 Wilton Crescent, London, SW1X 8SD; ☎020-7235 6961.

British Embassy: 14 bvd Roosevelt, 2450 Luxembourg; ☎22 98 64; britemb@pt.lu; www.webplaza.pt.lu/public/britemb.

US Embassy: 22 bvd Emmanuel Servais, 2535 Luxembourg; ☎46 01 23, fax 46 14 01.

Luxembourg Embassy: 2200 Massachusetts Avenue, NW Washington DC 20008; ☎202-265 4171.

Info-Accueil des Etrangers – Service Municipal: (Population Register), Bâtiment 'Petit Passage', 30 pl. Guillaume, 9 rue Chimay, 2090 Luxembourg; ☎4796-2751; fax 46 06 35.

Administration de l'Emploi: 10 rue Bender, 1229 Luxembourg, ☎478-5300.

Setting up Home

MOVING TO LUXEMBOURG is not as common an occurrence as moving to other EU countries and it is even rarer to buy a property there. As a result UK agencies are not geared towards such a move and little can be done from the UK. In Luxembourg estate agents exist and the British Embassy (and expats) will offer advice.

HOW DO LUXEMBURGERS LIVE?

LUXEMBURGERS TEND to live in small, rather than extended, family units. The majority (74%) buy rather than rent property and the trend towards purchasing homes remains upwards, especially the practice of buying a plot of land and building one's own house. The standard of living is high and Luxemburgers rarely go without when it comes to the comforts of life. The quality of accommodation is very good and most Grand Duchy homes are fully equipped with the everyday domestic appliances.

PURCHASING PROPERTY

THE PROCEDURES FOR BUYING A PROPERTY in Luxembourg are very similar to those in the UK. The greatest number of properties are advertised in the *Luxembourg Wort* newspaper (Wednesday and Saturday) and through estate agents (*agents immobiliers*) – the largest two being Rockenbrod and Immosol. For Sale signs (and To Let signs) are never displayed and a property survey is not required, but conveyancing must be carried out by a bona fide public notary. The standard of housing is high, but so is the cost. In Luxembourg-Ville expect to pay more than in the countryside. A deposit equal to one quarter of the price of the property is payable as well as high agents' fees. There is a transfer tax of 6% in the country as a whole, and 9% in Luxembourg City.

Finance

Mortgages can either be arranged through UK or Luxembourg-based banks. The type and number of home loans on offer are virtually the same as in the UK, but in the Grand Duchy applicants are subject to strict financial checks and insurance is a must.

Useful Addresses

Immobilière Betz et Hettinger: 76 rue des Romains, 2444 Luxembourg-Bonnevoie; ☎49 53 58-1; fax 48 29 54; mobile 021 14 13 76.
Immosol: 14 ave. de la Liberté, 1930 Luxembourg; ☎22 55 33; fax 22 20 08; e-mail contact@immosol.lu; www.immosol.lu.
Rockenbrod: 16 bvd. Royal, 2449 Luxembourg; ☎47 55 21; fax 47 55 29; e-mail info@rockenbrod.lu; www.rockenbrod.lu.

RENTING PROPERTY

RENTING IS STILL A POPULAR CHOICE in the Grand Duchy, especially on a short term basis. Furnished accommodation is not easy to find and Luxembourg-Ville itself is the most expensive, with prices one-third more than in the rest of the country. The easiest and quickest way to find a house is through estate agencies, which can cost two or three months' rent. Leases are generally fixed for three years, short term leases of just a few months are rare and require a deposit of one month's rent or more. Unfurnished means just that and light fittings, curtains or rods, carpets, kitchen cupboards and domestic appliances are not included. Furnished flats or houses for rent tend to include absolutely everything from furniture and fittings to lights and linen. Apartment buildings follow the German style of architecture with windows that can be opened in two directions and a communal laundry room in the basement.

Relocators

Relocators exist to ease the settling-in process for expatriates posted to foreign countries by their companies. They are rarely used by individuals because of the high charges. The following two relocators are members of the European Relocation Association:
Integreat Relocation Services: 2 rue Jean Jaures, 1836 Luxembourg; ☎26 44 16 73; fax 26 44 19 73; e-mail integreat@vip.lu; www.welcome.to/integreat.lu.
Settler International: 21 rue J.-P. Sauvage, 2514 Luxembourg; ☎43 15 96; fax 43 15 22; www.settler.lu.

UTILITIES

IN LUXEMBOURG-VILLE GAS, electricity and water are supplied and connected by one authority, the Recette Communale, which means bills, sent monthly, are charged on the same invoice. CEGEDEL supplies electricity to the rest of the country, with bills sent on a quarterly basis. Piped gas is available in Luxembourg-Ville, and the central and southern areas of the country; other regions rely on bottled supplies. For rural water connections contact the local Administration Communale. The domestic electricity supply uses three types of two-pin wall plugs: round pins with no earth connection, round pins with earth connections, and flat pins with earth connections.

Enquiries concerning the installation of new telephone lines or the renaming of old ones should be directed to the state-owned telecommunications company P&T. A charge will be levied for reconnection and monthly rental, in addition to the cost of the calls. Details of the telephone service can be found in the front of the telephone book – of which there is only one – on the green-edged pages. Dustbins are emptied everywhere once a week but only garbage placed in bins or the correct refuse sacks will be removed. A collection of larger items is held every month in the city and every three months in other parts of the country.

REMOVALS

THE COST OF MOVING is high, so don't take too much. Conversely buying new items in Luxembourg will be expensive, so take exactly what is needed. EU law states that legitimate household items can be imported duty free. Pets can be taken into the Grand Duchy (provided vets' reports, export and import certificates are in order). Rabies vaccinations are compulsory for dogs and cats. A number of companies specialise in removals to Europe and can advise on the red tape involved.

Useful Addresses

Capital Worldwide: Kent House, Lower Stone Street, Maidstone ME15 6LH; ☎01622-766380; peter.mcewan@skynet.be; www.capital-worldwide.com.

Gosselin World Wide Moving: Keesinglaan 28, 2100 Antwerp; tel+32 3 360 55 00; fax+32 3 360 55 79; e-mail com@gosselin.be; www.gosselin.be.

The British Association of Removers: ☎020-8861 3331; fax 020-8861 3332; e-mail info@bar.co.uk; www.bar.com can send you a list of removers in your area.

Department of the Environment, Food and Rural Affairs, will advise on importing animals from the UK. Call the PETS Helpline on 0870 241 1710 or see www.defra.gov.uk.

DAILY LIFE

LIVING IN A NEW COUNTRY normally means learning a new way of life, but in the case of Luxembourg it's more than that. Combine German efficiency with French flair, add a little essence of Belgium, a touch of *je ne sais quoi* from the Grand Duchy itself and you have the recipe for Luxembourg life. Foreigners make up more than a quarter of the population and tourism attracts more than four times the country's own number each year, mainly to the north and the Ardennes region. Needless to say the country is as cosmopolitan as anywhere in the world. But the people are rightly proud of what they have achieved and they are forever saying so. 'Mir woelle bleiwe wat mir sin' is the national motto and inscribed everywhere. It means 'We want to remain what we are'.

THE LANGUAGES

THE NATIONAL LANGUAGE of Luxembourg is Lëtzebuergesch. It is spoken throughout all walks of life and is closely related to both German and Dutch. Luxemburgers have adopted both French and German, and English is widely understood. French is the official government and administrative language; German, on the other hand, is associated with the less educated sections of the population, and is the language of the press and churches. Everyday conversation is usually conducted in Lëtzebuergesch.

SCHOOLS & EDUCATION

THREE SCHOOLS in the Grand Duchy are English-speaking: St George's, the American International School and the European School. Education in Luxembourg is compulsory between the ages of four and 16. Children leave primary schools at 11 and move to one of three establishments: the *lycée*, which is considered the stepping stone to university, the more practical and vocational based *middle school* or the *école complémentaire*, which treads a line between the two. Luxembourg does not have what we would call a university, but the Centre Universitaire, set up in 1969, offers one-year courses that include law, economics, arts, humanities and sciences. These courses function as a preparation for further study at other European universities. The language of instruction is French. The Centre Universitaire also offers a two-year course in computerisation and business, in commerce and banking, and in business control.

The other institution of higher education is the Institut Supérieur de Technologie, which offers a three-year diploma in engineering, and in computer science. Courses are mainly in French, a few are given in German. There is also a teacher-training college which is only open to Luxembourg citizens, the Institut Supérieur d'Etudes et de Recherches Pédagogiques.

Useful Addresses

St George's International School: rue des Marguerites, 2127 Weimershof-Luxembourg (tel/fax 42 32 24; e-mail st.georges@online.lu; www.st-georges.lu) 3-11.

European School of Luxembourg: 23 bvd. Konrad Adenauer, 1115 Luxembourg (☎43 20 82, fax 43 67 38) 4-18.

American International School of Luxembourg: 188 ave de la Fäiencerie, 1511 Luxembourg-Limpertsberg (☎47 00 20, fax 46 09 24) 3-19.

International School of Luxembourg: 36 bvd. Pierre Dupong, 1340 Luxembourg-Merl (☎26 04 40; fax 26 04 47 04; ☎admin@ci.educ.lu; www.islux.lu) 3-19.

Ministère de l'Education Nationale, 29 rue Aldringen, 2926 Luxembourg; ☎478-5100.

Centre Universitaire: place Auguste-Laurent, 1921 Luxembourg (science); 162a ave de la Fäiencerie, 1511 Luxembourg (for other subjects); ☎46 66 44-1; fax 46 66 44-508; e-mail informations académiques@cu.lu; www.cu.lu.

Institut Supérieur Technique: 6 rue Richard Coudenhove-Kalergie, Luxembourg; ☎4201 01-1.

MEDIA & COMMUNICATIONS

Newspapers/Books

OF THE FIVE DAILY NEWSPAPERS on offer in the Grand Duchy onethird of Luxemburgers buy one every day. The papers cover a wide political spectrum from the communist *Zeitung vum Letzeburger Vollek* to the democratic (and most widely read) *Luxemburger Wort.* The tabloid as we know it does not exist, but a ready supply of French and German papers fills the gaps. The Englishlanguage *Luxembourg News* is essential reading for expatriates. It includes news on politics and culture, a What's On section and a small ads section advertising cars, flats, furniture and jobs amongst other things. It appears every Thursday and costs €2.50. The same firm publishes the monthly magazine *Luxembourg Business*, price €3.72 (contact: International City Magazines SARL, 25 rue Philippe II, 2340 Luxembourg; ☎46 11 22; fax 47 00 56; www.news.lu and www.business.lu).

Television/Radio

Viewers are spoilt for choice and can tune into stations from France, Germany and Belgium. At one time there was no more widely-known radio station than

Radio Luxembourg. UK listeners can tune in only via satellite these days but in the Grand Duchy it is going from strength to strength. It is part of the *Compagnie Luxembourgeoise de Télédiffusion* and broadcasts programmes in French, German, English, Dutch, Italian, Portuguese, Spanish and Serbo-Croat.

Telephone/Post

Telephoning Luxembourg is easy as there are no area codes. Simply dial 00 352 and the number required. To phone Britain dial 00 44 and the number, minus the first 0 of the STD code; for the USA start with 00 1. The emergency number is 112 which covers fire, ambulance, duty chemists, locksmiths and other genuine emergencies. For police call 113. The telephone directory is available on-line on: www.annuaire.lu. The state-owned postal service is as quick and efficient as anywhere in the EU. Charges are slightly higher than in the UK and US.

Useful Addresses

Main Post Office: 8 ave Monterey, 2020 Luxembourg-Ville; ☎47 65-1; www.postes.lu.

P&T Luxembourg: Division des Postes, coin rue d'Epernay/place de la Gare, 2992 Luxembourg; ☎40 88-1; fax 48 12 14.

TRANSPORT

Roads

TO GET AROUND, a car is almost essential, and if you are a Luxemburger two is the norm. A total of 5,091 road kilometres, including 78.5 kilometres of motorway, comprehensively cover the Grand Duchy. Parking is at a premium in Luxembourg-Ville so taxis are a popular option. Alternatively the town's bus service is a cheap and easy way to get around. For travelling further afield hitch-hiking is acceptable and on the small roads getting a lift is relatively easy. Luxembourg has the worst accident statistics in the EU after Portugal and Greece, 18.5 fatalities per 100,000 inhabitants, so watch out!

Railways

Rail travel in the Grand Duchy is clean and on time, but limited. The Luxembourg National Railways (Chemins de Fer de Luxembourg – CFL) network links the capital to Esch-sur-Alzette in the south, to Wasserbillig (and onto Trier and Koblenz) in the east, and Clervaux, Ettelbruck (branch line to Diekirch) and Kautenbach (branch line to Wiltz) in the north. Luxembourg-Ville is on the main line from Ostend/Brussels to Basel: eight express trains run daily in each direction, and the journey to Brussels takes less than three hours. There are direct daily trains to various French destinations, including Metz, Nancy, Strasbourg, Paris, Lyon, Marseille and Nice. Other direct services include trains to Frankfurt,

Köln, Berlin, Vienna, Milan, Zurich and Geneva.
For information on railway and bus services see: www.cfl.lu, or contact 49 90 49 90.

Air

Luxembourg is easily accessible from Europe by land but a quarter of a million air passengers still use its main international airport, Lux-Findel, every year. It lies three miles east of Luxembourg-Ville and from here the national carrier Luxair operates three flights a day to London. British Airways has one scheduled daily service. Luxair flies two or three times a week to Manchester.

Most major European destinations are served from Luxembourg, as well as some major North American cities. Icelandair flies to Luxembourg from the USA, via Reykjavík; see www.icelandair.com.

Useful addresses

Luxair: Aéroport de Luxembourg, 2987 Luxembourg; ☎4798 5050; fax 4798 5499; www.luxair.lu.

British Airways: European Bank and Business Centre, 6th Floor, 6 rte de Trèves, 2633 Senningerberg; ☎0800 2000; fax 42 13 74.

BANKS AND FINANCE

THE PERSONAL BANKING system is similar to that in the UK. The majority of banks offer personal services including deposit and current accounts, loans, mortgages and insurance. There is no restriction on foreign nationals opening accounts, but the banks will require proof of identity and a letter of introduction from your UK bank. Accounts can be opened in the UK or in the Grand Duchy and no restrictions apply on money transfers.

Useful Addresses

Kredietbank SA Luxembourgeoise: 43 bvd. Royal, 2955 Luxembourg-Ville; ☎4797-1 (London office: Founders Court, Lothbury, London EC2R 7HE; ☎020-7600 0332.)

Dexia Banque Internationale à Luxembourg SA: 69 rte. d'Esch, 2953 Luxembourg; ☎4590-1, fax 4590-2010; e-mail contact@dexia.bil.com; www.dexia-bil.com. (London office: Priory House,

1 Mitre Square, London EC3A 5AN; ☎071-623 3110, fax 071-623 5833.)

Banque et Caisse d'Epargne de l'Etat Luxembourg: 2 place de Metz, 2954 Luxembourg; ☎4015-3676; fax 40 38 14.

Lloyds TSB Bank plc: 1 rue Schiller, 2519 Luxembourg; ☎4022 12-1; fax 40 21 67.

TAXATION

INDIRECT TAXATION in the Grand Duchy is renowned for being lower than in its neighbours, which means goods and services are somewhat cheaper. The tax authorities are the Administration des Contributions Directes et des Accises (income tax, excise duties and municipal business tax), the Administration de l'Enregistrement et des Domaines (VAT, stamp and registration taxes), Customs and the Communes (ground tax and tax on salary). People spending more than one tax year outside the UK are not liable to pay tax on earnings but will still be liable for tax on savings accounts and investments in Britain. It is advisable to inform the UK tax authorities of your decision to leave the country so that you are not considered liable for tax.

Income Tax

Foreigners working in Luxembourg are taxed on their worldwide income, that is they are treated the same as residents. The only exception to this applies to bank managers and experts in banking who are paid by a foreign company while working in Luxembourg; at the discretion of the tax authorities, such workers may receive special deductions on their income. You are considered a resident if you remain in Luxembourg for more than six months, or if you maintain a residence with the intention of remaining other than on a temporary basis.

Employees receive a tax card (*fiche de retenue d'impôt*) from their municipality which they then submit to their employer. There are three classes of taxpayer: Class 1 are single persons who are not entitled to child allowance, are not widows or widowers, and are under 64 years of age. Class 2 are persons assessed jointly (i.e. married couples); some widows/widowers and separated/divorced persons come under Class 2 as well. There is a further category Class 1a, for persons who do not come under Class 1 and 2.

Personal taxes are being reduced: the highest rate from 2002 will be 38%. The personal allowance increased to €9,667.85 in 2001, and is doubled for married persons liable to tax collectively. Tax bands now vary from 3% to 33% for those in Class 1. For married couples the rates are 3% to 22%. There are reductions for those who have children. On top of the regular income tax, there is an unemployment levy of 2.5% which is likely to remain in force for some time. You are obliged to file a tax return if your income exceeds €45,000 as a single person or €25,000 as a married person, or if you have self-employed income, or substantial income from investments.

Property Taxes

Municipalities levy an annual property tax (*impôt foncier*). The rate ranges from 0.81% to 8% of a notional income derived from the property, which is calculated at 4% to 6% of the standard value of the property, depending on the location and type of property. The tax is in any case not likely to exceed 2% of the actual value of the property.

There is a tax of 6% on the sale or transfer of real estate. This is increased by a further municipal levy (3% in Luxembourg) where the property is to be used for purposes other than housing.

Other Taxes

Dividends, excluding those from investment funds and holding companies, are subject to a withholding tax of 25%. There may be a reduction if your country of origin has a double taxation treaty with Luxembourg. Capital Gains Tax is charged on gains from the sale of art works, jewellery, etc, which you have owned for less than six months, on shares, and on profits from the sale of a house which you have owned for less than five years. The rate was 19.475% as of 2002.

The Net Worth Tax is payable at 0.5 per cent; everyone receives a personal allowance against tax of €2,500 (£1,500), along with exemptions for various personal items, and various thresholds for shares and other valuables. Your assets will be valued once every three years by the tax authorities. Large changes in your assets have to be reported to them. Estate duty is payable on inherited property, depending on the net value and the relationship between the deceased and the beneficiary. Heirs in direct line to the deceased pay between 2.6% and 4.7%. There are also inheritance and gift taxes, and a local business tax.

VAT

There are now four rates of VAT. The standard rate of value added tax (*taxe sur la valeur ajoutée – TVA*) is 15% and applies to electronics, alcohol, cars and clothing. VAT is levied at 12% on tobacco, lead-free fuel and most services; 6% on gas and electricity; and 3% on butter, milk, drugs, water, public transport and publications. No VAT is levied on banking, insurance, postal services and certain social and cultural activities.

HEALTH INSURANCE AND HOSPITALS

THE LUXEMBOURG HEALTH service is excellent and almost entirely private. Insurance premiums are normally paid by employers but it is advisable to take out extra private insurance. There are no private hospitals as such; the majority of hospitals are run by the state. The service is funded by the Caisse de Maladie (sickness fund). The E111 form (inside the leaflet T6 *Health Advice for Travellers Abroad*), is available from any post office, and entitles visiting British citizens to treatment, as long as they are resident in the UK. If you are already in Luxembourg you can have the E111 sent to you by International Services, Inland Revenue, National Insurance Contributions Office, Longbenton, Newcastle upon Tyne NE98 1ZZ; ☎084591 54811 *or* 44 191 225 4811 from abroad. Details are also available on the Inland Revenue website: www.inlandrevenue.gov.uk/nic/intserv/osc.htm.

SOCIAL SECURITY AND UNEMPLOYMENT BENEFIT

LUXEMBOURG'S COMPREHENSIVE social services system is administered by semi-public bodies (*caisses*). The two major benefit areas are pensions (old age and disability) and family allowance, and health (doctor and dentist fees, some convalescence and prescription charges). There is no provision for opting out, but all contributors benefit irrespective of nationality.

The unemployment fund is financed via supplementary income tax and a special unemployment tax. To qualify applicants must meet the following criteria: have worked in Luxembourg for 26 weeks (except students), be involuntarily out of work, domiciled in the Grand Duchy, and between 16 and 65 years of age. Unemployment benefit is 80 per cent of the average monthly gross salary for the three months preceding unemployment, but not more than 2.5 times the minimum salary for an unskilled worker, and payable for 12 months.

Useful Address

Common Centre of Social Security: 125 route d'Esch, 1471 Luxembourg; ☎401 41-1; fax 40 44 81.

LOCAL GOVERNMENT

CENTRAL GOVERNMENT has most power in the running of the country. Each commune has its own local council or *conseil communal*, elected by the residents, which deals with local issues. The majority of the wider-ranging issues, such as taxation, roads, transport and utilities, are centrally controlled.

CRIME AND THE POLICE

LUXEMBOURG HAS one of the lowest crime rates in the EU and it is not uncommon for Luxemburgers to leave cars unlocked. Burglaries and petty crime do exist but more violent offences are very rare. The Grand Duchy's police are armed but are relatively few in number.

RELIGION

THE PRACTICE AND HOLD of religion has been on the decline this century, but the overwhelming majority of Luxemburgers (97 per cent) still profess to be Roman Catholics. Religious instruction is taught in schools, but in the higher grades there is a choice between Catholic doctrine and a lay course in ethics and morality. Freedom of worship is an old tradition and both the Protestant pastor (Reform and Augsburg churches) and chief Rabbi are paid by the state, as are the RC priests.

Useful Addresses

Archbishop of Luxembourg: Archevêché, 4 rue Genistre, 1623 Luxembourg; ☎46 20 23.
Anglican Chaplain: Rev. C.G. Poole, 89 rue de Muëhlenbach, 2168 Luxembourg; ☎43 95 93.
Anglican Church: 5 ave Marie-Thérèse, 2132 Luxembourg; ☎43 95 93.
Chief Rabbi: E. Bulz, 2 rue M. de Brabant, Luxembourg; ☎44 25 69.

SOCIAL LIFE

OUTWARDLY LUXEMBURGERS may appear a little distant but once friendships have been struck they can give way to a surprising openness. There are of course a number of little rules and quirks to remember. Handshaking is very common, on meeting and parting; punctuality is also very important and if invited to someone's house it is customary to take flowers or chocolates for the host or hostess.

Entertainment and Culture

Luxembourg is not famous for its night life and much of the partying is at the instigation of the foreign communities. In the capital, the White Rose and the Pub in the Grund are just two bars under the English influence, and the Pygmalion has an Irish flavour. Beer is relatively cheap in the Grand Duchy and there are plenty of local brews to choose from, including the oddly named Henri Funk.

Thanks to active encouragement the arts are positively thriving in Luxembourg, as can be seen from the number of galleries, theatres and other cultural activities that abound. The number of professional artists is relatively small – expressionist painter Joseph Kutter and photographer Edward Steichen are two international exports.

The new music scene is not particularly vibrant but the classical variety is the first love of the true Luxemburger and every village and town has at least one band or a choral group. Cinemas are the popular form of entertainment among the younger generation and most films are subtitled rather than dubbed.

The nearest any Luxemburger gets to becoming excited about sport is by following football but the Grand Duchy's amateur team do not win many games and a draw is cause for national celebration. Needless to say attention is focused more on the German and French leagues.

PUBLIC HOLIDAYS

1 January	New Year's Day
March/April	Easter Monday
1 May	Labour Day
May	Ascension Day
May/June	Whit Monday
23 June	National Day
15 August	Assumption Day
1 November	All Saints' Day
25 December	Christmas
26 December	St Stephen's Day

Additional holidays are observed on Shrove Monday, in February, Carnival Monday in March, Biergerdag (Luxembourg-Ville only) in September, and All Souls' Day on 2 November; these are not official but many businesses close and services may be curtailed. Shops and firms traditionally close in the afternoon on Christmas Eve. If a public holiday falls on a Saturday or Sunday the following Monday is observed instead.

Retirement

LUXEMBOURG CANNOT GUARANTEE sun, sea, sand and sangria, but it does have beautiful countryside and a slow, relaxed way of life to offer those in retirement. Subject to meeting Luxembourg's entry and residence qualifications (see Chapter Two, *Residence and Entry*) one of the biggest disadvantages of retiring in the Grand Duchy will undoubtedly be the cost of living. A UK pension will not necessarily make ends meet and this should be taken into consideration. To arrange for pension funds to be transferred contact the Overseas Branch of the Department of Work and Pensions. Private health insurance is a must as a National Health Service as such does not exist. The languages could also prove to be a stumbling block, acquiring a good knowledge of either German or French would be strongly advisable. To avoid legal problems making a will is recommended. For further details the UK Department of Work and Pensions produces the booklet SA29 *Your Social Security Insurance, Benefits and Health Care Rights in the European Community* (available from any DWP office, or the DWP Pensions and Overseas Benefits Directorate, Newcastle-upon-Tyne NE98 1BA; ☎ 0191-218 7777; fax 0191-218 7293).

On the plus side the country is beautiful and the standard of living very high, also the English-speaking expatriate community (in excess of 6,000) is well-established and very helpful. Their experience can make all the difference to a successful integration into the Grand Duchy's way of life. Below is a selection of clubs for foreigners.

English-Language Clubs

American Business Association of Luxembourg (ABAL): Hotel Intercontinental BP 1313, 1413 Luxembourg; fax 45 56 83.
American Chamber of Commerce in Luxembourg: www.amcham.lu.
American Women's Club of Luxembourg: 51 rue Marie Adelaide, 2128 Luxembourg-Belair; ☎ 44 84 77; fax 45 19 93; www.awcluxembourg.com.
British Ladies' Club: BP 57, 6905 Niederanven; e-mail blclux@hotmail.com.
Ball Sports and Social Club: ☎ 30 81 75; www.balls.lu.
Hockey Club: tel/fax 47 02 89 (men); ☎ 44 08 37 (women).
Indian Association of Luxembourg: 20 rue Napoléon Ier, 8342 OLM, Luxembourg; ☎ 30 93 51.
Irish Club of Luxembourg: Ambassade d'Irlande, 28 route d'Arlon, 1140 Luxembourg; ☎ 45 88 20; fax 45 06 10.
Optimists Cricket Club: ☎ 45 55 24.
Rugby Club: ☎ 47 23 54.
New World Theatre Club: ☎ www.nwtc.lu.

Employment

THE EMPLOYMENT SCENE

WITH AN AREA of just 999 square miles and a labour force of 250,000, of whom about 87,400 commute in from Belgium, France and Germany, the Grand Duchy obviously offers finite employment opportunities. However, a constant demand does exist for skilled labour. Luxembourg has the lowest unemployment rate in the EU, currently 2 per cent. The biggest difficulty for anyone seeking employment will be the lack of a good knowledge of French and/or German; both are in common use and essential in commerce and industry. As far as obtaining work is concerned speculative enquiries can be made to firms in Luxembourg but it is advisable to make sure the company will be interested in the skills you can offer and that you correspond in either French or German. A full list of British companies in the Grand Duchy is available from the Luxembourg Embassy in London. Advertisements can be placed on the website www.annonces.lu.

RESIDENCE AND WORK REGULATIONS

AS A MEMBER of the European Community Luxembourg is subject to community regulations concerning free movement of labour, and UK citizens do not require a work permit. A passport is sufficient to stay for up to three months; beyond this period an Identity Card for Foreign Nationals is required (see Chapter Two, *Residence and Entry Regulations*).

SOURCES OF JOBS

Luxembourg State Employment Offices

THE STATE EMPLOYMENT service can assist EU nationals in finding work, especially during the summer, when there is a considerable demand for temporary staff in the tourist trade. You can initially try writing to the head office, to inquire about the possibilities. The head office is at: Administration de l'Emploi, 10 rue Bender, 1229 Luxembourg-Ville; ☎478-5300. There are also branches at Esch-sur-Alzette, Diekirch and Wiltz.

Newspapers

The job sections in newspapers can provide one of the most up-to-date sources of employment and also advertise your own particular skills. The English language *Luxembourg News* carries a well-read jobs column and adverts in Luxembourg's largest circulation daily, *Luxemburger Wort* can be placed through London-based publisher representative Powers International. Do not expect to find too many jobs in UK papers' sits vac columns, and if there are any, being UK based is likely to be a requirement. The specialist bi-monthly *Overseas Jobs Express* publishes a wide and diverse number of employment opportunities in Europe.

Useful Addresses

Luxembourg News: 25 rue Philippe II, 2340 Luxembourg; ☎46 11 22-1; fax 47 00 56; www.news.lu.
Luxemburger Wort/La Voix du Luxembourg: 2 rue Christophe Plantin, 2988 Luxembourg; ☎49 93-1; fax 49 93 384; or c/o *Powers Turner Group*, 100 Rochester Row, London SW1P 1JP; ☎020-7630 9966; www.publicitas.com.

Recruitment Information

The nature of Luxembourg's economy means that there will be most demand for employees will be in banking, computers, EC offices and secretarial work. However, it must be stressed that the highest qualifications are required. Details can be found in the directory, *Trade Associations and Professional Bodies in the UK*, available at most libraries.

Some Belgian publications also list Luxembourg employers, notably the graduate careers directory *Student Move Up* and *Executive Move Up* (see www.moveup.be). In Luxembourg a number of business groups can offer advice on employment.

Useful Addresses

European Parliament Recruitment Service: Bâtiment Robert Schuman, Plateau du Kirchberg, 2929 Luxembourg; ☎43 00-1; fax 43 70-09; www.europarl.eu.int.
Société Européenne des Satellites: Human Resources Office, 6815 Château de Betzdorf, Luxembourg; www.astra.lu.
Luxembourg Chambre de Commerce: Luxembourg Chambre de Commerce: 31 bvd Konrad Adenauer, 2981 Luxembourg-Kirchberg; ☎42 39 39-1; fax 43 83 26; e-mail chamcom@cc.lu; www.cc.lu.
Confédération du Commerce Luxembourgeois: 31 bvd Konrad Adenauer, 1115 Luxembourg; ☎43 94 44; fax 43 94 50.
Centrale Paysanne Luxembourgeoise (agriculture): 16 bvd d'Avranches, 2980 Luxembourg; ☎48 81 61-1.

Teaching English

Three schools are English-speaking but the thirst (and ability) to learn foreign languages means the need for private tuition is widespread. Only Luxembourg nationals can teach in state schools but private establishments may have vacancies. If you are a suitably qualified schoolteacher, then you can request information on teaching in schools from the European Council of International Schools (ECIS, 21 Lavant Street, Petersfield, Hants GU32 3EL; 01730-268244; www.ecis.org).

Au Pair Work

There is no special agency that deals with the placement of au pairs but positions can be found through general employment agencies. A potential employer must obtain an *Accord Placement Au Pair* from the Administration de l'Emploi. This is the contract specifying the conditions of the au pair's stay and is signed by both parties. It will require the host family to affiliate the au pair to the social security system and if the au pair falls ill they must guarantee board and lodging, and medical treatment. The contract must be concluded before travel to Luxembourg.

Tourism

Luxembourg receives around 800,000 tourists a year, as well as hosting conferences. You can try writing directly to hotels and restaurants. The Luxembourg Embassy will supply a leaflet *Hotels, Auberges, Restaurants, Pensions*, on receipt of an A4 SAE and 54p stamp. It is also worth asking the Luxembourg Tourist Office for the names of Luxembourg-based coach-companies, who employ tour guides in Luxembourg and elsewhere. The Centre Information Jeunes may be able to arrange a job or work experience in Luxembourg.

Useful Addresses

Adecco – Banking, Insurance: 4a ave de la Liberté, 1930 Luxembourg; 26 49 75-1; fax 26 49 75-339; www.adecco.lu.

Adecco – Industrial: 9 rue Joseph Junck, 1839 Luxembourg; 40 17 44-1; fax 40 32 07; www.adecco.lu.

Bureau-Service: 2 allée Léopold Goebel, 1635 Luxembourg; 44 45 04 (office work).

Centre Information Jeunes – Youth Information Centre: 26 place de la Gare, Galerie Kons, 1616 Luxembourg; 262 93 200; fax 262 93-203; e-mail cij@infojeunes.lu; www.cij.lu (student and au pair).

Canvas Holidays: East Port House, 12 East Port, Dunfermline, Fife KY12 7JG; 01383-629018; fax 01383-629071; www.canvasholidays.com (campsite and children's couriers).

Cercle de Coopération des ONGD: 29 rue Michel Welter, 2730 Luxembourg; 29 87 24; fax 29 87 25 (voluntary work).

Eurocamp: Overseas Recruitment Department (Ref SJ/02); 01606-787522 (campsite and children's couriers).

FM Recruitment: 153-155 Regent Street, London W1; 020-7287 5400 (catering).

Luxembourg-Accueil-Information: 10 Bisserwee, 1238 Luxembourg; 24 17 17 (general and au pair).

Manpower-Aide Temporaire: 19 rue Glesener, 1631 Luxembourg; 48 23 23 (general).

Manpower: 130 bvd J.F. Kennedy, 4171 Esch-sur-Alzette; 54 82 40.

MBR Services: BP19, 7701 Colmar-Berg; 85 94 74-1; fax 85 94 79 (farming).

ASPECTS OF EMPLOYMENT

Salaries

A MINIMUM SALARY rate for employees is fixed by Grand Ducal decree; for a worker without a family it is around €1,250 (£750) per month, and €1,325 for employees with a family. The rate increases 20 per cent for skilled/qualified staff, and is reduced to 60, 70 and 80 per cent for workers aged 15,16 and 17-years-old respectively. The average industrial worker earns €3,850 per month; a white-collar worker considerably more. Wages are normally index-linked and a 2.5 per cent rise in the standard-of-living index results in an equal rise in remuneration from the following month. What we would regard as fringe benefits, such as canteens and company cars, are not normally provided. Overtime has to be authorised by the Minister of Labour (Ministre du Travail) and is paid at rates between one and a quarter to two times the normal rate, or equivalent holiday is given.

Working Conditions

The standard working week in Luxembourg is 40 hours. Employees are not expected to work on Sunday but it is not uncommon for senior staff to work at weekends. Annual paid holiday of 25 days is obligatory and special leave is always granted for marriages, births and deaths. Maternity leave is provided for eight weeks before birth and up to 12 weeks after. A new mother can take a year's maternity leave and must be re-employed by priority in an adequate position.

Trade Unions

Between 50% and 55% of workers are members of trade unions. Strikes are very rare and industrial relations in Luxembourg are excellent thanks to extensive conciliation arrangements from the shop floor right up to national level. By law, employees can nominate one-third of directors on the boards of large companies (more than 1,000 employees) or have members on works' councils for smaller firms.

Women at Work

Unfortunately Luxembourg is no exception when it comes to women occupying senior positions – there are very few. However, more and more women are working in the Grand Duchy and constitute 45% of the current workforce compared with only 23% in 1970. These days more men draw unemployment benefit than women. The banking sector employs the highest number of women, but the jobs are for the most part at the bottom of the employment hierarchy.

BUSINESS & INDUSTRY REPORT

LUXEMBOURG IS a small, industrially developed country reliant on exporting, which at the same time has become one of the giants of world banking. Not only is it the world's number one for offshore fund management, it also ranks only behind the USA, France and Japan as an investment fund management centre. The wealth generated by the banking sector, as well as a still strong industrial sector, means that Luxembourg has one of the highest standards of living in the world. It was the only country in the EU to reach the original strict standards for European Monetary Union.

Banking & Finance

Banking is big business in Luxembourg, accounting for more than 15 per cent of the country's GDP. The state-owned Banque et Caisse d'Epargne de l'Etat is the country's oldest financial institution, founded in 1856. A favourable financial climate and a veil of banking secrecy saw the number of banks rise to 210 in 1999. Perhaps as a sign of things to come, there were only 196 banks in 2002. In particular, Luxembourg is the offshore fund management capital of the world, with some 3,086 funds comprising $354 billion in assets. Luxembourg has been heavily criticised by other countries trying to combat money-laundering. Changes in EU laws have eroded some of the financial benefits and loopholes previously offered by the Grand Duchy. The US and Luxembourg have concluded a treaty on limiting banking secrecy, and there are plans for the EU to make banking much more transparent in all of its member states, starting from 2003. In future any taxes on dividends paid in one state to residents of another EU state will be shared between the two countries concerned.

Media & Communications

The country has no state-owned TV broadcasting company but it is still responsible for the audiovisual diet of more than 120 million Europeans, mainly through the Compagnie Luxembourgeoise de Télédiffusion (CLT) and Société Européenne des Satellites (SES), whose satellites carry BSkyB. In 1931 the Luxembourg government granted CLT permission to broadcast from its territory, the company now transmits from 10 radio stations (including Radio Luxembourg) and six TV channels.

In 1988 a programme of tax-breaks was established for film-makers in what was described as an attempt to create a European Hollywood. By the end of 2001 $30 million had been spent attracting several small productions, but the project is still in its infancy.

Iron and Steel-Making

The iron and steel industry has undergone massive modernisation and rationalisation in the last 20 years. In 1970 the industry accounted for nearly one-third of Luxembourg's GDP. Today the total is nearer 11 per cent, of which the giant ARBED accounts for 10 of the 11 and employs one in 25 of the Duchy's population. The industry had to be severely rationalised after the heavy losses of the early 1980s, but is now highly profitable again. Three-quarters of production is aimed at foreign markets and as the EU develops ARBED is expected to join forces with a European rival.

Manufacturing Industry

The largest industrial employer after ARBED is the Goodyear tyre factory, with some 3,740 workers. Other major employers include Du Pont de Nemours (plastics), Villeroy & Boch (porcelain) and ELTH (thermostats). The Japanese audio- and videotape entreprise, TDK, was responsible for the largest ever foreign investment in the Grand Duchy. Its €175 million factory, which created 650 jobs, is seen as the jewel in the crown of Luxembourg's light industry sector. Manufacturing has seen its GDP share drop from 43 to 25 per cent in 20 years; nonetheless, diversification has worked well, and some €500 million is invested yearly in manufacturing industry.

Tourism

An estimated 800,000 tourists visited Luxembourg every year, attracted by the stunning ruins of medieval castles such as Clervaux, Vianden and Wiltz and footpaths/hikes through beautiful wooded countryside. The majority of visitors reportedly treat Luxembourg as a stop-off point to other destinations in neighbouring countries. This apparent under-exploitation means the industry has plenty of room to grow.

Agriculture

Agriculture provides little more than two per cent of Luxembourg's GDP and employs less than 3.5 per cent of the population. The Grand Duchy relies heavily on food imports, which in 1999 accounted for 10.6 per cent of the value of total imports. The principal crops are cereals, potatoes and wine grapes, the latter being the most well-known of the three. The 25 miles of vineyards along the Moselle yield 20 million bottles of high quality wine each year – most is kept for home consumption.

STARTING A BUSINESS

AS ONE OF THE EUROPEAN UNION'S most economically successful countries Luxembourg has proved that size does not matter. The Grand Duchy is geographically and culturally where France and Germany meet. But as far as its economy is concerned identification with either of these countries is a thing of the past. The country is well placed for the growth of the EU's single market, with low inflation (1.4% per annum), a proven record of strong economic growth and a highly trained workforce.

CREATING A NEW BUSINESS

A GOVERNMENT PERMIT is required to set up any industrial/commercial venture. This is issued by the Ministry of Small and Medium-sized Businesses – Ministère des Classes Moyennes. (A company is classed as small if annual turnover is less than €4 million and it has less than 50 staff. A medium-sized firm has a turnover not exceeding €16 million and no more than 250 employees.) In all cases the applicants must prove themselves to be of good standing, which usually requires professional qualifications and proof of experience. Applications must be accompanied by a registration stamp for €25. All new businesses must notify the Commercial Court's trade and companies register (Registre de Commerce et des Sociétés). In addition public and limited liability companies must appear before a notary and execute the *Acte de Constitution* (detailing the ins and outs of the company). Also all firms are required to register with the local VAT office within 15 days of starting, the Registre aux Firmes and join the Chamber of Commerce. The overall cost is not cheap, but most of the initial registration fees are tax deductible. The registration tax is 1% of the subscribed capital, notarial fees are a proportion of this capital. It costs between €400 and €2,000 to register in the Official Gazette (*Mémorial*) and registration with the *Registre aux Firmes* costs between €60 and €120.

Useful Addresses

Jordans International: 20-22 Bedford Row, London WC1R 4JS; ☎020-7400 3333; fax 020-7400 3366; www.jordans.co.uk and www.jordans-international.com. Can advise on setting up a business in Luxembourg.

Ministère des Classes Moyennes: 6 ave Emile Reuter, 2937 Luxembourg; ☎478-1.

BUYING AN EXISTING BUSINESS

NO RESTRICTIONS exist on foreign ownership, monopolies and acquisitions or mergers, other than those laid down in EU competition law. Commercial estate agencies (*agences immobiliers de commerce*) provide listings of firms for sale. For a limited liability company the transfer of shares to outside parties requires the consent of shareholders holding at least three quarters of the share capital. For public companies the transfer of bearer shares is effected by delivery of the share certificates. The transfer of registered shares must be recorded in the register of shareholders.

BUSINESS STRUCTURES

SIX TYPES OF BUSINESS entities exist in Luxembourg, of which the commonest two are the public company Société Anonyme (SA) and the private limited liability company Société à Responsabilité Limitée (SARL). An SA must have a board of at least three directors, two or more shareholders, and a minimum capital on formation of €31,000. The capital must be fully subscribed and at least 25% paid up. A SARL is limited by Luxembourg law to at least two shareholders and no more than 40, but public issues of bonds and shares are not permitted. The company is managed by one or more managers, subject to corporation tax and commonly used for medium-sized businesses. The others are the general partnership Société en Nom Collectif (SENC), the limited partnership Société en Commandite Simple (SECS), the Société en Commandite par Actions (SECA), and the co-operative society Société Coopérative.

FINANCE

A HOST OF FINANCIAL INSTITUTIONS in the Grand Duchy offer a wide choice of services. The privately-run Cedel clearance payments system provides for the administration and settlement of primary and secondary market transactions in international securities, bonds, equities, euro-commercial paper and notes. The system has more than 2,400 participants in 60 countries, and can also help to organise overdraft facilities. International payments can be made via the SWIFT network.

Investment Incentives

The Luxembourg government has stated that investments should promote the creation, rationalisation, extension or reorientation of firms. It promotes a diverse development programme which does not discriminate between foreign and national investment, although preference is given to high technology ventures. To this end the Société Nationale de Crédit et d'Investissement (SNCI) was set up. The SNCI is financed by state grants and can offer loans. It also takes up shareholdings in SA and SARL companies having a commercial or industrial objective.

The government itself provides cash grants of up to 15% of the total investment for research projects, and also interest rate rebates (on loans from subsidised credit institutions) on the cost of training, environmental protection, construction and market studies. On the export front the Comité pour la Promotion des Exportations Luxembourgeoises offers interest rebates on loans financing the export of goods. For the first eight years of trading 25% of the taxable income may be exempted from tax. Investment credit tax can be carried forward for four years and credits are available and may be deducted from corporate income tax.

IDEAS FOR NEW BUSINESSES

TWO SECTORS stand out head and shoulders above others as areas of potential growth – manufacturing and finance. Foreign investment is positively welcomed by the government. Tourism is expected to continue growing and the advantageous fiscal laws also mean establishing holding companies is as popular as ever. Other areas that are popular include health foods and recreation, and third world crafts.

RUNNING A BUSINESS

Employing Staff

THE LABOUR FORCE is skilled, well-educated and adaptable, and in addition the country has both skilled and unskilled labour from neighbouring EU countries. Contracts are usually a matter of collective agreement but employers must draw one up for each individual employee. The notice required on the employer's side ranges between two to six months, on the employee's side it can vary from one month for those with less than five years' service to three months for those with more than ten years. Severance pay is from one to three months' wages for manual workers with five years or more service. Non-manual workers are entitled to one month's salary for five years' service, rising to 12 months for more than 30 years in the job. The working day is eight hours but a flexible approach allows start and finish times to vary. Overtime is frequent, but regulated by the government. Employees are entitled to a minimum of 25 days holiday each year.

Conciliation arrangements at both factory and national level mean employer-employee relations are very good. Worker representation is required on the board for firms with more than 1,000 employees. Companies with more than 15 employees must provide workers' councils, which advise and conciliate in disputes. The law regarding the minimum wage depends upon an employee's age, skills and family circumstances.

The social security system operates a comprehensive scheme and firms are liable for certain contributions. Sickness insurance is contributed at a rate of 2.72% of gross remuneration for non-manual workers. Employers and employees alike pay 8% of gross remuneration, up to a ceiling of €70,000, to the State Pension Scheme. The employer is expected to fund the family allowance scheme by contributing 1.7% of salary (1.65% for temporary staff). Accident insurance is payable from 0.5% to 6% of salary depending upon the degree of risk in the occupation, and the unemployment fund is financed by company contributions, equivalent to 4% of corporate income.

Taxation

For foreign firms one of the key elements of the Luxembourg tax system is its tax-free treatment of holding companies. They are exempt from taxation on profits, capital gains and interest and dividend distributions. The heirs of non-resident shareholders are not subject to death duties or inheritance tax. The only tax liability is a 0.2% annual subscription tax on equity. As a consequence there are more than 7,000 holding companies based in the Grand Duchy. Other businesses, however, are considered resident for tax purposes if the registered office or central management is in Luxembourg. Resident firms are subject to several principal taxes on worldwide profits, but non-resident companies are liable only on Luxembourg source profits.

Corporation tax (Impôts sur le Revenu des Collectivités) is levied on a sliding scale between 20% and 30%. There are also municipal taxes on businesses, which vary between 8% and 12.5% depending on the municipality. The effective top rate is 40.25% in Luxembourg City. Businesses also have to pay a further 4% levy into an unemployment fund. Non-resident companies are entitled to a reduced rate where worldwide profits do not exceed the top rate. Corporate tax returns must be filed by May 31 in the year after the tax year. Advance payments are made quarterly.

The standard rate of VAT is 15%; reduced rates of 3%, 6% and 12% apply to some goods and services considered more or less essential (see Chapter Four *Daily Life*). Banking, exports, the postal services, some sanitary, educational, social and cultural activities, insurance and the letting of property are exempt from VAT.

Accountancy and Legal Advice

By law accounts must include the balance sheet, the profit and loss account before deductions and the proposed appropriation of profit (or treatment of loss) in the latest and preceding years. In addition a journal for the entry of day-to-day transactions and a record for the annual registration of the inventory of assets and liabilities are required. Auditing standards published by the Union Européenne des Experts Comptables (UEC) apply in the Grand Duchy where they do not contravene local laws. Independent auditors (*réviseurs d'entreprises*) prepare accounts for large and medium-sized firms, while smaller companies are looked after by statutory auditors (*commissaires aux comptes*).

The prospective business person in Luxembourg would be ill-advised not to seek specialist legal advice on setting up a business. The Luxembourg Embassy in London can provide a list of English-speaking solicitors in the Grand Duchy.

Useful Addresses

Deloitte & Touche (Luxembourg): 3 route d'Arlon, 8009 Strassen; ☎451 451; fax 451 452 401. Publish *International Tax and Business Guide for Luxembourg.*

Ernst & Young SA: B.P. 780, 2017 Luxembourg; ☎421 24-1; fax 421 24-421; www.ey.com.

Trade Partners UK: Website carries a country profile for Luxembourg: www.tradepartners.gov.uk.

Luxembourg Press and Information Service: 43 bvd F.D. Roosevelt, 2450 Luxembourg; ☎47 82 18-1.

Luxembourg Chambre de Commerce: 31 bvd Konrad Adenauer, 2981 Luxembourg-Kirchberg; ☎42 39 39-1; fax 43 83 26; e-mail chamcom@cc.lu; www.cc.lu.

Belgium-Luxembourg Chamber of Commerce in Great Britain: Berkeley House, 73 Upper Richmond Rd, London SW15 2SZ; ☎020-8877 3025; www.blcc.co.uk.

APPENDIX 1

PERSONAL CASE HISTORIES

BELGIUM

GORDON MCKAY

GORDON MCKAY IS 58 YEARS OLD and a partner in the management consultancy, Hastings McKay Associates. His family have long-standing connections with the port of Antwerp dating back to 1870, and Gordon made his first visit there at the tender age of three. After his studies in the UK, he started his career in the ship repair and maintenance sector in the port of Antwerp. He was then hired as a consultant for three months to a small temping agency in Antwerp called Creyf's and ended up staying for 13 years. By the time he left, Creyf's had become a major player in the temporary employment market and a listed company on the Belgian stock exchange. Creyf's now has branches all over Belgium and Holland, and in other countries. With his long experience in human resources and restructuring companies, Gordon decided to start up his own consultancy with a few associates. Hastings McKay Associates act as advisors to companies in the process of restructuring. They are also heavily involved in organising conferences and public events, which have included the Cutty Sark Tall Ships race at the Antwerp end, the World Diamond Conference, and many other events.

How do you find Belgian red tape?
Belgian bureaucracy is complicated, and it is essential to get the right advice, whatever you're doing. Hiring a local accountant and a notary will save you a lot of trouble, and ensure that you don't waste time because you haven't got the right documents or because you have been talking to the wrong people. To set up a national business in certain sectors of activity you may need three licences for the three different regions. Once you have started your business it can be difficult to alter things afterwards. The locals are generally good at reading between the lines and understanding which regulations really matter.

How were you able to build up your business?
Starting a business is basically not that difficult. As with anywhere it's who you know – your network of contacts – that matters. People are quite demanding in Belgium and want immediate results, whereas in the UK you have more time to do things. It's quite a high-pressure environment to work in. I might add that the euro is working out well here and should be very good for business.

How about Belgian workers?
Belgians are hard workers, and they put in a full eight hours a day. The greatest problem is the high social security costs, but this is offset by the greater productivity of the workers. Belgium is a small country, but people are very reluctant to commute to a job. Someone who lives in Antwerp will generally not want to work in Brussels, as if you were asking them to go to the other end of the world.

What advice do you have for someone starting a business in Belgium?
As I said, you need to first make the right contacts with the local people. Then make a checklist of what is required to start your business. It is absolutely necessary to proceed with caution, as mistakes can be very expensive to rectify later on. The question of languages is also crucial. If you are unable to speak Dutch or French you are at a big disadvantage. The more languages one knows the better. Command of both Dutch and French will definitely give you an advantage professionally and socially and the Belgians will respect you for it.

How do you find social life in Belgium?
Social life here is excellent, and I have a lot of Belgian friends as well as a lot of British friends. Belgian society is very close-knit and difficult to get into. Once you have managed to get into a circle then it's generally great. Going out here is somewhat cheaper than in the UK, and the quality of the service is very good. Finally, the great thing about living here is that you can get into your car and go more or less anywhere you like in Europe; you don't have to hang around waiting for a ferry or shuttle.

PETER BURNETT

Peter Burnett is 57. He read economics, Spanish and French at Cambridge, and then worked for the Ministry of Agriculture in the External Relations Section for 10 years. He has worked for the Council of the European Commission in Brussels since 1970 and specialises in translating from Spanish, French and Italian into English.

How did you find Belgian bureaucracy?
If you work for the EC you won't have many problems. The EC looks after its workers very well. I pay my taxes to the EC, so things are rather simplified. On

the other hand, I have to pay for my rubbish collection. In the past there have been occasional problems when the communes have tried to levy taxes they were not entitled to.

Was it difficult to find work?
After university I worked for the Ministry of Agriculture and developed an interest in translating agricultural policy documents coming from Brussels. Eventually the chance arose to work for the European Commission itself and I started work there at the beginning of 1970. I was involved in translating not only the texts of the negotiations for Britain's entry, but also press releases and other information, which even at this time had to be put out in English. These days I translate a wide variety of texts, whose subject matter can be legal, economic, scientific or whatever.

What are opportunities like now?
With the expansion of the EC the workload for translators has grown enormously and there is a steady demand for them. Interpreters are even more in demand. People choose to be either interpreters or translators. The interpreters are much more extrovert, more like actors, while translators are introvert backroom people. It's not enough to have language skills, however. You need to be able to understand the content of the texts. You may find yourself working all night with the people who are drafting the texts or with legal experts.

The growth area now is in Scandinavian languages and Finnish, since these are the countries entering the Community. Later on there will be a demand for Eastern European languages. In general there are not enough Britons working at the EC. Some of this shortfall is made up by Whitehall training 'parachutists', preparing certain new recruits specifically for jobs in the Commission.

How do you find social life in Brussels?
I knew the Netherlands and France quite well but Brussels was confusing. I couldn't recognise the local dialect as being French or Dutch. Brussels people don't have a clear identity and this makes them insecure with foreigners. This seems to be less of a problem with people in other Belgian cities. I tried to integrate myself into the local community from the start rather than mixing with expatriates all the time. These days I spend time with all sorts of nationalities, in particular Italians.

Have you any advice for those thinking of taking the plunge?
It's important to realise that everything in Brussels is political. If you want to work in the Commission it helps to have the backing of your own country's delegation. Outside the Commission itself, life is much easier if you have a multinational or international organisation backing you.

I would also recommend people to buy a flat or house as soon as possible after moving to Brussels, because in the end it is much more economical than paying a high rent.

APPENDIX 2

PERSONAL CASE HISTORIES

THE NETHERLANDS

ANN CAMPBELL-LORD

AMERICAN-BORN ANN CAMPBELL-LORD moved to Amsterdam to join her British husband who was working for Fokker at the time. She soon found that not speaking Dutch put her at a disadvantage in finding work, but her experience in written English proved an asset. She started writing for local English-language publications and moved into translating after studying Dutch. Later she added corporate teaching. We asked her:

How easy was Dutch red tape in practice?
It has always been very bureaucratic, but I believe that things have become easier over the years. Officials treat foreigners more courteously than they used to, but they do apply the rules more strictly because of the very large numbers of foreigners coming into the country.

Was it difficult to find work?
Many foreigners hope to find work straight away, and then find that they have start at the bottom of the ladder because they do not speak Dutch. Even college-educated people have found themselves working as chambermaids. Many get involved in translating, even though their Dutch is not much good. In the first place you need to work hard at making contacts and networking. Secondly, you need to have ingenuity and initiative in order to find a niche for yourself. If you have something to offer to the Dutch, then you will find work.

Was it easy to find accommodation?
It was much easier than I expected. I would advise foreigners to go to a *makelaar*

(estate agent). Many of them are very helpful, although there are exceptions. While you have to pay a commission, you don't have to take anything you don't like and in the end it will save you a lot of trouble. The other way to find a place is to look in the classified ads, such as in *Via-Via* magazine. Many foreigners sub-let (*onderhuren*) from other foreigners and find themselves having to move frequently.

How do you find the social life and the Dutch?

You have to learn to adapt to a very different culture. The best thing is to become affiliated to a club like the British Society; British clubs are especially welcoming. Social life in the big cities is very good, most of all in Amsterdam. Dutch people who have international connections are most likely to become close friends. The south of the country (Brabant and Limburg) is rather different. The people are more accommodating and easier to get to know.

What is your advice for those thinking of taking the plunge?

After looking at all the options, many foreigners have come to the conclusion that the Netherlands is a good place to start if you are going to live on the Continent. It's vital to understand that many things here are quite the opposite from in the UK. The Dutch take their social rituals very seriously and stick closely to rules and regulations of which there are many. Unless you ask precise questions, they will not necessarily tell you what you need to know.

SIMON EDWARDS

AFTER WORKING for the London-based architects Aukett Ltd. Simon Edwards went travelling and then joined them again to work for their joint venture, Aukett+Kokon, in the Netherlands. Aukett+Kokon is located close to Schiphol and mainly deals with large-scale developments with the occasional smaller projects. Simon is a qualified architect and works in a team mainly designing presentations for potential clients, using both computer- and hand-rendered images. He married a Dutchwoman after moving to Holland and now lives in Aalsmeer.

How easy was Dutch red tape in practice?

Surprisingly difficult. I came armed with a *Time Out* guide to Amsterdam which told me to go to the Aliens' Police (*vreemdelingenpolitie*). They sent me to the central population register, who then in turn sent me to the local town hall and finally back to the aliens' police. Then I had to have a social security (SOFI) number. It seemed as if I was unable to get the necessary forms without first having another form. In all it took about two or three months travelling between offices to get everything organised and finally receive my residence permit (*verblijfsvergunning*). On top of that I had to go back to London to have my birth certificate stamped at the Foreign Office. The registration process is certainly easier outside the big cities.

Was it difficult to find work?
There was no problem, as I was transferred from the company in London; I was asked to go to the Netherlands for a few days during which I was offered a permanent position. For people who don't speak Dutch it will be hard to find a career job. I find, however, that the Dutch are generally open to new ideas and will give you a chance to try them out. So if you have a good idea you may well be able to achieve something here.

Was it easy to find accommodation?
I got in touch with some rental agencies in Amsterdam before I came over, so they had something ready for me to look at when I arrived, and I found something straight away. In fact, I found that the rent was cheaper than what I was paying in London. If you are not prepared to pay above a certain amount, e.g. above £100 per week, then you will certainly have difficulties. I've now bought a house in Aalsmeer, which will work out cheaper in the long run.

How do you find the social life and the Dutch?
While it is true that the Dutch are very family-orientated, I have had a very good social life here (before my son was born anyway). I've found that if you go to bars and clubs and introduce yourself then people are generally interested in talking to you, something which might not happen in England. People will invite you to their homes once they have got to know you.

What is your advice for those thinking of taking the plunge?
If you can find a job, then you should go for it. The main frustration here is the language. I don't have much opportunity to speak Dutch; even though people will try to help you out, inevitably the conversation goes back to English. Other than that I can't think of any reason not to come here. I'm certainly going to stay!

BIBLIOGRAPHY

BELGIUM

Brussels, ed. C. Billen & J.-M. Duvosquel, Mercator (Antwerp).
Brussels: A cultural and literary guide, André de Vries, Signal Books.
Everybody eats well in Belgium cookbook, Ruth Van Waerebeek, Workman Publishing Company (New York).
The Factory of Facts: Luc Sante, Granta Books. American Belgian in search of his roots.
The Fair Face of Flanders, Patricia Carson, Story-Scientia.
Histoire de Bruxelles: biographie d'une capitale, Georges-Henri Dumont, Le Cri (Brussels).
Histoire de la Belgique, Georges-Henri Dumont, Le Cri (Brussels).
History of the Belgians, A. de Meeüs, Thames & Hudson.
In the Belgian Chateau, Renée C. Fox, Ivan R. Dee (Chicago). Academic politics in Belgium.
King Leopold's Ghost: a story of greed, terror and heroism in Central Africa, Adam Hochschild, Houghton Mifflin.
A Leap in the Dark: nationalist conflict and federalism in Belgium, Liesbet Hooghe, Cornell University Press.
Outrageous Fortune: the tragedy of Leopold III of the Belgians, Roger Keyes, Secker & Warburg. Defence of Leopold III's actions during World War II.
The Politics of Belgium: a unique federalism, John Fitzmaurice, Hurst.
Power and Politics in Belgian Education, 1815 to 1961, Vernon Mallinson, Heinemann.
The Sorrow of Belgium, Hugo Claus, Penguin. Classic account of the occupation by the best-known living Flemish writer.
A Tall Man in a Low Land, Harry Pearson, Trafalgar Square. Joky travelogue.
We Live in Belgium & Luxembourg, Fiona Cameron, Wayland. Social life and customs.
The Xenophobe's Guide to the Belgians, Anthony Mason, Oval Books.

THE NETHERLANDS

The Backroads of Holland, Helen Colijn, Bicycle Books (Mill Valley, CA).
Contemporary Explorations in the Culture of the Low Countries, ed. W.Z. Shetter and I. Van Cruysse, University Press of America.
The Diary of a Young Girl: Anne Frank, Penguin.
The Embarrassment of Riches: an interpretation of Dutch culture in the Golden Age, Simon

Schama, Collins.
Going Dutch, Dick Pappenheim, International Books. Guide to Dutch business culture.
Here's Holland, S. Gazaleh-Weevers, Here's Holland.com. Historical and cultural background.
History of the Dutch-speaking Peoples, 1555-1648, Pieter Geyl, Phoenix Press.
Inside Information, C. Gelderman-Curtis and R. Nyks-Corkum, Gelderman & Nyks. Consumer information and useful addresses.
Introduction to Dutch, W.Z. Shetter, M. Nijhoff..
Last Call, Harry Mulisch, Penguin. Leading Dutch writer's fictionalised account of the Dutch role in the holocaust.
The Low Sky: Understanding the Dutch, Han van der Horst, Nuffic/Scriptum.
The Netherlands: Prometheus/NRC Handelsblad.
The Netherlands in Perspective, W.Z. Shetter, M. Nijhoff,.
Reading Dutch: fifteen annotated stories from the Low Countries, ed. W.Z. Shetter and R. Byron Bird, Nijhoff,.
A Short History of the Netherlands, Rietbergen, Lamers & Seegers, Bekking Publishers (Amersfoort), 2nd ed.
The Simple Guide to Holland: customs and etiquette, M.T. Hooker, Global Books.
The Undutchables, Colin White and Laurie Boucke, White/Boucke Publishers. Observations on the culture and inhabitants.
The Xenophobe's Guide to the Dutch, Rodney Bolt, Oval Books.

LUXEMBOURG

Das Grossherzogtum Luxembourg: Portrait einer kleinen Demokratie, Michael Schroen, Brockmeyer.
Living in Luxembourg, American Women's Club of Luxembourg.
Luxembourg, the Making of a Nation: from 1815 to the present day, Christian Calmes, Imprimerie Saint-Paul.

Vacation Work publish:

	Paperback	Hardback
Summer Jobs Abroad	£9.99	£15.95
Summer Jobs in Britain	£9.99	£15.95
Supplement to Summer Jobs in Britain and Abroad *published in May*	£6.00	–
Work Your Way Around the World	£12.95	–
Taking a Gap Year	£11.95	–
Taking a Career Break	£11.95	–
Working in Tourism – The UK, Europe & Beyond	£11.95	–
Kibbutz Volunteer	£10.99	–
Working on Cruise Ships	£10.99	–
Teaching English Abroad	£12.95	–
The Au Pair & Nanny's Guide to Working Abroad	£12.95	–
The Good Cook's Guide to Working Worldwide	£11.95	–
Working in Ski Resorts – Europe & North America	£10.99	–
Working with Animals – The UK, Europe & Worldwide	£11.95	–
Live & Work Abroad - a Guide for Modern Nomads	£11.95	–
Working with the Environment	£11.95	–
Health Professionals Abroad	£11.95	–
Accounting Jobs Worldwide	£11.95	–
The Directory of Jobs & Careers Abroad	£12.95	–
The International Directory of Voluntary Work	£12.95	–
Live & Work in Australia & New Zealand	£10.99	–
Live & Work in Belgium, The Netherlands & Luxembourg	£10.99	–
Live & Work in France	£10.99	–
Live & Work in Germany	£10.99	–
Live & Work in Italy	£10.99	–
Live & Work in Japan	£10.99	–
Live & Work in Russia & Eastern Europe	£10.99	–
Live & Work in Saudi & the Gulf	£10.99	–
Live & Work in Scandinavia	£10.99	–
Live & Work in Scotland	£10.99	–
Live & Work in Spain & Portugal	£10.99	–
Live & Work in the USA & Canada	£10.99	–
Drive USA	£10.99	–
Hand Made in Britain - The Visitors Guide	£10.99	–
Scottish Islands - The Western Isles	£12.95	–
Scottish Islands - Orkney & Shetland	£11.95	–
The Panamericana: On the Road through Mexico and Central America	£12.95	–
Travellers Survival Kit: Australia & New Zealand	£11.95	–
Travellers Survival Kit: Cuba	£10.99	–
Travellers Survival Kit: India	£10.99	–
Travellers Survival Kit: Lebanon	£10.99	–
Travellers Survival Kit: Madagascar, Mayotte & Comoros	£10.99	–
Travellers Survival Kit: Mauritius, Seychelles & Réunion	£10.99	–
Travellers Survival Kit: Mozambique	£10.99	–
Travellers Survival Kit: Oman & the Arabian Gulf	£11.95	–
Travellers Survival Kit: South Africa	£10.99	–
Travellers Survival Kit: South America	£15.95	–
Travellers Survival Kit: Sri Lanka	£10.99	–
Travellers Survival Kit: USA & Canada	£10.99	–

Distributors of:

Summer Jobs USA	£12.95	–
Internships (On-the-Job Training Opportunities in the USA)	£18.95	–
How to Become a US Citizen	£11.95	–
World Volunteers	£10.99	–
Green Volunteers	£10.99	–

Plus 27 titles from Peterson's, the leading American academic publisher, on college education and careers in the USA. Separate catalogue available on request.

★ **Vacation Work Publications, 9 Park End Street, Oxford OX1 1HJ** ★
Tel 01865–241978   Fax 01865–790885

Visit us online for more information on our unrivalled range of titles for work, travel and gap years, readers' feedback and regular updates:

www.vacationwork.co.uk